I found him both physically very beautiful—the rich colours of his rosy cheeks and black hair and dark-blue eyes, the proud chin and craggy nose—and morally uplifting. I could think of him if I felt downhearted, and immediately be cheered. He was a rock. Sweetness, vigor, fierce intelligence. You would want him at your side in battle, or in a shipwreck.

—Fernanda Eberstadt

Peter Glenville

The Elusive Director
Who Charmed Hollywood
& Triumphed on Broadway

CAROL KING
WITH RICHARD HAVERS

Peter Glenville Foundation • Los Angeles

Printed in the United States of America

First published in the UK in 2010

Book design by Neal Colgrass

Library of Congress Control Number: 2011935889

ISBN: 978-0-615-50817-7

Published by the Peter Glenville Foundation
in Los Angeles

Contents

Quant Je Puis

"As Much As I Can"

Stonyhurt School Motto

Introduction

Peter Glenville was told to leave on the first day of production. The Broadway musical *Take Me Along* was mounting its tryout run in Philadelphia. Producer David Merrick, a control freak who liked firing people, was upset over Glenville's ability to outmaneuver him. As director, Glenville had called the show's choreographer a "disgrace" and replaced her—but her affair with an influential theater owner convinced Merrick to bring her back. In a pinch, Glenville let his preferred dance man finish the few routines he'd started. But Merrick didn't like the compromise.

Composer Bob Merrill gave Glenville the bad news inside of a Philly theater: "David's standing back there, and you're fired." Dashing as always, with brilliantined hair and a perfect tan, Glenville barely skipped a beat. "Do you know anything about the weather in Jamaica?" he asked. He walked out calmly and even stopped to shake Merrick's hand.

Diplomatic, charming, witty and razor-sharp, Glenville has faded from memory as quietly as he walked out of that theater.

Film and theater textbooks give no space to his impressive body of work; screenings of his films are hard to come by; "Oh, the one who directed *Becket* . . ." is sometimes heard from fans of film and theater history. Yet in his day, Glenville broke box office records on Broadway and in London. He directed Alec Guinness, Peter O'Toole, Richard Burton, Elizabeth Taylor and other post–World War II stars of stage and screen. He was a pillar and popular host in high society on two continents. And he held such ardent political views that he once funded an attempt to topple the despotic Duvalier regime in Haiti.

Perhaps he's harder to remember because his career was so varied. He worked with ease in such diverse repertoire that no artistic movement or even country ever "claimed" him. He directed middle-class, emotionally implicit plays by Terence Rattigan as easily as he staged a late avant-garde work by Tennessee Williams; he wrote a film script set in the 12th century as well as he played a seedy Cockney villain in the 1948 film *Good-Time Girl.* Meanwhile, he hopscotched from London to Manhattan to Mexico in order to avoid residency status and stiffer tax rates—which helped earn him a good living and maintain his place among high-flying socialites.

His complex family background and early career make him even harder to pin down. Glenville once admitted that Shaun Glenville may or may not have been his real father. Shaun did, however, save his life when Glenville's mother nearly aborted him with a handful of pills and a glass of gin; Shaun angrily threw her medicinal brew into the fire. Soon Shaun and his wife, Dorothy "Dolly" Ward—both wildly successful pantomime actors—handed over their son to be raised by a pair of alcoholics, Peter's aunt and his grandmother. Despite these obstacles, he enjoyed the benefits of wealthy celebrity parents, attending the elite Catholic college of Stonyhurst and matriculating at Oxford University. Elegant, moneyed and wickedly smart, Glenville left school in 1935 as the archetypal Bright Young Person—a socialite of the day who threw elaborate parties and magnetically attracted media attention. As artists, "their style [was] brisk, affected, outwardly impersonal, inwardly often deeply vulnerable," wrote one chronicler of the age. Shrugging off his childhood wounds and diving into acting, Glenville would soon discover how vulnerable he was.

"Perhaps as an actor he was forced too hard and tried too highly in his career," wrote one critic after Glenville took on highly demanding Shakespeare roles right away—and quickly suffered a physical breakdown. Diagnosed with an ulcer at the age of 22, Glenville took a full year off to recuperate. Yet this setback only led to his creative rebirth as a popular actor of mostly modern theater: he starred in plays by Noel Coward, Eugene O'Neill and Leon Gordon, and took roles in "quota quickie" films mandated by the government to ensure British content in movie houses.

But even that career would soon change. In 1944, Tyrone Guthrie invited him to direct for the storied Old Vic Company at a theater in Liverpool, where Glenville surprised audiences with modern and often foreign fare. When the war ended, he roared back into London, bought a fully staffed house in a fashionable part of the city, and established himself as a prominent West End director. He staged successful productions of plays by modern writers like Jean-Paul Sartre, Terence Rattigan, Graham Greene and Tennessee Williams. But like many British showmen—his parents included—Glenville yearned for success in America, and in 1949 he sailed to New York to direct one-act Rattigan plays such as *The Browning Version* and *Playbill*. A couple of years later, he was minting box office gold on Broadway with productions of Rattigan's *Separate Tables*, Georges Feydeau's *Hotel Paradiso*, and Fay and Michael Kanin's adaptation of *Rashomon*.

Described as "one of the most sought-after stage directors in America," Glenville aimed for yet another career—this one in Hollywood. Relying on his fame (and persuasive charm) to attract talent, he adapted *Becket* in 1964 with Richard Burton and Peter O'Toole in the leads. The film shook Hollywood with 12 Academy Award nominations, launching Glenville to the A-list and enabling him to direct stars like Alec Guinness in *Hotel Paradiso* and Elizabeth Taylor in *The Comedians*. But when the era of cinematic sex, violence, anger and method acting fully emerged in the 1970s, Glenville fell out of favor with critics. "I'm tired of beating my head against a stone wall," he said after his production of Osborne's *A Patriot for Me* fizzled on Broadway in 1969. A couple of middling stage productions and a thwarted *Man of La Mancha* film project later, Glenville, ever the gentleman, retired quietly into high society and the upper echelon of Republican circles.

That gentlemanly impulse was nothing new: it had long been a key and possibly a hindrance to his success. Described by one friend as "a bit bulldozer-like when he was younger," Glenville developed a fine sense of diplomacy during his career. Perhaps he would have gained more notoriety—and a firmer place in history—if his personality had been more aggressive, but it's a wonder to behold Glenville's diplomatic skills in his heyday. Writing to an angry agent who argued that his client, author Jean Anouilh, deserved a larger-size credit in the film *Becket—after* the film was finished—Glenville never lost his cool: "If M. Anouilh should choose to hold me responsible for the invention of the atom bomb it would be equally regrettable from my point of view, and I would be equally unauthorised to do anything about it." Glenville remained dignified even in the face of veiled threats from the agent, and Anouilh eventually backed down, admitting he had failed to read his own contract "with a fine tooth-comb."

Just as revealing is Glenville's duel with American censors, who objected to a character in *The Comedians* who dared utter a line about going to the bathroom to "faire pipi." Wrote MGM: "The Code people say that they personally still maintain the habit of urinating, but do not discuss it in polite society." Bristling behind his good manners, Glenville devoted nearly 300 words to a reply, including:

> What is 'polite society'? They cannot mean by this a society of either aristocrats or eminent intellectuals since members of the upper classes are quite intolerant of false refinements and circumlocutions. Amongst the socially privileged, it is certainly considered extremely common to use words like 'toilet' and 'powder room' instead of 'lavatory.' If, on the other hand, they are referring to every petty little housewife in the Baptist belt, the interesting question arises as to whether such rather limited outlooks have necessarily to be pandered to by the Code.

"The Code people"—then on the verge of losing their power in the 1960s—conceded that the line was "not a hanging matter" and approved it.

Glenville's diplomacy also translated into a directing style that actors loved. "He had very little ego, which is quite unusual for a top director," said one *Becket* actor. "He knew when to move things along and make a joke, he never shouted or put his foot down." Glenville even laughed it off when Burton and O'Toole were too hung over to get their horses facing in the right direction in *Becket*; the scene was tactfully postponed. Peter Ustinov explained how Glenville's "infrequent but telling sotto voces" affected his acting:

> It is very rare that one is able to work in an atmosphere of practically wordless intelligence, where every tiny indication is understood without fuss, and, as a consequence, one begins to rely on . . . oneself. That is a colossal privilege — the instinctive comprehension worthy of a sporting team . . .

But Glenville's understated manner also shrouded his accomplishments. Producer Hal Wallis took credit for bringing *Becket* to life, even though Glenville had gathered the all-star cast, written the script's first draft and made extensive edits along the way. Glenville argued justifiably for a credit with the Screen Writers Guild, but lost, and later watched Edward Anhalt—the sole credited *Becket* writer—take home the film's only Academy Award.

Glenville's diplomacy also concealed a good deal of tension. The duodenal ulcer diagnosed during his first year of professional acting recurred throughout his life, as did stress-related ailments such as rashes, boils, grippe-like illnesses and tension headaches. He was a lifelong chain-smoker to boot. Keeping his personal life private during a time when gays were punished by law no doubt contributed to his anxiety. By all accounts, Glenville had a close and easy relationship with lifelong companion William "Bill" Smith, the humbler and quieter of the two. As a Catholic, Glenville apparently reconciled his relationship through confessions. One friend said he was against any kind of flamboyant behavior, and "was as strict as a bishop of Boston." It was also suggested that his live-in relationship with Bill was platonic.

"It was obvious from his stories that he had had a painful damaging childhood," said a friend, who added:

> . . . and yet he had emerged from his early unhappiness not just successful but a whole, happy man, loving, fearless, sunny natured. He was full of contradictions . . . I imagine Catholicism was a lone source of moral stability and intellectual rigor to him, growing up with a capricious manipulative pantomime-star mother, and perhaps his politics provided the same kind of antidote.

If so, it was a successful one, for Glenville befriended Henry Kissinger, socialized with William F. Buckley and dined with

President Ford at the White House. And yes, he did contribute $20,000 to an attempted invasion of Haiti in 1966. But it didn't get much further than fishing boats filled with guns in the Florida Keys and would-be commandoes rounded up by a group of sheriff's deputies.

If only Glenville now had a sponsor to support his own invasion back into film and theater history. Creative, open-minded and adventurous, he was like a restless entrepreneur who spread his talents over acting, theater directing and filmmaking in two of the world's most competitive cities, London and New York. Complex and subtle, he forged hundreds of alliances in the film and theater worlds; he built the careers of stars, and yet he was undeniably a star in his own right. It is high time we turn a much-deserved spotlight back onto Peter Glenville.

Neal Colgrass
Los Angeles, 2012

Prelude

He's Leaving Home

January 17, 1922

The small boy was nervous. As he finished buttoning up his brown tweed suit, the one that his grandmother had bought for him at Barkers of Kensington, he stood and couldn't help but admire what he saw in the mirror. For a boy of 8, Peter Glenville was very conscious of his appearance and his new school uniform pleased him. But his thoughts about his appearance soon left him as his mind became filled with other thoughts, and not a few fears. Starting a new school at any age is more than a little frightening, but a boarding school that is hundreds of miles away from home is even more daunting. He was about to embark on a journey that was to shape his entire life in ways that a small boy's imagination could not begin to imagine, nor to understand.

Also from Barkers, Peter's grandmother had bought another tweed suit, two grey flannel suits for warmer weather, a dark blue serge suit for Sundays, handkerchiefs, socks, collars, shirts, pajamas, lace-up walking shoes, sports kit and underwear. It was everything a boy could need and it was all packed in a sturdy trunk ready for the 230-mile journey to his new school.

As he stood in his bedroom the one thing Peter did understand was just how much he would miss home, especially his toys and most of all, his books. Peter loved reading; tales of history and adventure were his favorites. Even more than reading them he loved his parents to read to him; they read so much better than his grandmother or aunt. The trouble was, Mamma and Papa were not always around—they were actors.

"Peter, come along, you need to eat your breakfast and we have to leave soon for the station." His grandmother calling up to him broke the spell of his thoughts. As he went down the stairs, nearing the kitchen, he could smell the bacon and eggs the housemaid was cooking; his grandmother insisted he eat it as he had a long journey but all the excitement had affected his appetite. Eventually he managed half of it before asking the maid to hide the rest. She grinned at Peter and he knew that yet again he would get his own way. His mother had taught him to always be polite and to make requests with a smile telling him it was amazing what a little charm—coupled with a dose of determination—could achieve in life.

Greencroft Gardens was in North London, not far from Finchley Road, and as Peter stood shivering on the pavement on that cold January morning, waiting for the family's car to arrive to take him to the station, he looked up at his home. It was a solid four-story building; the small windows at the top were those of the servants' rooms, and the two larger ones below belonged to his parents' bedroom and his room. There was the wrought-iron balcony outside his window and his eye followed on down to the arched entrance below with its glass-paneled front door. He knew it would be months before he was home again.

Peter and his grandmother climbed inside his parents' Rolls-Royce to be driven along the quiet tree-lined street in the area his mother called Hampstead, although his father jokingly referred to it as Camden. Peter's mother and father were actors and they were far from home working in a pantomime in Manchester; they had sent him a postcard and a letter, wishing him luck that he had read over and over again, just like all the others they had sent to him. A friend of his parents was driving the Rolls-Royce and as they drove along Peter ignored the customary stares of passersby—the knot in his stomach meant he was too nervous to even notice them. But it could have been worse: if it had been his mother she would have caused a stir, as she always did, particularly when she swept from her car, invariably wearing a long fur coat with her diamond rings glittering on her fingers.

As Peter and his grandmother walked through the stone arch a porter followed them with the large brown trunk straddling his sack-barrow. London's Euston Station with its Great Hall, vast coffered ceiling and sweeping double flight of stairs leading to offices at the northern end only seemed to add to Peter's sense of anticipation. After his grandmother purchased a single ticket they stood looking up at the station's vast departure's board. It showed the Stonyhurst train leaving from Platform 9 at 12:30 p.m. All around the station's concourse Peter noticed small groups of boys and their parents; on Platform 9 it was the same. After making their way along the platform the porter placed the trunk in the luggage van along with dozens of others. Peter's grandmother thanked him and gave him a tuppence.

Peter couldn't help noticing that he appeared to be one of the youngest—he was also one of the smallest. All around him older boys called out as they spotted a friend, elbowing their way through the crowd to swap stories about their month-long holiday. Some of the younger boys sniffed back tears as they said goodbye to their mother—and if they were lucky enough to have a father that survived the Great War—they shook hands with gruff men in suits, while listening to their pearls of paternal advice. Peter's grandmother bid him a tearful farewell and pecked him on the cheek, telling him to write as soon as he could. He did not cry.

As Peter climbed on board the train and searched the compartments for a seat, he instinctively knew he was at a disadvantage. "That one's bagged" and "No room" were the responses whenever he asked if a seat was free—whether a friend was really about to arrive or the large teenage boys just didn't fancy sharing a compartment with a small boy he was unsure. Eventually Peter found a seat, one on the same side as the platform, so Peter was able to watch his grandmother waving, while getting smaller, as the train drew out of Euston in a swirl of steam.

As he sat staring out of the rather dirty windows North London slowly slipped by as the engine gathered speed. As he clutched the small bag in which were his overnight clothes as well as some sandwiches and some chocolate he realized his hands were all sweaty. It wasn't long before Peter took the wrapper off his bar of Five Boy's chocolate, offering it round the carriage. It broke the silence. They began chatting, mostly about what Christmas presents they had been given and what they had done during their holidays. One boy had even been to Westminster Abbey to see the tomb of the Unknown Soldier. A priest dressed in a long black cassock swept down the adjoining corridor sliding back the door to ask if all was well. Peter nodded and noticed some of the slightly older boys muttered: "Yes thank you, Father." "He's a 'Jay,'" said one of the boys, "it's our nickname for the teachers."

The steam engine and its eight carriages soon left London's suburbs, snaking their way through rolling countryside filled with the bare skeletal shapes of winter trees; it was a strange sight for a city boy like Peter. He was more used to the hustle and bustle of the horses, carts and the occasional car seen on the Finchley Road. The train passed through large industrial towns with smoking chimneys and huge factories all nestling close to the railway line to make the movement of their materials easier. Peter saw the station names, which were all new to him; there was Rugby, Crewe and Preston before the train finally pulled into a small station where, on the platform, a large dark red sign with white writing proclaimed it to be Whalley.

Whalley is in the Ribble Valley on the banks of Lancashire's River Calder and as Peter got off the train he could see it was a small village of flint-stone houses. It was also snowing and as the station lay on high ground it was exposed to a biting cold wind that blew the smoke and steam from the stationary locomotive; there was a special smell that lived with small boys for the rest of their lives. Fortunately he did not have to struggle down the long flight of steps with his trunk; there were porters from the school there to do that.

When he got outside the station he saw a row of red coaches with "Ribble Motor Services" written on their sides. A man in uniform shouted in what peter would come to recognize as a broad Lancashire accent: "The last coach for Hodder Place." Peter knew one of the other boys that had been in his compartment was at Hodder so he followed him onboard the coach before sitting next to him for the four-mile drive to his new school.

As the coach made its way Peter watched the hilly countryside draped in a mantle of glistening snow, but already the winter light was fading. The bus passed through large iron gates coming to a halt on a tarmac forecourt outside a reddish, stone building that looked a little like a small castle with large windows. It was a Georgian building with two towers added that made it look like a castle. The boys all stood together on the tarred area outside the house; in front of them was one of the "Jays" who Peter soon learned was the Superior, or Headmaster. His name was Father Walter Weld S. J. (Society of Jesus); with him were the matron and a helper who was also a kitchen hand and odd-job man. Older boys pointed into the darkness telling Peter that here was the playground. Over there lay the Paradise Meadows—where he would learn to play rugby—and, pointing deep into the night, there was the River Hodder where they all went bathing in the summer. "Will there be enough snow for us to go tobogganing tomorrow in Paradise?" said one boy. "Perhaps it might even be cold enough for skaint on Observatory Pond," said another.

From there they were shepherded into the light of a large dormitory where each boy was shown a cubicle. Peter looked at his own small booth; it wasn't as big as his bedroom at home, but he felt happy that he wasn't alone and was surrounded by other small boys. Matron then took the boys over to a line of hand basins and lockers telling them it was the "wash place." The idea of washing alongside small boys was less appealing to Peter. As an only child he wasn't used to having to share.

After the boys unpacked the bags they had carried with them on the train, the matron walked them to the dining room for a supper of bread and butter and iced cake. Afterwards it was back to the wash place. Father Weld watched the boys brush their teeth, before they wriggled into their pajamas. Next came something totally new to Peter. He was used to saying his prayers by himself but all this was about to change. At Hodder the Superior led night prayers with the boys praying in unison. The Superior ended the prayer with the words: "Death is certain, but the time and manner uncertain, whether by a long disease or by an unexpected accident . . . be you therefore ready at every moment, seeing that you may die at any moment."

As the boys climbed into bed the matron reappeared to show the new boys one last thing before she turned out the lights. "Look under your beds." As Peter bent down he spied a cream-colored, china chamber pot, written on the side were the words "Quant Je Puis." The next day he asked one of the slightly older boys what it meant. "It's the school motto. It means, As Much As I Can."

1

Family Affairs

1913-1932

Peter Glenville, despite his unwanted entrance, went on to have a life more fascinating and more rewarding than most people could have imagined. It was a life that saw him live up to his school motto and do as much as he could and arguably more. He was extremely successful in the theater and cinema, working as an actor and director with some of the biggest names. His homes were stylish, filled with antiques and fine art. He traveled the world, living a life of luxury, dining in the finest restaurants. He dressed elegantly and mixed with the rich and famous. He counted not only actors and writers as friends, but also artists, politicians and even royalty. He found personal happiness, and was loved by both family and friends. He was intellectually curious, loved reading, music, history and learning languages. Most of all he loved people, and particularly enjoyed time with friends; he even liked meeting people with whom he disagreed. To everyone he was charming; Peter Glenville had a lust for life in all its many guises.

But Peter's story began on a less propitious note as he revealed through his own words, written for a memoir that he never completed.

Nothing had prepared her for this: she lay there in the large bed in her own house in Hampstead, strong, beautiful and frightened, for the first birth pangs had begun to grip. She was resentful. After all she had already at the age of 22, fought her way, albeit without any setbacks, to a position of what, in the London of 1913, could pass as the beginning of respectable middle-class affluence. She had four maids to carry out her commands and to which she paid ten shillings a week. Whenever she strode up the eight balustraded steps to her front door with its panels of coloured glass, she felt as safe as an animal in its lair. Outside was the world in which she could exercise her talents, her womanly allure, and her considerable will. She didn't analyse or even respect the world very much at all. It was merely an arena in which she could engage valiantly for money, fame and admiration.

It was an enclosed, prosperous, English world; easy game for a determined and healthy woman of honest, if self-interested, principles. She had ordered her affairs well. Her sitting room was enhanced [by] an assembly of fairly expensive copies of something she had heard called the Louis Quinze style with pink-and-blue upholstery. Her dining room was serious with its complete set of Jacobean-style furnishings from [an] established firm. . . . The coal fires cracked out a cosy welcome as she entered these rooms, and the sound seemed to suggest a connivance, a sympathy with her aims and progress. The skivvy blackened the grates at seven o'clock while she slept soundly next to her husband.

For she had also acquired a partner, masculine and a little unpredictable with his Irish humour, superstitious Puritanism, and bouts of bullish will power that contrasted—so oddly—with his usual concern for her wishes and admiration of her person. It was that sudden access of his will that had forced her in to this uncomfortable and unwelcome role of expectant mother; that had caused that scene with a current of considerable violence when he had discovered her drinking a glass of gin with a medicine in an elementary effort to persuade the embryo to vacate the premises it so pensively occupied in her womb.

He had a strong, thick-set physique, for he had boxed as a boy in Irish villages. At that moment his handsome face had flushed to a mauve colour and his dimpled chin had suddenly jutted forward in an unappealing and alarming way. He had snatched the glass of gin and had thrown it into the fireplace where the glass shattered against the background of burgundy tiles and the liquid had sizzled over the coals. She had been frightened, for her courage always collapsed instantly when she encountered physical danger; and he, seeing this fear in her eyes, had pushed her backwards across the room and she had fallen over the side of an armchair, [and] her feet had shot upward in an undignified way. Shaun, for such was his name, had muttered, 'Dolly, how dare you: It'd be bloody murder.' After a moment of silence she had let out a tiny, strangled scream, for she disapproved of swear words, and that was that. The scene had been melodramatic and inadequate. Neither had referred to it again. And, now, here she was, so unjustly she thought, condemned to this discomfort and pain, and, finally, to the deliverance of a distinct impediment to her career.

She so needed to conserve her figure and her energy and concentration for her next appearance in a few weeks' time before the public, as she called it. For she was already a star. A theatrical star, who had an admiring following in the provincial towns in the Midlands. She was already talked about for her exhilarating rendering of popular songs, her extravagant and fantastic costumes, and a fine pair of legs. However coquettish and vapid the lyrics she sang were, she gave them a resonance and defiant sincerity that belied their vacuity, and seemed to command applause.

She lunged strongly across the bed and rang the bell. Soon she heard a thudding of hurried footsteps on the stairs. After

> *a knock on the door a small and plain young woman in a cap and apron stood awkwardly on the threshold. Dolly turned with an exaggerated look of panic on her face and whispered, 'Tell Shaun to call the doctor and the nurse—it's started. For God's sake, quickly!' The woman retreated and Dolly turned back and gazed at the ceiling. The pain had already stopped and so she began to tot up her accounts both in terms of finance and of the general assets of her life. She enjoyed calculating in this way. It gave her a sense of order, even of mastery. Things looked—apart from this present and mysterious interruption of nature—good. She had never thought they would not. She had always had a good life, and, now, it was a better one.*

Peter was born on October 28, 1913, at his parents' home at 126 Greencroft Gardens, Camden in north London. His parents, Dorothy "Dolly" Ward and Shaun Glenville, were actors. Not just jobbing actors but one of the most famous couples to tread the boards of the music hall and variety circuit, appearing in revues and musical comedies; they were true celebrities. Among Dorothy's many admirers over the years were men in high places, including two Prime Ministers—David Lloyd George and Winston Churchill. The Glenvilles came to fame in the days before television and radio; even silent movies were in their infancy. Theirs was the heyday of the music hall, with its singing, dancing, comedy sketches and specialty acts like ventriloquists, impressionists, and even talking parrots; going to the theater was Britain's most popular night out.

The Glenvilles' talents weren't confined to music halls. They were renowned for working together in pantomime in mother and son roles. Small in stature, Shaun dressed as an older woman playing the "panto dame" that suited his talent for knockabout comedy and fast-paced gags, while Dorothy dressed in tights and shorts played the romantic hero; she was a "principal boy." For her it was the ideal role, given her glamorous looks and curvaceous figure. Unlike other principal boys Dorothy eschewed fishnets, although an admiring Mae West once gave her a large stock of them; Dorothy would wear as many as ten different pairs of tights in a show. With two performances daily it meant twenty changes; putting them on made her neck muscles ache.

For Dorothy there was nothing manly about playing a principal boy, as she revealed to *The Stage*: "When a principal boy swings one shapely leg forward and thumps a fist into the opposite palm, she is imitating some lost vision of man. When she adopts a resolute and deliberately unladylike stance, feet firmly planted apart, or hooks her thumbs nonchalantly in her belt, she is assuming postures which are meant to be recognized as manly but she is not trying to create an illusion of manhood."

Pantomime is a uniquely British form of theater. Although traditionally put on at Christmas and New Year, pantomime story lines usually don't refer to Christmas, but are based on children's stories such as *Jack and the Beanstalk*, *Cinderella* and *Mother Goose*. They are performed for a family audience and incorporate songs, dance routines, raucous slapstick and cross-dressing; pantomime is most children's introduction to the theater. Children love scrambling for sweets thrown into the audience, hissing at the villain and pointing out his sneaky moves to the hero and heroine with shouts of "He's behind you!" Parents laugh at the double entendre of the actors' lines and the political in-jokes that change from year to year. Pantomime is still popular in Britain, attracting top actors such as Sir Ian McKellen to don a wig, high heels, a skirt and rouge to play a panto dame. These days it's the latest TV soap stars that put on the tights to play the principal boy.

When Dorothy and Shaun were a double act, pantomime was at the height of its popularity, and the public adored them as its stars. Between the two world wars there would be as many as 500 pantomimes staged outside of London every Christmas season. Each of the thirty suburban theaters around

London staged a pantomime, and more than half the theaters in London's West End theater district did the same. Shows opened in late December and often continued through to the following March.

Both Shaun and Dorothy began working in the theater early in life. Shaun's first stage appearance was when he was two weeks old at the Theatre Royal, Birmingham in *Arrah-Na-Pogue, or the Wicklow Wedding*, a play by the Irish dramatist Dion Boucicault. Shaun's early introduction to the proscenium was because he came from a theatrical family. He was born plain John Browne at 27 Little Denmark Street, Dublin, Ireland, on May 16, 1884. His father Henry Browne was an actor and a comedian, who performed as "Harry Glenville," taking his stage name from Glenville House in County Waterford. Harry achieved considerable success and even worked with the first actor ever to be knighted, Sir Henry Irving. Shaun's mother Mary (née Lynch) was the manager of what was then the Mechanics Theatre in Dublin, and is now the prestigious Abbey Theatre famed for its promotion of playwrights such as William Butler Yeats and Sean O'Casey. At that time managers were also actors, and the current distinction between directors and actors didn't exist. Shaun's mother appeared as Mary Glenville, in both straight and comic roles, billed as "The Queen of Irish Comedy."

Harry and Mary had four children: Shaun, Matthew, Herbert and Katie. Matthew and Herbert followed their parents onto the stage, although with considerable less success than Shaun; Matthew moved into theater management running Scarborough's Theatre Royal and then Chesterfield's Hippodrome. Shaun spent his childhood steeped in the theater, learning how to sing, dance, make props and paint scenery at the Mechanics Theatre. He was taught to clog dance by an Irish champion and appeared in two plays each week as well as in farce and variety.

By 1901 Shaun had moved to England, taking on both comic and straight roles, appearing in pantomime for the first time in 1903, "[shining] brightly in an Irish character," the Baron, in

Cinderella at Coatbridge's Royal Theatre. He went on to make his London debut in a sketch in *Humpty Dumpty* at the Holborn Empire in 1906. Outside of the pantomime season Shaun spent the rest of the year touring as a comedian billed as "The Youngest Real Irish Comedian." He played Irish characters in his own sketches, and performed comic roles in dramas and musical comedies.

Dorothy was born on April 26, 1890, although in later years, conscious of her image and ever vain, she frequently gave her birth date as anything up to five years later. During interviews she was always evasive, saying: "I want audiences to enjoy the pantomime, not to wonder if I've got my own teeth." Having an adult son didn't always fit her image either as *The Sunday Times* critic James Agate recalled in 1935 when she was forty-five and her son twenty-two: "Dorothy, meeting some American managers and not particularly wanting to advertise herself as the mother of so bouncing a boy as Master Brabazon, Peter Glenville. Peter introduced himself as 'Mr. Brabazon.' All went well until Peter said, 'Isn't it about time you gave me a new sports car, darling?' and Dorothy answered, 'I give you too much as it is!' The Americans said nothing, but looked on in horror at what they obviously thought was a real-life scene from *Our Betters*." A play by William Somerset Maugham, *Our Betters* tells the story of an aristocratic married couple and their respective lovers. It seems Dorothy preferred a whiff of possible scandal to acknowledging her advancing years.

Unlike Shaun, Dorothy's parents had no theatrical roots, instead her Jewish father, Edwin "Ted" Ward and mother Eliza (née Millichamp), ran the Big Bull's Head pub in Birmingham, West Midlands. Dorothy's brother Leslie, three years her junior, later followed in her footsteps and made a living on the stage. By a quirk of fate, it was pantomime that drew Dorothy to the stage. When she was fourteen she went to see *Jack and the Beanstalk* at a local theater. Dorothy was so touched by the performance of the principal boy Ada Reeve that she cried when Reeve "sold" her prize possession, a cow called Jessie. Stagestruck, Dorothy left the theater determined to make her name in pantomime.

Dorothy always believed passionately in her roles, and her favorite was always Jack in *Jack and the Beanstalk*: "It's a part I can get my teeth into, not like Colin in *Mother Goose*." For her, the scene where Jack sells his cow for a bag of beans became the equivalent of Ophelia's mad scene in *Hamlet*, and she would always want to know how any of her rivals had sold the cow. The first time Peter watched her play Jack it was from a theater box and he became so agitated that he yelled, "Mummy! Mummy! Don't sell Jessie."

She made her stage debut in her hometown in 1905, playing the "Third Girl," Zenobia, in a pantomime based on the *Bluebeard* fairytale. Dorothy's introduction to the smell of the grease paint is symptomatic of the ambition, drive, determination and sheer force of character she exhibited throughout her entire career. She discovered that a friend of her mother, Lester Collingwood, was putting on a pantomime at Birmingham's Alexandra Theatre, and went to him saying, "I'm Ted Ward's daughter. Will you give me a job?" She sang for him and then found herself employed as understudy to the principal girl at a rate of thirty shillings a week. Yet luck as well as chutzpah played a part on her road to stardom. When the principal girl fell ill with laryngitis, Dorothy stepped in to take her place.

She won over audiences with her rendition of the song, "How'd You Like To Spoon With Me?" Peter later wrote that Dorothy sang the tune in a way never heard before: "Heretofore the lyric had been a simpering invitation flirtatious and inviting a smile rather than a response. Now, Miss Dorothy Ward, a tall girl, directed a question to the audience in firm, strong tones. A candid question: would they not like to spoon with her? A smile was on her lips that assumed but one reply. And yet, the hold of her head, the youthful but womanly purity of her interpretation of the lyric also suggested that an affirmative reply from the audience would be but a natural tribute and admitted no suggestion of compliance on her part. 'Do you admire me?' she seemed to ask, and, at the end of the song the answer was an unequivocal, 'Yes.' The applause continued long after she had finished." The next day the local newspapers talked of the "Birmingham girl's success"; Dorothy later referred to it as the happiest time of her life.

Following her success she began working for the playwright, producer and director Robert Courtneidge, making her London debut in April 1906 in *The Dairymaids* at the Apollo Theatre. It was the start of a long-running business relationship as both she and Shaun worked for him frequently. *Bluebeard* was the only pantomime in which Dorothy didn't play the part of principal boy, but the opportunity came around fast. In 1906 she was hired to play Dandini and the understudy for Prince Charming in Robert Courtneidge's *Cinderella* at the King's Theatre in Edinburgh. Fortunately for Dorothy, the actress playing the prince fell ill before the show opened. Dorothy was asked to pad out her then rather thin legs and take over. At sixteen she became the youngest actress ever to play principal boy and by the age of twenty she was well known as "The Best of Boys," earning £200 a week; a fabulous wage for the time. It wasn't just her glamour that endeared her to fans and critics, it was also her manner, as Agate recalled: "[She is a] really good sort, with no nonsense about her, and a hard worker. When you talk to her you feel that it's not her coiffeur but her sunny disposition which gives her that buttercup hair."

Unsurprisingly Dorothy's path soon crossed with that of Shaun. They met in 1910 in *Little Jack Horner* at Newcastle's Royal Theatre; Dorothy was principal boy, Jack, and Shaun played the panto dame—Jack's mother. On the last night of the run they announced from the stage that the hero had agreed to marry his mother. They married in 1911 at a Registry Office in Buckingham Palace Road, London; thereafter Dorothy would often introduce Shaun as, "This is my husband who plays my mother."

The couple crisscrossed Britain performing in Argyll, Brighton, Liverpool and Leeds; that is until Dorothy found herself pregnant. However, she continued working until she was six months' pregnant, but she was ill on more than one occasion early on in her pregnancy. She took time off "indisposed with a relaxed throat" and then again after a "turn," which may have been euphemisms to disguise morning sickness.

Despite the couple's breakneck schedule and Dorothy's evident determination that her pregnancy would not stall her career, Peter was born and named Peter Patrick Brabazon Browne in October 1913. Dorothy's mother was there to help at the birth, and went on to play a huge part in Peter's childhood; in essence she brought him up. Peter lived with her and Dorothy's sister Irene at the Shaun and Dorothy's home near London's Finchley Road. Grandmother and Aunt had moved in to bring up Peter as his parents were away from home for such long periods of time. The arrangement did have an upside. Leslie Ward's son by his first marriage, Patrick "Terry" Ward, lived there too. Terry was the same age as Peter, and the boys became fond of each other as they grew up together like brothers, sharing each other's company when Peter was home during the school holidays.

Shaun was appearing in the *Rienzi: Overture* revue at London's Empire Theatre in Leicester Square when Peter was born. Just a week later Shaun and Dorothy appeared in pantomime, starring in *Humpty Dumpty* at Manchester's Theatre Royal. The show opened on December 23, 1913, running until February 11 the following year. Despite the outbreak of the First World War in June 1914 Dorothy's first year of motherhood was when she finally began to be taken seriously as an actress and singer rather than just as a "principal boy." She was feted for her role as Louise, "The Princess of the Pictures," in Robert Courtneidge musical comedy, *The Cinema Star.* After touring the provinces the show opened at the Shaftesbury Theatre in June and Dorothy took London by storm. The press heaped plaudits on Dorothy for her "sprightly" dancing, "vivid personality," "vocalisation of beauty" and "voice of exceptional power," declaring her "a new leading lady." While Dorothy had already trodden the boards of London stages, this time critics sat up and took notice as never before. The *Daily Express* review was typical: "Miss Ward has made a name in the principal provincial cities as the ideal principal boy, but in London she is comparatively unknown. Well, she came last night, she was seen, and she conquered." In a world where the principal way to see a performance was still "live" on stage, it took longer to become a nationally recognized figure than when television arrived; equally stars shone for longer.

Despite the outbreak of the First World War the Glenvilles remained in constant demand. War made patriotic songs the order of the day, and Shaun had "a hit" with "Are We Downhearted? No–!" (1914). He traveled to France in May 1915 to entertain British soldiers with songs such as "Tommy's Learning French" (1915). As an Irishman, Shaun didn't face conscription at the outset of the war, but by August 1915 he held a commission in the Royal Highland Regiment, known as The Black Watch. As a 31-year-old married man, Shaun would have been one of the last considered for active military service. It may have equally been the case that he was deemed unfit for service as he had an operation in October 1915 that forced him to convalesce for two months before he returned to work in pantomime at Christmas.

Dorothy was famed for her English-rose looks, "red-gold tresses," "expansive smile," dazzling costumes and excellent voice. In his book, *The Melodies Linger On: The Story of Music Hall*, theater manager Walter Macqueen-Pope described Dorothy as "a handsome and striking woman, with auburn hair, wonderful carriage and fine figure . . . a great principal boy, something out of the Land of Romance. Tights become her, they are second nature to her and she understands pantomime and its topsy turviness. To see her as 'Jack' in *Jack and the Beanstalk* defy the giant outside his castle, wearing shining armour and then join in mortal combat with him in his own kitchen, clad in trailing clouds of gauze and silk, is to witness true pantomime. . . . Her husband is Shaun Glenville, a first-class star of the halls and a pantomime dame without equal; he knows how to sing songs, especially Irish ones."

She created a sexier version of the principal boy than had previously been seen; previously principal boys were attractive women, but corseted in cumbersome outfits made by theatrical costumiers. Dorothy caused a revolution when she insisted a dressmaker rather than a tailor should make her costumes. She wore specially made soft boots, and high-heeled court shoes that accentuated the curves of her "Junoesque figure." As Jack, Dorothy would never enter the same costume twice in a performance; she would ascend the beanstalk in one outfit and descend in another that was even more elaborate. She opted for figure-hugging opulent costumes made of lace, diamante, velvet, fur and ostrich feathers. Dorothy gave principal boys sex appeal.

Dorothy became so comfortable in men's attire that in 1916 she even risked prison when she strutted the streets of London dressed as man. She told the *Daily Mirror* newspaper of her bold escapade: "It all came about through a bet . . . the [theatre] company bet me a new girl's outfit that I would not go out in men's clothes. I went out from the theatre at nine o'clock dressed in tweeds, straw hat, gloves, stick and red 'Gilbert the Filbert' hair. I walked down Shaftesbury Avenue and the Strand. A woman heard me speak in my ordinary voice and spoke to a policeman. Two policemen came up to me and said, 'You're a woman aren't you?' And almost before I could speak they took me along to Bow Street [police station]. I told them who I was, and I had dressed as a man. I had a severe lecture, and was told I was liable to three months' imprisonment. Well, I have won my bet, and everything has ended happily."

Shaun and Dorothy were friends of composer Fred Godfrey, and Peter became a childhood friend of Godfrey's youngest daughter, Peggie. Godfrey wrote "Take Me Back To Dear Old Blighty" (1916) and "Bless 'Em All, The Long And The Short And The Tall" (1917) that were popular with British soldiers on the Western Front. Dorothy introduced one of his hits: "[In 1916] came 'Take Me Back To Dear Old Blighty,' which Fred Godfrey wrote in my house at Hampstead. I was due to sing it at Liverpool the next day, and there was no time to get the band parts written, so Godfrey himself came up with me and accompanied me on the piano." Shaun cut records of Godfrey songs including "Where Did You Get The Name Of Hennessy?" (1915) and "The Yiddisher Irish Baby" (1915), while Dorothy recorded "Blue Eyes" (1915) and "I Love My Motherland" (1916).

Songs are an integral part of pantomime, even more so when Dorothy and Shaun were stars. Dorothy used a group of children known as the Dorothy Dots to accompany her. She wrote in a 1924 edition of *Popular Music Weekly*, "Songs play a tremendous part in pantomime. . . . It would be a very poor pantomime indeed that did not depend partly on the big musical hits for its success. Songs are chosen for panto with the greatest possible care. Eleventh-hour successes are put in, and older numbers have to give precedence to the new ones, for success is the thing, and no principal boy can sing her way to triumph unless she has the right song to do it with. I have seen pantomimes ruined through a bad choice of songs of the year. In some cases, when those pantomimes possessed 'stars' of merit who were included in the production, the show has failed because of the poorness of the songs. I am not saying, of course, that the songs are everything, but they are of tremendous importance."

Songs were "tried out" in the early Christmas shows in Glasgow, and if they proved popular they appeared in pantomimes up and down the country. Success generated huge sales in sheet music so that people could play them at home on the piano. Shaun was also a songwriter, known for his Irish-themed songs. He penned "When An Irishman Goes Fighting" (1914) with Godfrey and solo he composed "He's A Credit To Ould Ireland

Now" (1916), "As Long As You're Irish You'll Do" (1916) and "Magee, Malone, McGinty and McGurk" (1922). His greatest success was "If You're Irish, Come Into the Parlour" (1919), which he wrote with Frank Miller. Many years later, in 1961, he performed it on a TV special with Bing Crosby as part of a medley of cockney songs.

Song writing and recording made the Glenvilles more money, but they were also adept at making money outside of the theater. Even then celebrity endorsement helped sell products and helped to make Shaun and Dorothy even richer. Dorothy endorsed a variety of products in newspaper advertorials, from tonics and toothbrushes to the popular Dr. Williams' Pink Pills. At two shillings and nine pence a box, the sugarcoated pink pills contained a combination of iron oxide and Epsom salts, and were touted as a general tonic "for restoring strength to weak nerves and new rich blood to the feeble and anaemic." In one ad under the headline, "How To Enjoy Life," Dorothy claimed: "I recognise how valuable Dr. Williams' Pink Pills have been in helping me to be well and keep well. What is good for the singer is good for the audience, that is why I willingly give public praise to Dr. Williams' Pink Pills; it is fully due to them."

Maybe it was the frenetic pace of Dorothy and Shaun's working life but for whatever reason they didn't register Peter's birth until April 14, 1919; almost six years after he was born. There has been some speculation that it could be because Peter's parentage was open to doubt. Even in his seventies, Peter told his cousin, Terry's half-brother, John Ward, and his wife, Janet, why he'd never written an autobiography: "People are always asking me to write my life story, but how can I with all the stories that go round about our family? I don't know who I am half the time." It's conjecture but perhaps Dorothy Glenville saw Peter as something of a detraction from her image as the "sexy" pantomime star.

According to Janet Ward, "Dorothy had a few affairs, including one with the Duke of Westminster, 'Bendor.' [Some people] think that Peter is his son, but I don't. I think he was Shaun's son, he was small like Shaun and had the same wicked sense of humour."

Hugh Richard Arthur Grosvenor, second Duke of Westminster, commonly known as "Bendor" after a racehorse owned by his father, was a colorful character and the antithesis of Shaun. A wealthy aristocrat, the duke was a ladies' man, war hero and politically active. He married his first wife in 1901 and was divorced by 1919; he went on to marry three more times. Known for having affairs, most famously a 5-year dalliance with the French fashion designer Gabrielle "Coco" Chanel whom he met in 1925, he was a daredevil, racing motorboats for Great Britain in the 1908 London Olympics. He was also a war hero, having been awarded the Distinguished Service Order in the First World War for commanding the Cheshire Yeomanry's Rolls-Royce armored car raid that destroyed a German camp in Egypt; he and his men then raced to the rescue of sailors aboard ship under siege by the enemy, 120 miles away.

An active member of the Conservative Party, he supported various right-wing causes in the run up to the Second World War, including the Anglo-German Fellowship. However, less noble was his membership of The Right Club, infamous for their anti-Semitic views. In 1931 he famously outed his brother-in-law, William Lygon the seventh Earl Beauchamp and leader of the Liberal Party in the House of Lords to King George V, as a homosexual. Homosexuality was a criminal offence and the Duke hoped to ruin the Liberal Party by his vindictive act. It was said that the King was horrified by the revelation, saying: "I thought men like that shot themselves." To avoid prosecution Lygon resigned and went to live abroad, a virtual exile.

Dorothy met Bendor when she was just sixteen, and working at the Folies Bergère cabaret in Paris. Famous for its showgirls and nude dancers it was hugely popular, and its often wealthy audience included European royalty. Dorothy and other English showgirls were chaperoned by an English governess; they lived in a private hostel for girls and took lessons in French. Bendor admired Dorothy sufficiently to give her a black leather jewel-casket that had her initials studded in diamonds on the lid. When Dorothy died in 1987 her estate was valued at £1.3 million. Speculation continues that she accrued such a large sum thanks to a lifetime pension from the Westminster estate. However, there are no details of how, when and where Dorothy and the Duke might have rekindled their friendship. Peter may well have liked the idea of this "noble" connection, but given his theatrical talent, mordant wit and strong physical resemblance to his father, it seems certain that Peter was Shaun's son.

Dorothy's penchant for rakish risk-takers was not confined to Bendor. In middle age, she was romantically linked to the Scotsman, Captain James "Jim" Mollison, a man fifteen years her junior, a dashing hero and aviation pioneer who broke records for flights from England to South Africa and Australia, and in 1932 was the first pilot to perform an East-to-West solo transatlantic flight. Mollison was a louche charmer as well as a notorious drinker and gambler. In 1932 he married aviatrix Amy Johnson, but they divorced six years later. Mollison was unashamed of his reputation, even calling his 1937 memoirs *Playboy of the Air*. Such was Mollison's affection for Dorothy that he dedicated his book to her and named his Bellanca 28-90 Flash aircraft *The Dorothy*. He chose to paint the aircraft in a garish fashion; its fuselage, fin and rudder were orange, and its wings and tail plane were green. Mollison's biographer David Luff speculated that Dorothy gave Mollison money toward buying the plane, and its color scheme may have been an affectionate nod to Shaun's Irish roots. It was actually painted that way because the Dublin-based Hospitals Trust, which ran the Irish sweepstake, had backed Mollison.

On Thursday, October 29, 1936, Mollison flew *The Dorothy* solo from Hardford Grace, Newfoundland in Canada, landing at Croydon Airport to the south of London the next day. The thirteen hour and seventeen minutes flight broke the record for an eastward crossing of the Atlantic. Dorothy was appearing in a revue at the King's Theatre in Edinburgh. She told reporters: "I am thrilled he got across, immediately my performance is over tonight I am rushing to London by train to meet him." She added how thrilled she was to have *The Dorothy* named after her: "I am terribly happy. It makes me feel that I in a small way have helped his success. Jim is a very dear friend of mine. I am proud and thrilled to know he has won through." On Sunday Dorothy and Mollison flew to Edinburgh where press photographers snapped them: Dorothy looking glamorous in a full-length, fox-fur coat and a jaunty William Tell-style hat. The following day, to loud applause, she led Mollison on the stage at the end of her matinee performance.

When Mollison's biographer interviewed Peter in 1990, he agreed that his mother and Mollison had a romance, but refused to believe they were lovers. "Remember, that at forty-six my mother was 'on the edge,' and therefore quite flattered by his attentions as he was by hers. It was no more than a highly geared mutual flirtation. She was very kind to Amy and admired the Mollisons greatly. Amusingly, whenever she recalled Jim, she would demurely refer to him as 'that splendid cad.'"

Even after Peter's death his close friend the actor Alec Guinness revealed in a letter to Peter's partner of fifty-one years, Hardy William "Bill" Smith, that he had heard gossip that Peter might have been "the son of an Irishman called Brown or Browne . . . a well-known and handsome boxer." When Guinness asked Bill if there was any truth in the story, he denied it indignantly. Given that Shaun's birth surname was "Browne," it seems likely that Guinness had been prey to a case of severe Chinese whispers.

Shaun turned a blind eye to Dorothy's liaisons, although not always, as Janet Ward remembered: "Dorothy had gone out one night and she had on a lovely white ermine fur coat and a white evening dress—she'd been out with some guy. When she came back and the taxi drew up, Shaun came down the stairs and whacked her on the chin. She ended up in the gutter with her dress no longer white. He knew she had affairs, but he adored her and she did look after him in his declining years."

Whatever the truth behind Dorothy's assignations she and Shaun were married for fifty-seven years until he died in his sleep in 1968. They last worked together in pantomime in 1957, appearing in *Dick Whittington* at the Liverpool Pavilion Theatre, forty-seven years after they first trod the boards together; Dorothy was just shy of her sixty-seventh birthday. For years after Shaun's passing Dorothy placed "in memoriam" notices in *The Stage*—"Always in my thoughts darling." In 1927 she told readers of her agony-aunt column in the *Sheffield Mail* her views on the art of managing a husband: "I'm sure that if wives would only continue to play up to the spirit of the little boy who wants looking after there would be a better understanding between husbands and wives and the spirit of give and take which is the essence of success in double harness would be more in evidence."

If Dorothy's weakness was rakes and cads, Shaun's was alcohol; it may have been the Irish in him. While Shaun was known for being able to learn a part in only three days he was also notorious for forgetting his lines during a matinee show after a liquid lunch, or even forgetting which pantomime he was in that season—looking around the footlights for *Mother Goose* when he was starring in *Aladdin*. His love of the bottle made for amusing stories. In *Roy Hudd's Book of Music-Hall, Variety and Showbiz Anecdotes*, he relates what happened when Dorothy bought a Rolls-Royce: "Shaun rang his pal [the comedy actor] Robb Wilton. 'The car's a beauty,' said Shaun. 'How do you fancy a spin in the country?' Robb liked the sound of this idea, and the two of them set out for a drive. They passed several pubs, and didn't pass several more, until eventually they decided it would be safer to spend the night at a hotel. Early the next morning Robb awoke to the sound of breaking glass.

He looked out of the window, and there was Shaun taking a sledgehammer to the headlights of the Rolls. 'What are you doing?' shouted Robb. 'My boy,' said Shaun, thinking of his wife's reaction to his night away from home, 'we're having the accident now!'" According to Janet Ward, "Peter had no home life. He lived with his granny and his aunt who were both alcoholics."

Shaun's appetite for whisky wasn't good for his health. Whether regarded as a mere jovial drunk or an alcoholic, toward the end of his life he seemed to need a tot to keep him going, especially before going on stage. Peter tried to wean his father off the booze on more than one occasion but with little success, as Janet Ward revealed: "Peter used to go on cruises with his father to try and dry him out. He used to lock Shaun up in his cabin, but it was impossible."

It was Dorothy who had the financial savvy, and her attraction to men proved useful in filling the family coffers. Janet Ward explained: "It took Dorothy all her time to keep Shaun in check. They were different days then in the music hall. They got paid at the stage door on a Friday night in cash. In about 1920 she was earning about £500 a week. She liked high-powered businessmen, and they told her what to invest in which is why she was always comfortably off. He spent it and she invested it."

Dorothy also liked to spend money, particularly when it came to clothes and jewelry. Even in her nineties she would sit in her easy chair at her home at Berkeley Court in London's Baker Street, clad in a fur stole, sporting a diamond brooch with perfectly coiffured hair and make-up. She even went to sleep wearing lipstick and powder in case she died during the night; the old trooper was afraid she would be discovered in a vulnerable or perhaps worse—a plain state. According to Roy Hudd, "One Christmas she was playing Colin, the miller's son in *Puss In Boots* for Emile Littler. At the dress rehearsal she made her first entrance in her 'poor boy' costume but wearing a positive fistful of diamond rings. She was very proud of how well she'd done, and wanted everyone else to know too. At the end of the run-through, Littler said, 'Dorothy, darling, you're supposed to be the poor miller's son. I think we should dispense with the diamond rings.' Dorothy said nothing, but on the opening night she came on with her hands behind her back and said, 'Here I am, Colin the poor miller's son.' She then waved her bejewelled hands at the audience and added, 'And look what the Good Fairy keeps giving me!'"

With two such colorful thespians as parents life wasn't always easy for Peter. Janet Ward said: "He didn't like his mother but he had to admire her determination. I think he was very fond of his father." Dorothy revealed her attitude towards bringing up her son in an article called "Treat your children as chums": "A practice I have adopted with great benefit is that of having little heart-to-heart chats with my boy. I do not mean lectures or homilies but little talks where we abandon the role of mother and son and become just chums. He appreciates them as much as I do and will come and say, 'Let's have one of our little chats mums.'" Perhaps this is why Peter enjoyed a far closer relationship with his parents as an adult than a child. As a theater director in London he would sometimes head for dinner at The Ivy or The Savoy with one of the playwrights he was working with such as Terence Rattigan; Dorothy would often join them. Peter's background was not that of the British upper classes; his access was gained through the combination of the wealth and the fame of his parents. But he grew to be a man of sophisticated, refined and intellectual tastes, one who later moved in society's highest circles, mixing with presidents, politicians and princes.

According to Janet Ward, Dorothy and Shaun "adored" Peter. Although their life in the theater meant they were rarely around, it provided considerable benefits. Their position on the British stage gave Peter an enviable wealth of contacts in the business. He also inherited Dorothy's looks, astuteness and sense of style, along with Shaun's wit, charm and wonderful sense of comic timing that made Peter a great raconteur. Moreover, his parents' prodigious success, and his mother's knack for making shrewd investments gave Peter financial independence.

One thing Peter didn't inherit from his mother was selfishness. When he grew up Peter entertained people with amusing tales about his parents, often told in an acerbic fashion. One such story was how Dorothy would send him biscuits when he was at boarding school, along with strict instructions not to share them with the other boys. Peter seems to have ignored his "dear mamma," and one of the first things colleagues and friends have said when asked about Peter is that he was kind and generous. Peter was astute with money, but at the same time he was quick to offer a loan or gift of money when friends or family were in need. He was generous when it came to giving gifts, not just financially but in the thought he put into choosing them. He was generous with his praise and encouragement to others, while being extremely modest about his own achievements, preferring to talk little about himself.

By the time Peter started boarding school in 1922, while Shaun and Dorothy were riding the crest of a successful wave; peacetime had brought even greater prosperity to the theater. According to respected theater critic Harold Hobson, "London playhouses were crowded, and every Sunday touring companies spread throughout the length and breadth of Britain from one 'date' to another, carrying with them a provincial version of the latest metropolitan successes." But the Glenvilles' horizons stretched further afield.

Shaun had visited America in 1907 as Shaun Glenville Luck, one of The Six Brothers Luck company, who performed pantomime, but as a couple the Glenvilles had not played on Broadway. In March 1921 they sailed to America on the *Mauretania* luxury ocean liner. They went to head the cast of *Phoebe of Quality Street*, a musical version of Sir James M. Barrie's play, *Quality Street*. Dorothy played Phoebe Throssel and Sean played Sergeant Terence O'Toole, a comic role invented for him. Barrie is most famous as the creator of the children's story *Peter Pan, or The Boy Who Wouldn't Grow Up*, but he was well known as a playwright, and *Phoebe of Quality Street* was a musical revival of a favorite with theatergoers. The show's first night was in May at Poli's Theatre in Washington, D.C., where it played to "a fashionable and distinguished diplomatic audience" that included President Warren G. Harding. The politician was so taken with Shaun's performance that he presented the actor with his portrait inscribed: "To Shaun Glenville. With many thanks for an enjoyable evening and many hearty laughs. Good wishes from the White House. Warren G. Harding."

The show was expected to go on tour, but such was the enthusiasm of its reception in Washington that the musical was immediately transferred to Broadway's Shubert Theatre. The transatlantic newcomers received positive reviews and the *Evening Journal* described Shaun as "a comedian of the robust type, with gifted Irish feet and a good singing voice." But it was Dorothy, billed as "England's Greatest Comedienne," who won over the New York critics. The *Evening World* said: "The golden-haired Dorothy Ward, from London, scored an undoubted success, she sang and danced with delightful spirit and was as pretty as a picture even when she was supposed to look worn and faded. *Phoebe of Quality Street* is attractive in its music and the lovely and melodious Miss Ward." *The New York Times* singled her out as "the most astonishing bit of casting that the current season has witnessed. She is a handsome and buxom young English woman, who looks like Mrs. Clare Sheridan, with just a dash of Margot Kelly . . . [with] considerable assets of voice and vitality."

The Shubert Organisation had booked the couple for only six weeks but they proved so popular they were signed up to play in the musical *The Whirl of New York* that toured St. Louis, Chicago and Boston. June saw them on Broadway playing at the Winter Garden Theatre, and the production ran until September. Dorothy played the part of a showgirl and fiancée of the heir to a large fortune, Cora Angélique, and Shaun her father, Doc

Snifkins. Dorothy received lavish reviews and *The New York Times* pronounced her the audience's favorite performer in the show saying she "plays the musical comedy queen with enough verve for two or three people." The *New York Review* was equally ecstatic about Broadway's new star: "Dorothy Ward, the auburn-haired English beauty the Shuberts brought over from England, scored the biggest hit any woman had made at the Winter Garden in years, and her reception can be only compared with that of Al Jolson or Blanche Ring." They conquered Broadway with the same mix of vitality and talent that made them so popular in Britain.

Dorothy and Shaun could easily afford the fees of £150 a year to send Peter to prep school at Hodder Place in Lancashire's Ribble Valley in northeast England. Hodder was the "preparatory school" for Stonyhurst College, situated a mile away. Stonyhurst is a Roman Catholic boarding school run in the Jesuit tradition. Shaun was a Catholic, and his wife converted to Catholicism, so Stonyhurst was a far from an unusual choice of school for their son. The Society of Jesus was founded by Saint Ignatius Loyola, and is the largest religious male order in the Catholic Church. The Jesuit priests that make up the order are famed for their missionary work, their love of cultural pursuits and their intellectual rigor that has led them to become advocates of human rights and social justice.

The Society of Jesuits established the college in 1593 at St. Omer in what is now northern France. During the reign of Queen Elizabeth I Catholics in England were persecuted, and the school at St. Omer was one of many schools catering to English expatriates. Ironically in 1762 the Jesuits had to flee from St. Omer to avoid persecution themselves and moved to Bruges in Belgium before settling in Liège in 1773. With religious intolerance in Britain a thing of the past the school moved back "home" in 1794 when a former St. Omer pupil gifted the Stonyhurst estate to the

Jesuits; this included Shireburn Hall, built in 1592, which became the college premises, and a large building close to the River Hodder, Hodder Place, which opened as a prep school in 1855.

The five academic years of the Stonyhurst are called Lower Grammar, Grammar, Syntax, Poetry and Rhetoric. Unlike most English public schools, it's organized horizontally by year groups known as "Playrooms" rather than vertically by houses. The head pupil is called "Head of the Line," with junior pupils being in Lower Line and the sixth form in Higher Line. The school prefects are known as the "School Committee." These conventions, used during Peter's time at Stonyhurst, are still in use today.

The school's surroundings are as impressive as its pedigree. It is located in breathtaking countryside; little has changed since the 1920s. The first time Peter passed through the gates of Stonyhurst he would have been met with the same spectacular vista: a mile-long drive that passes between two large, rectangular ponds leading up to a large stone building with an arch at its entrance capped by two cupolas. The place is steeped in Catholic ritual and tradition, having been attended by Britain's oldest Catholic families over the centuries. The rural surroundings are quintessentially English: the lush greenery of its sweeping lawns, duck-filled lakes and wooded glades are set against a backdrop of rolling hills. The Jesuits extended Shireburn Hall over the centuries and today it is one of the largest buildings under one roof in Europe and is listed Grade 1 by English Heritage for its architecture and setting. In a range of styles from the Elizabethan to the Victorian, Stonyhurst's eclectic architecture boast exquisite stonework, superb wood paneling, colorful tiled floors and wonderful stained-glass windows that adorn its classrooms, corridors, dining halls, dormitories and chapels. It is home to a number of precious artefacts, from the statues and oil paintings that generously populate its floors and walls, to a library that houses a copy of William Shakespeare's

First Folio. Peter would be proud that today his portrait, donated by the Peter Glenville Foundation, graces the hall of illustrious alumni.

When Peter was at school the college's vast grounds made Stonyhurst almost self-sufficient: fruit and vegetables from its garden, along with meat, butter, milk and eggs from its farm, fed staff and pupils. It even had its own water supply and electric generator. Boys fished the ponds and river while the grounds accommodated a nine-hole golf course in addition to rugby and cricket pitches and perfect terrain for serious cross-country runs. In warm weather the boys went bathing in the river, and when it was cold they went skating on the ponds and tobogganing on surrounding hills. Teachers accompanied the boys on walks along the river or through the woods. It all must have made a big impression on 8-year-old Peter, and as he grew up he would have gained an appreciation for art and architecture that helped to develop the strong visual sense he employed as a stage and film director.

The French motto, Quant Je Puis, meaning "As Much as I Can," is central to the ethos of the school; it was inherited from the Shireburn family, who originally owned Stonyhurst. The motto is emblazoned in stone above the fireplace in the college's Top Refectory dining room and is completely in keeping with the Jesuit tradition to provide an all-round education based on seven principles—finding God in all things, caring for the individual, showing love in deeds, building Christian community, engaging with the wider world, encouraging excellence, and cooperating in Jesuit mission. The principles are in accordance with the ignatian philosophy of a strong sense of duty, a concept of service for others, and the idea of being used by God.

When Peter was at Stonyhurst it had an enviable reputation, and former pupils included politicians, saints, sportsmen, archbishops, European royalty and five winners of the Victoria Cross, Britain's highest award for gallantry in war. Among his predecessors were Sherlock Holmes' creator Sir Arthur Conan

Doyle (the setting for Baskerville Hall in his novel *The Hound of the Baskervilles* was based on Stonyhurst), actor Charles Laughton, and *The Lord of the Rings* author J. R. R. Tolkien.

Peter's school days followed a strict regime. Each day began with a wake-up call provided by a large wooden rattle. There followed a busy timetable as a contemporary of Peter's recalled: "We got up at seven, got dressed and went to mass, every day. Breakfast was in one of two refectories; there was one for smaller boys and he would have been in that to begin with. For breakfast we had porridge, bread and butter and jam or marmalade. And one could have—if one's parents paid a little extra—something of a cooked breakfast. Then we had various periods of study, four different classes from about nine-thirty until ten. We had a break at about eleven, and if the weather was good we went outside, if not we played inside. There was then a fifteen-minute period of physical training under instructors and then lunch.

"After lunch there was recreation of one form or another. On a half-holiday there would be games, cricket and so on. On other days there would be a break then a period of classes from about three o'clock until tea. There was a break after teatime, and we studied as opposed to going to class, doing what would be called homework until five-thirty or seven. The boys would work in a big room called the Study Room. But fifty of the older boys had private rooms, and they went to their rooms; what they did was anyone's business as long as they behaved, got on with their work and there were no complaints from the masters."

Weekends were highly organized: "Saturday was a half-holiday so there were classes in the morning and then games in the afternoon until tea. There was a period allotted for letter writing in the evenings for the younger boys to remind them to write to their parents. On Sunday morning, there was mass before breakfast, some recreation and then there was a period of religious doctrine for about three-quarters of an hour in classes—one of two such classes a week. From midday until lunch we wrote essays on a set subject, which was boring if one didn't have imagination. In the afternoon we had games, which in those days in a non-Catholic school was unusual—we had lots of visitors in the holidays from the Education Department, and they thought it was wonderful. There wasn't much soccer, because the school changed to playing rugby in 1921, and we played cricket and tennis in the summer, or used the golf course, racquets courts or fives courts."

At Hodder boys were taught reading, spelling, handwriting, arithmetic, French, Latin, basic geography, religious studies and the catechism. When they went up to Stonyhurst the curriculum expanded to included Greek and science. At the age of thirteen they began studying for the Lower School Certificate exam, and then a year or two later for the Advanced Certificate, before specializing for the Higher Certificate in science, mathematics, classics, modern languages, history or English.

Peter reveled in the stable regime of a busy schedule, as his school records show. They also tell of an "all-rounder" which prepared him to be the "Renaissance Man" he became. He was strong academically and won prizes for debating, history, essay writing, poetry and religious doctrine—he won the elocution prize for ten years in succession. A musical child he played the piano and violin in the orchestra, and was known for his "remarkable" piano solos, playing the organ in church in his final school years. He became a member of the school choir that was a mixture of boys and priests, and was successively first treble and first bass. When he sang Felix Mendelssohn's *Elijah* aria to the school in 1927 the school magazine reported: "His transition to his encore left us speechless." Being a chorister was no light task, and during Easter's Holy Week they would sing for twenty hours.

But Peter had other interests. He had success on the field as a member of the Second XV rugby team. He exhibited leadership skills and became the president of the debating society, a prefect on the School Committee and Second Head of Line (the equivalent of deputy head boy). As was obligatory he was a member of the Officers' Training Corps and as Sergeant P. B. Glenville was credited as a First-Class Shot. The cadet force operated under the supervision of the War Office and is still a common feature in many public schools. Stonyhurst's corps was one of the top in the country; boys donned uniform to do parade drills, play in a band, shoot with rifles at the school shooting range, and go to camp for ten days each July to do military exercises with other schools including Harrow and Ampleforth.

The school was very self-sufficient in its outlook, partly because of a lack of communications and partly because of a recusant history that made it a haven for Catholics. Boys rarely left its grounds except for picnics on the nearby fells, playing sports matches against other schools, or taking a bike ride to a nearby village when they were older. During Peter's time Stonyhurst was a single-sex school; forty Jesuit priests and just a couple of laymen taught him. The only females he came into regular contact with were the infirmary's matron, domestic staff serving food and a preparatory mistress during his time at Hodder.

Peter's school days were a happy time, evidenced by the generous bequest he left in his will in recognition of "all of the advantages bestowed upon me in early life by the Stonyhurst Jesuit community especially the sense of values which was indeed a lasting legacy." Peter spent three-quarters of his year at school with just four weeks Christmas holidays, the three-week Easter holidays that began after Holy Week, and a seven-week summer holiday. Dorothy-and-Shaun visits were infrequent due to their working commitments but it was not unusual because other pupils' parents lived abroad. What was unusual was his parents' fame, so much so that their mere presence at Stonyhurst on speech days was sufficient to cause a stir. Shaun and Dorothy, in their white Rolls-Royce, would negotiate the long drive to the school while beeping the car's two-tone horn. In later life Peter joked that he would have paid to see his parents sweep up the drive in a humble family car like a Hillman Minx. Not that he didn't learn to like extravagance and later considered buying a Rolls-Royce: "They are so very important and dignified looking for a single person to dash around to theatre rehearsals and film studios in, though it is certainly a lovely feeling when one is inside!" For many children the actions of "over the top" parents can be an embarrassment.

During the 1920s Stonyhurst had up to 320 pupils; its small size helped to build a strong sense of community along with a spirit of bonhomie and friendship. A former pupil said: "It was a happy place, we were proud of it. I didn't know of any boy who grumbled that his parents had sent him there, there were other Catholic schools but we didn't know much about them. One was very happy there . . . there was a certain pride in the place."

Many of Peter's fellow pupils came from upper-middle-class homes and their parents would have been doctors, lawyers, civil servants, business owners or serving in the armed forces. His friends included Henry Flory who went on to become an investment banker, Philip Caraman who became a Jesuit priest, and William Devlin who became an actor. Some relationships lasted beyond Peter's school years, especially with Caraman, who edited the Jesuit periodical, *The Month* in the 1940s. He revived the paper's fortunes by employing distinguished writers, like Evelyn Waugh and Graham Greene. Alec Guinness was one of Carman's converts, enjoying a close mutual friendship with Peter. Caraman officiated at the Requiem Mass held in London after Peter died. Peter also became friends with one of his teachers, Christopher Hollis, who taught history at the college from 1925 to 1935. Hollis went on to become an academic, Conservative Party politician, and a leading writer on Catholic affairs. He was an inspiring influence on his Stonyhurst pupils and Peter corresponded with Hollis regularly after he left school.

Naturally the school had a very religious character with boys attending church regularly. Each day began with early morning mass, classes began with the catechism, and night prayers were said before bed. A priest was in charge of each Line, but there was also a "Spiritual Father," who gave talks and had a role outside of the daily routine; boys could go to him if they were in trouble and wanted consolation or help. The religious aspects of his education affected Peter profoundly: he attended mass throughout his life and always identified himself as a Catholic. As a contemporary said: "It's a pity everybody can't grow up in that atmosphere; there was a spiritual atmosphere pervading the place. Yet it wasn't a pious place, boys could be bad just as others. The whole atmosphere was one of religion: the chapel, the public church, there were statues about the place and pictures—there was a religious atmosphere. One grew up in it and of course it was very valuable."

Peter joined the Sodality of the Immaculate Conception of Our Lady confraternity when he was thirteen. As a Sodalist, Peter took part in an Act of Consecration, a holy rite in which he vowed to rise promptly in the morning, never neglect his morning or night prayers, have a great devotion to mass, never be unkind to others, not take part in unpleasant talk, renew his Act of Consecration daily, and show devotion to the Virgin Mary. On a practical basis he met with other Sodalists once a week, went to mass and prayed the rosary regularly, read books and pamphlets about the Virgin Mary, and visited the Blessed Sacrament in church after meals when at school and occasionally when at home. His devotion to the Virgin Mary continued all his life.

All the chapels had a considerable affect on Peter; particularly the beauty of the Sodality Chapel with its part wood-paneled walls that stretch up to an exquisitely painted ceiling, bright stained-glass windows that let in shafts of colored light. The altar crowned by a marble statue of the Virgin Mary is breathtaking. Being away from home for months at a time and caught up in the rigors of a strict routine, boys needed a refuge. He would have sat on one of its dark wooden pews and taken time to reflect.

Dorothy's celebrity and ever-keen eye resulted in her having a weekly newspaper column. In it she revealed that Peter's spirituality as a teenager was so strong that he was torn as to his future career: "Peter . . . is divided in his mind as to whether he will be a film actor or a priest. If he does decide to be a priest when he grows up both his father and I (we are Catholics) will be very happy about it. For some things I would like him to be a barrister but it is much too early yet for him to decide. I think a boy's mind changes each year on these things. At the same time it is important I think once the boy knows the really bent of his mind to allow him to follow it. Nothing is more foolish than to force a lad or a girl for that matter into an occupation which he or she strongly dislikes."

However, Peter's school days were far from focused purely on religion and reflected his confusion as to his career. Hodder contemporaries remembered him playing with a toy theater complete with electric lights, tiny figurines of actors, and a trap door where a ghost came up; Peter would impose an interval in his play to retrieve the ghost from under the stage. Actor and comedian "Wee" Georgie Wood, a friend of his parents, gave the model theater to Peter. Wood, who appeared in pantomime and music hall revues with the couple said that his gift to Peter was important because "according to Peter, Dorothy and Shaun [it] decided his vocation."

There is a tradition of Jesuit drama going back to the 16th century, so Stonyhurst was fertile ground for Peter's ambitions. The feast of the Immaculate Conception celebrated on December 8 saw a festive spirit at Hodder. The boys had a big breakfast of sausages and bacon, and at teatime scoffed on brandy snaps, toffee buns and cake accompanied by their favorite treat—Stonyhurst's own home-brew ginger beer that was kept under lock and key outside of feast days. During the evening the school put on a concert and a play, and in 1924 Peter played the lead role of Jack Deedes in *The Last Practice*; the following year he took the lead in *The Gipsy's Revenge*.

Peter moved "up" to Stonyhurst when he was aged ten and continued his interest in drama. Masters carefully weeded out potential actors: "Talent was spotted, as one of the masters would act as a producer and would be invited to take part. And talent was spotted in various ways among the small boys." The teachers saw Peter's talent and he appeared in plays staged in the Academy Room, with its full stage and tiered seating like a regular theater. He also saw a 1927 performance of Lord Alfred Tennyson's *Becket*; the story of the martyred Catholic priest was one Peter returned to when he directed stage and film versions of Becket's life. Peter stared in Gilbert and Sullivan's *Yeoman of the Guard* operetta. His size, and the fact that he was following in his father's footsteps, made him perfect for female parts in the male-only productions. Like his parents he starred in pantomimes as Cinderella, Will the Babe in *Babes in the Woods*, and Leopold the Waiter in *Ali Baba and the Forty Thieves*.

His most memorable role was that of Second Lieutenant Hibbert in the 1930s Shrovetide play, Robert Sherriff's *Journey's End*: "Hibbert is a small part, but difficult. . . . Glenville succeeded where most boys would have failed. In the powerful revolver scene he reached exactly the right pitch of emotion . . . in the tipsy revel he was remarkably good." *Journey's End* was first performed in 1928 with 21-year-old Laurence Olivier in the lead. The play is set in the trenches at Saint Quentin in France in 1918, and depicts the experience British infantry officers. When Stonyhurst staged the play, it was on a second run at the Savoy Theatre and it was unusual for schoolboys to perform a new play running concurrently in the West End. The school received special permission from the author to perform and adapt it by cutting "certain strong words" from the original script. The inspiration to do the play came from a Stonyhurst old boy, Colin Clive, who was then playing the lead role of Captain Dennis Stanhope. The Stonyhurst production caught the attention of the national press and the *Daily Express* reported: "The production was an example of the heights to which a stage production by young amateurs can rise. The twelve 'soldiers' were little children during the war: none of its tragedy can have reached their minds at the time. Yet throughout the play they acted with extraordinary conviction and confidence." The paper singled out Peter: "Hibbert, the nerve-wracked subaltern was played by P. B. Glenville, the son of Miss Dorothy Ward."

Peter's passion for theater was such that in his final year he wrote a letter to the school magazine suggesting a small improvement to the Academy Room. He wanted to hide the actors when they put on their make-up because "visitors are faced by a strange thing—a barrier composed of rococo screens, curtains, curtains of different shapes, sizes and hues, Peeping Toms, large apertures, and all the unbeautiful paraphernalia of the amateur's makeshift. . . . Surely our theatre is worthy of a more worthy stage door! I suggest that a light, strong, and fairly high wooden partition, after the nature of a folding screen, in sections if necessary, be made. Let there be one recognisable door therein. This structure might be kept . . . and erected before 'opening nights.' Failing this, let there be a rod with a sober curtain; it would be less unworthy than those antiquated screens." Today the Academy Room is just as it was in Peter's days; his suggestion was ignored.

Peter probably had his first exposure to films at Stonyhurst. It was the silent film era and pupils watched Charlie Chaplin comedies; early action fests including *The Charge of the Light Brigade*, *Oliver Cromwell*, King Baggot's *Ivanhoe*, *The Bewitched Boxing Gloves* and early Westerns including *Bad Buck of Santa Ynez*. Besides entertainment, in these pre-TV days, newsreels told boys of life in the outside world. The Grand National horse race, the Oxford and Cambridge boat race, the funeral of the First World War French commander Marshal Ferdinand Foch, and the signing of the Lateran Treaty in 1929 by Cardinal Pietro Gasparri and Italian Prime Minister Benito Mussolini recognizing the full sovereignty of the Holy See in Rome were all shown. Boys would have been aware of the Wall Street Crash of 1929 and Britain's departure from the gold standard in 1931, but as a contemporary of Peter pointed out: "It was very much a privileged existence." The Great Depression had little effect on the boys' sheltered existence.

However sheltered they were, Peter's school days shaped the rest of his life in ways that were arguably more marked than for a child who had a more conventional upbringing. Peter developed a faith that supported him spiritually and emotionally as well as providing hope whenever he felt down. The Jesuit system encouraged debate and aroused his sense of intellectual curiosity. He also learned to be a leader and to win an argument, which proved vital in his career as a director. Stonyhurst provided the stable environment that his parents were unable to because of their work. Most of all, Stonyhurst provided Peter with a nursery for his acting talent; a talent that was recognized and nurtured in the remarkable environment that is Stonyhurst.

2

Bright Young Things

1932-1935

In October 1932 Peter went to Christ Church College, Oxford; it was, and still is, one of Britain's most respected university colleges. Even today very few people are privileged enough to go to Oxford to study; when Peter went there he was in an even more privileged position. Peter went up to Oxford to study jurisprudence—the theory and philosophy of law—perhaps hoping to fulfill his mother's dream that her son would decide on a career as a barrister. Her dream was never realized, largely because Peter spent virtually his entire time at Oxford involved with acting and what spare time he had he figured prominently in the Oxford Union, the University's debating society. Not that his lack of studying was to hamper his progress; Peter was to benefit in untold ways from his time among the rich and privileged students he befriended, acted and debated with. He was very much one of the "Bright Young Things," a term made famous by Evelyn Waugh in his 1930 novel, *Vile Bodies*, when describing London's young and carefree aristocrats and Bohemians.

When Peter went up to Oxford there were twenty-two former Stonyhurst boys at the university. Drawn together by their common faith, many Stonyhurst old boys joined the university's oldest student bodies, the Newman Society. Their aim was to promote the Catholic faith, learning and culture within the university; they held parties, weekly meetings with speakers, an end-of-term mass and black-tie dinner. Speakers at the dinner included the authors Tolkien and G. K. Chesterton. Peter's friend from school, William Devlin was the Newman Society president in 1932, and Peter was an active member throughout his time at Oxford. Elsewhere the prominent Jesuit philosopher and Stonyhurst old boy, Father Martin D'Arcy, was Rector and Master of Campion Hall, a small college run by the Jesuits.

Christ Church is one of the largest of the University of Oxford's colleges as well as its most aristocratic with a raft of illustrious alumni including, thirteen British prime ministers, government ministers, bishops, the philosopher John Locke, religious leader John Wesley and the writer Lewis Carroll. At that time it was famed as a rowing college with many Old Etonians as students. The college, which sits in the heart of Oxford, bounded by its Meadow and the Rivers Cherwell and Isis, is an architectural gem with a Romanesque cathedral, gables, cupolas, cloisters and quadrangles, and a bell tower designed by Sir Christopher Wren.

Peter's arrival at Oxford coincided with a time of extreme economic hardship in Britain with unemployment standing at three million. While Oxford's students came from the middle and upper classes, they were aware of the effects of unemployment on the working class and many felt sympathetic to their cause. However, feeling sympathy is one thing, being affected by it is altogether different and it is doubtful that Peter and his contemporaries saw any material difference in their quality of life while at Oxford from those that had gone before. The problems of the Depression were felt everywhere in Europe, fuelling the growth of fascism and the rise of Hitler and Mussolini. Oxford students' involvement in these turbulent times extended to actively pursuing the pacifist debate that was going on in Britain, especially at the Oxford Union.

The Oxford Union is Britain's most prestigious debating society drawing its membership primarily from the university. Founded in 1823 it has gained a global reputation for the cut and thrust of its debates that are held in the Debating Hall. In Peter's day it was a series of benches overlooked by marble busts of three British Prime Ministers who all held office in the Union. The society has been an invaluable training ground for many politicians, including former Labour Party leader, Michael Foot, who was its president in 1933. Foot voted with the majority in the society's famous February 1933 debate "This House will in no circumstances fight for its King and Country." The resolution was passed by 275 votes to 153 causing a sensation and not a little consternation as far afield as Madrid and Santiago, in Chile; the British embassies cabled the Foreign Office in alarm when the story appeared in the local press.

The British press was scandalized by the students' sentiments. According to the *Daily Express*: "There is no question but that the woozy-minded Communists, the practical jokers, and the sexual indeterminates of Oxford have scored a great success in the publicity that has followed this victory. . . . Even the plea of immaturity, or the irresistible passion of the undergraduate for posing, cannot excuse such a contemptible and indecent action as the passing of that resolution." The paper's humorist started a series of articles about undergraduates who used scent in their baths and belong to the Oxford Union. *The Daily Telegraph* accused the undergraduates of "foul-minded disloyalty," and Churchill made a speech saying he was nauseated by "the abject, squalid, shameless avowal made in the Oxford Union." Such was the outcry regarding what was perceived as the students' cowardice rather than an altruistic show of pacifism, an anonymous critic sent the Oxford Union a box containing 275 white feathers, one for each vote for the resolution. Members of Sir Oswald Mosley's British Union of Fascists, commonly referred to as the "black shirts," tore up the minutes of the debate. Some even went as far as to claim that the students' apparent unwillingness to take up arms helped bring on the Second World War. Absurd, maybe, but it did encourage reports that Britain wasn't ready to fight.

In retrospect the students' attitude seems naïve. Hitler came to power as chancellor in Germany a mere ten days' prior to the debate but the specter of Nazi military expansionism had yet to rear its head. Some of Oxford's "bright young things" favored pacifism and disarmament as a route to avoid future conflict, believing Germany had been treated unfairly under the Treaty of Versailles. The heated debates at the Oxford Union revolved around foreign policy. It seems likely that Peter attended the King and Country debate, given he was a member of the Oxford Union and frequently participated in debates.

Throughout his time at Oxford Peter was a member of the Union. His love of debate had been nurtured at school and flowered at Oxford which all held him in good stead when he became a director. Many a Hollywood producer, agent, theater manager and actor felt the full force of Peter's rhetoric and his love of debating, and his skill at doing it, during the course of his career. He conducted his first debate in November 1933, opposing the motion "That this House strongly disapproves of Hitler's action in withdrawing from the League of Nations and the Disarmament Conference." He won. "Mr. Glenville contended that any attack on Hitler was quite irrelevant. It was not Hitler who was on trial. France had been using the League of Nations as a tool . . . He called upon the House to stand by the League, but at the same time to insist on a settlement which would give justice to Germany. A most convincing speech."

His "really good voice" and style of argument came in for praise: "Mr. Glenville gave a splendid performance. Sprawling exotically over the dispatch box, he was at times intimate and at other times stately and didactic, but at no time did he fail to hold his audience." But it was not universal praise. "Occasionally his efforts were a little too theatrical, but the vigour he introduced was refreshing and much appreciated by the House. He has certainly a future before him in the Union." His secret weapon was that he was "as good at appealing to the emotions of his audience as . . . convincing them by cold reasoning." Other debates that Peter took part in include the motions "That this House sees no hope in the Modern Theatre" and "That this conference would welcome the transference of power in India from the British democracy to the King in Imperial Council."

One of the many friends that Peter made at university was Paul Dehn, who went on to write plays, operettas and musicals for the stage and later wrote screenplays for films including *Goldfinger*; he won an Oscar for Best Adapted Screenplay for *Murder on the Orient Express*. One night he and Peter were walking home from a Union debate when they were attacked. Dehn wrote an article in the university's student newspaper, *Cherwell*, under the headline "Assault!" The two students met a group of Fascists on the street, fresh from a political meeting in the local town hall, who demanded to know if Dehn was the editor who allowed an article called "Blackshirts" to run in the *Cherwell*; Dehn admitted he was. An angry member of the group unleashed a volley of invective and pushed Dehn, who staggered backwards. Just at that moment some acquaintances from Brasenose College arrived and a fight with the Fascists broke out. At the end of "an epic contest," with shirts ripped and people stunned by violence, the Fascists got up saying, "Well, that was a damn good fight, you chaps. You can print anything you like about us now." Another Fascist undergraduate approached, begging them not to judge his colleagues by the fracas, claiming that Fascism stood for law and order. Dehn wrote: "We wish that we could believe him."

Dehn was also involved with the Oxford University Dramatic Society (OUDS); naturally Peter was also a member. The society was a place to make friends, and being a member of the OUDS for many was almost a way of life, certainly so in Peter's case. Its George Street clubrooms and bar were a genial meeting place for erstwhile young thespians. Members could read, eat, drink and laze over long Sunday breakfasts among witty companions who shared the same interest. It was so redolent of the times and would fulfill many people's idea of what life as a student in those halcyon days was like.

Then, as now, the OUDS could be a stepping stone to professional theater and many who made their first theatrical mark at the OUDS went on to successful acting careers. The OUDS put on two main productions each year: one in February at the Oxford New Theatre, and another in June in the open air, usually in the college garden or cloisters. Most of their plays were classical works as anything less than thirty years old was banned. Neither were women allowed to be members; professional actresses were brought in to play the female parts, which helped in raising the quality of the productions. During Peter's time at Oxford only 14% of around 1,750 under graduates were women. Professional directors, who were then known as producers, supervised and directed the society's plays.

Peter joined the OUDS shortly after John Gielgud staged his first play as a guest director, a production of Shakespeare's *Romeo and Juliet* in February1932. Aged only twenty-seven, Gielgud's reputation was growing after a decade of acting in classical roles as well as an emerging West End star. He engaged Peggy Ashcroft to play Juliet and Edith Evans as the Nurse. Among Peter's contemporaries in the OUDS were many future high-flyers: Devlin later joined the Old Vic; Hugh Hunt went on to direct the Bristol Old Vic theater school; Christopher Hassal became a notable lyricist for Ivor Novello's musicals; and George Devine became a director of the English Stage Company and co-founder of the Old Vic Theatre School and the Young Vic Company.

Gielgud brought his professional experience into play by paying vigorous attention to the scenery design and making sure the performance was one of fast-paced action. He drafted in his own costume makers, but best of all, Gielgud taught the students how to speak verse. The highly acclaimed performance, according to *The Daily Telegraph*, was enhanced because the OUDS "have cared to speak verse again, and have learned to speak it. By this their work is transformed." Gielgud raised the bar for the OUDS and Peter was to benefit from the society's new sense of professionalism.

Peter's OUDS debut came a year after Gielgud's success when he played the title role in Christopher Marlowe's *Edward II*. The press singled him out as a "promising young actor." *The Times* wrote: "Glenville . . . gave us some excellent acting as King Edward, and portrayed with real ability the King's alternating moods of defiance and weak submission." *Glasgow*'s *Bulletin and Scots Pictorial* praised his professionalism: "Glenville as the weak, defiant, effeminate King was magnificent throughout. His part seemed to fit him like a glove and there were none of those awkward moments, so common in amateur acting, when the spectator finds himself saying, 'That is Mr. Glenville, not the King.'"

A few weeks later Peter played the crafty Italian ecclesiastical politician, Cardinal Pandulph, to William Devlin's King John in Shakespeare's play of the same name. It was the last production at Oxford's New Theatre, before it was demolished. Peter won plaudits for his "polished performance": "The less important parts were unusually well filled. P. B. P. Glenville's Pandulph had dignity and command, and he dominated the third act even when he had nothing to say."

With acting consuming more of Peter's time than his studies it was appropriate that he concluded his first academic year by playing the hobgoblin, Puck, in the OUDS summer production of Shakespeare's *A Midsummer Night's Dream*. The Austrian actor and director Max Reinhardt, who arrived with a glowing reputation and grand ideas, directed it. Under his management Berlin's Deutsches Theater and Vienna's Theater in der Josefstadt had become two of the most prominent playhouses in the world. When he visited New York for his 1924 production of *The Miracle* in Madison Square Garden with its 2,000-strong cast, *Time* called him one of the "three outstanding dramatic institutions in the world today." His revolutionary staging techniques incorporated stylish scenery, dance music, and choreographed crowd scenes were all done on a gargantuan scale. He was also an advocate of site-specific theater that changed the relationship of the audience with the performers, fusing them together.

With a thick crown of swept-back hair and boundless energy, Reinhardt—an ostentatious showman—earned a reputation as "the Cecil B. DeMille of the theatre." He came to fame in 1905 for his production of *A Midsummer Night's Dream*, and perhaps it's not surprising that his lavish productions were often financial disasters; his version of Shakespeare's comedy almost left the OUDS in financial ruin.

Bucking tradition, Reinhardt eschewed staging the open-air summer production in the college gardens. According to author Humphrey Carpenter, Reinhardt surveyed the site saying: "'Very nice. But –' indicating the Headington rooftops in the distance—'that village over there must be removed.'" The production was staged at South Park, a large meadow on the slopes of Headington Hill that overlooks the city. In all aspects of the production razzmatazz ruled: costumes were flown in from Berlin, field telephones were installed to coordinate the actors' entrances and exits, electricity was laid on from Oxford, and a huge stand was built for the audience. Elm and beech trees that Reinhardt incorporated into the set surrounded the impressive stage; agile fairies flew down from the branches. Reinhardt even constructed a lake so that Bottom could see his reflection, and holes were dug so that Peter, as Puck, could disappear and reappear at will. Reinhardt even introduced unusual cast members—four Borzoi hounds—that caused consternation among the OUDS members. He appeared to regard the university as a playground for the rich, unaware that the society survived on its receipts from its productions along with members' subscriptions. Fortunately his opulent production just about broke even and arguably a success as the OUDS increased its membership.

Reinhardt's production wasn't merely unusual for its gigantic scale; his vision of the play was atypical. Peter had to play the imp as a demonic figure, which he succeeded in pulling off according to the press. "The keynote of the whole thing . . . was the mischievous enterprise of the fairy-folk in their dealings with the mortals—a keynote struck with peculiar emphasis by Mr. P. P. B. Glenville . . . as Puck. His was an extremely athletic performance, during which he must have run miles. If he did not literally set a girdle round about the earth, he came near it, in point of distance, during his evening's exertions!

"Puck was almost always on the scene, but not always visible. Early in the play he created a sensation by being swallowed by the earth, which seemed to open to receive him. It was quite half a minute before many of the audience realized that an enlarged rabbit hole had been arranged for him to dive into! Mr. Glenville dressed and played the part as a true child of faery nature, with the horns and hooves of hobgoblin, the alert cunning of a wild, half-human thing."

Peter's mother was very happy with it all according to an *Evening News* reporter. "Yesterday I met a very proud mother, Miss Dorothy Ward. She had been to Oxford, and she was proud because of the golden opinions that had been won by her young son, Mr. P. P. B. Glenville, for his performance as Puck."

When Peter returned to Oxford he expanded on his dramatic activities by becoming president of the Oxford University Stonyhurst Dramatic Society. He directed and played the lead in the society's production of Shakespeare's *Richard II* in December 1933 back at his old school. In February 1934 Peter also became the youngest ever president of the OUDS, winning the election by fifty-seven to fifty-one votes. "It was a great fight, and I am naturally delighted,"he told the university's magazine, *Isis*, who considered his theatrical pedigree a boon. "Glenville is the son of Miss Dorothy Ward, noted British actress. He is acquainted with many big shots in the dramatic world, so the OUDS should look forward to a rosy future."

Peter's next role was as Mephistopheles, the lead, in the OUDS spring production of Marlowe's *Dr. Faustus* that also starred 1934's Deb of the Year, Primrose Salt as Helen of Troy. Although the production staged at the local town hall had mixed reviews, Peter's portrayal of the man who sold his soul to the devil drew a positive response for its "definite dramatic *savoir faire*." *The Manchester Guardian* declared Peter's performance "an able piece of acting. The part is extremely difficult both in the physical appearance and in the suggestion of wickedness and corruption. . . . We did not like all his gestures nor his manner of walking, which was somewhat too sidling and coy, but in the essentials, in his speaking and in the impression he gave not only of evil but of torture and regret, he was brilliant."

Another highlight of the production were its masks, created by the young photographer and theatrical prop maker Angus MacBean. After the Second World War, MacBean became the official photographer for the Old Vic, Stratford Memorial Theatre, the Royal Opera House and Sadler's Wells, and was employed by theater impresario Hugh "Binkie" Beaumont to photograph all his productions for his company, H. M. Tennent.

The *Mephistopheles* cast went on to make history in April when the young performers embraced new technology by doing a radio broadcast of the play for the British Broadcasting Corporation (BBC). This was a first for the OUDS and according to *The Manchester Guardian*, "Nothing is so severe a test of ability to act in a poetic tragedy as a broadcast, and the performance last night was extremely good. . . . [Glenville's voice] is an instrument that he can control and direct."

Peter then took the opportunity to try out his directing skills at an OUDS "smoker." The society's smokers consisted of evenings where members performed their own Noel Coward-inspired sketches and songs, and were instigated to fill the group's coffers and help sustain it between annual productions. Young actors could try their hand at contemporary works and Peter directed Patrick Hamilton's murder story *Rope* that won favor with the *Cherwell*: "Over and above all, brooded Mr. Glenville the producer, like some deity whose unseen presence might be taken as a surety for success. His deft management of lighting, positioning and dramatic emphasis calls forth unqualified congratulation."

Peter also directed Paul Dehn's *The Masterpiece* at an OUDS night of one-act plays. For the *Cherwell* it was the best play of the evening: "[Dehn] was given brilliant support by Mr. Peter Glenville, in his dual capacity of actor and producer; Mr. Glenville's final lapse into madness, prolonged as it was by a very leisurely drawing of the curtains, became almost painful to watch. The use of a single table lamp to light the stage, so that all the emphasis was thrown upon Seddon's face, was an inspiration; and the other details of production which included a highly effective treatment of sound were equally well conceived."

In March 1934 Peter directed his own play, *Pass The Salt*, at a smoker. Among the students acting in the review was John "Jack" Profumo, who went on to become a Conservative politician and eventual Secretary of State for War, who achieved notoriety for his role at the centre of a sex and spy scandal. Profumo played the part of an Italian doctor, Meffi Siffilis, innocently singing

Britannia, Queen of the Sea. Another performer was Terence Rattigan, who was credited with writing "Wude Words" and co-writing one of the sketches. In Peter's second year they shared a flat at 6 Canterbury "Canters" Tenements in King Edward Street, a fashionable address among undergraduates. The duo soon established a reputation for throwing elegant, amusing parties in their digs. Rattigan and Peter formed a friendship at Oxford that was to continue throughout out their personal and professional lives.

Peter also brought the glamorous actor, singer, composer and dashing matinee idol Ivor Novello to one of the society's smokers. While on another occasion he broke the OUDS rules by bringing two actresses, Fay Compton and Gladys Cooper, to a smoker. It seems that for Peter, rank had certain additional privileges.

The OUDS summer production was Shakespeare's *Richard III* with Peter as the king. Nancy Price was in the role of King Henry VI's widow, Queen Margaret and for the first time in the history of the OUDS a woman directed the production; Hungarian actress and director Leontine "Leo" Sagan, who had trained under Reinhardt in Berlin. *Mädchen in Uniform* (*Maidens in Uniform*), Sagan's 1931 directorial debut was a shocking film about schoolgirls in the care of an authoritarian headmistress that remained censored until the 1970s.

Sagan had been invited to England by Hungarian director Alexander Korda's London Film Productions to make a film adaptation of Anthony Gibbs' novel *The Young Apollo*. Sagan was familiar with the OUDS, as much of the film was shot in Oxford, but it was while she was directing *Finished Abroad* that Peter invited her to direct *Richard III*; his theatrical connections were proving to be of benefit to the OUDS.

According to Sagan's autobiography: "I liked Mr. Glenville but felt doubtful about the invitation. I had never worked with amateurs and thought it might be an anticlimax after the West

End career on which I had launched myself. I did not know then that it was a great honor to produce for the OUDS." Sagan chose to stage *Richard III*: "This was a lucky choice, for Peter Glenville had wanted to play Richard since the age of ten."

Pretentiously prone to wearing Garboesque floppy felt hats and suits deemed mannish for the time, Sagan was known as a charmless, domineering individual who was apt to impose her will on her cast. Sagan's strident manner earned her the nickname "Saggybags" when she worked in London's theaters. She wrote of her time with the OUDS: "For two months I made Oxford my home so I could use every hour in which the undergraduates were free to rehearse.

When I could snatch a few of them I would drag them to their club, which was our headquarters. At night, between eight and twelve, and during the day, between two and three, we were allowed by the university authorities to rehearse in the cloisters. . . . Life at Oxford could be rather stormy at times. My young Richard had a fiery temperament, and the forty-odd students in the company did not always want to rehearse but preferred to rush off to sports or [the] pictures. It was rather comical that I, a woman, should have to act as a sergeant major."

At one particular rainy evening rehearsal Peter introduced Sagan to George Cukor. Cukor had already established a glowing reputation and had won an Oscar nomination for Best Director for 1933's *Little Women*. According to Sagan, "I discovered in the shadows of the courtyard a strange gentleman wrapped in an enormous woolen overcoat in the American style. Shortly afterwards Peter Glenville introduced me to George Cukor, the eminent Hollywood [director]. Our young and brilliant 'Richard' was not in vain a child of the theatre; showmanship was in his blood."

In spite of her bossy manner, or even maybe because of it, *Richard III* performed in Christ Church cloisters, was a success. *The Times* lauded Sagan for making the most of the open-air setting: "Sagan, has made the most of the geography of the place, and the processions, the entrances and exits through various arches, the noises from every quarter, the ingenious lighting, and the grouping of figures against the buildings are all designed to make a most harmonious effect, and to give at the proper times the illusion of a circumscribed stage, or of an open scene. Even the battle, a kind of entertainment which is seldom satisfactory on the ordinary stage, looked very well against shadowy walls."

But as the newspaper pointed out: "However much the producer may do, the play is really subordinate to the part of Richard, and it is a part in which vigour, maturity, and a full command of all the obvious devices of academic acting count more than anything else. From the beginning it was impossible to doubt that Mr. Peter Glenville would be able to hold his own, and as the play advanced he rose to all its great occasions with free and open rhetoric. The part has, of course, its inconsistencies. The Elizabethan villain was not only singularly blatant, but also a subtle Machiavellian who could use mysterious Italian devices to persuade anyone to his will. But the modern mind can hardly reconcile these opposites, and the modern actor can hardly hope to make plausible the scene where Richard successfully woos the Lady Anne. Mr. Glenville wisely played the straightforward villain and attempted no intricacies . . ." The *Yorkshire Evening News* speculated: "Glenville . . . is almost certain to become quite as famous on the stage as his father . . . It was the kind of performance it is quite impossible to forget."

Later in June 1934 Peter made his first appearance on a London stage when *Richard III* transferred to the Regent's Park Open Air Theatre. According to one newspaper the actors' performances were "generally above that of the ordinary amateur," and the 20-year-old Peter was picked out as a man to watch out by the *Daily Mirror*: "The chief interest of the production lay in the appearance as Richard of young Peter Glenville. . . . [He] gave a confident and accomplished rendering of the heavy role, and held the attention of the audience from first to last. His voice carries well, and it was clear that he had formed an intelligent idea of the character. . . . Glenville intends to go in for acting professionally, and . . . is likely to do well." *The Stage*, the newspaper for the theatrical profession, noticed Peter: "He is the son of Dorothy Ward and Mr. Shaun Glenville, and has the theatre in his blood—which should help him in his expressed decision to enter the theatrical profession. He is admirably equipped both in stage appearance and a fine resonant voice." Peter later joked about the experience, saying that the OUDS actors "were heard and not seen" when they had performed for BBC radio, and "were seen and not and not heard" at the open-air theater.

Whatever other ideas may have been considered as a career for Peter, either by him or his parents, it is clear that the theater was his only serious ambition. He got the chance during the summer vacation to join the Manchester Repertory Company for six weeks before returning to university in the autumn. American Broadway director, Carol Sax, was the one who gave Peter his chance and his landing the job won column inches in the press. His family connections and the fact that despite several offers to take parts in London's West End, he decided to go into rep "to learn the job in a workmanlike way" made him newsworthy. Peter was probably the first president of the OUDS to work a professional actor while still at the university. According to *The Manchester Guardian*. "Regarded as one of the most promising young actors Oxford has seen for a number of years . . . [Peter Glenville] is to play leading parts at the Manchester Repertory Theatre when the autumn season opens in the second week of September." It's interesting that there is no mention of Peter's parentage, which suggests he was starting to be taken seriously in his own right.

Repertory, or "rep," theater companies were the lifeblood of British theater. Based in provincial theaters, they staged classical productions as well as new works by aspiring British and foreign playwrights. They were centers of innovation for experimental stage design and allowed novice actors to learn their craft. A season of plays were staged, in rotation, offering new productions as well as bringing back old ones due to public demand. Working in rep was a grueling experience for actors who formed a stock company, a semi-permanent group of actors managed by a leading actor. While it provided regular employment, rather than the more erratic opportunities of commercial theater, the financial rewards were poor and the heavy workload was grueling.

Typically, a repertory theater company would do a new three-act play every week. In an average week actors would open on the Monday night having rehearsed the play the week before. On the Tuesday morning they would begin work on the next play; rehearsing Act One in the afternoon, before doing their regular nightly performance of that week's play. On the Wednesday they would rehearse Act Two and on the Thursday they would rehearse Act Three; on Friday they would run through the entire play. On Saturday there would be a second run-through in the morning. After a matinee and evening performances that week's play, Sunday was a day off, and on Monday it would start all over again with a performance of the play learned the previous week.

Formed in 1908, the Manchester Repertory Company was the first English Repertory Company; its great reputation was a magnet for talent. Among those who learned their craft there were Donald Wolfit, Sybil Thorndike and Wendy Hiller. At the same time as Peter was there so was Joan Littlewood, who later founded the Theatre Workshop and helped revolutionize British theater in the 1950s by premiering plays including Bertolt Brecht's *Mother Courage and her Children*. Peter was an advocate of rep as he revealed in *The Art of the Theatre*, his contribution to the 1934 collection of essays *Growing Opinions: A Symposium of British Youth Outlook*: "The English stage needs the service of intelligent minds interested in the theatre for its own sake. The theatre may be overcrowded, but it is with people who merely look to the stage to give them money and reputation. The stage needs more group effort, more repertory companies, with a permanent staff of artists and producers."

As the *Daily Sketch* recounted Peter's initial problem on joining the company was not learning his lines but something altogether more mundane. Under the headline "They have Met Their Peterloo" the paper went on: "A new Peterloo has been fought; this time behind the scenes of the Manchester Repertory Theatre. When the company assembled for rehearsal this week it was discovered that there were four Peters in the company —Peter Glenville, Peter Campbell, Peter Harrison, and Peter Carpenter. As Christian names are freely used in theatrical circles it was embarrassing. When anyone asked 'Where's Peter?' there was usually an answer, but the odds were three to one against it being the right Peter. The first decision arrived at was that Peter Carpenter was entitled to keep his name. He was only sixteen, and hadn't had it as long as the others. Of the three remaining Peters two had to go. Peter Glenville pointed out he was signed on first. So Peter Campbell decided to go completely Scottish, and plumped for Bruce. Peter Harrison concluded that if was going to lose the Peter he might as well let the Harrison go with it, so on next week's programme he will appear as David Markham." Maybe it was Peter's experience at the Oxford Union that allowed him to argue his case so well. Harrison continued to use "David Markham" as his stage name for the rest of his forty-year career.

Peter's first role in rep. was as the tutor Dr. Agi in Ferenc Molnár's romantic comedy *The Swan*. Dorothy managed to make it to the opening night but Shaun was appearing in *The Private*

Road at the Comedy Theatre, but the *Daily Mirror* did interview Shaun at a cast party, "He never expected, nor encouraged [Peter to] take up a stage career." Peter's parents would not have been disappointed in their son's professional début. The *News Chronicle* said: "Particularly praiseworthy was the performance of Mr. Peter Glenville," and the *Daily Dispatch*: "Glenville is a splendid young romantic actor who should do well."

Peter went to take on the leading roles in productions that varied from the showy to the classical: the bootlegger Antonio Perelli in Edgar Wallace's drama of gangster warfare in prohibition Chicago *On the Spot*; the young actor Jack Maitland in Ronald Mackenzie's tragic family drama *The Maitlands*; the poet Eugene Marchbanks in Sir George Bernard Shaw's comedy *Candida*; and a youth wrongly sentenced to die for murder in Percy Robinson's *To What Red Hell* in which he made "the most of his sympathetic part as the wrongly condemned Irish boy."

On Peter's return to Christ Church in October he was ebullient, as a writer at the *Isis* noted: "I almost died of a fit last Monday when Mr. Peter Glenville came into the office in the most pugilistic of boxing attire, meaning boxing-gloves. I thought at the least that he was coming to do me a mischief. I was informed, however, that he had taken up boxing again after an interval of many years, as he considers it will be an additional inducement to hesitating theatre managers in his future stage career. To prove his case, he then boxed his way out of the office, hitting the air wildly."

Peter also celebrated his twenty-first birthday with a sherry party at the OUDS clubrooms. The partygoers included Peter's father and friends from the OUDS and the Oxford Union. Among them were Sir Keith Ramsay-Steel-Maitland third Baronet of Sauchie, future stage and film actor Dennis Price, future leader of the Liberal Party Joseph "Jo" Grimond, and Nevill Coghill, one of the dons. Coghill was a literary scholar famed for his modern English versions of the works of medieval writers Geoffrey Chaucer and William Langland. He was also one of The Inklings, an informal literary discussion group whose members included the Oxford dons and authors Tolkien and C. S. Lewis. He was the first don to direct an OUDS production, going on to direct several while dominating the university's theatrical life for the ensuing decade.

The next month proved a turning point for Peter. At a party thrown by Oxford University Opera Club at the Town Hall Assembly Room to celebrate the first night of their production of Jean-Philippe Rameau's *Castor and Pollux* Peter met Oliver Esselte future ballet conductor Robert Irving, who was a member of the club, had invited Messel, a highly regarded theatrical designer, to the party. Messel had designed the masks for a 1925 London production of Serge Diaghilev's ballet *Zéphyre et Flore*, after which theater impresario Charles B. Cochran commissioned the 22-year-old to make masks for one of his revues. In 1932 his innovative use of white on white for Helen's bedchamber in Cochran's *Helen!* sealed his reputation. His ingenuity knew no bounds and his wonderful visual sense saw him create magical sets while he pastiched historical fashions from the medieval to the eighteenth century to create wildly dramatic, sensual and beautiful costumes. He was, by his own admission, "the enemy of everything utilitarian."

Messel, immaculately dressed, handsome and softly spoken with twinkling black eyes and a generous smile, had an easy manner, sense of fun and a talent for mimicry that made him a hit among the "bright young things." He received frequent invitations to society parties despite being an old Etonian; Messel was no snob, as the carpenters and technicians he worked with testified. His family was wealthy, well connected and artistic. His father loved gardens and antiques, and his mother was the daughter of Victorian cartoonist Linley Sambourne, and she herself worked as a cartoonist for the satirical magazine, *Punch*, in her teens. Messel grew up in a twenty-three-room house in London served by ten domestic staff, and in Nymans, a forty-room country mansion in Sussex. He went to London's celebrated Slade School of Art, before taking up theatrical design, although his first love was portrait painting. He painted numerous portraits of Peter throughout his life, one of which hangs at Stonyhurst.

Messel had been asked to do the costumes for the Opera Club's production but was too busy so he passed the job on to a friend, Derek Hill. Messel arrived at Oxford with a group of friends that reflected his society connections: style icon and an heiress to the Singer sewing-machine fortune Daisy Fellowes; the future Earl of Wickow, Billy Clomore; and classical composer and novelist Gerald Tyrwhitt-Wilson, fourteenth Baron Berners.

Messel "was the centre of an admiring group," as one University magazine reported; one of the group was Peter. It was the start of a friendship and working relationship, on both sides of the Atlantic, which lasted for the next twenty-five years. Shortly after this the 30-year-old Peter went to live at Messel's studio at 16 Yeoman's Row in Kensington until after the war. Among the OUDS members, homosexuality was often regarded as an affectation accompanied by little more than juvenile flamboyance.

Many of Peter's friends at the OUDS, including Rattigan, Wilson, Dehn and Price were homosexuals. There's no doubting the fact that these young men were drawn together by their love of the theater, but they ran risks, as homosexual acts among consenting adults were illegal in Britain.

In February 1935 Coghill directed Peter as the lead in *Hamlet*. The production marked the fiftieth anniversary of the founding of the OUDS and it was staged at the rebuilt New Oxford Theatre. The Art Deco building equipped with the latest technical apparatus, including a revolving stage, could seat 1,700 people, being twice the size of its predecessor, with a 45-foot-wide proscenium arch, and vast stage. It proved to be a problem for Coghill with his cast gave their soliloquies from separate platforms that were floodlit while the rest of the stage was in darkness, causing some confusion, especially when the lighting didn't synchronize. One member of the audience recalled that Peter "ploughed through it all with courage."

The Times criticized Coghill's staging but thought Peter showed "promise": "It was conditioned by a production which boldly, but not always successfully, sought to separate Hamlet's inner life from the bustling, vivid, melodramatic action around him, and Mr. Nevill Coghill, the producer, must share responsibility for some of Mr. Glenville's shortcomings. The 'To be, or not to be' soliloquy is not an easy one to bring to life, and the task was made no easier for Mr. Glenville by placing him in front of the rather disillusioning drop-curtain . . . in Hamlet's speech after the players have left him Mr. Glenville seemed embarrassed to find no throne into which he could plunge a dagger, and the theatrical climax of the speech eluded him.

"Wherever the producer tried to draw Hamlet out of the play he seemed to be creating more problems than Mr. Glenville was prepared to solve. . . . It may be said that Mr. Glenville, though unable to make good those scenes which brought him too far, so to speak, along the apron, made the most of the production's considerable merits. He chose to emphasize Hamlet's youth, doing all in his power to establish the portrait of an inexperienced student whose knowledge of life was to come to him in a single flash of revelation. In these opening scenes his performance was at its most sensitive and expressive. His responses to the king's smiling remonstrance's were pitched on precisely the right note of nameless suspicion, and from his encounter with the Ghost he drew its full double effect of suspicions miraculously confirmed and illusions suddenly and completely crushed. In the Queen's chamber his performance recovered an authority, which it had tended to lose in the soliloquies and in most of Hamlet's commentary upon life. It was, indeed, a Hamlet which seemed only to live fully in moments of violent perturbation, an effect largely due to Mr. Glenville's suppression of most of what is ugly and bitter in the part."

Peter once again used his connections to invite the critic Agate to speak at the OUDS dinner held following the last performance. Agate was unimpressed by both Coghill's interpretation of the play and the actors' performance. He felt the theater was less suited to the young actors, particularly so because their voices were not strong enough to full the huge auditorium: "I thought the costumes and music delightful and the acting weaker than in any OUDS production I have seen." But he joked: "Peter Glenville had one radiant smile and two beautiful legs, all three being obviously inherited from his mother, Dorothy Ward, his acting being very nearly as boyish but not quite so principal."

Peter left the jolly world of amateur dramatics in the knowledge that life as a professional actor would be very different outside the cozy quadrangles of Oxford. Shortly before he left, in his role as drama critic for the *Isis*, he wrote: "Oxford acting gives to those interested in the theatre an opportunity to realise what fun it all was when acting was an art, and when one would play Polonius one night and Hamlet another. But if you say that such opportunities still flourish in London, and you quote such names as Flora Robson, Gwen Ffrangcon-Davies, Cedric Hardwicke and Ernest Milton as giving the lie to my theory, then I repeat that in general it is true that real 'acting' is out of fashion. These names are of the very exceptional: if we judge the rest of them, we are only blinding ourselves to the fact that the names represent a depressingly small minority. What *is* true is that it is not the members of the true and small 'legitimate' group who make the big money, and that therefore, if the undergraduate thinks he is going to become rich on the stage, he must not hope to do this by acting.

"The fact that hundreds of thousands of people earn money on the stage should not unduly encourage successful amateurs to enter this profession of the seemingly great possibilities. And the reason is that ninety per cent of modern histrionic triumphs are gained by sex technique. The man who has sufficient charm or good looks, coupled with a technique for showing off these qualities at a moment's notice and in the most insinuating manner, is assured of the directors' attention. Indeed, when two years ago a prominent Oxford amateur actor wrote to one of the leading directors of repertory in England, asking him for a place in his company, and enclosing a photograph, the reply came, which would have come from any modern theatrical magnate, 'Unfortunately the public refuses to be moved by acting ability: good looks and a really fascinating appearance are essential to the budding actor.' The public pay their money to be emotionally stirred, and thus acting has now become, not so much the depicting of a character, as the technique of displaying all the sexual possibilities of the actor's own personality."

Was Peter being cynical or merely realistic? He was a handsome man, which would help him in securing certain roles. Slim, five feet nine inches tall with thick, brown hair, high cheekbones and grey eyes he was the epitome of the kind of leading man favored by both the theater and the cinema. His only physical imperfection was his goofy front teeth, although they certainly did not seem to affect his chances unduly. In any event his teeth were not fixed until 1959, when he was well past the acting phase of his life. Whether this would translate into the kind of parts that he had grown used to at the OUDS was anyone's guess. However, if we could have met the young Peter Glenville in May 1935, as he was leaving Oxford, we would undoubtedly have been impressed.

All through the 1930s it was lean years for British theater; the economy signaled an end to lavish productions, and the dazzling shows of the early 1920s. Theater managers increasingly relied on popular taste that looked to the theater to provide escapist entertainment. Plays of a light, frivolous nature were favored over experimental works that somehow reminded people of their difficulties. The extent of the problem can be seen from the fact that 150 provincial theaters closed down between the two world wars. Added to which the theater faced a new rival with the onslaught of "the talkies." The first film with sound to be shown in London was the Al Jolson musical, *The Jazz Singer*, and by the early 1930s talkies were a global phenomenon.

This was the world into which Peter was entering, no doubt well aware from what he heard from his parents and from his short spell working in rep. Peter argued in *The Art of the Theatre* that it was a temporary state of affairs: "Modern dramatists have acquired [the habit] of ministering to the moods of their audiences. It would be interesting to know how long it will be before there is a change of temperament and taste on the part of the public. For a long time now there has been a desperate cult of the Gay; a determined effort to be amused by the trivial, rather than absorbed by actualities. The most successful productions are all light, satirical, destructive, and refined to the point of effeminacy. Even the Shakespeare devotees show a marked preference for the Comedies, as opposed to his heavier and mightier works." Wishful thinking? The optimism of youth?

"[I am of] a firm conviction that acting talent is something inborn and not merely learnt. No star has ever achieved success without hard work and experience, but some people could never become good no matter how hard they worked." It's a somewhat flawed argument, and not one you would expect a seasoned debater to put forward. However, his relationship with

Messel was not to be underestimated, giving him a theatrical connection that was every bit as important as his parental connection.

The extent to which Peter ignored his studies in the pursuit of his art are clear, not least because he failed to secure a degree. There was a point in his three years at university when Peter decided to devote himself to drama at the expense of his studies, in the full knowledge that he wanted to become a professional actor. The connections he made with people in the theater during his time at Oxford, excluding those directly made through his parents, were invaluable, but so were his friendships with fellow students. Rattigan, Dehn, Devlin, Devine, novelist Angus Wilson, and actor and director Glen Byam Shaw would all feature in Peter's life.

However Oxford, the OUDS and the Union were not his sole benefactors during his university days. He obviously spent some time at least on his law studies and the knowledge gained, no matter how sketchy, would, in later life, help him tremendously. His letters reveal his sharp mind, logical thought process and remarkable persuasive skills that frequently helped get what he needed. Added to his razor-sharp mind is one asset that might just be the most important—Peter was immensely charming. Oxford, in addition to everything else it did, served as a finishing school for English gentlemen, and Peter was finished to perfection; he was able to rise above his middle-class roots to become a cultured individual. He may have been the son of an Irish panto dame and a publican's daughter who became a principal boy but Peter was suave and sophisticated—the epitome of class and elegance.

3

An Actor's Life

1935-1941

Shortly before he was to leave Oxford, at an after-show party for one of Dorothy and Shaun's productions, the *Sunday Times* critic Agate sat up until the early hours of the morning trying to dissuade Peter from taking the role of Dante Gabriel Rossetti in the tale of the Pre-Raphaelite poet and painter's love life in a production of R. L. Mégroz and Herbert de Hamel's *Rosetti* at the Arts Theatre Club in London's Great Newport Street. His "handsome beginning at Oxford," explained Agate, and his good notices from the OUDS meant he had garnered positive attention and was well placed to take on major roles on the London stage, but Agate cautioned the young actor that such roles may have come too early in his career. It was sage advice, but the lure was too strong for Peter to resist.

The role that Peter had been offered was with Nancy Price's People's National Theatre. It was an early example of his OUDS connections paying off; he and Price had worked together in the society's version of *Richard III*. Headquartered at the Little Theatre in London's John Adam Street until the building was bombed in 1941, the People's National Theatre staged over eighty productions at various West End playhouses in the years running up to the war. It aimed to bring new and experimental plays to the masses with cheap seat prices starting at seven pence. Known for welcoming newcomers the PNT gave many actors some of their first professional roles; besides Peter both Laurence Olivier and Peggy Ashcroft started there. Price hired Peter for the May 1935 production of *Rosetti* even before he had officially left university.

The following month Peter returned to the Regent's Park Open Air Theatre, the scene of his London debut with the OUDS. Once more Peter had a major role, this time as the powerful nobleman Orsino, Duke of Illyria, in Shakespeare's comedy of mistaken identity, *Twelfth Night.* The open-air venue gave theatergoers the chance to see Shakespeare in the summer when the West End theaters were closed and was a tradition established earlier in the century in what were then the Royal Botanical Gardens. It was formalized as the Open Air Theatre by impresario Sydney Carroll in 1933 who used an 80-foot lawn as the stage, set against a backdrop of hazel, sycamore and poplar trees that faced a semi-circular auditorium of deck chairs at the front with slatted chairs behind. Carroll persuaded many big names to appear in his productions, including Vivien Leigh, and Jack Hawkins. Peter appeared alongside veteran Shakespearians Sir Robert Atkins as Sir Toby Belch and Phyllis Neilson-Terry as Olivia.

The comedy's first night was touch-and-go, for no other reason than the vagaries of the English weather. Former Old Vic director Sir Philip "Ben" Greet opened the proceedings urging the audience "not to stampede if rain should fall." In front-row seats, were Peter's parents, fortunately for them and the rest of the audience it turned into a fine summer evening and was according to the *Daily Mirror* "an excellent performance" by Peter. *The Times* warmed to the actors' attention to the play's lyrical language and their recognition it was "to be heard," but felt: "Glenville, tempted by the Duke's enchanted lines, sometimes [carried] this excellent principle a little too far, even to the point of affectation." One wag remarked that Peter's posh accent sounded peculiar with his pronunciation of "a bank of violets" as "a bank of varlets."

Two months later, in August, Peter made his West End debut proper, at the Cambridge Theatre in Shaw's elaborate dance of the sexes, *Man and Superman*. Charles Macdona held the touring rights to almost all of Shaw's plays; his Macdona Players' lead actor and director was Esmé Percy who was a friend of Shaw, as well as being an authority on the playwright's work and known for the brilliance of her Shavian performances. Perhaps inspired by the experience that surrounded him, Peter's interpretation of the idealistic spurned lover Octavius Robinson found favor with *The Stage*: "Glenville was an agreeable Octavius as we have seen, giving a by no means unwelcome touch of manliness to the youth's sentimentality." In October Peter appeared in a contemporary play, Pär Lagerkvist's *The Hangman* at the Duke of York's Theatre. The Swedish writer's adaptation of his novella for the stage revealed his concern with the brutality of the Fascist dictators that were threatening Europe.

Peter's first six months as a professional actor had certainly been busy and possibly his next role felt a little like light relief. It was one that was to return him to his old stomping ground, Oxford, where he was welcomed as a star. According to the *Isis*, "the [Oxford] Playhouse has [a] surprise up its sleeve for you! No less a person that Mr. Peter Glenville, ex-President of the OUDS, has been secured by the Playhouse for its production of *Theatre Royal*. He is to play opposite that grand actress, Miss Haidée Wright, in the part that was played by Laurence Olivier in London. Book early to avoid disappointment!" George S. Kaufman and Edna Ferber's comedy about three generations of the American acting dynasty, the Barrymores, first opened on Broadway in 1927 as *The Royal Family*. When it transferred to London's West End in 1934 the title was changed to avoid confusion with Britain's royalty. Peter had a tough act to follow playing the flamboyant Hollywood actor and alcoholic Anthony Cavendish; London audiences had adored Olivier's swashbuckling performance as a thinly disguised John Barrymore, which saw him leap from a balcony in a typical display of pyrotechnics.

Peter joined the new Swansea Repertory Company in the winter of 1935, but the young company had a brief existence. His first production in Swansea was to be in Ashley Dukes' romance *The Man With a Load of Mischief* in the week commencing December 16. However, the company closed down the week before because of lack of interest, and because the man running the company, Arnold Taylor, was arrested for breaching probation conditions set down in 1933. The stint certainly would have helped in broadening his experience and it may have been as a result of heeding Agate's words, but Peter never got to act.

However, the next step in his career was certainly not one that Agate would have approved. The New Shakespeare Company invited Peter to perform in the Shakespeare Festival at Stratford-upon-Avon's Memorial Theatre, the Victorian Gothic theater had staged its first production in 1879, but came to prominence in 1919 under the direction of William Bridges-Adams. Its resident New Shakespeare Company became one of the most renowned in Britain and was the nearest thing the nation had to a national theater. The theater burnt down in 1926 and Britain rallied to contribute to the rebuilding fund and a new, "austere, boxy Art Deco" theater opened on the afternoon of April 23, 1932, the anniversary of Shakespeare's birthday, with a performance of *Henry IV*.

By 1936 the company was in the process of re-establishing its reputation by working with established Shakespearean actors and nurturing exceptional young actors like 22-year-old Peter. For him it was his big opportunity—it was also his biggest test. Despite the roster of well-established directors these were turbulent times in the company's history; the engagement proved to be extremely hard work for very low pay. Rehearsal time was sorely limited with just five weeks to master seven productions. The festival itself lasted from mid-April to the end of September 1935 with Peter and the other actors appearing in several alternating productions over five grueling months. Bridges-Adams had been replaced by the fresh-faced and somewhat ingénue Ben Iden Payne, who had served as director of the Abbey Theatre before working on Broadway. Having been away from the British theater for more than twenty years Iden Payne's adoption of a modified Elizabethan staging of Shakespearean plays—complete with Elizabethan costumes and scenery—were deemed to be old fashioned.

The festival opened with Iden Payne's *The Taming of the Shrew*, and *The Times* praised its Elizabethan horseplay. Peter performed "quite well" as the male romantic lead according to the newspaper but found his diminutive stature a problem: "He has fewer inches than become a Petruchio." *The Stage* picked up on Peter's nervousness in the lead role saying he was "handicapped by inexperience and a tendency to restlessness." Authors Thomas C. Kemp and John C. Trewin declared the production "work-a-day" and noted that Peter was "somewhat overawed": "His Petruchio was a hard-working fellow who strove valiantly for the upper hand but never gave the impression of being able to maintain it when the Paduan wooing was over."

Worse was to come. In Wyse's *Julius Caesar* Peter, as Marcus Antonius made a plausible and handsome young Roman with thick eyebrows, curled cropped hair and a leopard-skin flung across his toga, but it was insufficient to prevent him being lambasted by *The Times*: "Glenville seemed to have a clearer conception of Antony's mixed elements than he succeeded in conveying; his excitement lacked control, and his Forum speech was a series of beginnings that never gained coherence. Impulsive Antony may be, but he is also calculating, and even a demagogue needs a cooler head than Mr. Glenville lent his character." *The Stage* agreed: "Antony is not yet his part, for he suggested little of the crafty intelligence underlying the attractive, hail-fellow-well-met sportsman, and his delivery of the great oration went far too quickly into top gear."

Matters deteriorated two days later when Peter played the love-struck lead in Ayrton's *Romeo and Juliet*: "Mr. Peter Glenville is a young actor whose promise was marked in several performances of distinction with the OUDS, but, called upon to play several important parts on successive evenings, he is handicapped by want of experience. His playing is sincere, enthusiastic, and promising, but he is betrayed by technical insufficiency. His Romeo is well conceived, but clumsily executed," said *The Times*. *The Stage* was more generous: "Glenville is nothing if not wholehearted, a quality that should help him to distinction when he has learned to temper it with moderation."

Fortunately Peter regained his mettle to play the jester Feste in Iden Payne's *Twelfth Night* the next day, and *The Stage* pronounced him "successful as Feste, capering and singing with the right hint of soul-weariness behind his mask of folly." But there was a lack of balance between the comic performances of Peter, Roy Byford as Sir Toby and Geoffrey Wilkinson as Sir Andrews according to Kemp and Trewin: "In the kitchen scene, which should be the strict preserve of comedy, the trio seemed unable to decide who should be the life and soul of the party."

Three days later Peter appeared as Edgar in the opening night of Komisarjevsky's memorable staging of *King Lear*. Komisarjevsky had been director of Moscow's Bolshoi Theatre before moving to England. In the 1920s he introduced British audiences to Anton Chekhov's plays; he was still a daring choice as a guest director. His modernistic productions defied convention and frequently shocked audiences, but he guaranteed good sales at the box office.

His aim was to set the action "outside time and beyond geography" and in so doing his production declared the work of a great artist. The abstract scenery consisted of a single flight of steps and brilliantly colored lighting was used to affect the changes of mood in the narrative. It proved to be the *pièce de résistance* of the festival, which sorely needed a success having been criticized for its uneven acting and substandard productions. *King Lear* won praise for its rich and elegant costumes, fabulous staging and use of lighting. To modern audiences, it may not sound radical, but this was a stroke of groundbreaking modernity and breathtaking ingenuity. *The Times* pronounced it "a Lear worth making a long journey to see." Meanwhile Peter's Edgar was described as "played with tempered enthusiasm." For all the plaudits heaped on the production it was far from a glowing review for Peter.

By April 23 the pace was taking its toll, and Peter fell in for harsh words from *The Times* for his Claudio, a nobleman in Payne's *Much Ado About Nothing*: "Glenville as Claudio seemed unaware that Shakespeare gives some of his most contemptible characters the loveliest things to say." Luckily his playing of Hector in the Payne's *Troilus and Cressida* escaped any condemnation the following day.

Two weeks into the season Peter became ill and asked the management if he could give up playing Petruchio. It was all too much for a young inexperienced actor and Peter was suffering under the strain of playing multiple major roles night after night—three in the lead role. His progressively lukewarm reviews were tremendously disheartening; from being able to do little wrong while a student Peter seemed to be able to do little that was right. Agate's warning to Peter about overreaching himself too early in his career had come true. Peter never acted at The Memorial again.

As punishing as Peter found the schedule and demands made on him as an inexperienced young actor, the festival was a valuable experience; it's all too easy to take success for granted and for Peter some of the criticism he received must have been hard to take. However, he did appear in one of the most lauded productions of *King Lear* ever, all the while witnessing the revolutionary stagecraft of the genius Komisarjevsky at firsthand. He worked with respected old hands such as Ayrton as well as other younger talents including Trevor Howard, Rosamund John, Valerie Tudor, Pamela Brown and Wolfit.

For almost a year after the festival Peter did not work at all; it may have been because his illness was more serious than first appeared. In March 1937 he was diagnosed with a duodenal ulcer and advised to eat biscuits or drink Horlick's at eleven o'clock in the morning and bedtime, drink hot water first thing in the morning and last thing at night, never go for more than three hours without food, stop smoking and get exercise at weekends. At the age of twenty-three, Peter was young to suffer from such a complaint. It was likely exacerbated by his lifestyle, but the stress of performing may have been a factor. Life in the theater meant irregular mealtimes and there was the added fact that Peter was a chain smoker. Throughout most of his life he smoked seventy cigarettes a day, even between courses at lunch and dinner.

How much he heeded the doctor's advice is unknown, but he had recurring problems with ulcers for much of his life. He also suffered from a range of stress-related illnesses from boils to rashes to recurring grippe-like illnesses and tension headaches. Peter's calm exterior hid a nervous man whose health suffered from stress. The life he chose was full of stresses and strains, so why did he do it? Was it to prove himself to his peers, the critics and, perhaps most of all, his parents? Whatever it was, it certainly took its toll.

In May 1937 he returned to work Margate Repertory. He played a season as leading man in Leon Gordon's *White Cargo*, Coward's *Still Life* and Eugene O'Neill's *Anna Christie*. His reprisal of his Perelli role in *On the Spot* at Margate's Theatre Royal in Kent, complete with bow tie and moustache, saw him a favorite of *The Stage* once more: "Pirelli is played by Peter Glenville with much vigour, and the interest taken in the plot is largely due to the able way he acts."

In September he began a tour with John Baxter-Somerville's Repertory Players taking in the Channel Island of Jersey to play at the Springfield Theatre in another gangster drama, Barré Lyndon's *The Amazing Dr. Clitterhouse* and an adaptation of one of Dorothy Sayers' Lord Peter Wimsey detective novels, *Busman's Honeymoon*. During the latter play Peter's serious attitude to his role as the leading man got another young actor fired. The actor was Jon Pertwee, famed for his role as the Time Lord in the BBC TV series *Doctor Who*.

Pertwee bore Peter no ill will, and forty years later recalled that his grievance wasn't unjust. "In one scene I had to enter downstage left and warmly shake the hand of Mr. Glenville. It occurred to me that that it might be rather droll to have a raw egg in my hand on the first night. I, therefore, with a fresh brown one . . . secreted in my palm, shook Lord Peter's hand and chuckled merrily to myself when the yolk went up his sleeve and the white went down his trousers. The audience roared but Mr. Glenville didn't, and thought it to be a very thin piece of fun. Trembling with anger, and without my knowledge, he at once phoned Mr. J. Baxter-Somerville . . . and informed him that he would not remain any longer in a company where he was expected to perform with buffoons."

Baxter-Somerville flew to Jersey to find out what was going on. "But, as could have been expected, there was no laughter in the dressing room after, only censure and approbation. To no-one's surprise, including my own, I was . . . summarily dismissed." Unsurprisingly Pertwee's reputation led to a lean period in his working life. Peter's sense of professionalism shows he was more mature in his outlook than the still green 18-year-old Pertwee.

Against a backdrop of the spread of Fascism, and the continuing debate over appeasement, 1938 was a good year for Peter, not least because he joined the Q Theatre. It opened in 1924 near Kew Bridge in west London, hence its name, modeling itself along similar lines to other independent theatrical companies such as the Arts Theatre Club. Run by the dynamic husband-and-wife team of Jack and Beatrice de Leon, it was a small theater with big ideas, quickly gaining a reputation for trying out experimental plays and focusing on attracting new writers. Peter was aware of the theater during his Oxford days, as it was where Terence Rattigan's first play, *First Episode*, opened in 1933. Running the Q was a risky financial business; in some cases the plays transferred to the West End, but all too often they passed quietly into anonymity.

By the time Peter joined the Q it had become so successful that the trains were rescheduled at Kew Bridge station to take theatergoers home when a play ran until eleven o'clock. Jack de Leon attributed the theater's achievement to two factors: "the virtual non-existence of competition in the field of try-out theatre and the number of excessively short-lived plays in the West End. . . . The former resulted in an avalanche of new plays coming our way and the latter in a record of eight transfers out of the twenty-six new plays represented. Both factors combined to influence artists of star calibre to appear and to establish Q first nights as theatrical events which West End managements forewent at the risk of missing a potential winner."

The suburban theater nurtured acting and directorial talent. Peter Brook and Tony Richardson directed plays at the Q, and many of Britain's most famous actors started out there. Apart from giving aspiring newcomers a chance to tread the boards, the Q presented young thespians with the chance to learn about the theater from the ground up. Budding actors would often start by doing menial jobs, from selling ice cream at the intervals and painting scenery, to taking sandwiches to peckish performers in their poky dressing rooms. Novices could watch and learn, and if they were lucky, eventually gain a small part in a show. Many of Peter's contemporaries passed through the doors of this hive of activity including Devlin, Wolfit and Neilson-Terry; to have worked at the Q was a great thing to have on an actor's résumé.

With just 490 seats the theater was the very antithesis of appearing with the New Shakespeare Company and was certainly better suited to his young talents. In March 1938 Peter made an auspicious start in the lead role of the poetical American rancher Robert Mayo in Eugene O'Neill's *Beyond the Horizon*. *The Times* liked Peter but slated the play: "Glenville plays the part, though sometimes too picturesquely, with sympathetic self-identification with the dramatist's purpose, but the dramatist's purpose was stiff, and Robert Mayo seems to the end to have been imposed upon the scene as a kind of philosophic decoration of it." Throughout the summer Peter appeared in a variety of productions including Mary Frances Flack's *Blind Corners*, Edward Percy and Reginald Denham's *The Green Holly*, and a revival of John van Druten's *Diversion*. The latter saw *The Sunday Times*' Agate give Peter his stamp of approval: "Glenville is coming on hand over fist, and his performance in the first part of the third act is extremely good. Passivity is easy, and we are always told by the quietists that passion is a mere affair of shouting. Since, according to that school, acting is all an affair of whispering, I submit that rising passion must be a differentiation in whispers. And that surely calls for some doing? Whether it does or not, Mr. Glenville acts admirably."

For Peter 1938 ended with a return to radio, taking part in a broadcast of James Elroy Flecker's story of Hassan of Baghdad, *Hassan*. After initially over reaching himself, Peter, three years after leaving university, had achieved his dream of becoming, not just a professional actor, but also a busy one. Peter's personal life also appears to have been both happy and settled as he was living with the charismatic Oliver Messel. Messel's success had brought him money as well as fame, and he was known for driving a hard bargain with managements. He needed to pay for his increasingly lavish lifestyle and stylish white studio—no expense was spared in its decoration and he even had vicuna fur bedcover. Not that Messel's furnishings were always costly, his natural good taste meant he could transform an ugly Victorian mirror into an apparent Rococo gem with the aid of a little plaster and paint. His home was an eclectic mix somewhere between a colorful flea market and an exotic museum dotted with busts, his famous masks and large flower displays. The home that Peter and Messel shared was in Kensington, behind Harrods; perfect for Peter, whether he was appearing in the West End or out at the Q.

Messel's home was also his place of work and among the bric-a-brac he had tastefully assembled were easels, paintbrushes, paints and all the strange materials he used to assemble his creations. As much as Messel was a social dilettante, he was a meticulous perfectionist when it came to his work. He would often work all night staying awake with endless cups of black coffee toiling over a drawing board to make the deft sketches, poetic watercolors and carefully contrived scale models that helped him realize his costumes and sets. Sheets of designs would litter the floor, tables, chairs—and even the bed. Messel's nephew, Antony Armstrong-Jones, was a frequent visitor to the studio and remembers its creative chaos: "[My uncle] had a studio in Yeoman's Row where I first started to help him when I was six, in 1936. I used to soak bits of brown paper for masks."

Messel's sister Anne was a society beauty and Armstrong-Jones was her son by her first marriage. The young Armstrong-Jones married Queen Elizabeth II's sister, Princess Margaret, in 1960 to become the Earl of Snowdon and Viscount Linley of Nymans. Snowdon knew Peter well and described Peter as "part of the family"; Peter was invited to Snowdon's wedding to the Princess in Westminster Abbey.

Snowdon became a leading photographer in fashion, design and theater, and a portraitist known for his royal studies. Peter's mother was among those Snowden photographed for a portrait and he has cited Messel's artistic influence and contacts as helping him pave his way as a photographer: "He introduced me to theatre, to directors like Peter Glenville who in turn introduced me to Alec Guinness and so it snow-balled." The 24-year-old Snowdon's first engagement as a theatrical photographer was in 1954 when Peter invited him to take pictures at the try-out of his production of *Separate Tables* in Newcastle. Peter told Snowdon that he was on trial and if his photos were used he would pay him twenty-five shillings per still; Snowdon's pictures adorned the front of the St. James' Theatre in the West End throughout its run. Snowdon describes working with Peter as "Delightful. He couldn't have been nicer." Peter used Snowdon again to take the house photographs for the West End production of *Hotel Paradiso* two years later.

Messel's parties at Yeoman's Row were legendary—local urchins were fed on their leftover caviar and petit fours—and his studio was a haven for the biggest names in the theatrical and literary world; socialites, aristocrats and the avant-garde flocked to his door. Messel's increasing celebrity garnered him a growing social circle, with friends including the caricaturist and writer Sir Max Beerbohm, society hostess Baroness Catherine d'Erlanger, opera soprano Olga Lynn, and photographer and theatrical designer Cecil Beaton. All of these people Peter got to know as well, which in many ways was an extension of his university life. Peter's mother was not averse to his relationship, as she explained when she was interviewed for Charles Castle's biography of Messel. "I used to see Oliver with Peter when he had 16 Yeoman's Row. He used to have some wonderful parties; you met everyone there—all sorts of different people. There would also be a pianist and somebody that would sing very well (Olga Lynn, on many occasions). There was a high-society dame whose daughter ran off with a coloured person; that sort of thing wasn't done in those days. Oliver was always fond of coloured people and had asked him to the party. When he entered the room the old girl sat bolt upright, turned her chair around, and spent the rest of the evening with her back to him."

In February 1939 Peter returned to the West End to play opposite Leueen MacGrath in Mary D. Sheridan's *The Courageous Sex* at the Globe Theatre. "Glenville had the difficult task of representing a young author whose conversation did not often betray his talent, and this he executed with feeling and skill." The following month he moved a few streets away to the Phoenix Theatre, to take on another principal role, this time as the suicidal Raymond Lefort in Eleanor Kalkowska's *To Be or Not To Be* alongside Sylvia Coleridge and Gyles Isham. *The Times* rated him: "Glenville persuades us of Raymond's suffering in a performance that wonderfully is not monotonous."

March 1939 turned out to be the most propitious time in Peter's career when he was offered a wonderful opportunity for a young actor. In March The Old Vic's mainstay players were on a three-month tour of southern Europe and Egypt sponsored by the British Council and so the 38-year-old respected director, Tyrone "Tony" Guthrie, employed Peter among a number of new hires that he assembled to keep the theater open during the tour.

Guthrie first joined the Old Vic in 1933, the youngest director the company had ever appointed, after he had worked for the Scottish National Players, Cambridge's Festival Theatre, and the BBC, where he created some of the first plays for radio. The Old Vic governors were particularly attracted to him because of his work at the West End's Westminster Theatre directing plays by contemporary dramatists Luigi Pirandello and J. B. Priestley, as well as a popular production of Shakespeare's *Love's Labours Lost*. Guthrie made many changes, including reducing the number of productions and employing new designers and he also attracted a younger generation to the Old Vic; the company garnered the acclaim its governors craved. By 1939 Guthrie had instigated a number of changes at the Old Vic, particularly his relentless pursuit of crowd pullers including Laurence Olivier, Ralph Richardson, Vivien Leigh, Edith Evans and Sybil Thorndike that improved box-office receipts.

Peter's first appearance was one that had previously proved to be his undoing, *The Taming of the Shrew*. This time round he played Petruchio's foil, Lucentio, opposite Roger Livesey. Guthrie's production produced the piece as a "roaring knockabout Italian harlequinade, decked out with all the Commedia dell'Arte paraphernalia of fantastic clothes, clown's make-up, acrobatic tumbling and truncheon-beating" according to critic Audrey Williamson; many thought it to be one of Guthrie's most brilliant productions. Williamson's take on Peter was also positive: "Peter Glenville, who had suffered early in his career from some precocious forcing in big roles at Stratford-upon-Avon, showed a new gift for burlesque as Lucentio."

In April Peter was involved in the Old Vic's annual celebration for Shakespeare's birthday; a selection of famous scenes and speeches from the bard's plays rendered by past and present members of the company. John Gielgud opened the evening's entertainment with a soliloquy from *Hamlet* before rushing off to perform in the West End. The glittering cast included Peggy Ashcroft, Sybil Thorndike and Alec Guinness. Whether this is the first time Peter met Guinness, who was to become his closest friend, is unknown, but they were beginning to move in the same circles. Other young actors to take to the stage for the festivities were William Devlin, Anthony Quayle and Charles Hawtrey. Peter did a two-hander with Esmé Percy, performing the "Handkerchief" scene from *Othello*.

During the next five months world events were moving at a pace, and almost inevitably towards war between Britain and Germany. Hitler's forces invaded Poland on September 1, 1939. Two days later Prime Minister Neville Chamberlain took to the airwaves to announce that Britain was at war with Germany. The government anticipated Nazi air raids and gas attacks and the evacuation of children from Britain's cities began immediately. Cinemas and theaters throughout Britain were closed at once, which may have helped alcohol consumption rise by 50% in the first week of the war, however, the government soon backtracked. On the September 8 a tipsy nation was relieved to hear that theaters, cinemas, and football grounds in safe areas could open again over the weekend. A week later all the entertainment venues across Britain were allowed to re-open until ten o'clock in the evening, although the West End still suffered restrictions; venues within one-and-a-half miles of Leicester Square initially had to close at six o'clock hence plays had to be cut in order to finish before the blackout. Although going to the theater was fraught with problems, as transport became difficult, it helped maintain some sense of normality, and theaters put on fluffy productions to help keep up morale. Stars also found their salaries slashed—all actors took home the Equity minimum weekly wage of £3, 10 shillings and a percentage of profits.

The theater did benefit in one way from war. The fledgling television broadcasts by the BBC were suspended for the duration; although in 1939 it was only people living near to London that could receive the signal—less than 30,000 owned a television set. The hiatus helped stave off the inevitable moment when television would reign supreme. Theater was recognized as a morale-raising tool, and the Entertainments National Service Association (ENSA) was set up to provide entertainment for the armed forces. The outfit commandeered Drury Lane's Theatre Royal, and the first concert parties for troops took place only three weeks after the war started. From 1942 artists worked for six weeks a year in ENSA entertainments for the troops and in factories. Although the organization put on some notable productions—Laurence Olivier and Ralph Richardson performed Shakespearian plays for the troops in a six-week tour of Europe—and attracted music-hall stars including the singer Gracie Fields and Lancashire comedian George Formby, some of the shows were of poor quality; the standing joke among the forces was that ENSA stood for "Every Night Something Awful."

Peter's mother was among the first to join ENSA heading off to France to entertain the British Expeditionary Force.

She and Shaun continued to work in pantomime around the country throughout the war, but like all forms of theatrical entertainment it was hard hit. London pantomime's particular malaise was hit by the evacuation of many children from the capital to country areas where they would be safe from bombing. This deprived pantomime of its traditional chorus composed of youngsters and, more seriously, much of its audience. However, many children started drifting back to the cities when the air raids failed to materialize in 1939.

The cinema suffered too. The output of the British film industry fell drastically during the war. In 1938 there were 134 feature films made in Britain, by 1942 the number of films dropped to thirty-nine. The number of people working in film was reduced to one-third of pre-war levels as everyone from actors to technicians was called-up and half of the studio space was requisitioned.

Peter's first movie role was in the Warner Brothers-First National Productions melodrama *His Brother*'s *Keeper* released in January 1940. Directed by Roy William Neil, an Irishman who began his career in 1916 directing a number of movies in Hollywood before working in Britain where he made thirteen films between 1936 and 1939. Like many of Neil's films, *His Brother*'s *Keeper* is missing, believed lost; it's a film that tells the story of a gold-digging singer and dancer and her relationship with two brothers who fight for her love with Peter played the younger brother. The siblings make their living doing a music-hall act dressed in dinner jackets: the blindfolded elder one shooting an outline of bullet holes around his brother. It's a film that ends tragically, with a pile of dead bodies, although the *Monthly Film Bulletin* declared, "(It) is very well cast. Especially Peter Glenville as the idealistic Hicky and Clifford Evans as the elder brother brusquely devoted to the younger."

In March Ealing Studios released *Return to Yesterday*, in which Peter had a small role. It's typical of the kind of fare made in British studios during the war; it's a morale booster with the war as the central theme. *Return to Yesterday* tells the story of a Hollywood star who returns to England and faces the dilemma of whether to return to America or stay in Britain to help support his nation. Peter then played a minor role as a young Latin in another Warner Brothers film, *Two For Danger*; the comedy caper about an art theft opened in October. None of the three films were released in America; they were "quota quickies," low-budget films shot at a fast pace to meet the demands of the Cinematograph Films Act of 1927 that instituted a yearly allocation of British-made movies. The act was introduced to counter Hollywood's dominance of the film world in the mid-1920s, and help stem the decline of Britain's film industry. Studio managements didn't object because quota quickies could be filmed between larger productions and kept workers employed throughout the year.

Hollywood found ways round the act. The Warner Brothers' films Peter appeared in were made at the American company's Teddington Studios in West London. They bought the studios in 1931 to make films strictly for the British market—the American companies' British-made productions were included within the quota because a British film was defined as one in which 75% of salaries went to British subjects including a British writer. Quota quickies have generally been seen as cheap, sub-standard movies made to satisfy an artificial market and history has not been kind to them; although recently there has been a renaissance in interest for their cultural interest. However out of more than one hundred Warner Brothers quota quickies made at Teddington Studios only copies of thirty-three are known to survive. This was exacerbated when Teddington Studios was severely damaged in 1944 when a V-1 flying rocket exploded on the property destroying two sound stages, the administration block and other buildings. Sadly all the films Peter appeared in are among those that are missing.

As well as making these films Peter was still working in theater. In January he played Tony Howard in George H.

Grimaldi's *Behind the Schemes!* at the Shaftesbury Theatre, and was back with the People's National Theatre as Charlie Stubbs, a cockney criminal turned cabbie in Ernest George's drama set during the Depression, *Down Our Street*, at the Tavistock Little Theatre. Managers of theaters took to reducing the price of tickets to attract audiences into London but sales continued to plummet as the earliest Luftwaffe air raids began; by May there were only a dozen theaters open in the capital.

In July, with the beginning of the Battle of Britain, things got worse, although for Peter he was kept busy in a revival of Novello's drawing-room comedy *Murder in Mayfair* at the Q that found him back playing opposite Leueen MacGrath. *The Stage* said Peter offered "a clean straightforward study as Bill Sherry." Also appearing was Sarah Churchill who was less interesting for her performance than her lineage; her father Winston had become prime minister in May.

By August life for those working in the theater was dire according to author Harold Hobson: "There are bombing attacks in the south-east during the day, and the buildings in the centre of Folkestone are hit. Numbers of German aircraft fly up the Thames Estuary in the afternoon, and drop bombs in Essex. Forty-seven enemy machines are destroyed, and fifteen of our own. At night there is a six-hour raid on London. The enemy comes over in small numbers, or even singly, and drops a few bombs on the outskirts of Central London. But even this mild sort of attack is presenting London places of entertainment with a serious problem. As the bombs come down, so do the attendances in the West End theatres. Theatres and cinemas have not yet developed a satisfactory policy for tackling air raids. They expected air raids to be dangerous but of short duration. Consequently, from the beginning of the war, theatre programmes have invariably carried the information that, in the event of a raid, the audience could leave the theatre if it wished, but that the performance would in any case continue. . . . In some theatres, when the performance is over and the raid has only just begun, the players give impromptu vaudeville entertainments until dawn. In others they simply go home and leave the audience to amuse itself. The cinemas have a problem of their own. As soon as a siren sounds large numbers of people try to dash into the nearest cinema, and managers are perplexed whether they should let them in or not. The present tendency is to refuse admission after the raid warning has been given, but it is plain that the current state of affairs cannot indefinitely go on."

Only London's Windmill Theatre remained open permanently throughout the war. Its chorus girls, cast members and crew slept in the theater's basement, giving rise to its motto "We Never Closed." Given its showgirls often played nude, some wits gagged that the motto was "We Never Clothed." However, come September for many people in Britain, and particularly in London, things got much worse. The Blitz lasted from September 7, 1940, to May 10, 1941, and London was bombed for fifty-seven consecutive nights; more than 21,000 civilians were killed and more than a million houses were destroyed or damaged. Instead of going out at night Londoners went home early to sleep in basements or shelters if available, the less fortunate slept in tube stations.

Two days before the onslaught Peter and Messel opened Jean Cocteau's satire, *The Infernal Machine*, at the Arts Theatre Club on September 5. Peter played the vain Oedipus with Leueen MacGrath as the Sphinx and Jeanne de Casalis as Jocasta; Messel did the designs. Agate opined: "First three acts witty, after which the play peters out in a 'straight' version of the Sophoclean tragedy. Much too long. Peter Glenville, who appeared to have treated his torso with Cherry Blossom [boot polish], made a handsome Oedipus, and Jeanne de Casalis was pretty good as a sort of Beatrice Lillie Jocasta. But neither could look at the fourth act." *The Spectator* reported: "Messel's scenery sometimes gets in the way of the actors. . . . The name of Mr. Oliver Messel is printed as large as the author's. And however deplorable this may seem in principle, it must be confessed that the most satisfying memory of this performance is the décor. Mr. Messel shares with [Christian] Bérard the wonderful sense of colour and the modish Neo-Classicism which made *Seventh Symphony* and *Symphonie Fantastique* such a pleasure to the eye. Indeed, Oedipus' scene with the Sphinx might have taken place only a few yards from the romantic desert in which Massine set Berlioz's *Pastorale*, and Jocasta's superb red, white and blue bedroom is surely only up one flight from the Ball."

The production continued through October amidst the terror of the Blitz despite being staged in the heart of London in Great Newport Street, near Leicester Square. It was a miracle Cocteau's play found its way into London at all. Messel's costumes, masks and set for the play were hastily assembled under pressure when he was granted a few days' leave from the Royal Engineers regiment stationed at Aldershot where he was serving as a second lieutenant. He made the models for the play using plaster and cotton wool—already the scarcity of materials meant theatrical designers and costumiers had to be increasingly inventive. Messel's inventive flair meant he could do wonders with the most humble raw supplies: papier-mâché, sticky paper, cellophane, rubber sheeting or pipe cleaners. His dyed, gilded and sequined pipe cleaners would appear equal to the work of a goldsmith, jeweler or embroider once they emerged from his studio. Their glittering effect was sufficient to deceive audiences that his dazzling costumes and sets had been made from the most sumptuous materials.

Messel's genius was put to good use during the war. He rose to become a captain in the Camouflage Corps in Norwich, and was known for his ornate disguising of pillboxes as caravans, haystacks, ruins and cafes. His departure to the armed forces meant that party life at Yeoman's Row came to an end. Peter wrote to him a week after *The Infernal Machine* opened saying: "Last night an incendiary bomb fell on the studio next to mine and burned a hole through the floor above your bedroom."

The severe damage done to the house led to an invitation to Peter from Katina Paxinou. A star of the Greek Royal Theatre, Paxinou was performing in London when the war broke out. Peter wrote: "She is staying at The Ritz and she has asked me to go and stay with her every night in the shelter there. It is very gay (with King Zog) and you don't hear a thing so (far!) She wants to get a good play for both of us and go to America with it. Whether that is a sensible idea or not I do not know. After you left on Sunday I dined with [Lady] Elinor Smith. We were caught in the most terrific barrage, so we chased back to her place, opened a bottle of champagne, and talked the whole night about theatre, Byron, etc. It was rather fun." Yeoman's Row was in a poor state for a while as Peter told Messel: "Still no gas, but my electric heater has been attended to so that I can bathe."

The exiled King Zog of Albania wasn't the only illustrious name Peter mixed with while he stayed at The Ritz. Yeoman's Row may have been bombed but society life continued. At the hotel Peter would meet up with friends such as Messel's sister and her wealthy second husband, Michael Parsons, the 6th Earl of Rosse, and a friend of Messel's from Eton, the writer Harold Acton—further evidence that his relationship with Messel widened his social circle to include some of the most creative, cultivated, intelligent and affluent people of the day. Peter's cultivation of aristocratic circles and the intellectual elite continued throughout his life; a Filofax he left behind after his death reads like a who's who of European and American high society.

It was Messel's absence on military service that seems to have brought his personal relationship with Peter to an end, although the pair's friendship continued and they collaborated professionally. Peter had a lot to thank Messel for. Besides the people Peter met through Messel his mentoring helped form Peter's aesthetic tastes that would later encourage him to become a collector of art and antiques. Living with arguably the best theatrical designer in the world of his era obviously rubbed off, and enabled Peter to develop a visual sense that served him well as a director. Peter acknowledged Messel's talent, friendship and his influence when he was interviewed more than forty years later by Messel's biographer: "Oliver was a magician. He was effervescent, funny, egocentric, loyal, sophisticated, wise, childish but shrewd—and a beautiful sprite. All his work had a brilliant flair and evoked both the classical world of the past and a future world over the horizon. I was lucky enough to meet him when we were both young. After my enjoyable Jesuit education he taught me to appreciate through the eye and not just through the mind. To guide me in the visual world was a priceless event. His close friendship was another."

The respect was mutual. When Messel did his last play in New York, *Traveller Without Luggage*, in 1964 he complained: "It was appallingly acted and as the director didn't understand it very well, it didn't work at all. It needed Peter Brook or Peter Glenville or somebody that understood what it was meant to be."

Toward the end of September 1940 the fraternal theater-management duo Rocco and John Gatti took a bold step and re-opened the Vaudeville Theatre on the Strand with afternoon shows of Shakespeare's problem play, *All's Well That Ends Well*. The trade journal *Theatre World* bemoaned the general situation but praised the brothers' bravado: "The choice of the Londoner is now restricted to the delights of the Revudeville at the Windmill and the lunch-time ballet hour at the Arts Theatre Club, to which must be added the brave venture of Shakespeare at the Vaudeville, matinées only." Peter played the gullible romantic hero, Bertram, in a cast that included some old Shakespearian hands.

The Times was happy with Peter—and that any plays were being performed at all: "At the present time it is commendably bold to put on any play in Central London, even for afternoon performances only. . . . Glenville plays Bertram, and does succeed in suggesting that the detestable fellow is a real and enduring type."

The increasing intensity of the air raids prompted more theaters in London, Liverpool and Birmingham to close; potential audiences stayed at home rather than face broken water mains, fires and cordoned-off streets. The Shakespeare season at the Vaudeville struggled on without evening shows, with Peter opening as the carousing Prince Hall in *Henry IV Part One* on October 23. But going to the theater doesn't seem to have bothered Peter. In his autobiography Alec Guinness wrote that Peter had no fear of physical danger, maybe that was sheer bravado or maybe his religious faith gave him an ability to face whatever fate cast his way.

Peter was in the position of still working in the theater because he had been declared unfit for military service; his ulcer was the problem. When the war broke out Parliament passed the National Service (Armed Forces) Act, under which all men aged between eighteen and forty-one were made liable for conscription. The registration of men in each age group began in turn on October 21, 1939, starting with those aged twenty to twenty-three. By May 1940, registration had extended only as far as men aged twenty-seven and didn't reach those aged forty until June 1941. The Ministry of Labour and National Service wrote to the then 27-year-old Peter on December 10, 1940, saying: "I have to inform you that notification has been received that you have been medically examined and found to be permanently incapable of being placed in medical Grades I, II, IIa or III. You will, therefore, not be liable for service under the National (Armed Forces) Act 1939." Peter's reaction to this is unclear, but given what Guinness had to say it may not have sat comfortably with him, then again he may have been happy to continue to be able to work in his chosen profession.

Conscription was another blow for the British theater and cinema because it lost the services of many of its eminent actors and dramatists; Rattigan, Olivier, Richardson and Guinness all joined the forces. Fewer young actors were available, leading to lengthy casting calls, and musicals were hit by a shortage of chorus boys because children had been evacuated. Conscription didn't just deprive theaters of top-notch actors: stagehands and those who worked behind the scenes were thin on the ground. Although there was less acting work available, Peter was able to benefit from the shortage and his decision to stick it out in London despite the dangers, when some actors headed for the comparative safety of the provinces, proved to be a good one

In 1941 as the Luftwaffe continued to pummel Britain the Windmill Theatre continued to justify its reputation. In February it began to stay open to eight o'clock in the evening from Monday to Friday and until nine o'clock on Saturdays. On May 11, London endured its heaviest night of bombing; Westminster Abbey, the Houses of Parliament and the British Museum were all damaged. When the long summer evenings arrived the Blitz drew to a close, London's theaters made a partial return to normality, although they didn't resume their former late opening hours. Judged by wartime standards, the first week of June was a busy one for the London stage, with two new productions. Peter appeared in one of them, Emlyn Williams' *The Light of Heart* at the Globe Theatre.

While critics concurred that the sentimental play was not one of Williams' best, its hopeful and positive tone appealed to popular taste. Williams rewrote the play for its second run and decided to play the lead role himself. He was too young to play an old man, so where previously the bony-faced Angela Baddeley had played the dissolute actor's lame daughter, Cattrin, she was reinvented as his sister. Peter played her musician boyfriend, Robert, taking over from Anthony Ireland.

The production had mixed notices because some critics had quibbles with the rewrite and preferred Williams' first version. *The Scotsman* reviewed the play when it toured in Glasgow: "The change in the story . . . seemed rather strange at first, but familiar lines and incidents soon brought realisation of the resource of the author-actor." When it moved on to Exeter, *The Stage* said that the cast had a "fine reception from a crowded house." When it hit London Peter fell foul of *The Times*' comparison to the previous incarnation: "Glenville plays the girl's lover more realistically, yet on the whole less effectively than it was played before." But *The Stage* showered him with compliments: "Glenville . . . plays the part with a natural directness, which, while it does not suggest reserve of manner . . . is certainly most engaging. Mr. Glenville is shaping as one of our best *jeunes premiers*." *The Light of Heart* ran for 180 performances.

For Peter, it would turn out to be a fortunate move in that it was the first play he performed with H.M. Tennent Limited and Stephen Mitchell. Tennent owned the Globe Theatre and the company was run by the powerful impresario Binkie Beaumont. His productions dominated the West End and for Peter it meant he was on the radar of British theater's two most important managers; both were to prove hugely important to his career.

In December 1941, following Japan's attack on Pearl Harbor and America joining in the hostilities, things in Britain would slowly begin to change. For Peter the year ended on a high note; he was an actor in demand for the stage and had made it into films. After his less than auspicious start, with roles that were more demanding than what he had to offer, his professional life was looking more secure. His return to repertory theater had, in some senses, been a move back to basics. It allowed him to reposition himself to the extent that he was able to switch between classical and modern roles for some of the most pioneering and well-known contemporary theater companies of the day, while also working with many of Britain's leading directors and actors. After six-and-a-half years Peter Glenville could properly call himself a professional actor.

4

Victory at the Old Vic

1942-1945

Because Peter had not been conscripted into the armed forces due to his ulcer he was one of a handful of young actors that was able to work throughout the Second World War. Theaters were struggling to attract audiences but their civilian ranks were swelled by the presence of those in uniform—members of the British forces on leave and their American counterparts. As 1942 dawned Peter followed in his parents' footsteps by appearing at the London Palladium—Dorothy and Shaun had played there to packed houses in 1927 during their run in the hit musical, *The Apache.* The Palladium, normally a theater featuring variety performers, put on a benefit performance one Sunday afternoon in late January as a fundraiser for Esmond Knight, an actor wounded by shrapnel while serving as a lieutenant on the battleship *HMS Prince of Wales* during the Battle of Denmark Strait. During the action in May 1941 Knight lost an eye and was blinded in the other.

The theatrical world was quick to rally to his support and the Palladium show featured an impressive lineup designed to appeal to the widest possible audience. It included the celebrity couple of the moment, Laurence Olivier and Vivien Leigh, who somewhat aptly chose to perform the wooing scene from Shakespeare's *King Henry V*. At the other end of the theatrical spectrum popular comedians including Bud Flanagan and Tommy Trinder offered a series of sketches. Peter joined Emlyn Williams, Angela Baddeley and Sir Robert Atkins to perform a selection from Shakespeare's *The Merchant of Venice*. The sellout raised more than £4,500 for Esmond Knight, who although blind, returned to acting, at first on radio and then in films. Later an operation restored his sight and he resumed his career on the stage. In an ironic twist of fate he played the captain of the *HMS Prince of Wales* in the 1960 film *Sink the Bismarck!*

Peter also returned to the big screen in 1942 when Terence Rattigan asked him to take on a major role in Gainsborough Pictures' *Uncensored*, directed by his friend, director Anthony "Puffin" Asquith. The director had persuaded the Air Ministry to grant Rattigan a short spell of leave to co-write the script. Set during Germany's occupation of Belgium, *Uncensored* tells of how a group of Brussels inhabitants risked their lives by publishing an underground newspaper during the First World War, which was an appealing project for the British authorities in that it highlighted the courage of people under occupation that were prepared to fight for freedom. Based on a true story by Oscar E. Millard that tells of *La Libre Belgique* (*The Free Belgium*), the film included real documentary footage, and with cinematography by the talented Arthur Crabtree, *Uncensored* managed to create a realistic image of the Belgian capital under occupation.

Asquith, who had grown up in 10 Downing Street and was the son of the former Prime Minister H.H. Asquith, was the British film industry's first really outstanding director. A slight figure known for his charm and gentle politeness, Asquith was as an actor's director. He had directed the 1938 screen version of the playwright's *Pygmalion* that found financial and critical success on both sides of the Atlantic, and won an Oscar for its screenplay. *Uncensored* wasn't Asquith's first film with Rattigan; he had directed the 1940 screen version of *French Without Tears*.

Asquith was president of the Association of Cine-Technicians from 1937 to his death in 1968, and he used his political connections and directorial clout to help keep the British film industry afloat during the war. Both Asquith and his mother lobbied politicians to persuade them that the industry was important, explaining how films were important in keeping Britain informed, how they helped to raise morale and, more importantly, were a vital tool in the propaganda war. The government bought the argument, so much so that the Ministry of Information approved all films made during the war. The ministry monitored films to check that their message and their values were in the nation's best interests. Besides documentaries and public-information films, the industry produced features that idealized Britain while promoting the ingenuity and bravery of those fighting the Nazi regime.

For *Uncensored* Asquith assembled a fine cast that included Eric Portman, Irene Handl, Phyllis Calvert and Felix Aylmer, giving Peter the opportunity to work with a great film director as well as some excellent actors.

Handl and Aylmer had recently worked with Peter's father on the Warner Brothers movie *Dr. O'Dowd* a 1940 drama that was one of only two films in which Shaun appeared. He was cast as the lead—an Irish physician who has been struck off the medical register having been wrongfully accused of heavy drinking and later redeems himself during an outbreak of diphtheria. Unlike Shaun's doctor made good, Peter's role in *Uncensored* was far from noble. He got to play one of wartime's most detestable figures: a quisling. Peter played a disenchanted cabaret performer down on his luck, Charles Neele, whose first appearance in the film has him in a wig performing a comic song-and-dance skit that must have made his parents proud. He also sings and plays the piano with his stage partner, André Delage, played by Eric Portman. When Delage decides to leave their act, Peter's character is offended and worried that he will be unable to perform solo without the aid of his talented and popular partner. Delage's exit is because he is one of the patriots behind the campaigning newspaper. For no other reason that to satisfy his personal grudge, Peter's character turns over Delage and his accomplices to the Nazis to earn a reward—yet even they are horrified at Peter's character's traitorous act. Overcome with remorse, the quisling decides to donate his blood money to the church. He visits the local priest Father de Gruyte, played by Griffith Jones, and confesses his sins, which were driven by jealousy and hatred of his partner.

Typical of many wartime films, *Uncensored* was pure propaganda, so naturally the brave Delage and his love interest, Julie Lanvin—played by Calvert—manage to save the day and the lives of their fellow conspirators. They publish another edition of the newspaper bringing the guilt of those sentenced to death in doubt and the Nazis are made to look ridiculous. When *Uncensored* opened in July the critics liked it—and loved Peter. *The Times* gushed: "The most astute piece of acting comes from Mr. Peter Glenville as Delage's stage partner and his ultimate betrayer. Mr. Glenville creates a character odiously composed of jealousy, vanity, pettiness, and spite, and yet succeeds in making the creature's confession and remorse moving and credible."

London theater fared better in 1942. At the end of the year thirty shows were running compared to only sixteen in 1941, despite the fact that eight theaters had been destroyed or declared unsafe. However, the price of seats rose by as much as four shillings as theater managers tried to compensate for reduced revenues from traditionally profitable activities. Refreshments were rationed and chocolates hard to get, so sales during the intervals naturally dropped. The shortage of paper reduced the size of both advertising posters and programmes, which became just a single sheet of paper that also included instructions on what to do in the case of an air raid. Theaters warned audiences if an air raid was in progress by illuminated signs telling them they were free to leave for a shelter if they wished: "All we ask is that if you feel you must go you will depart quietly and without excitement." Frequently theatergoers stayed put to enjoy the performance; for many the need for entertainment outweighed the risks involved.

The demands of the war effort meant all kinds of materials were in short supply. The basics needed to stage productions were scarce, so costumes, makeup and the canvas and timber to create scenery were hard to obtain, and lighting for productions had to be kept simple as electricity rationing began. Actors on tour suffered from increasing difficulties in finding food and lodgings. Non-essential travel was discouraged in order to conserve fuel supplies, trains were poorly heated and privately owned cars lay largely unused because of petrol rationing; government posters asked the nation: "Is your journey really necessary?"

For Peter, travel was about to become unnecessary, as he was about to begin working for H. M. Tennent. The company had been founded in 1936 by Henry Moncrieff Tennent and following his death in 1941 Binkie Beaumont took over as managing director. It owned both the Globe Theatre and the Queen's Theatre on Shaftesbury Avenue and from his tiny office, tucked away on the top floor of the Globe, Beaumont oversaw a string of successes over the next three decades. His productions were known for their quality. It achieved its fearsome reputation because Beaumont employed top-line actors and sought out the best directors, composers, musicians, set designers, electricians and costume makers. A dapper individual with a cherubic face, he was always immaculately dressed, usually in a well-tailored dark suit. His love of the theater was genuine and his productions reflected his own exquisite taste: the words "H. M. Tennent presents" on a theater marquee was a guarantee of a top-notch production.

Beaumont regularly staged revivals of classic plays but was equally unafraid to dabble in experimental theater, particularly if he saw the chance to make some money. His passion and drive acted as a magnet and scripts by the world's most respected contemporary dramatists arrived at the Globe in droves; among those that Beaumont worked with were Noël Coward, Terence Rattigan, Christopher Fry, Jean-Paul Sartre, Arthur Miller, Peter Shaffer and Jean Anouilh. Financially shrewd and infamous for his hard-nosed negotiating skills, especially when it came to salaries, Beaumont usually got what he wanted. No actor, director or designer was willing to offend him with a refusal and so damage his or her theatrical careers. He would energetically pursue those he wanted to work with by wining and dining them in top London restaurants—and was willing to pay a premium for their services. Considered by many to be ruthless, he was also generous and appreciative, hosting extravagant parties at The Savoy hotel and showering a cast with gifts when a production reached its first anniversary. First nights were invariably followed by lavish celebrations at his Georgian house at 14 Lord North Street, Westminster.

Handsome, elegant and self-confident, he was well able to deal with the often-capricious behavior and swollen egos of some of the actors he employed. With his great sense of humor and charm many fell under his spell as the actor Robert Morley described. "Alone among the impresarios, he understands actors. In his office it is always they who play their scene; he is the friendly critic, the attentive audience, the committed fan. Beaumont never engages the actor, he makes sure that the actor engages him. . . . What actors admire most about him is his integrity."

Peter's wit and charm appealed to Beaumont, as did his acting ability. Beaumont was homosexual, which caused some people in the theater to criticise the influence of what they saw as Beaumont's "homosexual mafia." Whatever they may have felt his "inner circle" was an incredibly talented group, comprising John Gielgud, Terence Rattigan, Noël Coward, Peter Glenville, and Beaumont's partner, actor and writer John Perry.

Actor John Moffatt worked in seven plays for Beaumont and told the British Library's Theatre Project: "Binkie [Beaumont] and John Perry used the best directors and they cast the best actors for the parts." Any suggestions that there was some kind of homosexual cabal fails to take into account that Beaumont's loyal team at H. M. Tennent largely consisted of heterosexual men and women. It was somewhat a sign of the times when some sections of society were homophobic and failed to acknowledge that talent was what was important, not a person's sexuality.

Tyrone Guthrie once commented that when Beaumont's influence was at its peak he had the power to make or break almost any theatrical career in London. He was an impresario in every sense and nicknamed "The Czar of Shaftesbury Avenue." Perhaps the fact that one man had so much power wasn't good, but he entertained audiences with stylish quality productions known for their good taste and fine acting, and he kept many theater people employed.

Peter's working relationship with Beaumont was good, although he did sometimes complain of his meanness. Years later Peter confessed that he preferred co-producing plays with Beaumont than working for him because he was "infinitely more candid and more human to deal with as a partner than as an employer. He consults one over everything, and almost invariably defers to one's own opinion, except when he has a better idea—which he sometimes has."

One of Beaumont's production currently playing at the Theatre Royal in the West End was Shaw's *The Doctor's Dilemma*. It starred Cyril Cusack as the artist and womaniser Louis Dubedat opposite Vivien Leigh as Dubedat's wife; she was one of the most famous actresses in the world, thanks to her role as Scarlett O'Hara in the 1939 movie *Gone with the Wind* that won her an Oscar for Best Actress.

The Doctor's Dilemma was first staged in 1906 and was ahead of its time in its revolutionary handling of the thorny issue of medical ethics. It tells the story of Dubedat, a young man diagnosed with tuberculosis, whose doctor has to choose whether to treat him with his limited supply of an anti-toxin, thought to cure the illness, or whether to treat a colleague. At first, impressed by Dubedat's considerable artistic talent, he thinks he will save the young artist. As he becomes aware of Dubedat's infidelity, he opts to save his worthy, but boring, friend instead.

It was Laurence Olivier who suggested the play to Beaumont; he and Leigh had been offered the husband-and-wife roles for a pre-war radio broadcast, but it never transpired. Olivier was anxious that his wife should work as he was serving as an officer with the Royal Navy's Fleet Air Arm at a base near Winchester in Hampshire, while Leigh, who was both lonely and missing her husband, was living 50 miles away in the village of Warsash. Beaumont liked the script, and there had not been a major revival of the play since its first run, so he began rehearsals in the summer of 1941. Casting the crowd-pulling Leigh as the cuckolded long-suffering wife guaranteed full houses; her star status ensured press coverage. The popular photojournalistic magazine *Picture Post* featured the raven-haired beauty on its front cover.

Beaumont employed the society photographer Cecil Beaton, in one of his earliest theatrical commissions to do the décor; he would later design the costumes for *Gigi* and *My Fair Lady*. Besides Beaton the Motley Theatre Design Group to do the costumes, and Irene Hentschel, one of the few contemporary female stage directors to be successful to work on the production. With clothing and textiles rationed from June 1941, and the nation encouraged to "Make do and mend," it meant that hand-me-down theatrical costumes became the order of the day; actresses were allowed just three pairs of stockings every three months and two pairs of shoes per show. Strings were pulled in those hard-pressed times so that Leigh could be adorned in bewitching velvet dresses with high lace collars, ruffles and bows, beguiling veiled hats and sparkling jewellery; the latter on loan from a fashionable Mayfair jeweller. The Motleys' elegant Edwardian costumes and setting provided a sumptuous contrast to the dull fashions brought on by wartime austerity. Audiences, especially fashion-starved women, loved Beaton's photograph of the petite Leigh in her dressing room clad in a hat and veil; it became Olivier's favorite picture of her.

The production toured the provinces to good notices for six months before opening in London in March 1942. Accompanied by the Admiral of the Fleet, First Sea Lord Sir Dudley Pound, Olivier was there to watch Leigh receive one of her greatest ovations; the proceeds of the performance went to the Royal Naval War Libraries Fund. Critics adored the show, and Leigh; the box office was swamped with advance bookings. However, less than two weeks later, disaster struck creating a legend among theater folk for decades. Beaumont biographer Richard Huggett debunks the myth. Being a good Irishman Cusack celebrated his nation's saint's day on March 17 with a few whiskies at lunchtime before returning to the theater hoping to sleep it off before the evening's performance. Cusack's first cue was in the second act of the five-act play. Feeling sick and worse for wear, he fluffed his lines before his mind went a total blank and he began reciting lines from the one play he could remember, Synge's *Playboy of the Western World*. A distressed Leigh started to stumble over her lines. The curtain fell, Leigh returned to her dressing room, and Cusack's understudy Geoffrey Edwards, an old colleague of Peter's from the Q, took over.

Edwards had only just taken on the role as Cusack's understudy, having previously been covering the role of the doctor. Added to which none of the three understudies for the thirteen-strong cast had been through proper rehearsals, nor did Cusack's costume fit Edwards causing him to improvise by using his own clothes. Edwards, unable to remember all the lines, decided to avert further problems by reading from the script, which didn't go down well with Beaumont. The following day Beaumont summoned Cusack into his office and gave him two weeks' notice. An ashamed Edwards decided he had to go too. Some accounts suggest he was sacked; in fact he wrote to Beaumont on March 21 asking to be released on April 4 adding: "I should like to file also my gratitude to you for your kindness to me over the whole unfortunate incident."

On the same day Beaumont dismissed Cusack, he hired Peter to play Louis Dubedat for a salary of £10 a week (double the minimum) plus 0.03% of the weekly profits from the eight shows a week. Leigh received the same weekly wage, but her profit share was a heftier 30%. It was an ideal part for Peter, who had grown accustomed to playing the loveable rake. Photographs of Peter alongside Leigh show him sporting a goatee beard and moustache, looking every inch the handsome but amoral artist. Twenty-five years later *The Stage* still remembered it as one of theater's most "remarkable take-overs." At twenty-eight years old, the nervousness that saw Peter cast off the part of Petruchio at Stratford had gone. He was by this time a man who rarely got flustered, a characteristic that served him particularly well when he started to direct; his experience and maturity had helped him develop a cool head. In her autobiography Beaumont's secretary, Kitty Black, describes how Peter's capacity for calm in a crisis paid off in the production: "His considerable technique came in handy one afternoon when an air-raid warning sounded during a matinee and from far away the sound of the guns firing could be heard coming nearer and nearer as the invaders flew up the river. Stoically unmoved the audience never flinched until [Louis] Dubedat's line, 'My ears hear things that other people's ears can't,' when a ripple of amusement released the tension that was sweeping through the house."

Peter opened as Dubedat on March 28, 1942, and, as might be expected, his biggest fan, his mother, was in the audience for what was arguably the biggest night of his career thus far.

Fortunately the press warmed to the new Dubedat. *The Times* said: "Mr. Glenville, an improving actor, draws Dubedat with persuasive liveliness. Indeed, none of the changes can be said to weaken Miss Irene Hentschel's admirable production." Although *The Observer* was more restrained in its comments: "Glenville's Dubedat is much livelier than the predecessor (perhaps a dying man should not be quite as lively as all that)."

Nevertheless, not everything went to plan. In February the following year Peter contracted jaundice and was hospitalized for a week. His understudy became ill too and audiences arriving at the theater were met with a notice: "Owing to the indisposition of Mr. Peter Glenville the part of 'Louis Dubedat' will be played at this performance by Mr. John Gielgud who has taken it up at very short notice."

In August 1943 Gielgud wrote to Shaw about his experience: "Did anybody tell you that I dashed on at twenty-four hours' notice and played Dubedat for a few performances in January when the actor [Peter Glenville] and his understudy were both ill. I greatly enjoyed myself when I knew the words, which wasn't until about the fourth performance. The earlier nights I held the book under my blanket in the death scene, and, as I believe old actors say 'winged' the lines as best I could. I am told my conception of the part was superior to my execution of it, and of course I am far too old. But it is a part."

The play eventually closed in April 1943 having been a huge success, breaking box-office records and taking £3,000 (£300,000 in today's money) or more in a week. Leigh's star status helped, but it was also a play of quality by the most eminent dramatist of the time rather than one of the prevalent trashy "naughty" comedies playing in London's theaters. The production made a profit of £28,000 and Beaumont was ecstatic, saying: "I shall never speak disrespectfully of Shaw's plays again. There is as much money to be made in him as Shakespeare."

Among the American serviceman who arrived in England in 1942 was Storekeeper, First Class Hardy William "Bill" Smith;

Storekeepers are the navy's supply clerks, and Bill worked with the Admiralty in London in a liaison capacity on Anglo-American Reciprocal Aid. During Peter's run in *The Doctor's Dilemma* he met Bill and the two of them began a professional and personal relationship that lasted for the rest of Peter's life. Their meeting was at a ball held at Mayfair's Londonderry House, given by society queen Edith, Marchioness of Londonderry, wife of Charles Vane-Tempest-Stewart, the wealthy 7th Marquess of Londonderry, and a cousin of Winston Churchill. Slim, with brown hair and green eyes Bill was a handsome man, he dressed immaculately and was equally gracious. The perfect gentleman, together he and Peter cut a dashing pair.

Born Harold William Schmidt on December 1, 1916, in New York, Bill was one of two children; his sister, Maddy, was three years younger. Their parents, Lucy and William Hardy Schmidt, had run a successful cigar business on Long Island, before losing it in the aftermath of the Wall Street Crash, so they moved to Jackson Heights, in New York; following which Bill's father died and Lucy Schmidt later remarried.

A friend of theirs in later years, TV producer Tom Seligson, said that on the surface, Peter and Bill's partnership seemed an unlikely one: "They were from completely different worlds. Peter, of course, was from this theatrical English family, and I believe Bill was from Queens. On the surface, you'd never imagine them together." But like Peter, Bill had a great visual sense and after graduating from high school he went to work in the fashion-garment industry.

Also like Peter, he changed his name. In 1943 he legally said goodbye to Harold William Schmidt to become Hardy William Smith; it was a move designed to distance himself from the Nazi connotations of a German-sounding name. His parents' financial demise affected him, and like Peter he loved the good life and fine things. Their partnership allowed both of them to represent themselves as gentleman of good standing, and over the years Bill even acquired an English accent. Born into the Lutheran Church, after the war Bill sought for spiritual meaning; Peter's faith served as an example to Bill and he converted to Catholicism in 1957.

Perhaps, above all else, to begin with what they both had in common was a love of the theater. When Bill returned to civilian life, he studied at the Old Vic theater school for a year, acting the part of Tom Wingfield in a production of Tennessee Williams' *The Glass Menagerie*. He went on to attend several London art schools, studying painting and design, and familiarizing himself with theatrical costume and décor. He would sit in on rehearsals of plays Peter was directing and was present throughout their production. Bill chose to stay in England, renewing his visa every three months and in 1952 he even applied for British citizenship, but it was never granted.

Within the theatrical world they were known as partners, in every sense of the word, with Bill widely accepted as Peter's respected right-hand man. Talked of by family and friends as both shy and kind, his personality was just the opposite of Peter's gregarious, flamboyant nature—Bill was happiest behind the scenes, organisingtheir domestic and travel arrangements, as well as acting as Peter's assistant. He sometimes gained formal recognition, credited as "assistant to the director" on *Romeo and Juliet*. He was a sounding board for Peter too, reading plays and discussing ongoing projects. Given that Peter appeared to be calm to his work colleagues, and his task as a director was often to soothe ruffled feathers and smooth the way in negotiations, Bill was the steady rock that Peter leaned upon when he came to unburden his problems. Bill was vital in Peter's career as well as a huge emotional support to him.

After *The Doctor's Dilemma*, Peter made a return to films in the now forgotten musical, *Heaven Is Round the Corner* released in April 1944 and produced by J. Arthur Rank's British National Films. It was the worst year for British wartime film production; a mere thirty-five films were made. It starred Scottish musical-hall comedian Will Fyffe and singer Leni Lynn. The latter plays a girl driven from her home on a farm by the war so she heads to Paris where she falls in love with a man from the British Embassy. The war puts an end to their romance for three years until they are once again reunited on the farm. It's another "lost" British film, and no print is available.

Peter's next film, *Madonna of the Seven Moons*, has survived, although contemporary critics were scathing of its labyrinthine and hugely implausible plot, audiences loved it. In modern times it has undergone a minor reassessment gaining credit for its strong female roles, which were relatively uncommon when it was made. It was one of Gainsborough Pictures' melodramas, and its extravagant costumes and sheer romantic escapism appealed to an audience tired of war. Despite the fall in British film production, audiences were desperate for entertainment and headed for movie theaters in record numbers. In 1945 cinema admissions climbed to almost one and a half billion—a record figure that has never been equalled. From the summer of 1944 the "doodlebug" V-1 flying bombs and V-2 rockets rained down on London. Despite the arrival of these new deadly weapons, and a resumption of a "blitz," Londoners put on a bold front, enjoying themselves wherever and however they could.

For his role in *Madonna of the Seven Moons*, Peter once again drew on his considerable experience of playing the cad. He had a lead role as the sinister Sandro Barucci, a Florentine gigolo and younger brother of a jewel thief. The film saw Peter encounter former colleagues Nancy Price, who played his scheming mother, Mama Barucci, and Phyllis Calvert as the schizophrenic Maddalena Labardi, who lives a double life. It was a bizarre role for the Calvert, a huge star who had made her name in "honest-woman" roles in such classics as 1943's *The Man in Grey* and 1944's *Fanny by Gaslight*. In *Madonna of the Seven Moons* she acted the part of a deeply religious and respectable Roman middle-class wife of a wine merchant and mother, who was raped as an adolescent by a gypsy. The incident made her develop an alter ego, Rosanna, a wild, sensual gypsy. When she adopts her Rosanna identity she disappears from the family home in Rome to head for Florence where she becomes the mistress of Sandro's nefarious brother, Nino, played by Stewart Granger. Another big name, Granger was a popular romantic lead, having made his name opposite Calvert in *The Man in Grey* and *Fanny By Gaslight*. Like Peter, he too had an ulcer that made him unfit for military service.

For Peter's first appearance in the film he's clad in a tight-fitting T-shirt that he soon swaps for a well-cut suit and flashy tie. Peter played the silver-tongued greasy charmer with great panache, but the oily Latin lover meets a suitably sticky end, when he is stabbed in the back and killed by the wildcat Rosanna when he attempts to seduce her 17-year-old daughter, played by Patricia Roc, who has come to the bandits' hangout, the "Seven Moons" of the title in search of her deranged mother. In his death throes Peter's character manages to launch a stiletto at Rosanna and she is fatally wounded. The final scene had to be shot six times, because Peter repeatedly forgot that the Board of Censors wouldn't pass any seduction scene unless the seducer has at least one foot on the ground.

Today the film's plot seems ludicrously far-fetched, and even in December 1944 it was criticized for its Home Counties' theatricality. The *Monthly Film Bulletin* said: "Artistic settings beautifully photographed are a pleasing feature of this lavish production, hut they cannot disguise the crude melodramatics of the story nor the fact that the film drags, despite its bursts of robust action. The players act well to a certain degree and yet they somehow fail to give convincing studies of the Italian characters they are meant to portray." *The Times* was less generous: "In spite of the Italian setting and much self-conscious flashing of knives and teeth, the film and the cast remain invincibly British." It was the directorial debut of Arthur Crabtree, and his lack of experience showed through, prompting some of the criticism. Having worked as a cinematographer he was one of those who had helped to create the distinctive elegant look of Gainsborough Pictures' costume melodramas. Despite the carping, *Madonna of the Seven Moons* was box-office gold, and audiences lapped up its exoticism.

By the time of the film's release Peter probably paid scant attention to the reviews; he had already moved on to bigger and better things. In the summer of 1944 Tyrone Guthrie invited him to direct for the Old Vic. This was a welcome return following his appearance with them at the Shakespeare Birthday Festival on April 22, 1940. The war necessitated radical changes to the company, particularly after the Old Vic Theatre in Waterloo Road was bombed in 1941. Fortunately in 1940, when the air raids in London began, Guthrie transferred the company to the relative safety of the Victoria Theatre in Burnley, Lancashire. But the move did little to aid the company's precarious financial position as falling box-office receipts saw it struggle to compete against those with deeper pockets. The rise in the Old Vic's fortunes in 1944 were thanks to the Council for the Encouragement of Music and the Arts (C.E.M.A.); the government realized the importance of giving the company funds to help preserve British cultural life.

Peter's productions helped the company back on the road to success as his friend and mentor, Guthrie, recognized in his autobiography: "For a year or two the Old Vic trod a distinctly thorny path. In this game of theatrical politics we seemed to have been completely outmatched; our prestige waned; it became harder and harder to get actors we wanted because they all preferred to work for Beaumont. The one feather in our cap was the reopening of the Liverpool Repertory Theatre, which had closed after the severe bombing of Liverpool in the winter before. We operated it for four years successfully and very profitably. For a period, under the direction of Peter Glenville it was, I think the liveliest theatre in the country."

Sadly the achievements of Laurence Olivier and Ralph Richardson, who were recalled from military service and asked to become joint directors of the London Old Vic, have dwarfed those of Peter. Whereas they began a series of magnificent productions at the New Theatre (now Noël Coward Theatre) on St. Martin's Lane that are regarded as the most illustrious in the company's history, starting in 1944 with *Peer Gynt*, *Arms and the Man*, *Richard III* and *Uncle Vanya*, Peter was making a directorial debut that has disappeared into the mists of theatrical history. Peter's productions were staged at the Liverpool Playhouse in Williamson Square, far away from London and the nucleus of the nation's theatrical orbit, which meant they escaped the attention of national newspaper critics.

Peter not only directed but also performed under Guthrie; between them they assembled a strong company of players including, Nancy Price, Eileen Herlie, Mary Ellis and the German-Czech actor Frederick Valk. Tanya Moiseiwitsch, the London-born daughter of the celebrated Ukrainian classical pianist Benno Moiseiwitsch, designed many of the sets and costumes. Fresh from an apprenticeship at Dublin's Abbey Theatre and a stint at the Oxford Playhouse, her work on the season's productions rapidly gained attention and she went on to work for the Old Vic in London and in West End commercial theater. Peter would work with all of his Liverpool Old Vic contemporaries throughout his career.

Prior to the season opening Peter wrote to the local press: "I have been influenced by the fact that there are many brilliant modern classics which English audiences are seldom, if ever, given an opportunity of seeing. . . . Of course, in presenting such plays we run the risk of losing a section of the audience that is interested only in seeing established successes, but we hope and believe that we may be doing a service to such playgoers as have a more catholic taste and whose curiosity goes further afield."

Many of the productions were written by foreign playwrights and Peter lamented the lack of contemporary British talent: "We should have been pleased had we been able to present a higher percentage of new British plays, dealing with contemporary themes. But where are these plays? It is understandable that in times of great events serious works of art reflecting such times do not appear at once. Great events take some digesting. . . . It is not to be expected that the experience of the last five years will be transmuted into artistic experience until they have been 'recollected in tranquillity.' Meantime, we believe that in this season the first production of two new plays will acquit us of neglecting the rather grim present, and remembering only the spacious days that are gone."

Peter's directorial debut came in August 1944, staging a revival of Henrick Ibsen's *John Gabriel Borkman*. Mary Ellis, an American opera singer turned actress, had found fame in Ivor Novello's musicals and she recalled rehearsing for her part as Ella Rentheim in her autobiography: "Rehearsals were in London. Despite the V-1 and V-2 bombs every few hours, the days were seething with activity. The spirit of make-do, and survival, and national exuberance and sacrifice made the atmosphere of the scarred city almost more seductive. My first morning of rehearsal was ushered in by the huge bomb blast at Smithfield Market."

Peter was faced with a problem brought about by the disparity in the ages of Ellis and Nancy Price. Their characters were twin sisters but the 64-year-old Price was seventeen years older; Peter chose to make Price the older sister, rather than the twin, which, according to Ellis, took much of the meaning and tension from the play: "Frederick Valk played John Gabriel Borkman and his European accent didn't help. However, nothing could take away the thrill of working in that play. I only wish I could have played it again later. Peter Glenville, who was directing, held me properly in check and the smaller theatre was a restful exercise."

Peter and the rest of the cast stayed at the Adelphi Theatre in Liverpool, which Ellis described as "amazingly comfortable." The company were glad to be away from the rocket attacks: "I welcomed the idea of a night without wailing sirens, so when on our arrival we had one of the worst night-raids, I suspected the Luftwaffe of disliking actors. A small orchestra of elderly gentlemen in the [hotel] lounge played the *Warsaw Concerto* every evening with more emotional verve than accuracy."

The play received a "rapturous welcome" according to the *Liverpool Echo*, and the *Liverpool Daily Post* praised Peter's "brilliant" direction of Ibsen's tale of tortured souls and suffering: "This reopening of the Old Vic season should be long remembered. It is something of a challenge to Liverpool, as well as an encouragement. It dares our playgoers to see greatness in gloom and to enjoy being depressed."

The crew swiftly moved on to rehearsals for a new production named *Lisa* set to open in September. This was another string to Peter's bow; *Lisa* is his adaptation of Ivan Turgenev's novel *A House of Gentlefolk* into a three-act play. *The Stage* was enthusiastic about Peter's first and last attempt as a professional dramatist, and praised its visual style, which was in part due to a little help from a friend: "Mr. Glenville has made a first-rate job of this adaptation, and its first performance made a deep impression. He has succeeded admirably in catching the nuances of the period. With equally deft craftsmanship he has presented the central theme of the book—the one love affair of the gentle religious daughter of this *House of Gentlefolk*, and the shattering consequences which befall when it is wrecked. An inner stage is used with the greatest ingenuity for some of the scenes—a device made possible by a particularly imaginative set after designs of Oliver Messel." The *Liverpool Daily Post* also praised *Lisa* for its music, something to which Peter always paid close attention: "The play has an imaginative, poetic quality, and music is used, all through its various scenes to establish them successfully on the romantic plane to which pathos delicately inclines them. Mr. Glenville has made a great success of his adaptation. A dramatist who can show such feeling for the finer shades of atmosphere and character should also be able to do great things with a theme of his own."

In October Peter directed the British premiere of Noël Coward's melodrama *Point Valaine* that first played on Broadway in 1935. It tells the story of a lonely widow on a West Indian Island and Moiseiwitsch's sets with their verandas gave the play a suitably tropical feel, but insufficient to win universal critical favor The *Liverpool Daily Post* felt that the war had dated the play and didn't seem in tune with times, pronouncing it "a tropical storm in a teacup," while the *Liverpool Echo* felt Ellis' performance, the sets, lighting and Peter's direction "a triumph." Beaumont and Coward both came to the standing-room-only opening night and the playwright was impressed paying "a deserved tribute to the brilliant production of Peter Glenville." Despite the play's mixed reception, Coward was so enthusiastic that Peter was asked to direct a West End production of the play three years later.

Come November Peter returned to acting under Guthrie's direction in *Uneasy Laughter*. The play was an adaptation, by Guthrie's wife, Judith, of Leonid Andreyev's circus melodrama *He Who Gets Slapped*. Peter's lead role as Funny the Clown who gets slapped, won plaudits for its vividness with the *Liverpool Daily Post* declaring it "acting that refuses to be forgotten."

For the Old Vic's Christmas production Peter directed Sheridan's comedy of manners, *The School for Scandal*. Mary Ellis played the wife of Sir Peter Teazle opposite the 62-year-old Henry Edwards, one of Britain's first-ever film stars, adding a touch of faded glamor to the event. *The Stage* praised Peter's "delightful production . . . [with its] atmosphere of a Rowlandson print." The *Liverpool Echo* called it "a welcome reversion to the classics—welcome also for the pleasure afforded the eyes by the colourful dresses and settings by Tanya Moiseiwitsch." The *Liverpool Daily Post* declared it an "outstanding success": "It has great pace, sparkle, and gusto, though the tempo is varied with a genuine instinct for satirical and emotional effect."

In January 1945 Peter moved on to direct revivals of O'Neill's 1921 tragedy *Anna Christie* and Robert Marshall's 1901 farcical romance *His Excellency the Governor* in May; neither production made much of a mark, appearing dated to reviewers.

In March 1945 Peter took the lead in *Hamlet* directed by Peter Ashmore; it was recognized as one of the most outstanding Shakespearian productions during the Old Vic's tenure at Liverpool. According to *The Stage* "it made a deep impression. Mr. Glenville's distinctive contribution is a sense of deep animation with an almost athletic vigour, neither of which qualities are allowed to overshadow the essential moodiness nor interfere with the poetic Hamlet." He came in for some criticism for his hurried delivery but the *Liverpool Echo* was still impressed: "Mr. Glenville had so saturated himself in the part and worked so hard at it that he deserved the triumph which the dramas' patrons decided was his due." The *Liverpool Daily Post* liked his "very intelligent and very expressive performance" and his "prodigal exuberance": "All of us who saw it will remember Peter Glenville's first Hamlet because it was so alive and emotionally rich." In April he performed under Guthrie as Face in a modern-dress version of Ben Jonson's *The Alchemist*. It was performed "with an *obbligato* of air sirens" according to the *Liverpool Echo*, which praised Peter and his fellow for giving their characters "life and meaning."

It was June, shortly after the war ended in Europe, when Peter left the Old Vic, saying he might join "a producing unit which is being planned to deal with plays of an unusual type." With hindsight, his departure proved to have been a wise move. The company underwent a sea change after the war becoming bogged down in squabbles that went on for years. Although Olivier and Richardson had created a quasi-national theater, and their efforts recognised in 1947 when they both received knighthoods, some felt that the actors had gained too much power and in 1949 their contracts were not renewed. The changes in a post-war Britain were to be as significant in the world of the theater as they were in everyday life. Peter avoided years of political backbiting, leaving him free to make his mark elsewhere.

5

A New Direction

1945-1949

Change for Peter also included a new home. He took a lease on a house at 23 Brompton Square in one of London's most fashionable and expensive areas. An elegant Georgian mews house with four stories, basement and garden, it overlooks a tree-lined garden at the heart of the square. It was an ideal location for shopping and eating out, but close enough to the West End to make going to rehearsals or the theater easy. The house served as an office too, and it was where Peter would sometimes audition actors. A short stroll away from the elaborate Baroque Catholic Church of the Immaculate Heart of Mary, or Brompton Oratory as it is usually known, Peter could see its large, vaulted dome from the back of his new home and it was where he regularly attended Mass.

Complete with domestic staff, including a butler, the house perfectly suited Peter's desire to live in the style to which he'd grown accustomed. With his taste for fine food and clothes, dressing in cashmere waistcoats, handmade calf leather shoes, tailor-made shirts, suits and even silk dressing gowns, 32-year-old Peter was every inch the man about town. With his brilliantined hair and a tan supplied by a sun lamp when he wasn't able to acquire one naturally, his new abode fitted the image of the stylish, affluent English gentleman he was obviously keen to project.

Peter's earliest peacetime job was acting in one of post-war theater's first successes, Mary Hayley Bell's thriller *Duet For Two Hands* staged at Shaftesbury Avenue's Lyric Theatre. An actress turned playwright, Hayley Bell was John Mills' second wife, and originally her husband directed and acted the lead in her play. Mills was a star, principally for his many war-hero roles in movies that included 1942's *In Which We Serve* and when he stepped down from his lead role in September 1945 it was Peter who replaced him as the young poet that lost his hands in an accident and by a miracle of surgery is given a new pair. The play's central premise is based on the fact that the hands' previous owner was a murderer.

Peter was still appearing as the maimed poet when he made his London directorial debut with William Saroyan's morality play *The Time of Your Life* at Hammersmith's Lyric Theatre in February 1946. It brought him back into the H. M. Tennent fold under the banner of its new offshoot, The Company of Four. Beaumont had taken the lease on the leaking Lyric as the London home of his new company that was to present experimental theater and give work to actors returning from the armed forces. The project was the idea of Sir Rudolf Bing, who was then the general manager of the Glyndebourne Opera, but he lacked theatrical experience and called on Beaumont for help. Quickly grasping the possibilities and enlisting regional theaters in Brighton, Cambridge, Bristol and Cardiff as touring venues, Beaumont's idea was to take productions to the provinces for a month prior to a four-week run at the Lyric. Completing the managerial team were Tyrone Guthrie, who was managing the company's venue at the Bristol Old Vic, and Murray MacDonald, a former director of Salisbury's Garrison Theatre. It was the quartet of managers that inspired the name "The Company of

Four." Beaumont's lively and capable secretary Kitty Black was appointed assistant administrator.

The Lyric's location in an unfashionable area, far from the West End, failed to draw the customary theatergoers and the venture got off to a slow start. Emlyn Williams teased Beaumont that The Company of Four was attracting "an audience of two." By August 1946 it had lost £12,000, which was close to half a million pounds in today's money, prompting Guthrie and Bing to make a hasty exit. Happily for Peter, his production was their first success although it strayed from the Company of Four's original aim by not touring in the provinces initially.

The Time of Your Life had originally opened on Broadway in 1939 to great acclaim, winning the New York Drama Critics' Circle Award, and a Pulitzer Prize for its author. It was set in Nic's Pacific Street Saloon, Restaurant and Entertainment Palace on San Francisco's Embarcadero waterfront. Tanya Moiseiwitsch was asked to create a set with the feel of a honky-tonk bar; the £300 it cost was the most the company had spent on any of its productions. The play depicts a slice of life at the saloon; a home to prostitutes, seedy gamblers, a pintable fanatic, cops, a sailor, tourists, loafers, an Arab harmonica player, drunks and other seedy characters. Peter described it as comment on the natural virtues, simplicity, and individuality of the humbler classes in America: "Saroyan clearly thinks that pity, love and understanding do far more to effect a happy society than the truncheon, pen and statute book."

It took Peter three months to assemble a large, international, cast of twenty-seven people hailing from Britain, Canada, America, Czechoslovakia, Germany and the West Indies. Among the motley cast were three dancers appearing on the straight stage for the first time, Prudence Hyman, Walter Crisham and Donald Reed whose skills were needed for the dance numbers. Crisham, an American, was the most famous of the trio and was a star of musicals such as Henson's Gaieties and *Sweet and Low*. They danced along to "mean and melancholy" boogie-woogie piano numbers played by West Indian pianist Willie Wilson that he composed for the play.

Among the cast was William "Biff" McGuire, a young actor making his professional debut, who was one of three American G.I.s hired to add authenticity. The Tony-nominated actor remembers how he started out in the play: "I caught the last month of the war in Germany. There was a point system then. You had to have eighty-six points at the end of the war to go home. You got so many points for being wounded, and so many points for battles. I had about fourteen points, so I knew I'd have to start another war or something if I wanted to get home. They set up a situation where you could go to England and study. I studied acting, directing, radio and television in Swindon."

When McGuire heard about the play he headed to London to catch Peter performing in *Duet For Two Hands*. He sent a note to Peter's dressing room and was told to come back stage after the performance. McGuire was impressed: "Peter was a handsome man and seemed wonderful in his role in what was a strange play. . . . I went back stage and met Peter and Bill and told him what I'd been doing and that I wanted a part in his play. Peter said, 'Go ahead.' So I performed a set piece from *The Amazing Dr. Clitterhouse* that I'd done at university. I did the dying scene in the dressing room—and without managing to break too many things." Peter offered McGuire the part of a sailor in his new production. Despite the war being over, costumes were still in short supply, so he borrowed Bill's naval uniform.

The sheer scale of *The Time of Your Life* and its rambling nature as the narrative shifts from one character's story to another's meant the relatively inexperienced Peter had a big job on his hands. One critic acknowledged the enormity of Peter's task suggested it was "not at all like a play but like a production."

Peter decided that he needed something to pull in the crowds and so he placed his father in the role of The Drunkard—a part with no lines. However, he wanted to keep this a secret from his first-night audience as Kitty Black recalled in her autobiography: "As we couldn't arrange the billing to give [Shaun] his proper status, we decided he should appear anonymously and the cast list was completed by 'The Drunkard.' Shaun made his first entrance immediately after the curtain rose, was recognised by the delighted house and got a huge round of applause."

According to McGuire, Shaun got up to his usual antics, often arriving too early or a little late for a scene because he had ducked out for a swift drink at the pub next door. Usually, it didn't matter, given the nature of the play, which is set in a bar and has a large cast that wanders off and on. Not that Peter was there to see all of this because he was still acting in *Duet for Two Hands*. For the opening night of *The Time of Your Life* Peter raced across London changing out of his costume in the taxi to arrive in time to catch the last act. Afterwards Kitty Black joined him and his parents for supper at The Savoy so she could tell him what he had missed. They danced the night away and then headed down to Fleet Street to pick up the first editions of the newspapers.

Even though critics didn't all warm to the play's hokum philosophising, they liked Peter's direction. *The Observer* said: "The piece . . . formless and often tedious, is redeemed by Mr. Saroyan's eye for character, by the subtleties of Mr. Peter Glenville's direction, and by a group of alert performances." *The Evening Standard* reported: "The acting in this play is surprisingly and consistently excellent, for which much credit must be given . . . to Mr. Glenville, who produced it so brilliantly."

Peter's ploy certainly worked and the reviewers adored Shaun. *The Times* said: "The Drunkard who, through the beginning, the middle, and the end of the play has nothing whatever to do with it, is an excellent turn, for though unnamed in the programme the practised style of Mr. Shaun Glenville breaks down anonymity. But perhaps there is also a sense in which The Drunkard also symbolises the play. Its life is life as it might appear to a tipsy man in a moment of comic despair."

The Star declared Shaun's performance "enormously amusing" and the *Evening News* loved The Drunkard "who hiccups his way in and out." The *Daily Mirror* summed up the general feeling: "This, under Mr. Peter Glenville's direction, is one of the best productions of the Company of Four season at the Lyric. This miraculously catches the atmosphere of the honky-tonk scenes and does its best to conceal the vacuity of Mr. Saroyan's tough whimsy."

The production was a watershed in encouraging theatergoers to head towards the fringes of London and the Company of Four's fortunes began to change. Within a year it was staging groundbreaking productions including Cocteau's melodrama *L'aigle à deux têtes (The Eagle Has Two Heads)*.

For McGuire the production was not without a serious hiccup. One evening, at the end of a performance, two American Military Policemen arrested him because his working papers were not in order; Black thought the young actor was a Canadian. McGuire was taken off to prison where he spent three months. He says it was thanks to Peter, Shaun and Hyman's efforts that he was eventually released. Despite it all McGuire has fond memories: "Peter was very kind to me as a young individual and very welcoming. . . . He had aplomb and style . . . and as a director he was excellent. He had a wonderful eye for editing and for a picture that would be beautiful to behold by the audience." Peter's efforts to help the young actor when he was in a tight hole was typical, his kindness was such that fifteen years later he came to the aid of another member of the cast by lending him money to set up a floristry shop in Los Angeles.

It was at the Hammersmith Lyric that Peter gave his last stage performance. True to form, Peter played the bad guy. He played the actor John Wilkes Booth, the man who assassinated President Abraham Lincoln, in Peter Yates' tragedy, *The Assassin*. Gielgud had taken an option on the play the year before, but Beaumont baulked at staging a verse drama by a new playwright that needed a cast of almost thirty people in the West End. The

Company of Four provided the ideal opportunity for a tryout, as well as allowing Beaumont to get sponsorship from the newly formed Arts Council. He managed to fill the cast with a large number of actors fresh out of the armed forces and the play opened at Cardiff 's Prince of Wales Theatre in September before touring in Cambridge and Brighton before its London debut at the Lyric in October.

Beaumont's first instincts proved right, and critics were unimpressed by Yates' verse. The *South Wales Post* set the tone of ensuing notices: "Peter Glenville, as Booth, had an appallingly heavy part, all acted in the key of high tragedy." When the production opened in Brighton it fared no better. The *Brighton Herald* opined "that it fails on the stage is no reflection on the acting and excellent elocution of Peter Glenville as Booth."

Despite the critics Peter cut a dashing figure sporting long sideburns and a moustache. His swansong as the Southern patriot was convincing in its sheer, wild-eyed bravado and the highlight of the production. It was a demanding role, requiring Peter to recite dozens of lines of what critics derided as "mediocre" blank verse, all of which he managed to handle eloquently. *The Scotsman* said: "The idea and construction of the play are more notable than Mr. Yates' verse. Indeed, apart from the glowing periods which Peter Glenville speaks with a good deal of fire and spirit, it is only now and again that the other characters seem . . . to 'drop into poetry.' The interest of the play, which has a lengthy cast and a chorus of solemnly chanting commentators, belongs entirely to the character of Booth, and permits Mr. Glenville, as Booth—vain, boastful, fanatical, exulting in his crime, and haunted in his dying moments by the ghost of Lincoln—to give a commendable bravura display."

Not long after this Peter played his last major role in film. Significantly, it was one of the first British films to tackle social problems. The *Good-Time Girl*, shot in 1947, was eventually released in May 1948 at a time when the British cinema was free from the shackles of creating features that portrayed a nation worth fighting for; instead it could lift the lid on society's malaise as Britain redefined itself under the new left-wing Labour government.

Good-Time Girl was a Gainsborough Picture and it reunited Peter with his friend from the OUDS, Dennis Price, and a colleague from *Uncensored*, Griffith Jones, when it was made at Shepperton Studios in Surrey. A far cry from the glossy costume melodramas that had dominated its wartime output instead it was based on a true story. Told in flashback, the chairman of a juvenile court, played by Flora Robson, it tells a cautionary tale to a young runaway, played by the future British blonde bombshell Diana Dors. Robson relates the story of another runaway's descent into criminality, the 15-year-old Gwen Rawlings played by Gainsborough Pictures' stock player, Jean Kent. Unsurprisingly, Peter's character, the sharp-suited but seedy cockney spiv, Jimmy Rosso, is one of those instrumental in her downfall.

Rawlings is portrayed as the victim of abuse as she fends off a violent father and a series of lustful men. When she runs away from home and takes lodgings she becomes acquainted with her neighbor, Rosso. He helps her get a job as a cloakroom check-in girl in a nightclub where he works as waiter. The pair become involved in a fracas at the club and are both sacked. Rosso persuades her to pawn some jewellery that, unbeknown to her, is stolen goods. After she is caught she realizes that Rosso has set her up. The juvenile court sends her to school for delinquent minors for three years where, rather than reforming, she picks up more bad ways. She escapes only to pursue a life of crime before ending up back in jail.

Gainsborough Pictures' switch to contemporary social issues was largely thanks to Sydney Box, its newly appointed head of production. Such was the realism of *Good-Time Girl* that its release was delayed by the British Board of Film Censors until a new opening was shot and some of its more violent scenes axed; even then it was banned by some local authorities.

Although the film pointed out society's failure in tackling the roots causes of female delinquency, audiences responded well to its brutal message. It struck a chord with the public and Robson received letters from worried mothers who saw her in the film and wanted advice on their wayward daughters.

Perhaps the criticism Peter incurred for his cut-glass accent in *Madonna of the Seven Moons* stayed with him because in *Good-Time Girl* he manages a more than plausible cockney accent, carrying off the role as a nasty, low-life piece of scum with self-confidence. This role highlights the obvious fact that as a film actor Peter was typecast as the bad guy; For whatever reasons it seems fair that Peter was not considered to be the kind of actor that was romantic lead material. That being the case it is arguable that he would not have made it to the top as an actor on stage or screen; had he continued acting he would always have been in the shadow of other "leading men." He failed to achieve the level of fame as an actor that Shaun and Dorothy did, and in spite of the financial independence his parents' wealth afforded him, his ambition was redirected. Peter was a man driven to achieve and eager to try new things. Pursuing a career as a director was a natural next step.

In September 1947 Peter directed the London debut of Coward's *Point Valaine* at the now-defunct Embassy Theatre on High Holborn. He worked with actors Mary Ellis and Audrey Fildes from his Old Vic productions, as well as designer Tanya Moiseiwitsch. *The Stage* enthused: "Mr. Glenville soaks himself in a play until he lives in the environment and he knows the characters as well as members of his own household. As he understands their mental and facial reactions so completely, he frequently directs his actors so that they score their greatest effects when they have no lines to deliver. . . . Mr. Glenville's direction . . . displays masterly psychological insight."

The paper was less enthusiastic about Peter's next production, Shaw's *Major Barbara*, which he directed for Arts Council and took on a tour of mining towns in South Wales before opening in London at the Arts Theatre in March 1948: "The play is treated with a facetiousness that jars and misses much." Perhaps Peter was spreading himself too thin as March also witnessed the premiere of Aldous Huxley's murder story *The Gioconda Smile.* It was Huxley's first play for seventeen years, and excitement ran high. It had a strong cast headed by Pamela Brown and Clive Brook. Since Brown's stage debut as Juliet opposite Peter's Romeo at The Memorial, the red-haired, honey-eyed beauty had won praise for her work in Gielgud's 1947 production of Oscar Wilde's *The Importance of Being Ernest*, as well as in films. The 59-year-old Brook was best known for playing opposite Marlene Dietrich in the 1932 movie *Shanghai Express*.

The Gioconda Smile opened at Leicester's Opera House to acclaim and following a successful provincial tour it arrived at the Old Vic's temporary home, the New Theatre, in early June. Brook as a man wrongly accused of murdering his wife and Brown as a jealous spinster proved a winning combination and the play was transferred to the Wyndham Theatre. The rising young critic, 21-year-old Kenneth Tynan pronounced: "Brook gives one of his richest, sulkiest performances. . . . [Brown] is undoubtedly the loveliest murderess on the English stage."

What was becoming apparent was that Peter had a flair for directing plays by contemporary dramatists and he was soon at work on two other projects, Jean-Paul Sartre's *Les Mains Sales* (*The Dirty Hands*) and a double bill by Terence Rattigan. Peter seemed to prefer working on cutting-edge projects rather than classics or revivals; contemporary playwrights also seemed to enjoy working with him. His intellect, charm, ability to put together a great cast and build a team were his strengths, as was his openness to handling new material and patiently shaping it for production along with its author.

It was something Peter clearly enjoyed: "I used to entertain quite a few general ideas about the function of the director in the theatre. Now theorising about it no long interests me. I prefer to get on with the actual business of directing, and empirically to discover new musts and must-nots with each new play. I like arguing about is (this) production or that performance, and I quite enjoy small talk about possible casting, disasters and achievements." Peter's move into directing came at a propitious moment; the concept of actor-managers was no more—the era of the director was dawning.

With the end of the war creative relations between Britain and America were renewed, as were those with Europe; the cutting edge works of Sartre, Anouilh and Brecht became popular. Sartre was very much in vogue in Paris, and an exponent of the new philosophy of Existentialism. *The Listener* called him "the most discussed author in the world," and his political melodrama set in Illithya, an imaginary Central European country, *Les Mains Sales*, was his most discussed play. The multi-talented Kitty Black translated it into English, calling it *Crime Passionel.* The play tells the story of a bourgeois young revolutionary and member of the Proletarian Party, Hugo, who is called to assassinate the party secretary. The tension in the play arises because the young idealist and a poet cannot easily bring himself to shoot a man he has grown to love. Hugo procrastinates—and a modern version of *Hamlet* ensues.

The Company of Four acquired the rights to the production in the same month the play caused controversy when it opened at the Théâtre Antoine in Paris in April. The French right wing welcomed it as anti-Communist because of its depiction of Communists as muddled fanatics, while left-wingers attacked it for the same reason. The Cold War was beginning and Europe was jittery; the divisive play was not staged again in France until 1976.

According to Kitty Black, Peter was not the first choice. Peter Brook, who had directed Sartre's *Huis clos* in 1946, was originally slated to direct it but he was too busy. When it opened at the Lyric in June 1948 it was an instant success. *The Times* reported: "The piece has been so tactfully produced by Mr. Peter Glenville that the best scenes seem not to have been prepared but to be taking shape as the actors proceed." The *New Statesman*'s critic declared it: "The most exciting play that has come my way for nine months." The *Evening Standard*'s reviewer agreed: "I consider this a remarkable and fascinating play."

When Beaumont held a party a month later at his home at Lord North Street to celebrate the play's success with the visiting French cast, Noël Coward was in attendance and enthused: "It's the best produced, best acted and best translated play I've ever seen." Sadly, when it transferred to the Garrick Theatre in August Roger Livesey left the to appear in a film and was replaced by Basil Sidney; the magic was broken. It was also a hot summer, which kept the crowds away and the production only ran for a few weeks. The Company of Four had to pay a hefty 15% royalty to the Hungarian owner of the play's English-language rights and couldn't justify keeping it open.

Peter's next production enhanced his reputation still further. It also began one of the most important creative partnerships of his entire career. His friend and former Oxford housemate Terence Rattigan asked him to direct *Playbill*, a double bill of one-act plays, *The Browning Version* and *Harlequinade*. The wunderkind Rattigan was by this time a very popular playwright having come to the fore in 1936 with *French Without Tears* that ran for more than 1,000 performances. It was a feat repeated by *While The Sun Shines* at a time when no other dramatist had done so twice. In 1946 *The Winslow Boy* chalked up 476 performances so the prospect of more plays caused great excitement and anticipation.

The Browning Version is a study of failure in a public school and depicts the downfall of a disillusioned housemaster, while *Harlequinade* is a study of success and is a comedy set on the stage of a "rat-hole" provincial theater before and during the dress rehearsal of *Romeo and Juliet*. Starring Eric Portman as the schoolteacher Andrew Crocker Harris and Mary Ellis as his wife Millie, the production was a highlight of both their careers.

Critic Harold Hobson talked of *The Browning Version* as "what many people consider to be the masterpiece of English playwriting of the middle of the [twentieth] century": "There was not in it a single sentence that would itself surpass the emotional level of a railway time-table. There was hardly a word that would be out of place in giving an order for a pound of vegetables. Yet such was Rattigan's craftsmanship, and so fine was the quality of his feeling for an unloved, middle-aged schoolmaster compelled by heart weakness to abandon an already failing career, that when Eric Portman asked the solitary schoolboy who had thought fit to give him a parting gift to pour out a dose of medicine to cover his emotion, the audience could not restrain its tears; and when his wife cruelly remarked that the gift was not a sign of affection or respect but merely a piece of astute policy to get a higher mark in an examination, a visible thrill ran through it. At that moment Portman hesitated whilst polishing his glasses. The action was barely perceptible, but Portman made it show how the whole pride of a man's life can be killed in one blow."

In spite of Rattigan's track record, Beaumont turned down the chance to stage *Playbill*—he was unconvinced by the concept. To make matters worse, the director of *The Winslow Boy*, Byam Shaw, rejected Rattigan's invitation to direct it. Then Gielgud refused to take on the role of Crocker-Harris, saying he didn't want to appear in anything second rate. Naturally, Rattigan was disheartened. When the play opened to rave reviews in September 1948 Gielgud obviously regretted his refusal and wrote to some friends: "I have had a baffling year. The Rattigan plays which I let go are the most enormous success, and I fear it was a great error of judgement on my part not to do them."

Byam Shaw's error proved to be Peter's good fortune and Rattigan showed his appreciation by dedicating *The Browning Version* "To Peter Glenville with gratitude." It was Mitchell's London Theatrical Productions that decided to back the show and according to Rattigan biographer, Geoffrey Wansell, Portman was persuaded to join the cast over drinks one evening at the playwright's Albany flat. Peter suggested that he, Rattigan and Mitchell should dress up in dinner jackets "to look very distinguished" and when Portman came through the front door and saw the trio he said: "I can't resist this, I'll do it." Peter knew how to charm and get what he wanted. Portman had spent eight years acting in films and *Playbill* was to be his return to the stage.

Peter began working on *The Browning Version* as early as February 1948, when Rattigan was still wondering what play should complete the double bill. Peter even suggested using his one venture into playwriting, *Lisa*. Rattigan was unconvinced, saying he couldn't see it as a "great big thumping success."

When *Playbill* premiered in Liverpool in July *The Stage* wrote: "Rattigan . . . has many successes to his name and, judging by the enthusiasm of the first-night audience, he has struck oil again with his latest plays." The play's Liverpool reception suggested all was going smoothly but in August Peter left to holiday with his mother and Bill at Castello San Peyre at Opio on the French Riviera. At this point Rattigan started to become nervous as his letters to Peter reveal. He told Peter that there had been ructions among the cast when the tour hit Manchester Opera House and that Portman had "reduced the entire company to tears and hysteria" over the weekend.

More worryingly Ellis reported that Portman had "grossly underplayed." Rattigan surmised that Portman's wobble was because he couldn't wait to get back into films and he blamed the shift in his performance on the fact that some producers from the Rank Organisation had been in the front row. Rattigan finished his letter with some well-placed flattery: "I thought you had better be *au fait* with the situation so that when you return refreshed and invigorated by *le soleil* you will have the famous forefinger ready to wag in Eric [Portman's] face. It is a brilliant forefinger as I know and indeed if I didn't know that I would be far more depressed about the turn of events than I am."

Peter's prompt reply to Rattigan's "rather disturbing letter" shows his calming influence; a talent as a director he needed in abundance: "My own conjecture about the situation is perhaps not quite the same as yours. My guess is that Mary [Ellis] faced with the opera-house grandeur and no prefects in front, gave a Tourneur rendering, which would put the whole play out of key and make Eric seem an old duck and chips. Watching Eric work my instinct is that any change of attack, particularly in the first play, would only be effected by the most minute graduations. Mary however is keeping middle Europa gas compressed in that salient frame with the greatest difficulty.

"As regards the lurid background of the weekend which tends to bias one's view against Eric I think we should be careful not openly to put it in its probable proportions but to separate it entirely from questions of performance. We know that Eric is a highly geared, stupid and inflammable lady with more talent than judgment and that unpopular blasphemies against Mistress theatre (who has in the past been so elusive as far as he is concerned) are rather his line.

"We also know that when ruffled, drunk or fatigued he can be thoroughly rude. So far I have never seen it affect his performance. Now we also know that Mary by now is, in her unholiest of holies, bitterly resentful of his predominance, his success, his notices, his blasphemies and his dressing room."

Peter warned Rattigan that it would be unwise and unfair to placate—and thereby encourage—Ellis. He advised Rattigan that he should be more wary of "Mary's histrionics than Eric's," which he had already chatted about to her in a "sugar-coated" fashion. Peter promised he would smooth things out on his return to the tour when it opened in Leeds.

In her autobiography Ellis recalled: "All of us had some hard times with Eric, keeping him, literally on the rails" but that they had "a splendid rapport in the play." She said of her time in the show: "Even the hours after the play at night in a hotel suite, thrashing out line changes and benefiting by the criticism and direction, and tireless working towards perfection that seemed to galvanise Peter Glenville, Rattigan and all of us, into continual work."

When *Playbill* opened in London in September it was a smash hit. *The Stage* called it "a very remarkable double achievement" and Peter's direction "impeccable." *Playbill* did more than add to Rattigan's popularity and bank balance; it established him as an eminent playwright and he acknowledged that *The Browning Version* was "his passport to heaven." Eric Portman won the Ellen Terry Award for Best Actor and Terence Rattigan won the Ellen Terry Award for Best Play; it was the second year running Rattigan won the prestigious award. Such was the acclaim that critics began to compare Rattigan to Shaw, Barrie and Somerset Maugham.

Peter was clearly astute in financial matters and his friendship with Beaumont may have been a factor when, in August, he and Bill set up Hardy William Smith Productions Limited to provide for tax efficiencies. They realized there was more money to be made from producing plays than directing them and Hardy William Smith Productions Limited would be behind a number of plays that Peter directed, including *Hotel Paradiso* and *Rashomon*. However it was not all success and among their failed projects were attempts to make films of the life of St. Teresa of Avila and Jean Giraudoux's play *The Enchanted*. Nor did they confine their production support to just plays directed by Peter. In the summer of 1950 they tried to convince Maurice Evans to stage Frederick Knott's *Dial M for Murder*. Sadly they failed, although the play premiered in London in June 1952 and then had a successful Broadway run with Evans in the lead. Knott went on to write the screenplay for the 1954 Hollywood movie directed by Hitchcock. It would have made them a good deal richer. In March 1954 HWSP bought the rights to Angus Wilson's *The Mulberry Bush* for £50 and it was eventually put on at the Bristol Old Vic in September 1955 by "an arrangement" with Peter, which meant they collected some royalties. It was probably too much for Peter to juggle his own projects along with trying to put a play into production.

Peter returned to work for H.M. Tennent at the end of 1948 to do a no-expenses-spared revival of St. John Hankin's Edwardian morality play, *The Return of the Prodigal.* It opened in November at Brighton's Theatre Royal with sets and costumes by Cecil Beaton. A week later it transferred to the Globe to some considerable anticipation; it was the first West End production Peter did for Beaumont. The starry cast included Sybil Thorndike and Audrey Fildes, with Gielgud in the lead role as Eustace Jackson, it was his first appearance on the London stage for two years.

Perhaps there were too many expectations around Gielgud's long-awaited return and Hankin's comedy was too insufficient to fulfill them. *The Times* lamented: "Gielgud makes his return as the engaging ne'er-do-well of a commonplace Edwardian social comedy. He gives a gay, charming, and highly accomplished performance, but the part puts no sort of tax on his rare powers as an actor, and we are left wondering what attracted him to it." Gielgud himself had reservations about the production and in a letter to Christopher Fry about his play, *The Lady's Not for Burning*, he wrote: "The one week we had [on tour] in this play was barely sufficient, and I didn't feel at ease on the first night."

Only Beaton's décor found favor with the critics as a "feast for the eyes." The production ran for sixty-nine performances before it closed having lost more than £4,100. Beaumont was disappointed but didn't blame his cast; instead he put it down to audience's lack of good taste as he explained in a letter to Beaton "it is caviar and something that only appeals to us and the small group who are still interested in style, convention and manners." This helps to explain why he gave his rising young director another chance. By then Peter was ranked as one of the top six directors in Britain and Beaumont asked him to direct what was his most expensive production to date, the £8,000

Adventure Story. The polished production was to prove an adventure in itself, a nerve-wracking roller-coaster ride for its playwright and Peter.

Beaumont regretted not staging *Playbill*, and he hoped to rectify matters between himself and Rattigan by putting on his most ambitious work to date as well as his first attempt at an historical epic. By 1949 his gentle, drawing-room comedies and film screenplays were earning him £30,000 a year, or approximately £2.2 million today. Rattigan's reasons for writing an historical epic were relatively straightforward: "It has been too quiet—and I'm to blame as much as anyone. We need something larger than life to wake it up: action and violence, drama and spectacle."

Adventure Story tells of Alexander the Great's descent from fiery idealism into materialism when his genius becomes corrupted by power. Rattigan saw it as a story of what happens when a man gains the world but loses his own soul in the process. Staged so soon after the Second World War, inevitable comparisons were drawn between Rattigan's Alexander and Hitler, and *Adventure Story* verges on political allegory. It was also a huge production. Three hours long and with twelve scene changes, its sweeping historical canvas stretches from Asia Minor, Syria and Persia (now Iran) to the gates of India. Beaumont's no-expense-spared approach included a colorful map painted on the stage's drop curtain to keep audiences *au fait* with the hero's conquests by spotlighting locations from to Delphi to Alexandria.

Rehearsals began in December 1948 and it opened in Brighton a month later before going on a six-week tour and then transferring to the West End. Such was the anticipation that on the day of its London opening thirty people were queuing outside the theater at six o'clock in the morning; three hours later the queue had swelled to a hundred.

Beaumont wanted to hire Moiseiwitsch but she was unavailable, so he turned to the Russian, Georges Wakhévitch.

Raised in Paris, Wakhévitch had made a name in films during the 1920s, as well as designing for theater, ballet and opera. His dignified sets and almost space-age black-and-gold costumes were topped and tailed by extravagant jewellery and platform-soled boots and shoes. But Rattigan complained that they "overload the play" and advised his designer: "The director sees the play on a much more sombre and simple note." Eventually they reached a compromise and Wakhévitch won praise from critics for the touch of movie glamor his "sumptuous and simple" décor brought to the stage. The *News of the World* said the play was "a winner": "Peter Glenville's production is full of colour and the settings are conceived with cinematic vision."

Rather than use excerpts from classical pieces such as *The Planets* as was normal in a classical play, music was composed for the production by Benjamin Frankel. He had made a name for himself arranging scores for film and the theater, and became a major British composer, best known for his chamber music. Peter commissioned him on the strength of hearing a phrase of music he had written for the 1947 film *Mine Own Executioner*. *The Scotsman* praised Frankel's "remarkable" music for the play.

The production's most striking aspect was its large cast of eleven men, six women and seven extras. Beaumont was keen to cast Paul Scofield, a rising young actor, as Alexander. It was the 26-year-old's first starring role in the West End, having played for three years at the Memorial Theatre's Stratford Festival; his performance as Hamlet had given rise to claims that he was "the next stage star in the Olivier class." Scofield certainly had bags of potential with his distinctive sharp voice and leonine good looks; he warmed to the part, growing his hair long and dying it blonde. But it was a huge challenge, requiring him to depict Alexander as he grew from a petulant boy into a warrior and finally arrogant despot. The exhausting role required him to memorize 11,700 words and according to Scofield's biographer, Garry O'Connor, "It was a mammoth trial of strength. . . . Paul proved himself equal, in an impressive display of his range from Hitlerian displays of monomaniacal rage, atrocity, to philosophical detachment, gentleness, tender and violent passion, weeping self-pity and gnawing self-doubt." Yet Scofield's youth and relative inexperience proved problematic.

Beaumont was eager to give another unknown young actor a big break, a fellow Welshman, named Richard Burton. A few years earlier the 18-year-old Burton had gone to Oxford University's Exeter College for six months; permitted this special term of study because he was an RAF cadet. Peter's former mentor, Nevill Coghill, spotted Burton's potential when he appeared as Angelo in the 1944 OUDS production of Shakespeare's *Measure for Measure*. Coghill invited Beaumont to the production specifically to see Burton; also among the audience were Terence Rattigan and John Gielgud. Beaumont wasn't disappointed and suggested Burton look him up if he decided to taking up acting when he finished in the RAF. Burton went on to serve as a navigator until 1947, although he secured leave in 1946 to act in an adaptation of *The Corn is Green*, one of the first for British television.

After he left the services Burton decided to ask Beaumont if his offer still stood. His company had a scheme in which it put promising young actors on a one-year contract and Beaumont offered the 23-year-old Burton £500 for a year. He thought that *Adventure Story* could bring Burton to the fore, and the young actor impressed Peter. In October Peter hired him to play Alexander's close friend Hephaeston, but after only a few rehearsals, he sacked Burton. According to Peter he dismissed Burton because the script called for Hephaeston to be taller than Alexander; Burton was several inches shorter than Scofield. Rattigan's script also hinted a homosexual attachment between Alexander and Hephaeston and there have been suggestions that Burton was too heterosexual for the part. Beaumont sent a smarting Burton off to audition for a part in *The Lady*'s *not for Burning* directed by Gielgud—both the play and Burton became a success.

Peter later admitted that Burton's personality didn't fit that of the diffident Hephaeston and both he and Rattigan felt that Burton was unsuited, both physically and emotionally, to the role of the unassuming adviser Hephaeston. The author was quick to write a letter to Burton apologizing for their miscasting gaff: "I hope you realise how very distressed I feel at what has happened. The fault was entirely mine and Peter's, for a bad misreading of the character, and it is sad that it should be you who have to suffer for it. Binkie will have told you the lines on which we both now feel Hephaeston should be played, and as this new approach involves a physique and personality different from yours, a change is essential. There was never any criticism of your performance, which was excellent. You must try to forgive us for our incompetence."

Rattigan then did Burton a favor: "Tolly de Grunewald asks for you to get in touch with him at once. He wants you for a part in the film *Now Barabbas*. I understand it's a good one, and I've no doubt you'll make a great success in it. Anyway I wish you the very best of luck, and can only hope that we'll be associated again in the future, in happier circumstances." Burton followed up Rattigan's advice and his fiery acting, wonderfully resonant deep voice, darkly masculine good looks and striking green eyes saw him start to catch the critics' attention. The rest is history.

Another of the cast new to the limelight was Scofield's wife, Joy Parker. Peter hired Parker unbeknown to her husband, who was in Rome when she auditioned for a part. Peter cast her in the role of Roxana, a part that didn't require her to say any lines but perform a dumb show. Among the Greek Soldiers was another young actor destined for a big future, Stanley Baker. But Peter and Beaumont didn't just consider young talent for the stellar production. The final line-up was packed with names that would attract audiences. Gwen Ffrangcon-Davies was hired as Alexander's mother the Queen Mother of Persia, Cecil Trouncer as Cleitus, Devlin as the Persian ruler Bessus and Robert Flemyng as Philotas. The return of the esteemed classical actress Ffrangcon-Davies to the West End stage to play her tenth queen after seven years of working in South Africa with her own theater company was an event in itself.

To direct such a massive production headed by a young actor was a colossal task and it is a measure of Peter's talent and Beaumont's trust and respect for Peter's abilities that he had landed the job. But it was a task made more difficult because *Adventure Story* wasn't the only production Peter was staging. Following *Playbill*'s spectacular reception in Britain, Peter was the obvious choice to open the play on Broadway, and while he was working on *Adventure Story*, he had to go to New York to begin casting.

Before *Adventure Story* opened in Brighton he spent almost three days in the theater, working continuously. The sets were erected only two days before the opening night meaning that the actors began rehearsing at midnight and continued the next day and night without sleep. They eventually got to bed at dawn, before rehearsing again at two o'clock on the afternoon of the opening night. Despite what seems like a formidable task and the stresses for both actors and director the first-night capacity audience were not disappointed in the play. *The Sunday Times* review was typical: "a brilliant company directed with great skill by Mr. Peter Glenville, probably our most successful [director]."

The notices continued to be very positive after it went on tour playing to packed houses. "Peter Glenville's direction with its broad sweep and sure sense of tempo gives [the cast] all their movements," said the *Birmingham Evening Despatch*. The *Stratford Herald* declared: "A big play is produced in a big way by Peter Glenville." While *The Scotsman* enthused: "It is magnificently produced by Peter Glenville and nobly spoken by a company which contains some half-dozen stars of the London stage." The *Edinburgh Evening News* summed up: "Peter Glenville's production was a work of art."

By the time *Adventure Story* arrived in London in March, Peter had managed to cut the running time. Rattigan gave Peter a gold coin to mark the occasion, with a note saying: "How I have loved it!" When the final curtain fell there were cries of "Author!" and the cast took eight curtain calls. *The Star* declared: "The play is produced to perfection by Peter Glenville." The *Sunday Chronicle* enthused: "[*Adventure Story*] is the best new play presented in London in the last decade." But some had reservations about what they saw as Rattigan's presumptuous attempt to retell a historical story that even Shakespeare hadn't attempted. Some were unimpressed by Scofield: "The part is tremendously long, and Mr. Scofield has yet to find intermediate tones between his piano and his forte." *The Observer*'s reviewer wrote scathingly: "Some of [Scofield's] intonations, sharp ending of sentences and other mannerisms suggest a first-rate cartoon of how Olivier would handle the job."

None of this caused any problems at the box office and business was brisk the next day. But only a week after the show opened Rattigan was unhappy, particularly with his leading man. He wrote to critic Harold Hobson: "The reason I have been worrying over *Adventure Story* is . . . I feel the play, production and performances need quite a considerable amount of polishing and tightening up, and as Peter Glenville is busy on another play . . . we haven't done nearly enough work in the six weeks we have been out. Scofield is a very inexperienced actor, brilliant some nights and on other nights, having no technique to fall back on, quite hopelessly mechanical and artificial. It isn't that he doesn't try or that he doesn't understand the part, but this is the first time he has ever had to sustain a long part (*Hamlet* was only played once or twice a week at Stratford) and he needs continual guidance and coaching." He was reassured when Peter was able to join rehearsals again: "It's a great relief and very popular with the company who are naturally feeling rather neglected."

Despite the work Peter put in, Scofield's performance remained erratic in quality throughout the run. Some blamed Peter's direction, but the role of Alexander was probably too large for Scofield at such an early stage of his career, it required an actor to play the full gamut of emotions. Moreover, *Adventure Story* was a lengthy play with a prologue, followed by ten scenes and an epilogue. Scofield was at the centre of the action, unused to performing at such a gruelling pace, while being expected to consistently be on top form. Most of all, *Adventure Story* was an experiment for Rattigan, and it was unwieldy, a fact Rattigan later acknowledged: "I wasn't ready . . . [it lacked] the language of the poet and the perception of the philosopher."

By May audiences were distinctly thin and *Adventure Story* closed in June. Beaumont was hugely disappointed and blamed patchy reviews that criticized Scofield and lamented the play's length. But he realized that the theater was a large venue and although it was in the West End, it was on a side street and so lacked passing trade. The lavish production needed six months of playing to capacity houses to cover Beaumont's costs. Yet he had put on a groundbreaking play as Hobson pointed out: "[*Adventure Story* is] a play, which besides being exciting, witty, and moving, is the most adult political comment of the contemporary theatre. Mr. Peter Glenville has [directed] with splendid spirit and drive."

For Peter, his "mastery of stagecraft" was recognized as critic Brian Harvey pointed out: "The last twelve months have seen Peter Glenville not merely consolidate his reputation as a [director], but also achieve real maturity in the theatre. . . . Perhaps as an actor he was forced too hard and tried too highly in his career. These parts left him with a touch of extravagance and flamboyance in style, which it was too late for him to control, and which made it difficult to cast him, especially in modern plays, once he was past the prime of his juvenile days."

The author and director's roller-coaster experience on *Adventure Story* wasn't just as a result of its cast and crew.

Rattigan's former partner, Kenneth Morgan had killed himself in February when the play was on tour. Peter was with Rattigan when he heard the news. They were drinking tea in the author's suite at Liverpool's Adelphi Hotel when a porter delivered a note to the author. According to Rattigan's biographers Michael Darlow and Gillian Hodson: "Rattigan read it, obviously very shaken. Then he handed it to Glenville, telling him to burn it when he had read it before the police arrived. The note told Rattigan that Ken Morgan had committed suicide." Bizarrely, Rattigan's reaction to Morgan's death was to conceive a play based around a suicide attempt. When he and Peter were on their way to the theater to see the *Adventure Story* that evening Rattigan told Peter in the lift: "The play will open with the body discovered dead in front of the fire." Rattigan's idea became 1952's *The Deep Blue Sea*, which ironically met with more success than *Adventure Story*. Peter was shocked at what he saw as Rattigan's cold-hearted creativity, although he acknowledged that writing the play was likely an act of catharsis to help deal with his grief.

While he was directing *Adventure Story* Peter was also putting together another production that opened in Manchester in April. It was his own translation of Leo Tolstoy's *The Power of Darkness*, which had never been performed in Western Europe. He hired Georges Wakhévitch to do the sets and costumes and the play brought Peter back into contact with Stewart Granger. Since they had worked together on *Madonna of the Seven Moons* there had been significant changes in Granger's personal life. He had divorced his first wife in 1948 and was courting the petite beauty Jean Simmons, who was also booked to appear in *The Power of Darkness*; by 1950 the rising star was rated as the number four box-office attraction in British cinema. The combination of two movie stars who made a handsome couple on and off stage, and the interest around their relationship, should have pulled in the crowds.

Granger describes in his autobiography how their collaboration came into being: "Peter was a very persuasive young man and, although I had my doubts after reading [the] lugubrious, bloody drama, he triumphantly pointed out that Jean's part answered all our doubts about her stage acting capabilities; she would have an important leading role but the character [Akulina] was a mentally-retarded peasant girl. . . . Peter arrived one evening with Tolstoy's grand-daughter who fascinated us with her story of how the play had come to be written. Apparently it was a true story and the character I was to play [Nikita] had died in Siberia while serving a life sentence for murder. She didn't know what had happened to the girl. Peter also brought along with him a Russian set designer [Wakhévitch] who had made brilliant sketches for the production; with all this excitement we were hooked."

The production had four sets and a large cast, so there was some nervousness over the cost. Granger offered to co-produce it and put up half of the money. When the play opened in March at Manchester's Opera House there was standing room only and it went on to break box-office records, but it toured to mixed reviews. Granger, concerned whether they would fill the theater and cover their costs, doubted it should open in London at the Lyric—a large venue on Shaftesbury Avenue.

His instincts proved right. Audiences giggled at what was meant to be tragic, and the critics panned it. *The Times* lamented: "A courageous, well meant performance which almost wholly lacks the peasant quality. . . . The disastrous weakness of the present performance is that throughout it is namby-pamby. None of the principals can conceal the telltale marks of civilization. They are bound accordingly to be outside the characters they are playing. While Mr. Stewart Granger is being goaded by the farmyard Lady Macbeth to kill his illegitimate baby with a spade it is the actor rather than the man who tremblingly approaches a situation which he clearly feels to be rather too strong for his audience. . . . Miss Jean Simmons is colourlessly correct as the lustful Akulina, best when she is spitefully triumphing over the wife she has supplanted."

With doubts about it lasting the week the leading actors cut costs by drawing the minimum salary; it managed to limp on for a few months before closing. Granger's verdict on Peter was that "our director, who was initially responsible for the idea, on reading the notices, left town, and we didn't see him again during the run." There is no denying that fact that Peter was juggling too much at this point in his career. Like many people trying to "make it" in whatever their chosen career there can be a tendency to take on more work than can be properly handled. Those that reach the top have the luxury to pick and to chose; Peter would get there but for the moment he was stretching himself too thin.

Peter had left London to face the greatest challenge of his directorial career to date and unquestionably his biggest opportunity—a Broadway opening. There is no doubt that Peter's decision to abandon acting and concentrate on directing was astute. He was never a great actor although he could have made his living as one, but he clearly wanted more than just "a living." He was already proving he was a far more capable director, although his ability to do more than one production at a time was in question. Peter had talent, but he was fortunate enough to know people who believed in him and give him a chance. He just needed to be careful and not overreach himself.

6

Broadway Success

1949-1951

For British actors the lure of Broadway was strong. It started around the middle of the 19th century and with the rise of the director it was natural that they too should want success on the American stage. A triumph in London's West End was a dream for many, but conquering Broadway brought international recognition and the financial rewards that accompanied it. Shaun and Dorothy had made the transatlantic crossing in the 1920s and by the 1950s a steady stream of actors and directors headed for New York, while some went further west to Hollywood. Some made the move on a more permanent basis, attracted by the glitter and glamor; they also enjoyed being feted by the many Americans who loved the British. In the early 1950s Britain was still in the grip of food and fuel rationing. While London seemed to share a single, low-wattage light bulb, New York, and especially Broadway, was the epitome of bright lights, big city. Having found a cozy niche in Binkie Beaumont's West End empire, Broadway theater meant forging new relationships and different working practices. For

Peter it was exciting, but also daunting, with the added frisson that there was no guarantee of success.

Besides being so very different to the West End, Broadway was the theatrical epicenter for an entire continent. As many as a thousand hopefuls would turn up to audition for a Broadway musical, all vying for half dozen vacancies; Tyrone Guthrie compared it to a slave market. This was in sharp contrast to London where after five years a director was acquainted with just about every prominent actor, and many of the lesser ones. Casting actors in London for Peter was a relatively speedy and efficient process; he knew their work and their personalities. But casting in America proved to be a nightmare, and for much of 1949 Peter attempted to find the right actors while trying to keep everyone happy. He was there to direct Rattigan's double bill of one-act plays, *The Browning Version* and *Harlequinade*, *Playbill*.

The problem was compounded by the fact that both Broadway and Hollywood competed for the best actors. Actors were drawn to the West Coast to act in films and the burgeoning TV industry; they could earn more money working on screen than on Broadway as well as considerably more fame. The film industry's love of youth meant that a thespian needed to achieve success early, if they failed they were seen as washed up and often left the profession altogether. For Peter there was an added complication, he was looking for English actors, or at least actors who could convincingly pass for English.

Casting for *Playbill* began in January and both Stephen Mitchell, the British producer who owned the rights to the play and Peter wanted to use Eric Portman to reprise his role, and if he was unavailable then either Richardson or Gielgud. However, Rattigan and the American backers, Jack Wilson and the New York Theatre Guild, felt the play needed a well-known name to American audiences, in order to make the production more secure. Rattigan and the backers got their way when Maurice Evans signed a contract in May; he also agreed to co-produce the play. British-born Evans had become an American citizen in 1941 and had a strong reputation on Broadway as a Shakespearian actor; he was particularly well known for his cut-down version of *Hamlet* that he performed for G.I.s.

Rattigan was hopeful that Mary Ellis, an American, would return home to reprise her role as Millie Crocker Harris/Edna Selby but she wasn't available. In June while Peter was holidaying in Rome, Rattigan wrote several times suggesting Eileen Herlie, Isabel Jeans or Martita Hunt before he was eventually convinced that Edna Best would be best, because "Glenville could work well with her." Best, who was British, had the advantage of being familiar to American audiences having appeared in movies that included 1948's *The Ghost and Mrs. Muir*.

Having got the casting largely finalized several things conspired against the play, including Rattigan's father suffering a stroke in June, making him reluctant to leave for America. Peter was dissatisfied with the terms he was being offered and asked for an increase. He wrote to Rattigan saying it was "highly dangerous" to leave the remaining casting and décor to Evans. Meanwhile Evans was unaccustomed to dealing with living authors and impatient to begin auditions; he claimed there were a limited number of English actors available and they may gain an advantage by starting auditions early. Rattigan and Mitchell agreed to pay Peter's fare to New York on the understanding that Evans would pay Peter's expenses.

He arrived in New York in July, immediately cabling Rattigan: "Décor should now be Okay. Casting difficult but Evans now very cooperative. My percentage agreed providing London management pay return fare London New York." Mitchell was affronted. Rattigan wrote of Mitchell's outrage to Peter: "Stephen's face [went] purple at suggestion of paying your fare."

Peter used his famous charm to sweet talk Bertha Belmore into playing Dame Maud Gosport; her agreement came as a surprise to Evans who didn't think she would do it for the money they had to offer. Peter explained to Rattigan that Gosport's had conceded to doing the role because "she is an old friend and has been in a couple of flops, [so] it was all very successfully negotiated." Within a few weeks he had cast all but two parts, those of Mrs. Gilbert and Jack Wakefield.

Peter was unhappy to hear about Mitchell's ire. He felt he had done a great job with the casting so far and was irritated by Mitchell's quibbling about money. He wrote to Rattigan: "As regards the enpurplement of Stephen's face, I am *ici a dire* that I am only interested in hearing effusive congratulations at successfully negotiating the plays from something worse than death and also, let's face it, on the question of terms, had Evans been obdurate, it would have been a question either of Stephen doing something his end regarding the percentage, or of my leaving the building. I thought that as Evans had agreed to look after the more considerable financial angle this end, Stephen would be pleased at only having to concern himself with the return ticket. I am myself looking after all my personal expenses during production in America, which is I understand, far from usual. So much for the royal purple!" Eventually Peter won out and Mitchell paid for his return fare. Peter agreed to a fee of $2,500 (around $50,000 today) in advance and 1% of gross from the first twenty-five weeks of the run and 1.5% thereafter.

However, the final casting went anything but smoothly as Peter reported to Rattigan: "The English-speaking actors in New York . . . are all rather soft, sentimental and lacking in any sex threat." Peter went to Hollywood, staying at 9166 Cordell Drive, the home of his movie-director friend George Cukor, and auditioned ten actors a day. It was tough going: "All the English types are soppy." Finally Peter managed to recruit Patricia Wheel and Ron Randell, but come September, and the start of rehearsals, he was missing being able to bounce around ideas with Rattigan, his "Dearest T," and was "beginning to get the big itch to be back [home]." Nevertheless he had to remain in America for the next two months.

Peter struggled to get his cast to appreciate Rattigan's humor: "*The Browning Version* is in fine form . . . [but the cast are] relying on lines rather than character, all very deliberate and somewhat melancholy. Sooo . . . much finger wagging and new rehearsals. Edna was beginning to play it with a huge voice and very vulgarly and distinctly out of the bottom drawer. They all lack the faintest touch of sophistication and as I explained to them the real comedy comes not from the gaps on exit lines but from the satiric point of view from which the characters are observed. But alas I was speaking in some foreign tongue. However it does some good I think."

The show had a two-week run in Boston before opening at New York's now demolished Coronet Theatre in October. It received warm notices, but as sometimes happens with transatlantic transfers, what does well in London fails in New York.

Peter revealed his disappointment and frustration to Rattigan: "It's odd . . . the business isn't better. I don't honestly feel that the performance as it stands could ever have been a smash-hit type, but one would feel with [the] notices, especially when compared with those of other plays, would have induced Mrs. Public to press in . . . presumably the double-bill element doesn't appeal: and yet . . . and yet the *en dit* on the shows is excellent."

Rattigan was alarmed that some journalists viewed *The Browning Version* as a depiction of life in an English school rather than a study of character, prompting him to write an article on the different reception his plays had in Britain and America. While audiences responded well to idea of *The Browning Version* the double bill deterred them. By the end of November the show had accrued losses of $13,833.65; Evans responded by cutting actors' salaries and canceling the royalties. But "saving" a show to prosperity is impossible without an audience eager to buy tickets, and it closed in early December after running for sixty-nine performances.

Despite this disappointment on Broadway Peter spent the next two years working almost constantly in America. A casualty of this move across the Atlantic was that Peter did not get to direct both his parents in the kind of show he watched them in as a child. He had wanted to do a pantomime, but the project was postponed because of *The Browning Version*. There was no hint of intellectual snobbery from Peter and his desire to work with his parent reveals his respect for their stagecraft.

Peter's next Broadway production *The Innocents*, William Archibald's adaptation of Henry James' novel *The Turn of the Screw* opened at the Playhouse in early February 1950. The Victorian tale of terror and the supernatural is set in a rambling English country house and centres on an overly sensitive young governess who is alone in the house with an earnest housekeeper and her two motherless charges, an 8-year-old girl and a 12-year-old boy. The children are under the malign influence of the ghosts of a sinister valet and his paramour, a governess he drove to commit suicide.

This time casting was easier; just four actors and two extras. Beatrice Straight played the governess Miss Giddens, Isobel Elsom the housekeeper Mrs. Grose, and he brought over two child actors from England, David Cole and Iris Mann, to play Miles and Flora. Both Elsom and Straight were strong character actresses and familiar to Broadway audiences. Critics found their performances in *The Innocents* faultless. Peter also made a valuable contact while working on the play: Jo Mielziner. One of the 20th century's most influential stage designers, Mielziner was already a legend. In 1931 the usually caustic Dorothy Parker wrote in *The New Yorker*: "I do not believe that there is half enough screaming about Mr. Mielziner. Show me, that's all I ask you, anybody better in our theatre." Mielziner came to *The Innocents* after designing sets and lighting for Arthur Miller's *Death of a Salesman* in 1949.

Born in Paris in 1901, Mielziner grew up in an artistic family, and the family emigrated to America where he made a name for himself designing costumes and sets, but his flair lay in his ingenious use of lighting. After he read the script he approached Peter with a novel idea of creating the lighting first and then the scenery. The latter was almost secondary; it comprised a staircase, windows and some furniture. According to Mielziner Peter happily gave him free reign: "For a production so dependent on mood and the suggestions of ghostly figures either seen or felt in the background, and with an imaginative director who planned well ahead, this reversal of the designer's usual procedure proved very effective. This is the kind of play that calls out for magic in the lighting. During most of the scenes it was desirable to have actors playing in [a] moody, shadowy atmosphere. Except for brief moments, the actors had to be covered by some brighter source of light. To cover every one of their acting positions would have necessitated far too many individually controlled lights. My solution was to use two follow spots, handled in such a subtle manner and with outlines so soft that most people in the audience were unaware of the technique."

The result was that most of *The Innocents* was performed in a twilight world punctuated by spotlights on the main characters, whose huge shadows were cast on to the backdrop, to create an otherworldly atmosphere that was perfect. Mielziner and Peter went on to become frequent collaborators.

Reviewers loved this ghost story for adults. *Time* said: "With the help of Jo Mielziner's fine period set, Alex North's effective music and Peter Glenville's perceptive staging, *The Innocents* inhabits a different world from the usual, or even the unusual, thriller." *The Stage* praised the production's "mounting atmosphere of mystery and terror": "The whole has been craftily knitted together by Peter Glenville's deftly under-emphasised direction." *The New York Times* declared it a triumph: "Under Peter Glenville's imaginative direction, the performance is a work of art. To give the story its proper tone and environment,

Jo Mielziner has designed an ominous but beautiful living room, which we may as well describe as a masterpiece. His lighting arrangements are masterly also. And Alex North, who wrote the score for *Death of a Salesman*, has composed a witches' chorus that is pithy, practical and terrifying."

Mielziner's haunting set won him his sixth Tony Award for Best Scenic Design and fourth Donaldson Award from *Billboard* magazine. Peter won the George Jean Nathan Award and New York Critics' Circle Award for Best-directed Play. When the play closed in June its success awoke interest in Britain and soon there were plans take the production to London under Peter's direction using Mielziner's set and North's score.

In August the New York Theatre Guild invited Peter to direct *The Curious Savage* a play by John Patrick. It opened in Wilmington, Delaware, to mixed notices, prompting Peter to do a hasty revamp by rewriting as making cast changes. The lead, Patricia Collinge, left and her understudy, Marie Carroll, took over when the show moved to Boston. Peter signed movie star and "First Lady of the Silent Screen," Lillian Gish, as the lead. She memorized the seventy-page script that was being rewritten as she was learning her lines and made her debut on the show's last night in Boston. Peter joked: "'Plays,' someone once remarked, 'are not written. They are rewritten.'" When it opened at New York's Martin Beck Theatre (now Al Hirschfeld Theatre) in October, Gish's performance as Ethel, an eccentric and extremely wealthy widow committed to an asylum by her avaricious stepchildren, was labelled "lovely, humorous and touching." But the critics were scathing about its topic of life in a mental institution, regarding it as in questionable bad taste. *The Curious Savage* closed in November, running for a paltry thirty-one performances.

Peter then directed *Romeo and Juliet* on Broadway for a limited run of six weeks. It is memorable for the casting of Olivia de Havilland and Jack Hawkins as Juliet. Peter was conscious that he had to create "an American *Romeo and Juliet*" and wanted to use as many American actors as possible. Fully aware of the problem he would have casting such a costume ensemble work, having auditioned 200 character actresses for *The Curious Savage*, yet his major challenge on *Romeo and Juliet* turned out to be his leading lady.

De Havilland was a huge star having appeared opposite Errol Flynn in a series of swashbucklers as well as winning two Academy Awards for Best Actress. But she had only appeared in one play: Max Reinhardt's *A Midsummer Night's Dream* at the Hollywood Bowl sixteen years earlier. The $150,000 *Romeo and Juliet* was to be her star vehicle and Broadway debut, which is why Peter was drafted in. As a rising director who had experience, albeit as an actor, in Shakespearian productions he was deemed to be perfect. His old friend Oliver Messel was hired to design the sets and costumes.

In his autobiography Jack Hawkins highlighted the challenges Peter faced: "The problem was that . . . Olivia . . . had limited stage experience. Peter had, therefore, to concentrate his efforts on her performance. To complicate matters, Olivia was at that time married to an author [Marcus Goodrich], who for some reason made it his job to protect Olivia from press publicity. The result of his very efficient endeavors was that when we were ready to open, the American press was just not interested. This obsessive protection also succeeded in working Olivia into a frightful state of nerves."

It opened in New York in March 1951 at the Broadhurst Theatre on West 44th Street. The critics deemed De Havilland's verse speaking poor and insensitive, and Peter's direction drew mixed reviews. Hawkins, Watson and William Smithers came in for plaudits, as did Messel for his exquisitely painted backdrops evoking Renaissance Verona. Smithers' Broadway debut as Tybalt won him the 1951 Theatre World Award as one of the Promising Personalities of the Year. Years later Peter privately expressed scepticism about De Havilland's talent for the stage.

Despite the lacklustre reception to *Romeo and Juliet*, the mere fact Peter had been invited to direct De Havilland—one of Hollywood's all-time greats—on Broadway indicates how the he had gained respect within the industry in a relatively short pace of time. And it was a respect that didn't just bode well for his career in America, it enhanced his standing at home in England. He had established his name on both sides of the Atlantic, and his love affair with New York began.

7

Working With Giants

1951-1955

Peter returned to Britain and the press speculated what the rising director might do next; there was even talk of Peter returning to the Old Vic. In August 1951 *The Times* reported that he would direct Donald Wolfit as the aging roué Lord Ogle by in *The Clandestine Marriage*. However, Peter never went back to the Old Vic; perhaps his experience of *Romeo and Juliet* deterred him from tackling Shakespeare, because he never directed a play by the bard again. Instead, he went home to take up an offer too good to refuse: Binkie Beaumont offered him the chance to direct Tennessee Williams' *Summer and Smoke*. Peter's stint on Broadway had served him well. He went there thanks to his working relationship with Rattigan. Spending time in New York meant he got to know American actors and playwrights, and he became a known quantity; this must have helped Beaumont persuade Williams that Peter was the right man for the job.

Unsurprisingly Peter was thrilled at the chance to direct one of the world's leading playwrights and told *Theatre World*:

"[Williams'] plays appeal to me very strongly because they challenge the realistic conventions of the theatre. Tennessee has an impressionistic approach and hates the cumbersome realism of the old-fashioned box set with its three walls and ceilings. His plays, often performed in a skeleton setting that can suggest so many different places by a mere change of the lighting plot, are a [director's] dream, because the author bears imaginative effects in mind when actually writing the script. They are not superimposed afterwards by a director wishing to attract attention by the novelty of his treatment."

Summer and Smoke debuted Off Broadway in October 1948, but had little success and lost $70,000. It caused heated debate among critics and theatergoers alike: some saw it as amateurish and dull, while others pronounced it a masterpiece, comparable to his earlier plays *A Glass Menagerie* and *A Streetcar Named Desire*. Williams spent the summer of 1951 in Rome rewriting the play, after which he felt it had, "a straight, clean dramatic line for the first time, without the cloudy metaphysics and the melodrama that spoiled the original production." However he took so long that Peter and John Perry opted to use the original version for the sake of expediency when the play went into rehearsals in mid-October.

Set in a small Mississippi town during the First World War, it tells the story of a lonely, neurotic spinster, Alma Winemiller, and her misguided devotion for the local rebel, John Buchanan, Jr., who is reluctant to follow in his father's footsteps as the local doctor. Peter told *The Stage* what he saw as the chief problem with the play: "Each scene is at the same time an episode in itself and a link in a chain. The more orthodox method of central plot development is not employed, but neither is the technique merely episodic. The author selects a series of incidents and self-contained situations, each of which in turn brings home his theme of change of heart and illustrates the milieu in which he is interested. Directors and players are set the problem of giving unity of dramatic style and atmosphere to the whole. Whilst giving each scene its particular flavour and point there is always the danger of allowing the underlying mood of the play, its unifying element, to disappear or slip out of key. There is need of a distinctive dramatic style, otherwise much of the effect will be lost."

His solution was to use unrealistic lighting, and a set and music that gave an impressionistic view of life in the Deep South in 1916. Reece Pemberton's skeletal set of beautiful transparencies, the mosaic of lighting and the "pale washes of background music" were hailed as "imaginative" and "diaphanous" by some, while others found it "confusing."

Peter cast William Sylvester as the wayward Buchanan and Margaret Johnston as the fragile and frustrated Winemiller. Sylvester was an American who moved to England after the Second World War, making his London debut in 1948. His portrayal of the young physician in *Summer and Smoke* with his sultry sex appeal helped establish him as a virile leading man. Johnston had come a long way since her portrayal of Kitty Duvall, a prostitute with romantic dreams, in Peter's production of *The Time of Your Life*, and had been declared a triumph for her depiction of Elizabeth Barrett in the 1948 stage production of *The Barretts of Wimpole Street*. She was well suited to conveying the edgy nervousness of the repressed clergyman's daughter and her performance in *Summer and Smoke* was one of the most outstanding in her career.

It opened at the Lyric Theatre in November 1951 and was well received, even drawing comparisons with Chekov. Peter's direction drew favorable comments for its "delicacy" and the *Sketch* said: "Peter Glenville has ordered the stage with the air of a man at home way down with Tennessee." *The Times*' response was typical: "Margaret Johnston gives as the frustrated woman a performance of much distinction. A certain monotony is perhaps inevitable, but all that accomplished acting can do to combat monotony is done. Mr. William Sylvester's fascinatingly reckless young doctor is exactly the contrast needed, and the company responds well to Mr. Peter Glenville's admirable production." The play was a hit and transferred to the West End in January 1952.

Williams wrote to Peter in November expressing his gratitude: "The report on '*S. & S.*' is the most gratifying thing that's happened to me in a long time. I can't tell you how enormously I admire your work on the production, not only as the director but also as a person, your understanding, your patience and sweetness. It was a completely happy experience working with you, and I shall always be indebted to you for restoring my faith in the play, and this isn't just the usual sentimental testimonial after a successful opening but what I would have felt regardless of how it had turned out. You are the top man on the totem pole!" Peter was captivated by Williams' work; his sympathetic understanding and sensitive handling of *Summer and Smoke* began a working relationship with one of the outstanding dramatists of the 20th century.

By the time *Summer and Smoke* transferred to the Duchess Theatre, Peter was in rehearsal for the world premiere of a satirical comedy about an ant colony, Sam Spewack's *Under the Sycamore Tree*. Like Williams, Spewack was an American and one half of a husband-and-wife writing team who wrote screenplays for films, but they were best known for co-writing the book for Cole Porter's 1948 musical *Kiss Me Kate*.

The colony's inhabitants live happily in accord until its principal scientist, played by Alec Guinness, synthesizes two young ants into human beings so their queen can observe the emotions of love. Diana Churchill played The Queen, Peter Bull The General, Ernest Thesiger The Chief Statistician, and Eric Porter and Daphne Anderson the mad scientist's subjects, The Boy and The Girl. Messel designed the sets and costumes for what Spewack called a "farcical fable" set in the queen's throne room in an anthill under the sycamore tree of the title.

A production meeting the immaculate standards and starry casting prized by Beaumont along with a wacky story aroused a lot of interest. The press was fascinated and Messel's inspired designs whetted their appetite even more according to Peter: "The play was a satire on the human condition. The action was described as taking place in the maze of rooms and corridors of a vast and modern hotel. The dramatis personae were a swarm of ants behaving more or less as ants could be comically perceived to behave. The text was funny and imaginative. I discussed a possible production with Oliver and he agreed to work on the play if, instead of a hotel, the action could take place in a real ant colony below ground; and if all the characters could be dressed to suggest humanised ants; and so it was done naturally with the author's consent . . . and the final effect was a feast of fancy and wit."

Messel's imagination ran riot. He twisted together 300,000 pieces of felt, 700 feet of wire and countless pieces of silk, gauze and furry oddments to construct the throne room complete with a settee in the shape of a centipede and a pastiche wasp-skin rug instead of a tiger-skin one. There was spontaneous applause when the curtain rose at its opening in Edinburgh and the audience saw Messel's brilliant set framed in the twisted roots of a tree. His whimsical sets and colorful costumes were called "a miracle of invention."

After a six-week tour it opened at London's Aldwych Theatre in April where, despite Messel's "deliciously fantasticated décor" and the "easy flowing yet convincing" "imaginative direction" by Peter, the production came in for harsh criticism. Critics didn't like Spewack's vision for the play, finding it muddled. They praised its witty dialogue but felt its observations on American life too alien for a British audience. It was Guinness' performance that saved the day: "Let Alec Guinness play twenty parts in his next picture and he surely cannot be more devilishly clever nor more delicately funny than in the one part he plays in this American 'farcical fable,'" gushed Cecil Wilson in the *Daily Mail*. Hobson wrote in *The Sunday Times*: "Mr. Guinness shows supreme accomplishment.

There is no sign of effort anywhere; this is a performance of complete mastery. It reveals for the first time on the stage, in a single evening, the versatility of the Guinness of *Kind Hearts and Coronets*."

Under the Sycamore Tree was the first in a string of collaborations between Peter and Guinness. They knew each other from the Old Vic but became friends when they both went on holiday to the Italian island of Ischia off the north coast of Sicily. Guinness was with his wife Merula, son Matthew, and a friend, actor Ernest Milton. Peter was with Bill. In his autobiography Guinness wrote of Peter and Bill's "bright good humour" that "heralded . . . the commencement of a long, close friendship with both of them." The men were drawn together by work, their love of the theater and cinema, a shared sense of fun and their witty black humor.

They both shared a deeply held faith and would stay up until the early hours discussing religion. Peter's Catholic beliefs would have a strong influence on the Anglican Guinness, who later converted to Roman Catholicism. Guinness also became a good friend of Bill's, and Peter with Guinness' family. Peter and Guinness' correspondence reveals the strength of their friendship and Peter's role as a trusted confidante; it shows them chatting about mutual friends and family, and enjoying a mutual passion for art, literature, theater and cinema, sharing opinions on what they had read or seen. They talked of problems and illnesses, finances and holidays. All human life is in those letters and for them that included religion, whether that was to recommend the life of a saint or share reflections on a particular passage in the Bible. On a professional level their relationship made for some of Peter's best work.

Peter had little time to reflect on *Under the Sycamore Tree* because he was in rehearsals for the British version of *The Innocents* produced by Mitchell's London Theatrical Productions. His success with the show on Broadway made him the ideal choice to open the play in London. He cast Flora Robson as the governess, Jeremy Spencer and Carol Wolveridge as the children, and Barbara Everest as the housekeeper. Robson was the finest British character actress of the day, and Peter had worked with her in *Good-Time Girl. The Innocents* opened at Brighton's Theatre Royal in May before heading for Her Majesty's Theatre in the West End in July. Peter's deft hand created another hit, and Robson's stabilising presence when working with the children was a real asset. *The Stage* raved: "There was a thrilling experience at Her Majesty's . . . when Peter Glenville [directed] *The Innocents*. . . . Flora Robson could not have bettered her portrayal of the terror-stricken governess. What astounded everyone however, was the amazing degree of maturity witnessed in the performances of those two exceptional juveniles, Jeremy Spencer and Carol Wolveridge. It was an evening of many excitements."

The production coincided with a revival of interest in the works of Henry James. Capitalizing on the mood of the moment Peter then directed Dodie Smith's adaptation of the James' *The Reverberator*, which was retitled, *Letter From Paris*. Brenda Bruce and Nicholas Hannen played Francie Dosson and Mr. Probert, and Messel designed the scenery and costumes. Set in Paris in the 1880s, *Letter From Paris* tells the story of some Americans who marry into French society. When it opened at the Aldwych Theatre in October 1952 it was panned by the critics, who hated Smith's adaptation. *The Stage* judged that Peter "did everything possible for the play." Messel's costumes and sets inspired by the work of Impressionist painters Édouard Manet and Pierre-Auguste Renoir were seen as the only redeeming feature. It ran for a pitiful three weeks before it was taken off.

Peter and Bill spent Christmas Day 1952 in London at a party at Beaumont's house. Gielgud wrote of the bash: "Last night there was a great tamasha at Lord North Street. St. Johnnie [Perry] is fairly perky . . . Mrs. Lunt [Lynn Fontanne] was looking terrific last night with one tit provokingly popping in and out. Noël [Coward], Joyce [Carey] and Adrianne [Allen] disciplining strictly in 'The Game' and me slyly flirting with Graham [Payn] and P[eter] Glenville whenever their husbands' backs were turned!"

In October the 49-year-old Gielgud was convicted of "persistently importuning men for immoral purposes" in a public lavatory in Chelsea. In slang this was known as "cottaging" and referred to homosexual men looking for sexual partners. Gielgud's biographer Sheridan Morley revealed that the actor had even been warned off by some charitable detectives and told to watch his step. Nevertheless, Scotland Yard's so-called "Pretty Police"—young plain-clothes policemen selected for their looks and stationed in urinals to entrap homosexual men—caught Gielgud in a honey trap. The arrest of the actor caused a scandal that was made worse because he had been knighted only months earlier.

Homosexuality was illegal and gay men who performed sexual acts, even in total privacy, were at risk of going to prison. According to the critic Harold Hobson: "No one, of course, who had any connection with the London theatre at the end of the war, and in the years immediately following, could be unaware that homosexuality was very prevalent in it. Nevertheless, homosexuality was still not socially acceptable. The most famous of London theatrical clubs continued to ban from membership anyone even privately known as homosexual. The result was naturally a lack of frankness. The outward forms of correct bourgeois behaviour were scrupulously observed, and homosexuality was officially secret. . . . The English homosexuality in the theatre was that of English gentlemen, impeccable in social behaviour, and it was never referred to in public. . . ."

When he was arrested Gielgud was rehearsing N. C. Hunter's play *A Day at the Sea*. The play was to open five days later in Liverpool and when the news of his arrest broke, Beaumont worried that his production would bomb. But there was little time to replace the actor and Beaumont decided to see how the tour panned out; if it suffered he would pull Gielgud from the show. On the opening night Gielgud received a standing ovation when he came on stage. When the play transferred to London Beaumont was still nervous, in part because of their friendship, because some sections of the press declared the actor a "homosexual menace." He arranged for a Rolls-Royce to collect Gielgud from the front of the Haymarket Theatre on the first night. But Gielgud had guts, and refused Beaumont's offer, saying: "Nonsense, I shall leave through the stage door like any other actor."

There was a crowd of some 300 people at the stage door, and there was no knowing if there were troublemakers among them. Beaumont quickly formed a guard of friends and staff, which included Perry and Peter, to escort Gielgud to the waiting car. When Gielgud nervously made his exit, he met a cheering crowd. The hastily improvised guardsmen slowly made their way around the corner to the car amid applause and requests for autographs as Gielgud was clapped on the back. His talent meant more to the public than his indiscretion.

The incident says so much about Peter; he was there for his friend in need. It also took great courage to support Gielgud so publicly; the majority of the theatrical community defended him, but they were far less overt in their support. Others were far from supportive, including the leading choreographer Frederick Ashton who said: "He's ruined it for us all." Noël Coward wrote in his diary: "Did [Gielgud] not even think for a moment think about what trouble his little indiscretion would cause the rest of us? England, my England, has always been full of intolerance and bigotry. Just when things might have started to improve for us all, John goes and does something so utterly careless that it will do us harm for years to come, at least among those who still think our private sex lives are any of their bloody business." Such was the climate of fear that Gielgud's lover, interior designer Paul Anstee, burned all his letters in case they should be incriminating.

In 1954 Gielgud was invited to play the lead in a Stratford Memorial Theatre production of Shakespeare's *The Tempest* in New York. British Embassy officials in Washington warned him off, saying he was unlikely to get a visa, intimating that Buckingham Palace would regard such a refusal as an embarrassment because of his knighthood. It was six years before Gielgud appeared on Broadway again.

Peter was conservative by nature, living in a glamorous rarefied bubble protected from ordinary life, but he was also discreet. He felt his sexuality was his own business and nothing to do with thc public at large. However, his rallying to Gielgud's side reveals that Gielgud's friendship was more important to him than public vilification. Unlike Gielgud, Peter was not promiscuous. Family and friends have all said he strongly disapproved of such behavior. However, in keeping with the times, Peter and Bill appear to have never been photographed together at a public event such as a premiere, and what photos exist of them as a couple are snaps belonging to family and friends.

For Peter, 1953 was an auspicious year. Hardy William Smith Productions had its first hit, when the company joined with Beaumont to co-produce Graham Greene's first play, *The Living Room*. Peter had enormous respect for the literary giant, so much so that he was nervous. In a tribute to Greene shortly after his death in 1991 Peter wrote: "I found it positively intimidating when I was working with him (as a director on his first play) that he would listen patiently to suggestions and proceed to amend or alter with simple interest and enthusiasm. Of course when he did not agree (which invariably meant that you were, in fact, wrong) he would gently point out your mistake with a quiet smile."

Whatever his literary achievements, Greene wanted to be known as a dramatist, and while his plays failed to achieve a similar level of success to his novels *The Living Room* was the happy exception. Unusually, it premiered abroad, in Sweden.

According to Greene's biographer, Norman Sherry, Sweden was chosen because Greene was desperate to win the Nobel Prize. As a tactic it failed. The play transferred to Edinburgh in February, went on a short tour and opened in the West End in late March at Wyndham's Theatre on Charing Cross Road.

The play tells the story of a strict Catholic household in contemporary London inhabited by two spinster sisters, Teresa and Helen Browne, and their brother James, a former priest confined to a wheelchair. Their niece, the 20-year-old Rose Pemberton, comes to visit after her mother dies, and the family is thrown into turmoil when she embarks on an affair with a married man. Faced with condemnation and the loss of her lover, she commits suicide.

Greene came to write his play in middle age, taking over three years to complete it, and given his stature as a novelist there was a lot riding on it. He was nervous and not all went smoothly during the production but the cast managed to pull it off. There were also concerns that it wouldn't be long enough—it fell fifteen minutes short—and it was impossible to lengthen it. In one of his autobiographies Greene revealed how this was solved: "by raising the curtain a little late, by imperceptibly (to those in the bar) increasing the interval beyond a quarter of an hour, it was possible to pass the minimum two hours which to a theatrical management remain . . . necessary."

Dorothy Tutin played the sexually liberated niece and Eric Portman the aging, crippled priest. Although this was not Tutin's London debut Peter was credited as "discovering" the 23-year-old because the part established her reputation. When the play opened she was declared "potentially great." Kenneth Tynan described her as "ablaze like a diamond in a mine." Tutin was famous throughout her career for her purring but croaky voice, compared by one critic to "a turtle dove with laryngitis." Peter helped her acquire her trademark by urging her to intensify the emotional temperature of her performance by raising her voice.

Greene was thrilled by the play's success, enjoyed being on tour and wrote to Bill: "I have so enjoyed being with you and Peter in Edinburgh and Glasgow. I can imagine that having a play produced might be an awful ordeal, but with you two it was fun from beginning to end." Greene thought more highly of Peter than even the Oscar-winning, and recently knighted, film director Sir Carol Reed, who directed the author's own adaptations of his work—the classic thrillers, *The Fallen Idol* in 1948 and *The Third Man* in 1950—as he confided in a letter to a friend during the play's production: "Carol is just not up to [Peter's] standard. Peter is quite remarkable. It's a wonderful thing that he is doing here." It was the start of a lifelong friendship between them, and Peter must have enjoyed the fact that his career was bringing him into contact with the English-speaking world's premier writers.

Peter spent much of the rest of the year in Paris, with his friends, film producers Denise Tual and husband Roland. They introduced him to Jean Cocteau; recent winner of the Nobel Prize for Literature, François Mauriac; actor, director and mime artist Jean-Louis Barrault; the widow of Jean Giraudoux, Suzanne Boland; the Proust heirs; and author Julien Green as well as other prominent directors, actors and the leading literary and artistic figures. Peter adored the company of creative and literary people, and revelled being among the intellectual glitterati of the French capital.

But the trip was about more than meeting interesting people. In January 1953 Peter saw the Paris debut of Samuel Beckett's *En attendant Godot* (*Waiting For Godot*) at the Théâtre de Babylone: "I was taken to the first night of *Godot* in Paris by a close friend, Denise Tual. . . . I was most moved and strangely disturbed by the play. It was in a tiny theatre—almost the size of a large room—and the impact of the acting was consequently both intimate and intense. I was particularly struck by the economy of the movements of the actors, which gave the slightest gesture a dramatic impact: a turn of the head, the lifting of a shoelace, for instance. Of course, there was no clowning, no choreography to speak of, and no professional comedy tricks. The result was a complete concentration on the play and on the characters themselves (rather than on the actors as performers)."

Bill was equally enamored with the play and suggested to Peter that Hardy William Smith Productions secure the British rights from the Irish playwright. The theatrical impresario Donald Albery was also interested and suggested he co-produce it with them at one of his theatres. They acquired the rights for £125 (around £7,000 today) after seeing off other interested parties from both sides of the Atlantic. Peter wrote to Bill enthusiastically of his victory "the rights are in the *poche*."

Peter was too busy to direct the play because of his other activities, so they agreed to find a first-class director. He still wanted to be involved and suggested offering the parts to Alec Guinness, Ralph Richardson, Wilfred Lawson and Robert Helpmann, but leading actors were reluctant to appear in what was deemed an incomprehensible play. In 1994 Peter wrote to Beckett biographer James Knowlson: "Alec [Guinness] . . . accepted and was very interested. I talked to Ralph Richardson and he, too, seemed interested, but indicated that he would like to meet and talk to Beckett."

Although grieving from the death of his brother, Beckett met with Peter in London. "[Beckett and I] lunched at my house in Brompton Square. I cannot remember our conversation at all. However, there were no problems or difficulties. I admired the play. He wrote it. It remained to cast and produce it. He was a little taciturn which . . . was understandable in view of his grief about his brother.

"We then took a taxi to the Haymarket Theatre where Ralph [Richardson] was performing. . . . Then a sad and farcical scene took place for which I blame myself for not having in some way foreseen it. Remember, I did not know Beckett at all well. We were shown into a splendid dressing room and Sir Ralph, resplendent in a fine silk dressing gown, greeted us with enormous courtesy and suggested a glass of sherry. Beckett who seemed to grow rather distant declined. Upon which Sir Ralph expatiated upon such subjects as 'Waiting on God,' 'Which God,' with what expectations? etc. All this was in a mode that was far from Beckett's way of thinking or writing. Then, after a quick further exchange of courtesies, Beckett murmured to me that he and I should retire to the nearest pub. Once outside he said that he didn't think the old boy had anything in common with the play.

"And that is where I was both foolish and short-sighted. Sir Ralph of course would have been magnificent in the part. All it needed was a late night that with a couple of whiskies and a few laughs. Ralph had a wonderful and strange instinctive imagination—almost as strange and instinctive as that of Beckett himself. But it was not best exercised in entertaining a visitor from across the Channel over a glass of sherry. So, dumb and daunted, I expressed my disappointment and after a glass of beer, I saw Beckett on his way. . . . I thought (absurdly) that the bottom had fallen out of my ideal cast, and later transferred the option I still held to Peter Hall. . . . I had not met Beckett before this meeting, or indeed, alas, since."

Richardson said his decision was "one of the greatest mistakes of my life." Peter, too, realized the enormity of his mistake: "I regret deeply not having directed the first English production of *Godot*. It was entirely my own fault. I should have persisted and persuaded Beckett to meet Sir Ralph under more relaxed circumstances. I thought the two great theatrical figures would never 'get on.' I was wrong."

Peter's instinct was accurate, and he saw in *Waiting for Godot* what others failed to recognise. Perhaps his desire to stage the play using leading actors he was familiar with was misplaced, and motivated by his Beaumont training to assemble a cast that would draw in the crowds.

Waiting for Godot is one of the dramatic masterpieces of the 20th century and its English-language version premiered in

August 1955 at London's Arts Theatre under the direction of the 24-year-old Peter Hall; the production made his name as a cutting-edge director. Had Peter directed it his name would have gone down in the history of theater never to be forgotten; today few people know that Peter was the director who gave up waiting on *Waiting for Godot.*

Contemporary plays posing serious questions appealed to Peter, and when those questions touched on religion they were even more fascinating, which made Bridget Boland's *The Prisoner* perfect. The Anglo-Irish Catholic writer's gripping drama about a Catholic cardinal in a totalitarian police state behind the Iron Curtain was co-produced by Beaumont and Hardy William Smith Productions.

The play was a hot potato during the Cold War because its central character—a priest and Resistance hero—is arrested, charged with treason, and psychological tortured into making a phoney confession in a staged public trial. The play calls to mind the fate of Cardinal József Mindszenty, who at the time of its opening remained incarcerated in Communist-ruled Hungary. Mindszenty achieved international fame in 1948 when he refused to let Catholic schools be secularized, leading to him being charged with treason. After his arrest the Hungarian government released a "Yellow Book" listing the cardinal's confessions. At a show trial Mindszenty declared his statements to be null and void because they were made under duress; he was sentenced to life imprisonment in February 1949. Despite the contemporary parallel, Peter insisted the play was not political but an acute study of character.

The role of the cardinal—The Prisoner of the play's title—demands great skill and stamina because he is on stage throughout; Guinness agreed to do the part for a limited run of sixty performances. The play had an "alarmingly" successful six-week tour of Ireland, Scotland and the Midlands before opening at London's Globe in April.

Although it has a cast of nine there are only three speaking roles; it is almost a two-hander as The Prisoner and The Interrogator meet in a struggle of wills. Noel Willman played The Interrogator and Wilfred Lawson that of the other speaking part, The Cell Warder. A staunch character actor of stage and screen Lawson's most celebrated role was as dustman Alfred P. Doolittle in the 1938 film of *Pygmalion*. Peter took a chance with Lawson because he was an alcoholic and stories of Lawson's drunken exploits were rife. Lawson's behavior on the set of *The Prisoner* was no exception and Peter had problems keeping him in check. But he valued Lawson's considerable talent and like others in the theatrical world Peter did his best to keep him in work.

The Prisoner's strength lies in its incredible subtlety and the slow build up of tension to a climatic finale. It explores the conflict of minds between The Prisoner and The Interrogator; never depicting scenes of physical torture. It follows the slow deterioration of the cardinal's spirits under the relentless, calculated pressure of interrogation that cause him to question his sanity and to grapple with his faith.

According to Peter: "[The priest has] a sort of inferiority complex, and desire to cleanse himself and to become respectable that made him enter the church. This, of course, is only a half of the truth about the spiritual odyssey of the cardinal's life, and The Interrogator—by putting his finger on this initial weakness in the Cardinal's background (which he discovers through finding out his lack of love for his mother)—manages to distort this half-truth, and represents to the cardinal that the whole foundation of his life and career as a Minister of God, is based on pride, and was never a true vocation."

The cardinal agrees to having betrayed the Resistance and to having accepted money from foreign countries to create a secret arsenal, but refuses to ask for the mercy of the court and collapses, pleading for God's mercy. Having been sentenced to hang the cleric becomes a pitiful figure during his dramatic demise. This causes the interrogator to regret the efficiency of his work. On the day of his execution the interrogator informs his former prey that the government has decided that he should live because his death would turn him into a martyr. The priest will be freed but his former flock will always doubt him. The interrogator offers to kill the cardinal, as he thinks that the priest would find such a future untenable, but the cardinal refuses, accepting his fate and the suffering he will endure as the penance for his life of deceit and vanity. The ardent Communist then questions his role in events and his almost religious fervor for a political doctrine.

The somber play was a huge hit and Guinness' performance a tour de force. The *Daily Express* pronounced it "the performance of the year in a play worthy of his remarkable art" and said Peter had "directed the play with humour and terrible pity." Reviewers praised Willman for bringing "a smooth, diabolic charm to the secular Torquemada" and Lawson for his "Shakespearean richness."

Around the time *The Prisoner* was opening Bill was looking to break out on his own as a producer and was in New York negotiating the American rights to co-produce the play with Beaumont, having secured Guinness as the lead. Bill wasn't well at the time, and was suffering from insomnia and shingles. The combination of his illness and Peter's voracious energy meant he found it hard to know what Peter wanted him to do regarding selling the play in America. He wrote to Peter: "I find it a little difficult to keep up with the facts on things. You are like a racing car that now and then lets off a puff of smoke and little oil in my direction and I have to sift the cloud and try to see what direction you have gone. I never seem to have any advance information or map of your destination. . . . It's a big rat eat race here and if I'm going to survive even another fifteen minutes I really have to sharpen my teeth."

He was confused by Peter's hasty and vague correspondence as to what rights to *The Prisoner* their production company actually owned: "It is so difficult for me to think or function or be of help. Is it not possible for [your secretary] to send me copies of correspondence you must have on these matters? I think I could be more helpful than you imagine. I'm in the darkest dark that has ever been and you seem to be going to Dior children's parties which doesn't make a good business partnership if one is to try to be part of it and perhaps a little helpful."

Peter replied to Bill suggesting that he approach Roger Stevens and the Playwrights Company with the idea, and explained that he had already spoken to Stevens about Bill: "This will put the ball firmly at your feet, as having an important property and a big star at your disposal to offer him you can ask for anything you may want to secure from him. If you are as clever as I think you are, you will use this situation to your advantage." Sadly, despite Guinness' willingness to play on Broadway, the play's merits, Bill's talent and Peter's belief in the project and Bill's ability to sell it, *The Prisoner* was never staged on Broadway; all very disheartening, particularly so for Bill.

Following the disappointment over *Godot* and the success of *The Prisoner* in the West End Peter staged one of the most popular plays of 1954, Terence Rattigan's *Separate Tables*. It's a double bill, *Table by the Window* followed by *Table Number Seven*, but unlike *Playbill*, its two halves were conceived as a unity. The plays portray the interaction of a group of lonely characters staying at the shabby Beauregard Private Hotel outside of Bournemouth on England's south coast. "Separate Tables" refers to the practice of seating single guests at their own tables in the dining room, which Rattigan uses as a metaphor for fear of emotional intimacy. *Table by the Window* focuses on the troubled relationship between a disgraced politician turned journalist Mr. John Malcolm, and his ex-wife, the glamorous 65-year-old Mrs. Anne Shankland. *Table Number Seven* is set about eighteen months later, and deals with the touching friendship between a repressed spinster, Miss Railton-Bell, and a retired army officer, Major Pollock, who tries to prevent his fellow guests from seeing a copy of a local newspaper report on his trial for molesting women in a movie theater and its guilty verdict. The secondary characters—the hotel manager, staff and permanent residents—appear in both plays.

Rattigan's play infers the major's offence was a homosexual one, with references to "nudging" in the movie theater and lines such as: "I'm made in a certain way and I just can't change it. It has to be in the dark you see, and strangers, because—." Staged after the furore of Gielgud's arrest, there were few in the audience unused to the guiles of dramatists attempting to avoid censorship. They would have realised that Rattigan's dialogue referred to something other than making unwanted advances towards women. When the characters of the play gather at the hotel in judgment of the major, the character Charles Stratton, a student doctor defends him: "The Major presumably understands my form of lovemaking. I *should* understand his, but I don't. So I am plainly in a state of prejudice against him, and must be very wary of any moral judgments I may pass in this matter. It's only fair to approach it from the purely logical standpoint of practising Christian ethics, and ask myself the question: 'What harm has the man done?'"

Rattigan made it a plea for sexual tolerance, having conceived the play following Gielgud's arrest; he wanted to make the major's offence a homosexual one, but he knew that such a script would not pass the censors at the Lord Chamberlain's Office. Established in 1737, the Lord Chamberlain's Office received and studied scripts of every play, revue, pantomime and operetta before granting a licence to perform. The censors would sometimes suggest amendments in the name of decency, propriety or diplomacy, and in some cases refused to license a piece. Sexual or blasphemous references and toilet humor often fell foul of the censors and getting a script passed could be an arduous process, requiring delicate negotiations, patience, tact and rewrites. Rattigan was motivated by his desire to see his play on the stage and chose to portrayed the major as seedy heterosexual rather than a homosexual.

Critics failed to allude to Rattigan's hints and veiled suggestions in their reviews; only Tynan chose to flout convention by acknowledging Rattigan's intentions. His review took the form of a duologue between A Young Perfectionist and Rattigan's invention Aunt Edna, "whom Rattigan has described as the 'universal and immortal' middle-class playgoer." Tynan bemoaned the fact that Rattigan was forced to infer the major's actions—and what he saw as the playwright's appeasing of Aunt Edna:

"Y.P.: . . . I regretted that the major's crime was not something more cathartic than mere cinema flirtation. Yet I suppose the play is as good a handling of sexual abnormality as English playgoers will tolerate.

"A.E.: For my part, I am glad it is no better.

"Y.P.: I guessed you would be; and so did Mr. Rattigan. Will you accompany me on a second visit tomorrow?

"A.E.: With great pleasure. Clearly there is something here for both of us.

"Y.P.: Yes. But not quite enough for either of us."

Homosexuality was such a taboo subject at the time that even Tynan was forced to be oblique in his criticism of Rattigan's obfuscation and refusal to address the topic openly. According to writer Michael Billington: "*Separate Tables* is more radical han many of the loudly trumpeted plays that preceded it. *Table Number Seven* . . . marks a historical watershed in that it unequivocally puts the case for charity and understanding in dealing with what at the time would have been called 'sexual aberration': it is a milestone not just in the history of queer theatre but in the shifting nature of public tolerance and shows the capacity of art to anticipate legal reform."

Originally Olivier and Leigh wanted to play the leading roles and asked Rattigan to postpone the production to fit in with their schedule, but he would not wait. Instead Peter assembled a fine cast headed by Kay Walsh and Eric Portman. The play reunited Peter with a colleague from his days at the Regent's Park Open Air Theatre, Phyllis Neilson-Terry as Mrs. Railton-Bell, along with Jane Eccles as Lady Matheson, Beryl Measor as Miss Cooper, and Basil Henson as Charles Stratton. Rehearsals went smoothly as the *News Chronicle*'s critic revealed: "[*Separate Tables*] is likely to be one of the high-spots of the autumn season. . . . I have seldom attended a more soothing rehearsal. Producer Peter Glenville hardly raised his voice above a purr as he directed his cast."

However, disaster struck when Walsh abruptly decided to leave. It was fourteen years since she had appeared on the stage having concentrated on films, achieving star status with her brilliant character study of the eccentric spinster in the 1951 movie *Encore*. *The Stage* reported that Walsh "asked to be released from *Separate Tables* because of a disagreement with Peter Glenville, who directs, Stephen Mitchell, who presents the bill, and the author over her interpretation of her part in the first play, *Table by the Window*." Playing the aging Mrs. Shankland didn't sit well with the 42-year-old Walsh as Rattigan told the press: "It's psychological—no woman likes to play a part beyond her years."

Margaret Leighton stepped in to deliver one of the best performances of her career: "I wasn't considered because my film work was expected to keep me busy too long. But by one chance in a million we finished ten days early. Then I was determined on a holiday. But I went dancing one evening and Peter Glenville . . . saw me. The next day Rattigan called me and asked me if I could get the lines in ten days. I read the first play, and rushed over to rehearsal. I've been going ever since."

Separate Tables had its first performance in Glasgow in August, followed by a provincial tour before opening in London. It got an enthusiastic reception in the provinces. "No other dramatist today can match the sureness and economy of effort with which Terence Rattigan conveys character and both the short plays included in this bill bear witness to the fact," said the *Manchester Evening News*. *The Manchester Evening Guardian* raved: "Rattigan is courageous here, and persuades us, as Chaplin and a very few others have managed to do, that the cheap, the spoiled, even the ridiculous, can strike near to tears. If he does not get quite home to deep tragedy, he succeeds . . . to move and to disturb." Audiences loved it. The cast were given numerous ovations and curtain calls, with the curtain continuing "to rise and fall for several minutes."

The London critics were virtually unanimous in their enthusiastic reception. *The Sunday Times* said that along with Fry's *The Dark Is Light Enough* it was one of two plays in London that "would render distinguished the theatrical season of any capital in the world." The *Sunday Graphic* felt the double bill was "the two best British plays of the year." The *Financial Times* wrote: "The plays are most beautifully performed and produced with a most unobtrusive discretion by Mr. Peter Glenville." *Plays and Players* said: "Peter Glenville has directed these plays so that the cast give the performances of their lives. This is the sort of production which should be sent abroad as an example of the English Theatre."

As 1954 ended *Separate Tables* was on many "Best of the Year" lists in the newspapers. The *Morning Advertiser* declared: "From every point of view the best new dramatic work of the year was *Separate Tables*." And *The Stage* called it "perhaps the most dramatically effective evening of the year." The production continued to run throughout 1955 and when the *Evening Standard* held a poll of London theatergoers, they picked *Separate Tables* as one of the top ten London plays of the year, but the run took its toll as Leighton revealed: "After we'd been doing *Separate Tables* for eighteen months . . . the director Peter Glenville came to see me and said my room looked as though I'd been doing a split week in Stockport instead of a hit in the West End." *Separate Tables* broke the record for the longest run at London's St. James' Theatre with 726 performances; at the end of it run in June 1956 it had banked £250,000.

Those abroad took note, too. When the American Actors' Equity Association held the Clarence Derwent Awards—the oldest awards on Broadway—in April 1955, Beryl Measor won the gong for Best Supporting Actress for performance as the housekeeper in *Separate Tables*. It was a good night for Peter—the actor's award went to Noel Willman for his interrogator role in *The Prisoner*.

The American appetite was whetted: *Separate Tables* transferred to Broadway in 1956 and Harold Hecht and Burt Lancaster secured the rights to make the 1958 movie. *Separate Tables* was one of the highlights of Peter's career and more excitement was ahead.

The Prisoner's theatrical success prompted Peter to think that it might be possible to turn the play into a film. While the immediate post-war years had seen the British film industry produce some creative and prestigious movies, audience numbers at movie theaters dropped significantly. This was partly down to changing social circumstances but also because of the inroads made by television. By 1955 the industry was concentrating on producing populist comedies and Second World War dramas, which meant that *The Prisoner* represented something of a commercial risk.

Peter's enthusiasm for the project put him back in touch with Sidney Box with whom he had worked at Gainsborough on *Good-Time Girl*. Box's B & D Film Corporation and Columbia Pictures Corporation were behind the film, with Box as executive producer. As a former documentary-maker, the gifted Box had courage as a producer and a taste for the experimental. Like the *Good-Time Girl*, *The Prisoner* shows that he had the nerve to tackle contemporary issues and as his biographer, Andrew Spicer, reveals, Box had some interesting ideas too. He suggested casting Guinness in both the role of *The Prisoner* and *The Interrogator*—a move that would have been very avant-garde. Box brokered the vital financial and distribution deal with Columbia Pictures, which was no mean feat given that *The*

Prisoner was regarded as an art-house movie that made few concessions to prevailing box-office taste.

Bridget Boland had experience in writing screenplays and adapted her play for the screen, while Lawson and Guinness returned to reprise their roles as The Prisoner and The Cell Warden, and Jack Hawkins took on the part of The Interrogator. Since playing in *Romeo and Juliet* Hawkins had become a star following his role as Ericson, the determined captain of the Compass Rose in 1953's war movie *The Cruel Sea*. Hawkins said of *The Prisoner*: "I found this one of my most rewarding acting experiences—if not financially—but then Alec and I were amateurs on the production side of the business, but we both loved to act."

Guinness and Hawkins were brilliant; Guinness played the broken cleric to perfection and Hawkins excelled as the cunning interrogator. According to Guinness, "Playing the cardinal was a risk of course; people kept warning me I'd finished my career. . . . [*The Prisoner*] did well, though I think one or two people went in to it thinking they were going to see me and Jack Hawkins in a comedy."

Peter's home in Brompton Square hosted a constant stream of visitors from wig makers to set builders as he set about preparing for his directorial film debut. Peter and Boland work on the top floor with a designer to create a shooting script, the bedrooms were inhabited by wardrobe people for clothes fittings for the leading artists, and the drawing room was used for conferences between the producers. Downstairs, the dining room was used to interview actors for the minor roles. Production began in late November 1954 and was wrapped before Christmas. The film was made in black-and-white film; with exterior scenes shot on location in Belgium, and the interiors at Pinewood Studios in Iver Heath in Buckinghamshire, to the west of London.

Like the play the film concentrates on the duel of wills between the two protagonists, but Boland added a sub-plot to the film that follows the fortunes of a young couple, one a guard at the prison and the other the wife of a political fugitive. There are some fleeting scenes of the harshness of daily life under Communist rule, presumably to add an extra dimension beyond the prison walls and to temper what would have otherwise been a static, claustrophobic piece. The touch of romance sets the film in its social context and depicts how Communism affected the general population.

Peter persuaded Boland to put in a rewrite after The Interrogator offers to shoot the cardinal: "It is a fairly subtle point, but a very important one, to my mind. . . . The Interrogator is merely horrified, as a man, at what he has done to another—and brilliant—man. His success in destruction has been too great; the pain he has caused has been too appalling, and the victim has been to considerable a person to allow him any satisfaction in what he has done. And out of sheer humanity he offers to kill him, as one would put a dog out of its misery.

"Now, originally, this same attitude carried through into scene 2, but to my mind—from the moment that he offers the cardinal this means of escape, out of a human motive of pity, and the cardinal refuses, he should realise finally that he his up against something more than a man, and something that looks suspiciously like being a soul, a spirit, a what-have-you—but certainly something of which his party took no account in their calculations.

"In other words, as a man trained in psychiatry he would realise that the cardinal's values ultimately have triumphed over the ordeal to which he has been subjected, and the fact that he could refuse death, and accept the heavier sentence, is what makes The Interrogator realise that he has been defeated—defeated not by pity for human weakness and pain, but by the realism that the values of the other man, and his spiritual independence, give him a strength which triumph over his apparent defeat and humiliation.

"In other words, his 'real sting' has not been drawn, and it is this new awareness of the cardinal's inner strength that converts him, not to any positive belief, or to Catholicism, but away from his confidence in the ethics of his own cause."

The Prisoner is one of three stage plays Peter brought to the screen, but his film debut was the toughest to bring to cinematic life. In 1958 Peter told the *Los Angeles Times*: "[*The Prisoner*] was a dialogue play . . . very cerebral, very concentrated, very difficult to make and still get variety in camera angles and movement." Boland's screenplay required Guinness and Hawkins to draw on all their expertise and talent to create the dramatic tension and when the film premiered in Britain in April 1955 it received a warm reception.

Reviewers admired the leading actors' performance but were unconvinced by Peter's changes to expand the scope of the drama beyond the prison walls. *The Times* said: "*The Prisoner* is not a film as the purist understands the word. It is based on a play and it remains a play throughout; it is dependent upon quality of dialogue and acting; it is a static rather than a moving picture, and what action there is takes place within the brain and the hidden springs of impulse and motive.

"That is not to say that a director like Mr. Alfred Hitchcock could not have pulled out a trick or two which would have made *The Prisoner* a film in fact as well as in name, but Mr. Peter Glenville has not been so ambitious. Indeed, his few excursions outside the prison and the room where the examination is held make for weakness rather than strength."

The *Daily Mirror* saw it as a moving tale of life behind the "Frontier of Fear" and the *Daily Express* as "a wrestling match of the minds that symbolises the dilemmas of our time." Cardinal Mindszenty was still imprisoned in Budapest. His defiance made him a symbol of the struggle between East and West during the Cold War. The West and the Roman Catholic Church looked upon him as martyr fighting to stem the atheistic evils of Communism.

However, somewhat bizarrely, *The Prisoner* managed to offend both pro- and anti-Communists alike. The Italian film board banned it for being "anti-Catholic" and in Ireland the censor banned it for being "subtly pro-Communist and tending to the subversion of public morals." Peter felt this was because "clerical sympathies might be affronted by the presentation, however sympathetic, of a prominent church dignitary as a fallible human being."

It was rejected from the Cannes Film Festival as being "anti-Communist" and a possible embarrassment to the Communist delegates, who were attending the festival for the first time. It was withdrawn from the Venice Film Festival because it was deemed "politically dangerous." In Britain, Cardinal Bernard Griffin wrote to Guinness and authorized the star to use the following extract: "This is a film which every devout Roman Catholic should see."

When the film premiered in America eight months after its British release there was a blaze of publicity. Peter arrived in New York two weeks before the film opened and wrote an article entitled "The Prisoner's Case; British Drama Dissects Clash Between Priestly and Totalitarian Credos" for *The New York Times*: "I have always thought that anything a director of a film has to say should be said in the picture itself. However, on account of the preliminary publicity that has been given to *The Prisoner*, there is a possibility of a misunderstanding as to its theme and subject matter. I feel it might serve some purpose to clarify this matter a little. . . .

"I was definitely surprised on arrival here last week to be asked point-blank, 'Which side of the fence is the picture on, Catholic or Communist?' The answer, quite honestly, is that the film does not in any essential sense concern itself with either of these issues. What moved and excited all the contributors to the film, including myself, about Bridget Boland's script was the dramatic story between a man of God and a man of the State. The one, a prince of the Church, the other a high government official, an intellectual and State Interrogator. . . . They are both prize fighters in the realm of the spirit, the politics of the one and the religion of the other are implied but are not in any sense defined or discussed in the picture, which illustrates the struggle of the man of the state with the mind and soul of the man of God whose independence and prestige he wishes to destroy. . . .

"Although the statesman wins his victory by cunning psychological pressures, he finds that in the end he has, in fact, fortified the spirit of the man he had momentarily broken. He, the persecutor, discovers within himself instincts of pity and remorse that make him realise he can no longer consider himself a proper servant to the implacable dictates of his party. The inference is that persecution is more truly destructive to the persecutor than the victim. One is left to wonder at the end who, in fact, is the prisoner.

"Although the implied sympathies of the film are anti-totalitarian, the real arena of the story is human and psychological. . . . Naturally, I hope that the film will succeed in provoking thoughts and opinions on a variety of subjects, but what it directly sets out to do is to move and excite telling a dramatic story." Peter's protestations about being neutral are at odds with the language he uses; he implies, strongly, which "side" he was on. Readers would have been unaware of the strength of Peter's faith, which makes his remarks totally explicable.

American critics were unanimous in their praise. *The New York Times* said: "The drama and its execution are beautifully done in every way. With a trenchant script by Bridget Boland . . . [and] strong direction by Peter Glenville." In its first ten weeks at New York's Plaza Theatre, the film took more than $100,000, and *The New York Times* voted it one of 1955's Ten Best Films.

The debate surrounding the film encouraged people to want to see it: eighteen months later Columbia Pictures was still distributing *The Prisoner* to British film societies when Cardinal Mindszenty was freed from gaol during the Hungarian uprising in October 1956. It was nominated for five British Academy of Film and Television Arts Awards (BAFTAs) including Best British Film and Best Film from any Source. Guinness and Hawkins were both nominated as Best British Actor for their performances, and Boland was nominated for Best British Screenplay.

In America the movie won the 1955 National Board of Review Award for Best Foreign Film. It also won the Grand Prix Award from the Office Catholique Internationale du Cinéma (International Catholic Office for Cinema) for illustrating "the final victory of the soul—strengthened by the grace of God—upon a destructive ideology."

For Peter the recognition from a Catholic body was especially meaningful. It no doubt also resonated for Guinness, who converted to Roman Catholicism a year after its premiere; it was Peter who recommended Guinness see a Catholic priest—evangelical efforts that were rewarded when his friend asked him to be his sponsor. The Bishop of Portsmouth accepted Guinness into the Church in a private ceremony held in the priest's attic.

Guinness wrote: "Peter Glenville acted as my sponsor and, in the ritual of those days, was required to stand with one of his feet on one of mine. Our faces remained solemn but I fear that we were shaken by silent giggles, which became almost uncontrollable when the Archbishop put on an abnormally low mitre, which looked like a paper hat from a Christmas cracker. His Chaplain, an elegant young man, straightened it for him, saying, 'Excuse me, Grace.' Peter had to hold his foot down very hard."

Following Peter's shift to films he was asked to write an article on the differences between directing in the theater and cinema for the journal of the British Film Academy: "From my limited experience in film studios, it seems to me that the major problem for the director is that of choice and selection. There is an *embarras de choix*. The difficulty is not, as in the theatre, to overcome the physical and technical limitations of the machinery, but rather to decide with tact and taste between so many glittering possibilities. . . . A pretty composition in a sequence that calls for stark ugliness, a face meaninglessly distorted by extravagant angling, a clever shot seen through the whirring blades of an electric fan—these self-conscious essays into the rococo can be as damaging to a story as can dullness and flatness.

"One engrossing tool the cinema affords the director, which is entirely denied him in the theatre, is the sound track. Whereas I firmly believe that dialogue should be limited to the bare essentials in the best type of film script, there is no doubt that the use of sounds, cleverly orchestrated, can be used to magnificent effect in telling a story on the screen. . . . Contrariwise, I have found that in the theatre recorded sound cannot be mixed satisfactorily with live dialogue."

Peter's comments reveal his distaste for Hitchcockian artistry and his belief in the need for a compelling soundtrack. His films bear this out as Peter's oeuvre as a film director is stagey, especially to modern eyes, and while his films have been called "club-footed dramas" they are most assuredly about story-telling. In 1955 the concept of the *auteur* director had yet to arrive, but the French New Wave was around the corner and when it did arrive cinema changed forever. Besides his use of a strong cast Peter had an eye for detail and paid close attention to everything from the soundtrack to the sets, and his considerable organizational skills allowed him to produce films on deadline and within budget.

He was working with some of the world's top writers and had assembled a core team of talented people that he felt he could work with well in both theater and film. He used the financial savvy he inherited from his mother to earn money beyond merely collecting a salary; it was Hardy William Smith

Productions that was key to his financial independence and consequently his artistic freedom.

Clockwise from top left: Peter in his role as Richard III in the OUDS summer production of 1934; Peter, the young thespian; Peter in the 1940s; Peter as Puck in the OUDS 1933 production of *A Midsummer Night's Dream*; Peter, back row second from left, as Second Lieutenant Hibbert in *Journey's End*, Robert Sherriff's play at Stonyhurst in 1930.

Clockwise from top left: Peter with Vivien Leigh in *Doctor's Dilemma* in 1942; Peter directs life-long friend Alec Guinness, probably in the 1956 London stage production of *Hotel Paradiso*; Peter directs Anthony Quinn in the first New York staging of *Becket*, 1960; Peter again directing Guinness in *Hotel Paradiso*.

Clockwise from top: Peter directs Simone Signoret and Laurence Olivier in *Term of Trial* in 1961; Peter directs Peter O'Toole and Richard Burton in the film adaptation of *Becket* in 1963; Peter (white sweater, right) directing Burton and O'Toole in *Becket*, when the actors were too hung over to face their horses in the same direction; Peter with the Duke and Duchess of Windsor, probably in New York in 1967; Peter cozies up with Angela Lansbury.

Top: Peter with columnist Aileen Mehle, a.k.a Suzy, and William "Bill" Smith (photo by Christopher Little). Right: Peter, probably in the 1970s.

8

To Pay Tax, or Not To Pay Tax

1955-1959

In the autumn of 1955 Peter returned to New York to direct a Broadway production of a play he had seen in Paris and to which Hardy William Smith Productions had secured the English-speaking rights. *Island of Goats* was British poet Henry Reed's adaptation of Italian writer Ugo Betti's 1946 play *Delitto all'isola delle capre* (*Crime on Goat-Island*).

Set after the Second World War in a remote mill-house on a desolate island in the Mediterranean, Goat Island, it tells the story of a young man, Angelo. A former prisoner of war, Angelo goes to the sun-scorched island to see the place his deceased cellmate spoke of and to meet his widow, sister and daughter. Angelo's presence jolts the women out of their sheltered existence and one by one he seduces them—and ends up trapped in a well for his efforts.

Peter asked the Motley sisters to do the costumes and Mielziner to do the lighting and scenery. Lithuanian-born actor Laurence "Larry" Harvey headed the five-strong cast. Harvey had already made his name on the stage and screen in Britain and the show was his Broadway debut. When it opened in October at the Fulton Theatre things augured well as Harvey received thirteen curtain calls and the cast went off to the Dakota for their first-night party. The next morning they were stunned as the critics loathed it; *The New York Times* headline was particularly scathing: "Man Mumbling From a Well; Ugo Betti's *Island of Goats* Is Deep And, in Truth, It's Also Dank and Dull."

It closed after only four days and was Peter's greatest failure. As he later admitted the production contained "all the ingredients for disaster." Peter felt that Americans didn't take to contemporary Italian plays heavy with symbolism, Broadway wasn't the right place to stage it, and neither he nor the rest of the cast and crew were the right people for the job. But it wasn't a complete catastrophe. Harvey's seven performances in the show won him a 1956 Theatre World Award for a Debut Performance On or Off-Broadway.

In January 1956 Mitchell and Rattigan were in New York to negotiate a Broadway production of *Separate Tables*. It opened in the autumn, and Rattigan sold the film rights to Hecht-Lancaster Productions for $350,000. Meanwhile Peter was working on three other projects including a film for Metro-Goldwyn-Mayer (MGM) in Hollywood, *Raintree County*—an "intense psychological drama." He spent part of the summer in France with scriptwriter Irving Ravetch working on a film adaptation of D. H. Lawrence's *Sons and Lovers* for Columbia Pictures, starring Montgomery Clift; Ravetch's script for *Sons and Lovers* never made it to the screen. Nor did Peter direct Raintree *County*—that honor fell to Edward Dymtryk and, ironically, it starred Clift. Peter's other ongoing project was for the stage, a vintage French farce, *Hotel Paradiso*, an adaptation of Georges Feydeau and Maurice Desvallierès' 1894 play *L'Hôtel du libre échange*.

In July 1956 he wrote in *Plays and Players* about how he stumbled on the French playwright's work: "Four years ago in Paris, I was sitting at the Deux Magots with a friend who taught modern languages at the Paris university. I invited him to the theatre and asked him to choose the play. Without hesitation he suggested that we should see the Feydeau farce that was currently playing. He was astonished when I confessed I had never heard of M. Feydeau and that I would prefer to see a more serious piece that would give greater opportunity to the actors. 'But all French actors admit that if you can play Feydeau well you can play anything,' he exclaimed. 'Anyway, he is our theatre's greatest humorist and the father of French farce. Let's go!'

"Since that evening I have seen five productions of Feydeau's plays and have read the others. I found every one of them immensely funny: funny in a direct, robust and merciless way—an antidote to gloom and excessive cerebration. Feydeau provokes the loud, spontaneous laughter that happens in life when an arrogant and censorious person slips on a banana skin at a solemn moment. . . . Such laughter may be childish but—like a child's laughter—it is full blooded, thoughtless, and refreshing as a week at the sea. . . .

". . . [Feydeau's farces] are as exquisitely dense as a Swiss clock. Marcel Achard describes their technique as '*la poesie comique de la table de logarithmes*' [the comic poetry of a logarithm table]. No word is spoken that does not further the logic and the movement of the action. There are no loose ends, and, however outrageous the happenings become, they are always the necessary outcome of the monstrous infernal machine set in motion by the follies of the characters themselves.

"The plays are therefore impossible to cut without omitting some essential point about which it is proper for the audience to be informed. Without logic there can be no belief and without belief there can be no true laughter in the theatre. There is very little wit in the plays—at any rate in the modern colloquial sense of the word. The characters talk in the flat direct tones of the class and milieu they represent. However dizzy and breathtaking the rhythm of their actions seem, the basic reality of their reactions is always there. I once challenged a member of the cast of *Hotel Paradiso* to quote one line of her part that she had not spoken herself at some time, in similar circumstances, in real life. She failed to do so." *Hotel Paradiso* turned out to be a labor of love for Peter.

Guinness was equally impressed by the French writer and wanted to mount one of his farces in London; he and Peter took Barrault into their confidence. He advised them that *Hotel Paradiso* was the most likely to appeal to an English-speaking audience. Rather than using an existing adaptation, Peter and Bill had spent the summer of 1953 in Capri adapting it along with some other Feydeau plays. Hardy William Smith Productions staged the play in conjunction with Binkie Beaumont.

Set in *la belle époque* in a shabby hotel in Montmartre, the play is a mad, frolicking farce where no door remains unopened for long. Its hero is the downtrodden Benedict Boniface who, tired of his overbearing wife, Angélique, escapes to the rundown Hotel Paradiso for an evening tryst with his neighbor Marcelle Cot. She is bored of her dull engineer husband, an architect, Henri. Sparks start to fly when Boniface and Marcelle find that Henri has been sent by the sanitary authorities to investigate ghostly noises at the same hotel. Things get worse when the Boniface's friend, M. Martin, a stammering provincial barrister and widower, arrives at the Hotel Paradiso with his four young daughters. The situation deteriorates still further when Henri's nephew, the priggish student, Maxime, turns up with the family's maid, Victoire. Things go bump in the night and there is a police raid as the curtain falls on the second act.

However when Guinness read Peter's translation for the first time he was shocked, and disappointed, because he didn't find it funny. The actor returned the script to Beaumont saying he wasn't interested. London's leading producer would have none of it and gave the script back to Guinness suggesting that he must have been having a bad day when he read it and was blind to its comic potential. Guinness sought a second opinion and invited a few friends to his home so he could read the script aloud to them. To his surprise they roared with laughter before he even reached the end of the first act.

Guinness agreed to play the henpecked Boniface, and Martita Hunt his gorgon of a wife. Peter assembled the rest of what was a dream team. Cartoonist Osbert Lancaster was hired to design "doll's house set which [offered a landing], an enormous winding staircase, and a clear view into two impeccably sordid bedrooms." Worth played the runaway wife, Frank Pettingell her pompous husband, and Douglas Byng the tongue-tied lawyer. Two less well-known names among the cast were Kenneth William as the earnest student and Billie Whitelaw as the saucy parlor maid. It was 23-year-old Whitelaw's London debut and she had fond memories of the show: "Alec Guinness and Irene Worth and Douglas Byng and Martita Hunt were the stars, with Peter Glenville directing like a ringmaster and Martita with those enormous bat's-wing arms swooping down on me in the wings and muttering hideously indiscreet things about the rest of the company. It was wonderful. Eccentric, but wonderful."

But Guinness' doubts about the play's comedic quotient continued during rehearsals. He was new to farce as were Worth and Hunt, and none of them could envisage an audience laughing. *Hotel Paradiso* was completely different to the comedies they appeared in before—its humor arises from a series of madcap situations rather than from the dialogue. Peter encouraged his downhearted troupe to increase the pace to a breakneck speed, an admonition that made them even more miserable. Guinness in all his twenty-two years as an actor had never been so unhappy about a production.

To the stars' astonishment, everything went well on the first night at the King's Theatre in Glasgow. As the production made its journey south via Newcastle and Birmingham it garnered more favorable notices and when it opened at Winter Garden Theatre (now New London Theatre) in Drury Lane in May it received eight curtain calls as well as glowing reviews. "Peter Glenville has directed *Hotel Paradiso* at so breathtaking a pace that the dust on this musty piece has little chance to settle," said the *Evening Standard. The Stage* found no fault with Peter "the ingenious translator": "Peter Glenville's translation of the play . . . is beyond criticism and his swift direction is impeccable." Reviewers loved the set too. "It's a multiple set so hauntingly, so bloodcurdlingly designed by Mr. Osbert Lancaster that one can almost hear the gargling next door."

In a move completely out of character for London critics they confessed to laughing themselves. "Styled by director Peter Glenville with top-grade actors and whirlwind pace [*Hotel Paradiso*] is so funny I had to stop looking at the stage. I shut my eyes—and it was a joy to hear so much laughter," said John Barber of the *Daily Express*. His colleague on the Sunday paper, Derek Monsey also got the giggles: "[Directed] by Peter Glenville with a brilliant disregard for reason, this essentially boring piece kept the audience close to hysterics, finally captivated me and had Eartha Kitt laughing herself almost out of her stall."

It was widely labeled the funniest theatrical entertainment to hit the London stage in years. The "masterpiece of mickey-taking" with its mix of "outrageous complications" and "knockabout pace" had all "the old magic of the early slapstick film." Guinness was credited as having "the finesse of Chaplin" and the *News of the World* dubbed him, Hunt and Worth the "New Keystone Cops." Peter and his cast celebrated with a party at his house in Brompton Square. *Hotel Paradiso* had a limited run because Guinness had to leave in November to make a film. Peter tried to persuade American actor Bert Lahr, famous for his role as the Cowardly Lion in *The Wizard of Oz*, to come to London to take on the role. Lahr, fresh from his success playing Estragon in the Broadway premiere of *Waiting for Godot*, had other commitments; but Glenville got his actor the following spring when the *Hotel Paradiso* opened on Broadway with Lahr as Boniface.

Only a few days after *Hotel Paradiso* opened in London, John Osborne's *Look Back in Anger* premiered at the Royal Court—

it was the very antithesis of French farce. *Look Back in Anger* was a huge success and represented a watershed in British theater; it initiated the "angry young men" and introduced kitchen-sink realism. With critics growing tired of verse drama, religious plays and drawing-room comedies, *Look Back in Anger*'s fresh ideas appealed greatly and seemed to reflect the whole notion of a "popular culture." It also said something about a post-war Britain and its changing role as the fulcrum the British Empire. *Look Back in Anger* spawned a host of harsh, gritty realistic plays and films set in dingy, working-class areas that dramatized the trials of everyday life among the masses. It was Rattigan who suffered most from the outpouring of working-class angst, mostly because of Osborne's comment "Look Ma, I'm not Terence Rattigan!" when he was challenged about the vulgarity of his play. Osborne was the exact opposite of Rattigan's crafted slices of middle-class life and it took years before revisionist criticism led to an appreciation of his work. Peter's own reputation suffered slightly by association with his collaborator, but unlike his friend he continued to work with new faces and fresh talent.

Peter headed to New York in July. The American Actors' Equity had agreed to let five British members of the original company of *Separate Tables* reprise their roles on Broadway: Portman, Leighton, Measor, Neilson-Terry and Hallatt; with an opening scheduled for October Peter had to audition for the supporting players. It was also a time of interesting behind-the-scenes activity by Peter, Rattigan and the New York producers.

Eric Portman told reporters after the play opened that he had looked at the dramas on Broadway ahead of time and came away cheered: "I kept seeing plays about dope fiends and people slashing peoples' faces and pregnant women and people washing out their socks in the kitchen sink. I said to myself, 'Now, really we can't have much more of this.' And I thought our plays would stand a very good chance." He said only a few lines were altered and performances were "moderated out . . . a trifle" for the

American offering. Portman's assessment of how the play was adapted fails to accurately represent the struggle to arrive at the final script, and his own role in the eventual outcome of that effort. It was Portman who played Major Pollock, the retired army officer who pleaded guilty to the charge of molesting women in a cinema in *Table Number Seven*.

Rattigan and Peter were unsure whether American audiences would be as alert as British theatergoers to the allusions in *Table Number Seven* to homosexuality. They discussed making the major's offences overt. In August 1956 Rattigan wrote a lengthy letter to the show's American producer Robert Whitehead outlining his desire to change the script: "Before I start I had better tell you that Peter [Glenville] is wholeheartedly on my side. In fact I think he had arrived at exactly the same view himself, quite independently, and it was at our first meeting on his return from New York that in discussing the play and its likely impact on American audiences that on mentioning my idea to him I discovered that he had also had the same idea, but had hesitated to bring it up. After thinking about it for some days we put it to Stephen [Mitchell] at lunch today and he is in complete agreement (with Peter's suggestions).

"Now let come to the point. I want to revert to my original idea for *Table Number Seven* and for which, because of the Lord Chamberlain, I was forced to find a considerably watered-down substitute. The play as I had originally conceived it concerned the effect on a collection of highly conventional people of the discovery that one of their number was a sexual deviant; and that deviation I had naturally imagined as the one most likely to shock; the one most likely to be outside their sympathetic understanding; the one which the Major would be most ashamed of their finding out and the one which the whole part of the character of the Major was originally conceived. Obviously homosexuality." Rattigan's letter relates how he thought his changes worked "fairly well" but was concerned that they may not work so well for an American audience: "you must remember that I was writing for an audience that has been conditioned for over three hundred years to the acceptance of a fairly vigorous censorship and which was thereby enabled to perceive—certainly in the early part of the run—exactly what I was really driving at. They fully realised that the Major's peccadilloes (in the cinema) were in fact only symbolical of another problem of which, at that time (just after several prominent cases) they were most sensitively conscious. An English audience knew my problem and accepted the fact that I had to skirt around it. They got the full impact of the play, as I subsequently learnt from many conversations.

"An American audience, on the other hand, not conditioned to censorship and to the evasiveness to which British dramatists are now forced, may well take the Major's stated offence not as a symbol at all, but as a literal fact. If they do, then, in my view, the play will lose the dramatic impact that it had here."

Rattigan rewrote a new speech for the character of Mrs. Railton-Bell that made the nature of the major's offence crystal clear. However, the rewritten script was never performed; Portman and Whitehead objected to the revisions. Portman was homosexual and afraid for his own reputation. Ironically, the decision to stick to the version performed in London may have in fact enhanced the play's resonance. Rattigan said in an interview with *The New York Times*: "In a way this turned out for the best. If I had written the man as a homosexual, the play may have been construed as a thesis drama begging for tolerance specifically of the homosexual. Instead it is a play for the understanding of everyone."

At its Broadway opening the notoriously hard-to-please New York critics raved: "The craftsmanship and the writing are enormously expert. The acting is brilliant," reported *The New York Times*. *Time* said: "*Separate Tables* . . . brings quicksilver to a Broadway season still lacking in blood. A big London hit [it] is as much stunt as drama in effect, as much production as play in appeal . . . as staged by Peter Glenville, both productions are consistently adroit theatre, full of gaudy character acting and authoritative ensemble playing." *Newsday* was impressed: "Under the fastidiously brilliant direction of Peter Glenville, the performers make up one of the most skilful and knowing groups that has hit these shores in some time." New York's *Saturday Review of Literature* wrote: "The performances as expertly guided by director Peter Glenville are masterpieces of discretion." One columnist even went so far as to exhort every member of the Actors Studio in New York to "pay out five dollars to see some first-rate acting instead of standing around in jeans studying his subconscious." It's a remark that in itself highlights the crossroads at which actors were assembling. America, like Britain, was changing and this was a challenge for directors, just as much as players. Peter, in his forties, was from an older generation, and the gap was widening between him and those who espoused the trend for Method Acting.

Whatever the theatrical undercurrents the Music Box Theatre's box-office was buzzing: tickets were reserved as far ahead as the following March and advance sales totalled over $200,000. Within a month it was taking more than $31,000 a week. It played to capacity for the first six weeks of its run, setting an all-time house record. Peter's contract agreed that he would be paid $3,333.33. The breakdown was $1,000 upon signing, $1,000 at the end of second week of rehearsal and the balance at opening of the play. He also received a percentage of the gross weekly box-office receipts, which on some occasions amounted to more than $400 a week ($5,000 today).

Separate Tables ran for almost a year and beyond the financial benefits for Peter it meant recognition from his peers. He received the first of his four nominations for a Tony Award for Best Direction and despite the fact that he did not win, for this play or any of the others, it was still a great achievement.

Separate Tables garnered a slew of Tony nominations: Rattigan for Best Play, Portman as Best Actor, William Podmore as Best Featured Actor, and Neilson-Terry and Measor vied for Best Featured Actress. Leighton won the Tony for Best Actress.

As *Separate Tables* was running on Broadway, Rattigan was writing the screenplay; Peter chose not to direct the movie telling the press he was unenthusiastic about repeating the assignment he'd already done twice. Meanwhile he was considering directing four other projects: a Broadway musical *A Carriage for Alida*, a West End adaptation of the Japanese film *Rashomon*, a film of John Braine's *Room at the Top* and a screen adaptation of Du Maurier's *The Scapegoat*. None of the projects transpired—at least in their original form. Peter directed *Rashomon*, but on Broadway, not in London. Conflicting film and stage commitments prevented him from directing *Room at the Top* that made it to the screen in 1959 directed by Jack Clayton while *The Scapegoat* also premiered in 1959 directed by Robert Hamer.

Missing out on *Room at the Top* was a disappointment, but Peter's refusal to direct *The Scapegoat* turned out to be a little more sensitive. *The Scapegoat* was a pet project of Guinness', and he was keen to work with Peter. But Peter disliked the script and asked for a fee $100,000. This frustrated Guinness, who felt that Peter's demand was outrageous, but he could afford to be choosy. Whether he really imagined that on the basis of having directed only one film he was really worth so much, or he knew that by asking for such an extravagant sum Guinness would blanche and so make turning down his friend that much easier, is not known.

Instead Peter went on to direct the New York production of *Hotel Paradiso*. After a short provincial tour, the play opened on Broadway in April 1957 at Henry Miller's Theatre, co-produced by Hardy William Smith Productions and H.M. Tennent with American backing. Byng reprised his role as Martin, but the rest of the cast were new to their roles.

Lahr played Boniface opposite Vera Pearce as his battle-axe wife, Angela Lansbury took on the role of the highly strung Marcelle, and John Emery played her slow-witted husband Henri. Lancaster again did the set. Like Peter, Lansbury was a Brit abroad. She and Lahr were the two big names in the cast, and she already had two Oscar nominations for Best Supporting Actress. Making his Broadway debut was James Coco as the professor, Tabu.

Preparing for the show took its toll on Peter. When the play was on tour in Washington, D.C., he visited a doctor who diagnosed him with a range of gastrointestinal problems and having more than one duodenal ulcer, the root cause was tension. While Peter invariably appeared calm on the surface, he was evidently stressed; life on tour and the prospect of a new Broadway production were behind it.

However, critical applause was unanimous, and reviewers were impressed by Lahr's clowning. "God must have laughed when he invented Lahr," said *The New York Times*. "Last autumn Mr. Glenville gave us a superb example of his serious method in his neat direction of *Separate Tables*. It is extraordinary to find the same man doing an equally distinguished job on a farce from the old school. It begins with one of those obsolete curtains that display advertisements—this time in French . . . but Mr. Glenville's recreation of old theatre is not precious or patronising. His actors plunge head-first into a slam-bang performance that goes at high speed, like the silent movies of very many years ago." The play raised belly laughs for 108 performances, finally closing on Broadway in July.

Peter's next project was *Me and the Colonel*, his first Hollywood movie. His $35,000 (somewhere close to $500,000 today) and 10% of the net proceeds puts into perspective his demand of $100,000 from his friend Alec Guinness. Among its cosmopolitan cast were Curt Jürgens starring as a Polish colonel and Danny Kaye as a Jewish Polish refugee. Peter had a role as the bearded British Submarine Commander who makes a swift cameo appearance in the closing minutes of the movie. He hired Wakhévitch as art director.

In *Me and the Colonel* Kaye played S. L. Jacobowsky, a Jewish refugee stranded in a Paris hotel in the spring of 1940. The mild-mannered, gentle and ever-resourceful Jacobowsky has arrived at the French capital via Berlin, Vienna and Prague. He is a man resigned to life on the run from the approaching Nazi army and plans to flee to Spain. Jürgens plays the aristocratic Colonel Tadeusz Boleslaw Prokoszny, a thick-skulled anti-Semite, womaniser and snob. They become unlikely travelling companions when the ingenious Jacobowsky acquires one of the last available cars in Paris, a Rolls-Royce and together with the colonel's sidekick, Corporal Szabuniewicz played by Akim Tamiroff, they drive to St. Jean de Luz on the Spanish border where the colonel is to rendezvous with a British submarine bound for London. The colonel is driven by his desire to deliver some important documents to the Allies; Jacobowsky by his desire for survival. En route the trio pick up the colonel's girlfriend Suzanne Roualet played by Nicole Maurey. Their picaresque adventures are amusing and poignant, and both the colonel and Jacobowsky exhibit bravery.

Aided by a nun played by Hunt, the pair manage to escape to England by which time the colonel has overcome his bigotry, and the men form a warm friendship based on mutual respect.

Location filming took place in November 1957—in Lyons, Nîmes, Arles and Marseilles—before the film unit moved to the Columbia Studio in Los Angeles in December. Location shooting proved gruelling; they worked day and night filming scenes that would have ordinarily taken two days to shoot so that they could meet their schedule. Yet the shoot wasn't without an upside. He chose Château de Castille in Provence as the location to shoot some exterior shots; Cubist art collector Douglas Cooper and his lover, art historian and Pablo Picasso biographer John Richardson, lived in the house at the time. Cooper and Richardson were part of the artist's inner circle, and frequently entertained him. When Peter was filming at the château, Picasso was staying there and Peter had his photo taken alongside the artistic genius. Peter treasured the experience and kept the photo displayed on a table in his study for the rest of his life.

Back in Hollywood Peter told the *Los Angeles Times*: "*Me and the Colonel* . . . is based . . . on the actual experiences of a Polish colonel, as told to Franz Werfel. It happened to be done as stage play first, but it is ideal as a film. Sam Behrman wrote both the play and picture, and I think his script is superior to the play. Usually you lose a little something, but in this I think we've gained. The exodus from Paris, for instance—the crowds, the strafing . . . we show it on the screen." Of his first time filming in Hollywood he said: "I am enjoying it because I am enjoying the film—and it's what we're doing and whom we are that counts."

Who they were was important. A star of stage, screen and radio, Kaye was touted as "the world's greatest clown" and known for his rubbery features and tongue-twisting comic patter. But he had experienced uncomfortable brushes with authority. During the Second World War the Federal Bureau of Investigation investigated him for draft dodging, and in McCarthyism's heyday he came under scrutiny for supposed links to Communist groups. None of the allegations were ever substantiated and Kaye was never charged.

Kaye's straight role in the gentle comedy was an unusual one. With his famous red hair tinted grey and sporting a moustache, Homburg, business suit and furled umbrella, his appearance and demeanor were a far cry from his previous roles. It was also his first black-and-white movie—Peter and William "Bill" Goetz, the producer, chose to spurn color because it would have made the film "a little operatic." Taking on the part of Jacobowsky was a risk—more so because the film handled the topic of anti-Semitism, albeit with great sensitivity. Peter said of his star: "This is Danny's first genuinely straight part . . . he uses both pathos and drama. He is not a funny man in any way; the comedy comes out of what he thinks and says. It's a switch."

Peter was more worried by the casting of Jürgens as he admitted years later: "An element I ultimately felt deeply wrong with *Me and the Colonel* was that Curt Jürgens was a German and to anybody with any sensitivity he was a million miles from being a Pole."

The film was hardly conventional commercial fare and when it premiered in New York in August 1958 some disapproved of its marriage of anti-Semitism and comedy. *New York Times* film critic Bosley Crowther asked: "Can you imagine anything more surprising for a light comedian to try to play?" But others felt that Kaye's delicate performance and Peter's sympathetic direction saved the film from being offensive. *Time* said: "Not a part in the whole picture falls, and not one double-talked song or double-sung talk issues from the Silly Putty that is Kaye's usual movie face. The result of this hold-down of his celebrated talents is the most appealing and one of the funniest films Danny Kaye has ever made. . . . Less surely handled by Director Peter Glenville or either of the principals, *Me and the Colonel* would tip over into maudlin sociology or an embarrassing joke."

Fortunately the industry agreed with *Time*. *Me and the Colonel* was voted one of the year's ten best American films by the 1958 National Board of Review and won the Writers Guild of America Award for Best Written American Comedy of 1958. It received Golden Globe nominations for Best Film Promoting International Understanding and Best Motion Picture Comedy; Kaye won the 1959 Golden Globe Award for Best Motion Picture Actor in a Comedy/Musical.

What Peter hoped to do next was to shoot an MGM production of *I Thank a Fool* starring Ingrid Bergman. His plans went awry when he was involved in a car accident on March 8, 1958; he turned on to what he thought was a one-way road—it wasn't. He collided with another car, and suffered a fractured humerus, bruises and cuts. After a convalescence of almost two months he was offered the chance to return to London to stage Spewack's *Once There Was a Russian*, starring Charles Laughton but refused, telling the actor: "I do like it . . . I don't intend to let myself in for eight performances a week run ever again. I am just too old to get bored that much. Another thing, my next two years are completely booked up. I am rather sad, because I have always wanted to work with you."

An excuse? Possibly, because Peter, in an unusual move, directed a stage adaptation of a film, the Japanese movie *Rashomon*, on Broadway. Hardy William Smith Productions co-produced the drama with David Susskind and perhaps the possible financial benefits involved were more appealing. The stage adaptation was written by husband-and-wife team of Michael and Fay Kanin and was based on two stories written by Ryunsoke Akutagawa. A courtroom drama, it tells the tale of the murder of a samurai and the rape of his wife that took place in a Japanese forest more than 1,200 years ago. The story is told from four different viewpoints: by a bandit charged with the crimes, the raped woman and her slain husband, who speaks to the court via a medium, and a passing woodsman who watched the events unfold. Their different accounts of what happened leave the audience to form their own opinion.

The Kanins and Peter decided to emphasise the play's exoticism with a Japanese period set and incidental music. They opted not to use Asian actors because *Rashomon* was such offbeat proposition they felt they needed big stars to attract theatergoers. Peter's own explanation of their decision was that since the characters "are totally unaware that they are Oriental. . . . It would be pointless to call on Oriental actors to portray the parts." The Caucasian cast were, however, made up to appear Japanese. The cast was headed by Rod Steiger as the Bandit, Claire Bloom as the Wife, Willman as the Husband and Tamiroff as the Woodcutter. Steiger and Bloom was a casting of opposites. Steiger was a rough and ready type, who had made his name in 1954's *On the Waterfront* playing a lawyer with mafia connections. Bloom was an elegant Englishwoman and classically trained actress who had played the Stratford

Memorial Theatre and the OldVic. She won worldwide acclaim after starring opposite Chaplin in the 1952 film *Limelight*.

Peter's first thought was to hire Mielziner to design the scenery, but he also talked to Messel who said he would like to do it. Mielziner volunteered his services as lighting designer, normally he designed both lighting and the scenery, but he believed in both the play and Peter and decided to make an exception. Messel was less humble, insisting on being billed above Peter and Mielziner. Messel had recently been made a Commander of the British Empire and perhaps it made him more conscious of his status and worth, whatever it was he found giving life to the stage version of a widely admired film "a headache." Peter could be very firm when he wanted to, but on this occasion Messel proved more so.

Messel's sets portrayed the crumbling ruins of the Rashomon temple gate and courtroom in the ancient Japanese capital of Kyoto and a bamboo forest set against Mielziner's translucent green sky, along with his costumes they were, as usual, breathtakingly beautiful—a fact acknowledged by Peter: "His set consisted of the most magical Japanese forest that actually moved; the trees themselves seemed to come to life. He also produced a great elevator that emerged from the pit of the theatre, supporting a witch surrounded by her cauldrons of incense . . . the leading female character was led on horseback by her husband through [a revolving Japanese forest with] glades and trees that glided gently by as the couple progressed towards their fateful encounter with the bandit. Nearby was a ruined temple, later to be battered by a tempestuous rainstorm. It was formidable challenge for a designer, magnificently mastered."

Besides Messel and Mielziner's contribution the music was a definite plus for the production: "*Rashomon* is completely beautiful theatre, whose colour coalesces with the strangeness and sorcery in the music of Laurence Rosenthal to bewitch the spectator." *Rashomon* was the first of many productions on which Peter collaborated with Rosenthal. He had studied piano and composition at New York's Eastman School of Music before going to study in Paris for two years. Peter called upon the 33-year-old Rosenthal thinking he was an expert in Japanese music. He wasn't, but soon became knowledgeable about it.

Rosenthal describes Peter as "a marvellous director and a brilliant and honest man": "A very good friend of mine, actress Beatrice Straight, told me about *Rashomon*. I said, 'Do you realise I adore Japanese films? Is there any chance I could speak to David Susskind?' She spoke to Susskind who rang Leonard [Larry] Bernstein to find out about me. Susskind said, 'Larry thinks a lot of you,' and arranged a meeting with Peter.

"I was a fledgling composer. I met Peter and was very impressed. He was very handsome, elegant and beautifully spoken—the essence of refinement and civilisation. I was immediately taken with him. During our meeting he had to take two phone calls, one from Lillian Gish and the other from John Gielgud—I knew I had moved into a stellar atmosphere and was a bit overwhelmed. Peter talked about his feeling for the play and the music he envisioned. He wanted something exotic that would evoke Japan.

"We discussed the play over several meetings, and I had the first taste of the magic of working with him. The incidental music was to cover moments to allow smooth scene changes. I didn't know what the music was doing, what was its essence, motive and atmosphere. Peter advised me to look at the script, and said to look at the tea-ceremony scene in purely poetic terms and think of achieving that result. We worked that way for years, and the longer we worked together, the less we had to say as we were on the same wavelength and in harmonious synch in our tastes and impulses."

Rosenthal wrote the music for the duel scene between the samurai nobleman and the bandit but when they tried it out in Philadelphia they realized the music was too long—practice had made Steiger and Willman faster and more efficient. Rosenthal remembers that Peter handled the revisions very cleverly by organizing two recording sessions; one that the cast could work with on an ongoing basis and another that was used when the duration of the action was finally decided. Rosenthal says: "Peter was thrilled with the score and talked of its 'bewitching sorcery.' I felt very flattered. It was a great experience and sealed our personal friendship." Rosenthal has since been nominated for twelve Emmy Awards—and won seven—two Golden Globes and two Oscars.

When the medieval whodunit had its tryout in Philadelphia, *Variety* admired its acting and "exciting entertainment." But when it opened at Broadway's Music Box Theatre in January 1959 it met with mixed reviews. Comparisons were inevitably—and detrimentally—made with the film. *Time* declared: "*Rashomon* . . . is essentially a stage remake of the eight-year-old Japanese film classic, and some of the charm and power of the film has spilled away in transit. . . . Under Peter Glenville's firm direction, this misanthropic drama thrums with barbaric violence, yet unfolds with the stylised gravity of ballet. Rashomon is rich in theatre craft—Jo Mielziner's doom-dappled lighting, Laurence Rosenthal's eerily instrumented score, and Oliver Messel's turntable forest of disenchantment. Apart from a U.N.-like babel of accents, the brilliant cast often achieves a triumph of mime over matter. Radiant, in white kimono, as netted moonlight, Claire Bloom is part lotus flower, part flower of evil. Noel Willman's samurai is a bred-in-the-bone aristocrat, and Rod Steiger's bandit a bite-to-the-bone outlaw."

Bill wrote to his friend, film producer James "Jimmy" Woolf: "Business is marvellous with lines at the box office all the time and standing room sold out all last week even at the Sat[urday] matinée and great bravo receptions. Maître d's are bowing and scraping while front tables are cleared for one." The production's success lead Bill to profess his desire to produce films rather than plays, which are "illusive qualities and one can hardly ever make a son." Peter received his second Tony nomination for Best Direction and Messel was won a Tony for Best Scenic Design and Best Costume Design. The show finished its six-month run in June 1959 and the on-stage relationship between Steiger and Bloom blossomed into an off-stage romance, they were married in September.

When *Rashomon* closed Peter had only a few weeks before starting rehearsals for his first Broadway musical, *Take Me Along*. It was a radical shift in artistic direction for Peter and no one seems to know why he took it on; perhaps it was the challenge of the new. He had played music at school, his parents were singers and no doubt some of their musical talent must have rubbed off on him because when the production opened in October it was a huge success. Based on Eugene O'Neill's play *Ah, Wilderness*, *Take Me Along* is a musical comedy set in Connecticut, New England the early 1900s. The story revolves around the coming of age of a 17-year-old boy, Richard Miller. Its cast of stars included Jackie Gleason, Una Merkel, Eileen Herlie, Robert Morse and Walter Pidgeon, whose return to the stage after twenty years was an event in itself. Rosenthal returned to work with Peter to write the incidental music and leading American designer Oliver Smith did the sets.

The music and lyrics were composed by Bob Merrill, who had written a string of pop hits including *(How Much Is) That Doggie in the Window?* (1952). *Take Me Along* was only his second musical—he later went on to write the lyrics for Julie Styne's music for the smash hit *Funny Girl*. The book was written by Joseph Stein, who later did likewise for the classic musical *Fiddler on the Roof*. The show's backer was David Merrick; by the 1960s he was staging half a dozen musicals or plays simultaneously and by 1966 he employed 20% of Broadway's work force. His penchant for publicity stunts respected no boundaries. When he staged *Look Back in Anger* at the Lyceum Theatre in 1957, a woman climbed on the stage and slapped the lead actor on the face, apparently incensed by his character's misogyny. Three weeks—and many column inches and ticket sales—later, Merrick confessed to hiring the woman for $250.

His biographer subtitled his book, *The Abominable Showman*, which says something about the man.

Merrick battled with Gleason and Peter on the production; quibbling with his star about billing and money. The pugnacious Gleason was then a huge TV star and was used to drawing a salary to match. He asked for $5,050 a week for *Take Me Along*—and got it, making it the largest amount paid to an actor on Broadway at that time. He also demanded a private carriage on the train that took the cast on its tryout tour. But Gleason didn't stop there, he insisted the carriage have a well-stocked bar and that Merrick hire a Dixieland band to entertain him en route. Merrick indulged his star, and Gleason brought in the crowds—and the cash.

Peter's clash with Merrick was over artistic interpretation. Peter became unhappy with the choreographer, Onna White, informing Merrick that her dance steps were a "disgrace." He persuaded Merrick to fire her and hire a young choreographer of his own choosing, Herb Ross. Peter then went off on holiday, leaving his problems behind. Merrick was evidently unamused by Peter's absence at a critical point in rehearsals and after a few days Peter received a wire ordering him to return to New York at once.

When Peter returned Merrick told him to sack Ross and reinstate White. Understandably, Peter was flummoxed by what seemed a capricious decision by Merrick and suggested a compromise: White could resurrect the scenes she had done, and Ross could finish the scenes he had started. What Peter didn't know was that White was having an affair with one of the theater owners, who had stepped in to protect his lover. Merrick's apparent capriciousness came from his desire to appease the owner, not because he doubted Peter's judgment.

When the show had its tryout in Philadelphia, Merrick had not forgotten Peter's outmaneuvering and asked Merrill to sack his "son of a bitch friend." Apparently Merrill pointed back to the back of the dark theater and said: "David's standing back there, and you're fired." Peter who seemed to take it all in his stride simply said: "Do you know anything about the weather in Jamaica?" After saying goodbye to Merrill he walked up the aisle to the back of the theater where he shook Merrick's hand before walking out.

Merrick's biographer alleges that Merrick's tactics in hiring and firing were often a way of asserting his control over staff, who would then have to sue him to get paid. Sometimes this came to pass, but on occasion Merrick would re-employ someone once he felt that he had taught them a lesson. In Peter's case, the incident ended with no hard feeling, and it appears it was the last time Merrick attempted to bully Peter. By the end of the year they were working together again on *Becket*, and in December 1959 Peter wrote to him: "Just a note to say that I'm very happy we're going to be together again." In 1961 Merrick sub-let Peter's house in Brompton Square, which he used when he visited London and the arrangement helped Peter when it came to avoiding paying British taxes. Given the nature of Peter and Merrick's personal and professional relationship, perhaps the story of Peter's sacking is apocryphal, but it reveals the industry's regard for him as aan archtypical English gentleman as well as one with a cool head.

As the winter approached, Peter was in demand on Broadway, but his motivation for working on Broadway was not just artistic or down to the rise in popularity of British actors and directors. He was avoiding returning to Britain to avoid paying tax. His accountant advised him that a visit to Britain would be "in practically all cases fatal, because even if one is [t]here for only a few days, one is bound to answer the telephone and do some business on it, which enables the Revenue to say that one carried on one's profession during the year. For this reason it is best to stay out of the country for a complete year in order to avoid any argument." His accountant wrote to Peter saying he wanted to show he was "emigrating with a view to permanent residence in the U.S., even though you may change your mind in five years' time and come back here to live. Where there is a any doubt as to whether a person has gone to reside abroad permanently, the Revenue regard him for three years as still resident here and tax him accordingly."

Peter took his advice and went on to direct Robert Anderson's *Silent Night, Lonely Night* in December at Manhattan's Morosco Theatre. Despite a top-notch cast headed by Henry Fonda and Barbara Bel Geddes and "glorious" sets by Mielziner, Anderson's story of a couple who meet one Christmas holiday at an inn in a small New England town failed to win much favor. The *New York World-Telegram* said: "Before carping intrudes, let it be emphasised Henry Fonda and Barbara Bel Geddes handle [the script] handsomely. If nothing mattered except their silken delivery under Peter Glenville's sharp direction, all would be well." Peter's direction was praised for its "exactness," the actors lauded for "splendid performances" and the production regarded as "technically triumphant." The problem was that the play was regarded as "a bore." Times were changing and so was the taste for straight drama. The show ran for 124 performances and closed in March 1960.

Dorothy flew to New York to see the opening night of *Silent Night, Lonely Night* and *The Stage* reported that her son's commitments would keep in him in America for the next two years. This doesn't quite tell the whole story. Bill had bought a house in a Landmark Building in Manhattan's Upper East Side at 18 East 68th Street between Fifth Avenue and Madison Avenue; it was to be their new home. The Beaux Arts townhouse was built in 1904 for luxury-home furnishings magnate and philanthropist Henry T. Sloane. The imposing five-story residence has a sixth story at the rear and was built on a plot 36 feet wide by 100 feet deep. Known as the Henry T. Sloane Mansion, it comprises approximately 19,300 square feet, with stunning terraces and ceilings, fifteen bedrooms, seventeen baths and eleven fireplaces. In 1941 *The New York Times* reported that the mansion was notable for "the spaciousness of its rooms, its marble staircase and its costly wood panelling . . . it serves as an example of the type of home which leaders in business and the social world of a generation ago put up in an era of gracious living." Its arched, wrought iron entrance is crowned by square-headed windows with panelled pilasters on the first floor, wrought-iron railings above the third floor, and a balustraded parapet in front of fifth story.

Peter's success brought with it a lot of money and accompanying high tax demands. Peter's creative solution when faced with the possibility of a huge tax bill was to cease being a resident of the United Kingdom, but this did not mean he become a United States resident, he had non-resident alien status. Ever careful with his cash, Peter began to investigate ways of minimizing his income tax payments in 1958. He was canny with his earnings from working on Broadway: "Apart from my living expenses while I am [in America], all dollars I or my company receive are sent straight back to a very greedy Bank of England, where they are speedily transferred into English pounds, and as none of us are allowed to leave money in America, outside investment is out of the question. The only possibility in this respect that I have is when I do a play myself, and wish to invest money in the show. In this case I arrange my contract so that I receive less money for my directorial fee, and the amount I should have been paid is put into the production. Even this is a dodge, and would be very frowned upon by the Bank of England if they knew."

He considered setting up a company abroad, somewhere like Curacao, Jamaica or Switzerland. In 1960 he set up an offshore company, Maximilian Productions Limited, in Bermuda, which paid his income to the company rather than himself. He chose to have payments made to him as a director deferred, choosing to invest productions and receive royalties instead. By 1962 he had bank accounts scattered around the world in Britain, America, Holland, France, Mexico, the Bahamas and Bermuda.

Many of Peter's choices regarding where to shoot films

were dictated by his need to spend time in no particular place and so avoid being declared a resident. He spent little time in Hollywood: on *Summer and Smoke* and *Me and the Colonel*. His remaining films were made abroad, albeit for American studios. He would make other films in a variety of locations and countries, all part of his plan to avoid paying tax. Peter's taste for the good things in life was expensive and it meant he tried to pay as little tax as he possibly could, albeit legally. Tennessee Williams even referred to him as the director "who lives like a prince." Peter and Bill always travelled first class and such was their taste for luxury that when they were in London and had to travel abroad by plane they would buy champagne and smoked-salmon sandwiches from Fortnum & Mason rather than eat airline food.

His move to America was part motivated by a desire to continue his extravagant lifestyle. It led to a globetrotting existence as he jumped on planes and boats never spending too long in Britain to avoid being deemed a resident nor in America to threaten his non-resident status. Bill was unable to spend more than ninety days in Britain because he had to keep renewing his visa. Indeed when Peter had his spat with David Merrick and "went on holiday" it may have been because he needed to exit the United States in order to re-enter to protect his status.

Having a home in New York made Peter's life easier. He was frequently directing on Broadway and working for Hollywood studios. Because Bill was an American they could buy a property in Bill's name without any problems. Peter's focus had changed. He was looking at America as a place to work and to live. In later years Olivier and Gielgud would say he had sold out to Hollywood and wasted his talent. If he had continued to live in Britain and work in classical and commercial theater it may have enhanced his reputation still futher, but Peter's love for the fine things in life and his love affair with Manhattan, as well as his connections through Bill's family, meant it never happened.

9

A Bishop, a Trial and a Musical

1960-1963

In 1960 *The Times* called Peter "one of the most sought-after stage directors in America." It was a well-deserved reputation as he consistently brought out the best from his casts and crews on award-winning material. But it was a talent that was to be almost entirely absent from the West End stage as Peter only ever directed one more play in London, preferring instead to concentrate on Broadway and films. With the advent of the still-to-be-named Swinging Sixties, Peter was hard at work on another play about a priest; his passion for the piece would consume much of the next four years and, arguably, it was his finest achievement.

Jean Anouilh's *Becket ou l'honneur de Dieu* (*Becket or The Honour of God*) was first performed at Paris' Théâtre Montparnasse Gaston Baty in October 1959. Set in 12th-century England, the play explores the relationship between Thomas à Becket and Henry II, Duke of Normandy and King of England, and the conflict that arose between them after Becket became Archbishop of Canterbury. Their power struggle ended with Becket's murder in his Cathedral at the hands of the king's followers. Its theme of the clash between church and state, and the motivations and psychology of two historical figures appealed to Peter both intellectually and emotionally.

Anouilh based his work on erroneous information, making Becket a Saxon when the cleric was Norman. Realizing his mistake he decided to let it pass which only adds to the dramatic tension of the piece. In Anouilh's work Becket and the king are friends, pursuing wine, women and song together, but when Henry appoints Becket to the Bishopric, hoping he will protect the interests of the crown, the strength of their relationship is tested. Becket has a spiritual experience, becoming a man who puts God and the Church before himself, the Crown, friend and country. Henry is affronted that Becket stands against him and hurt by what he perceives as his rejection by a man he loves. The king makes clear to those around him that he wants rid of Becket. However, when his nobles murder the priest, Henry is heartbroken and proceeds to make penance for his actions; realising that his friend made the right choice in choosing God over state.

Undeterred by Anouilh's poetic licence Peter was captivated by the dramatist's skill: "One of the interesting things about this play is that although it is set in a colourful, historical background, its actual style is very modern and lively and witty and scenes in which ideas cascade like fireworks alternate with moments of tremendous passion and drama. It is really quite unlike the average historical spectacle in which romantic platitudes are delivered in vibrant and measured tones!" Nevertheless his enthusiasm for the dialogue failed to stop him asking Anouilh for rewrites.

It was the winter of 1959 when Peter began casting and by June 1960 he had his two leading men. Olivier originally wanted to play the king, but Peter was unconvinced he would find someone in New York to play the cool, cerebral Becket, so he pursued Olivier to playing Becket, while casting Anthony "Tony" Quinn in the showier role of the king. Both actors turned down lucrative film offers, in part because Quinn was keen to work with Olivier.

Olivier's decision dumbfounded the critics, who perceived Becket an ideal role for the actor who always looked so "kingly." Before the play even opened the critic Harold Hobson lamented: "For [Olivier] will not play Henry, a character absolutely and utterly made for him, at least in New York. He has been hesitating for months, but now his decision is said to be final. He has elected to play Thomas Becket. I cannot believe that this is simply because in America the reigning dramatic method makes it difficult to find a player with the controlled grace that Becket needs. (We could find him in England. The part of Becket would be the great opportunity—and great test—of Peter O'Toole.) There may be qualities in Becket that appeal to Sir Laurence at levels of consciousness below that of active reason."

Despite working so often on Broadway, Peter seems to have had a low opinion of American actors and frequently found casting plays difficult. Peter's situation was exacerbated by Hollywood luring the cream of American talent to California, while the rise in the popularity of television also took actors to the West Coast. However, it seems unlikely that a top American actor would have been attracted by the role of Becket. What seems more likely is the fact that Peter just preferred British actors; perhaps it was his own classical training that encouraged this view.

Although Peter had known Olivier for more than twenty years, *Becket* was the first time they worked together. In 1972 Peter talked to Olivier's biographer Logan Gourlay: "What was extraordinary was that when we did *Becket* [Olivier] was then established as a great actor, if not the greatest actor on the English stage, and he had successfully directed several productions himself, but he had never tried to take over in any way or even suggest what I should do as director. From my point of view he was the ideal. First of all he had all the technical equipment to do whatever was required. I could have asked him to play it this way, or that way, *à la française* or any way, and he would have been able to respond. He welcomed direction. Unlike all the young actors of today he would even ask me to give him a reading on a line. Because he thought I had a certain facility with readings—different ways of interpreting or emphasising lines—he'd suddenly turn to me and say: "I'm not happy with my reading, let's hear another." Funnily enough, this didn't mean he was losing confidence as an actor. It meant the opposite, because he knew that whatever the reading he could accept it and makes it his own, modify it or broaden it—or just discard it.

"Nowadays the young actors from the modern schools don't believe in readings. They believe in happenings, or visceral events. If you give them a reading they scream and say they don't even want to hear it. But Larry [Olivier] has such command of his craft that he could listen to any suggestions—any variations in interpretation—and make use of them if he wanted to. That's real professionalism." Peter's dismissive attitude to youth is because he was a firm believer in a classical training and he was averse to the Method Acting approach favored by many young American actors.

The Mexican-American Quinn was a good choice as Becket. His swarthy good looks and rugged charm saw him in a clutch of roles that drew on his own passionate and volatile nature. Peter believed his "huge presence" and "expansive gestures" would be right for the King. A two-time Oscar winner, Quinn virtually guaranteed a first-class production as well as significant box-office interest. He wrote to Peter saying how he was excited as prospect of starting *Becket*: "I saw Olivier in *Rhinoceros* and went backstage afterwards. We both behaved like two shy schoolboys. I think this is good for both of us and the play. I must say he is certainly an easy person to love."

But Quinn was nervous about playing opposite Olivier, whose brilliant reputation was intimidating. His concept of Olivier as "an easy person to love" was to be tested, as Quinn sought to match Olivier's skill. According to Peter: "Tony had a great desire to strike up a close relationship with Larry. But Larry didn't encourage it. He was polite but cool. He was professional but he didn't invite any 'rapping' sessions. . . . Larry is a fairly reticent man and he was having none of that. However they got on quite well together, but . . . they came from very different schools and occasionally it was obvious. . . . Henry and Becket have a close relationship in the play, with Henry saying: 'I love you Thomas. You don't love me, etc.' At one stage during rehearsals Tony turned to Larry and said: 'My God, Larry, I hope they're not going to think that we're sodomites—a couple of buggers.' Larry smiled thinly and said: 'My dear chap, I hope they do. Didn't you know that in the Middle Ages at the time of the play all the men went at that kind of thing like hammer and tongs?' It took Tony a moment to realise that Larry wasn't being serious."

There is a story that Quinn was so impressed by Olivier's speech delivery and enunciation that he asked how he did it. Olivier told him that he used to walk on the beach reciting Shakespeare with his mouth full of pebbles like the Greek orator Demosthenes. Quinn is said to have sent to California for pebbles and walked about Broadway with a mouthful, saying his lines while almost choking.

Peter debunked the story: "It's a marvellous story but I'm afraid it is apocryphal. Tony did know, however, that he needed speech direction and he took it willingly. I had to teach him all the boring things that are part of the basic training in England but are not taught in America at all, like not joining a consonant to the next vowel and so on, but I'm afraid we didn't include the pebble method. . . . I must say in fairness to Tony that he finally made a good Henry—bold and powerful. Of course he could never have played Becket."

Quinn himself didn't see his relationship with Olivier as sycophantic and in his autobiography he wrote that Olivier was the one seeking his attention. It was a turbulent time for Olivier; his divorce from Vivien Leigh was granted a few months into the show's Broadway run. He was also missing his new love, and future wife, British actress Joan Plowright. According to Quinn, Olivier was lonely, confused and "desperate for companionship": "There was something pathetically endearing about [Olivier] and rather sad. . . . The poor man tailed me like a puppy dog."

Written years later, Quinn's take on the relationship may have been motivated by Olivier's subsequent performance as the King for which he achieved fine notices. Quinn admitted he found trouble in matching Olivier's "immense scale, his exaggerated rhythms." During rehearsals Quinn even considered quitting, but Peter persuaded him to stick it out and let Olivier test him, pointing out that what Quinn identified as "screaming and yelling" was "projection" for Olivier. It was sound advice because it was Quinn's performance that grabbed the attention of awards judges rather than Olivier's; he was nominated for the Antoinette Perry Award for Best Actor in a Drama and for a Tony as Best Actor in a Play.

With the exception of Olivier it was an all-American cast so that there would be little difference in the accents of the actors. Peter found the process a trial: "It is a slow and laborious job and one has to wade through dozens of inadequate performers and then, every now and again, someone really talented comes along." Peter said it was the "most tricky casting assignment" he had ever had and it was "a tough job to find thirty authoritative actors . . . within a realistic budget." The nature of the play and its two heavyweight leads caused difficulties: "Largely it is a play of intellectual argument and high cerebral voltage and this is indeed a difficult area. With two such superbly cast stars there is a danger of the rest of the cast appearing to be inadequate."

Actors in auditions who read the dialogue in a "slow and measured way . . . lost the wit and even the meaning of the scenes. The actors who tackled it with a quick, modern, relaxed rhythm immediately were understandable and the scenes began to crackle with life . . . most of [the] Bishops were [boring] in the readings. Most of them droned on like parsons, whereas what is really required is the quick cut and thrust of clever politicians."

Peter finished casting in August 1960, declaring: "I feel I have seen every actor in America." Once more, he was ill with ulcer problems. He was also exhausted.

There was little rest as he was soon preparing his new team for their roles, writing to Quinn: "My only suggestion at the moment is that you should not delve too deeply into the actual Henry II of history. The true Henry was obviously a many sided man and a dramatist could present him in one of several ways, particularly since the details of his personality elude one in the political hurly-burly suggested by the chronicles of the times.

"Anouilh is the first to admit that he did not rely on precise historical research in the creation of his characters. He merely took the basic story of the relationship of the two men and the political and religious issues, which constituted the background of their friendship and subsequent quarrel, and then proceeded to give them flesh and blood with the license of a creative writer. . . .

"As I am sure you have observed, Anouilh's Henry is a simpler and in some ways more primitive Henry than that of history. He is cunning, sharp-witted, humorous, vigorous and has the direct, uninhibited, emotional reactions of a child. A child, moreover, who is used to getting his own way. Of course the Normans in general, and Henry in particular, are presented as being more primitive and unsophisticated than the Norman rulers of England actually were. However, this contrast between the urbane and polished intellectual refinement of Becket and the rugged primitivism of the King of this play is an essential part of the pattern, and indeed their friendship is, in a way, the attraction of opposites who supplement each other. Becket is in many ways a man of intellectual passion, whereas Henry is a whole-hearted man who can suddenly cry out, 'Oh, my Becket!' like a wounded animal and who can rage on the floor and weep."

He forewarned Quinn: "Keep in trim, as for the first scene you will face your public stark naked!!!"

David Merrick produced *Becket*, making it clear that he and Peter had got over their earlier differences; they called upon their winning team of collaborators, Laurence Rosenthal, Oliver Smith and the Motley sisters to create the incidental music, sets and costumes. Smith's set modelled on that of the original Parisian production won a Tony for Best Scenic Design and the Motleys' lavish outfits won a Tony for Best Costume Design.

The production went smoothly, the only problem was with the text of the play. Peter was unconvinced by Lucienne Hill's translation that he found "a little too correct and not easy on the tongue." He wrote to Anouilh about his concerns, volunteering to undertake the revisions himself, which he would then pass on for the author's approval. Peter was a master at getting his own way and his request illustrates his persuasive skills; neither was he averse to a spot of fawning or name-dropping: "Quite apart from wishing to catch your tone as far as possible in an adaptation, I am very anxious not to have long discussions when the actors suddenly discover that the syntax and vocabulary of some of the sentences defeats them and makes it difficult to make their point. Sir Laurence [Olivier] has already mentioned this matter to me and took it for granted that I would be working on the English version. Naturally, I reassured him on this. Although he does not speak French, he had the actor's insight to realise that some of the robust humour of the part of the King seemed lacking in the translation, and that it did not seem quite so good a part in the English script as it did when played on the stage. Of course, this may momentarily have helped our casting, in that it propelled him into accepting the part of Becket rather than that of the King which, as you know, he originally wished to play."

Peter succeeded; mentioning Olivier's concerns clearly helped. Peter made significant changes to the dialogue that previously he claimed to admire. As Peter's friend film producer Denise Tual once observed to Bill: "[Peter] has a brilliant talent to switch to his advantage what is not really his." But Peter was facing a problem that may have motivated his tinkering with the author's text. He was "seriously worried about the length of the play" knowing that "with all the transport and commuter problems [in New York], no audience would stay in the theatre for over three and a half hours." Peter went on to cut some of the historical details that were not directly connected to the action and asked Anouilh to rewrite a couple of scenes in shorter form.

When *Becket* premiered on Broadway in October 1960 at the St. James Theatre on West 44th Street it failed to find universal approval. Reviewers acknowledged its "flashes of brilliance" but spoke if its "lack of unity." Peter admitted that by cutting an hour from Anouilh's three-hour-and-forty-minute script had damaged the play. But his choice of leading actors won plaudits, and Olivier took seventeen curtain calls on opening night, but the mixed reviews saw the show soon ailing. Peter offered to take a pay cut of 25%, although by the end of October he was still earning $900 a week (around $10,000 today) from his share of box-takings. However things began to improve and the big name actors attracted the crowds allowing *Becket* to run until March 1961 when Quinn left to make a film.

The show became Olivier's longest ever stretch on Broadway and he wrote to Peter to thank him "so infinitely much for the very great pleasure, respect, interest, fun and lovely cosiness of working with you. I had wanted to, as you know, for a very long time and it was so lovely for me to find . . . such instructive guidance and help beyond my dreams, because I was aware that they had built themselves up during the years. Thank you my dear dear Peter so deeply much for all your kindness and so much that was enchantingly delightful."

But the show was not over. Peter suggested taking it on tour and because Olivier was still available he took on the role of the King. He approached Gielgud to play Becket but he was busy, and eventually cast Arthur Kennedy as the cleric. One of Hollywood's finest players, Kennedy had won one Best Actor and four Best Supporting Oscar nominations between 1949 and 1959. He had also gained recognition in Arthur Miller plays on Broadway. The change in lineup worked wonderfully well and it broke box-office records in many cities. The production returned to Broadway in May for a short run at the Hudson Theatre, and became me profitable for the first time.

Before it started out on tour Olivier was nervous about his new role and after the production opened in Boston wrote to Bill: "[It] went very nicely last night, and I am greatly relieved that it's over and I was rather dreading it. It was lovely having Peter holding one's hand with such firm understanding and guiding pressure." The role switch won the critics' approval although, inevitably, he outperformed Kennedy, and it was Olivier's interpretation of the King that suggested his relationship with Becket was homoerotic. *Time* said: "Anouilh's Henry is . . . for an Olivier a fat part . . . Olivier catches him in a whole succession of picturesque moments and shifting moods. As against Quinn's clod-like vigour, Olivier's Henry has an easy swagger, a skipping verve; he can be cruel, capricious, ironic, every inch a king less for greatness of will than assertiveness of whim; and one who loved Becket, not just because of lifelong loneliness—domineering mother, dried-up wife, hen-brained children—but because Becket expertly pleased and amused him. And with scene after scene of pageantry thrown in, the part becomes a Field-of-the-Cloth-of-Gold day for Sir Laurence. The play gains by the switch also, emerging a livelier theatre piece. . . . But its playful side eats into its prayerful side, leaving Becket half snuffed out. If clear-spoken, Arthur Kennedy—who has not yet worked into the part—seems much too sober and colourless. With this second try at Henry, it becomes Henry II's show."

Olivier was a natural as the King and had Peter cast him in the role when the play first opened perhaps it may have had a warmer reception initially. The industry recognized *Becket* as an artistic success, and it gained five Tony nominations and won the Tony for Best Play. Peter's interest in the play was such that before it even opened he was thinking of making it into a film. He started exploring the possibility of acquiring the film rights as early as February 1960 and for the next four years he worked tirelessly to bring it to the screen.

Meanwhile Peter returned to a play he knew well, Tennessee Williams' *Summer and Smoke*, this time as a film for Paramount Pictures. Hal Wallis Productions had bought the film rights for $100,000 in 1952, shortly before its successful off-Broadway revival at the Circle in the Square. He decided to buy the rights following the successful film adaptations of Williams' *The Glass Menagerie* in 1950 and *A Streetcar Named Desire* in 1951. Wallis was a Hollywood titan and the legendary producer was behind 1930's *Little Caesar* and 1942's all-time great, *Casablanca*. Wallis had a feel for what would be a commercial success; frequently artistic considerations came second—he produced many Elvis Presley films.

A Hal Wallis Production attracted the cream of Hollywood talent. Laurence Harvey was hired as the tearaway doctor John Buchanan Jr., and Geraldine Page played the Southern spinster Alma Winemiller. Harvey had come a long way since his Broadway debut in the disastrous *Island of Goats*, gaining fame as the womanizing protagonist in *Room at the Top*. Page played Winemiller in the 1952 stage revival of *Summer and Smoke*, a performance that won her the Drama Critics Award. Since then she'd earned an Oscar nomination for her part opposite John Wayne in 1953's *Hondo*. Peter told the *Los Angeles Times*: "The first time I saw Geraldine Page, I was looking for someone to replace Margaret Leighton in *Separate Tables*. She looked kind of strange and sleazy with that mop of hair. But when she's acting, you can't take your eyes off her. People thought I was crazy when I wanted her to play the elegant girl of the first play. But I took her down to Elizabeth

Arden and to the best shops, showed her the latest collections, worked with her on makeup and hairstyle. And of course, she was wonderful."

Among the supporting cast was Rita Moreno as Rosa Zacharias, the Latin spitfire who seduces the wayward physician. She made her name as a concubine opposite Yul Brynner in the 1956 musical, *The King and I.* Una Merkel played Winemiller's unstable mother, and John McIntire played the patient father to a wayward son, Dr. Buchanan.

Harvey found difficulties mastering a Southern accent and Peter hired Louisiana-born voice coach Marguerite Lipman to help, it was the start of a lifelong friendship between Lipman and Peter. Whenever he and Bill visited London they stayed with Lipman and her husband Mark and she helped organize Peter's memorial service when he died: "He was autocratic in everything but with enormous charm, and so good looking one was hypnotised by his good looks. Everyone fell in love with Peter as far as I could see. He was very good with the crew and he noticed everything. Actors loved him, he always went to the person and talked to them quietly—he didn't scream across the set to say they'd done something wrong. . . . He was always hugging, very tactile. . . . He knew what he wanted but he wasn't vain in any sense. He was very decisive about everything about dresses, rooms, everything . . . he didn't miss a trick. You could tell when he was disapproving but, curiously, we never had a cross word. We were very, very close."

James Poe, who had worked on *Cat on a Hot Tin Roof*, and Meade Roberts, who worked on the adaptation of *Orpheus Descending* into the 1959 movie *The Fugitive Kind*, wrote the screenplay. Peter's take on *Summer and Smoke* was more than just a literal adaptation of play; he transformed it significantly with the author's approval: "Tennessee's road was the creation of a dreamlike stylisation. Ours was a realistic presentation of the physical passion and violence." Filmed in large-format Panavision, the movie has a lavish feel. It is full of color, music and crowded scenes that range from seedy cock fights at a gambling house to Moreno flouncing her skirts as she dances wildly at a drunken party.

His lively interpretation of the bittersweet tale of unrequited love was too much for some. *Summer and Smoke* drew mixed reactions from reviewers when it had its first showing in November 1961. The *New York Herald Tribune* found it "one of the better American films this year" while *Films in Review* thought it "confused and meaningless." *The New York Times*' Bosley Crowther said: "[The] few wispy moments, when the theme of frustration comes clear and one can see what Mr. Williams was pushing in this intimate, agonised tale—are pretty much drained of their intensity by the over-powering blasts of hot, thick fumes that come out of a seemingly always torch-lit production crowded with noisy characters, gingerbread scenery and bright costumes . . . [it is full of] melodramatic explosions that are made monstrous on the giant screen."

Peter wrote to Wallis, saying: "I am so glad that *Summer and Smoke* went well in Hollywood. [Laurence] Larry H[arvey] must be particularly pleased with his really splendid press. It is a pity about Mr. Crowther, but as I have disagreed with practically every notice he has ever written on any film I am not too surprised to be on the other side of the fence from him with regard to this one. It is also interesting to bear in mind that he considered Tennessee's *The Fugitive Kind*—the fate of which we all know—to be a great picture and a major achievement!"

But for *The Times* Peter's film was anything but "pageantesque": "In general film-makers tackling Mr. Williams' work, with or without his assistance, have tended to play up the violence, but in *Summer and Smoke* . . . Peter Glenville unexpectedly, and very effectively, goes in instead for understatement: this must surely be the quietest Tennessee Williams film yet made. . . . Every refinement that superior taste in setting and costume design can give is there: perhaps, indeed, because the familiar small-town American scene in the 1900s has been observed on this occasion by an Englishman the effect is somehow sharper, stranger and more revealing (to a European eye at least) than ever before. The film, in colour and wide-screen, is constantly a pleasure to look at, and moves relaxedly but with complete certainty until very near the end: in only three films Mr. Glenville has shaken off all traces of the theatre from his handling of the medium."

Critical opinion was divided about Harvey, who some felt was miscast, but unanimous regarding Page's virtuoso performance: "[*Summer and Smoke*] is still very much an actor's play, and here Mr. Glenville meets his only major misfortune: the casting of Mr. Laurence Harvey as the young doctor on the slippery path. Mr. Harvey is smooth and personable, but convinces neither as the iconoclastic wastrel with an insatiable thirst for experience of all sorts nor as the sadder and perhaps wiser man his father's death makes him. To set against this, however, there is a superb performance from Miss Geraldine Page as Alma . . . it is unmistakably her film."

Page was Oscar-nominated as Best Actress and netted National Board of Review and Golden Globe Awards. The film earned Oscar nominations for Best Art Direction and Best Score, and Merkel was nominated as Best Supporting Actress. More nominations came from the Directors Guild of America and the Venice Film Festival. The National Board of Review voted *Summer and Smoke* one of the ten best films of 1961.

The filming of *Summer and Smoke* finished in the spring. In the summer Peter told the *Los Angeles Times* how he felt about Hollywood: "I just wish I could take my house around. Some people seem quite happy with a suitcase, but I am not. I find that I can't work in a hotel—I have to have some little nest around me where I can rummage and build a fire."

In Peter's case the nest consisted of a rented hillside house overlooking Hollywood's Sunset Strip and southwest Los Angeles, a pile of trunks "filled with books and oddments and the things that I have collected along the way," and a dog.

Ever an animal lover, Peter's aged boxer had died. So he had a twelve-week-old pug, Fluellyn, sent from England to keep him company. To relax, Peter admitted he enjoyed reading history books: "The preoccupations of the stage and screen deal with the present moment, and the next moment is so different from this one. Everything is so transitory. The reading keeps a sense of balance."

He felt Hollywood was conducive to creative work and, like many Englishman abroad, he appreciated its climate: "Once here any Englishman enjoys the open air. To be able to pop into the pool all the time—it's wonderful. In London you have to make an appointment to play tennis."

Peter denied his work was a crusade "for anything other than quality": "I don't think a director should be saying anything. The job is to interpret a work well, providing you are in sympathy with it. If you are not, then you don't do it. . . . I am for example, a Roman Catholic and would probably not accept a violently anti-Catholic play. You have to admire, be excited by the creation of the writer."

When asked about the "sick" state of American theater he responded: "The so-called sick plays are a very natural reflection of that trend of interest in the society itself—an intense preoccupation with the solo soul, psychoanalysis. I don't think it is a bad thing. It has made for some great roles." He did concede that the need for box-office success was restricting: "You can't appeal to a small section of the public and be a success. And for the public, going to the theatre is not an everyday thing. It usually means going to a restaurant for dinner and then paying a high price for tickets. They only go to see the things that the paper tells them are an absolute must—the smash hits."

Peter then started to work on a movie for Warner Brothers, *The Devil in Bucks County*, based on Edmund Schiddel's 1959 novel satirizing life in an artists' colony. The project was cancelled by the autumn and Peter was paid $50,000. Peter was given opportunity to return to the West End to direct Rattigan's *Man and Boy*, the story of a ruthless businessman, Gregor Antonescu and his inability to love. It was based on the Swedish match manufacturer, financial genius and swindler, Ivar Kreuger, whose machinations were exposed by the Wall Street Crash in 1929.

Rattigan wrote to Beaumont in September asking if the impresario could arrange for Peter to take over the director's role from Glen Byam Shaw: "From the beginning I told you that I wanted Peter Glenville. The information given me was that his tax position prevented him from doing the play in England. When we decided on doing an English production I agreed to Glen's reading the play only because I presumed he was unavailable. I now find that this is not so. He has read the play, is wildly enthusiastic about it, he says he thinks it is my best and, as he has already done three others of mine, two of which were great successes (it's a generous judgment) and in a week's close talks, in Venice and Paris, seems to see the play exactly as I see it.

"In other words, such changes as he wants me to make in the play are designed to strengthen it rather than water it down. His first words—on meeting me in Paris after a very quick reading of the play—went straight to its heart. After compliments—told above—he asked whether Gregor's inhumanity was God-given or man-given. In a week's talks with Glen I had hardly got beyond discussing what coloured shirt the boy should put on (if, indeed, he should put on any), whether or not he had masturbated (or how I could make it unequivocally clear that he had not been masturbated by a prefect), and what is the semantic difference between girlishness and effeminacy.

"Peter's first question is the most important question the play should try to answer. All the rest is subordinate. Glen had never, in a week's passionate talks, got anywhere near it. Nor, I sincerely believe, ever would . . . [Peter] would like to direct, and I am now utterly determined he shall."

Byam Shaw was sacked but in October Peter wrote to Rattigan with "very disappointing news": "Frankly, I am told that the penalties and dangers of accepting such an assignment in London are too serious to be sensible. The real problem is that I am trying to establish my past and future intention of non-residence. If I embark on a theatrical project within a month of the termination of my official three years' absence, apparently it will cast a doubt on my whole intentions on the matter. Furthermore, when I film *Becket* in France there is a strong probability of my being called upon to do a certain section of it in London. As this is a Hollywood film being made in Europe I can, apparently, get away with this work in London without it affecting my overall position. However, it seems the situation would change very considerably if I had already undertaken a totally English theatrical production. As you probably know, when you are taking up a position as a genuine non-resident your movements and business activities are open to scrutiny and interpretation by the [Inland] Revenue chaps. . . .

"Not only do I love the play incidentally, so does Bill, whose judgement I trust because he has almost always been right. He was immensely enthusiastic about it. But it would have been such wonderful fun to work together again. I am sure that if you have a strong and honest production of the play it will be an important theatrical event. Lovely, too, for you to deliver such a strong body blow which can surpass the formless shock tactics of the New Wave writers with their boring anti-middle-class snobbery."

Peter then wrote to Beaumont saying he had consulted a lawyer in America and an accountant in London to say that taking on the production would cause "grave practical and financial penalties" for him and even rehearsing the play in Dublin wouldn't work as fees from royalties and profit participation would all be subject to the maximum level of English tax. He also told Beaumont he had entreated Rattigan to "consider engaging an evocative, new look, non-realistic American designer [saying], 'If ever there was a play that deserved not to have a box set with French windows opening onto a sun-lit village, it is yours.'" Beaumont wrote to Rattigan saying Peter's news came as "a complete bombshell": "In all my talks, he had I must admit, stressed that he would be making a great sacrifice but it never appeared that there was any doubt that he would be available." Rattigan lamented the lack of Peter's direction but Peter's tax affairs were so complex that they may have played a part in his decision.

In October Peter headed for Dublin and Paris to begin filming *Term of Trial*. The screenplay was based on a novel of the same name by James Barlow, and the black-and-white film is a gritty story set in the north of England, telling of a schoolteacher and a man of principle, Graham Weir. He's also a conscientious objector who refused to fight in the Second World War whose career stalled as a result. Weir is stuck in a school where the majority of pupils are surly, misbehaved and disinterested, with a French wife, Anna, who treats him with disdain. The tedium is partly lifted by one of his pupils, Shirley Taylor, a shy girl with some ambition who Weir agrees to give some private tuition. She develops a schoolgirl crush and on a school trip to Paris, Weir rejects her advances. Humiliated, the teenager, egged on by her shrewish mother, accuses him of indecent assault. When the case comes to trial, the girl confesses that she has fabricated the story and Weir goes free, but his wife still regards him as an effete coward. In order to save his marriage, and appear to be the man his wife wants him to be, Weir abandons his ideals and pretends that he did have an affair with his pupil.

The producer John Romulus sent the proof pages of Barlow's novel to Peter who was impressed after he read the book. John and his brother James felt likewise and their company, Remus Films Limited, bought the rights to make a picture for Warner Brothers. Peter adapted the novel into a screenplay while he was at the Venice Film Festival in the summer of 1961 and developed the character of the schoolmaster's wife "into a woman who is less a fishwife and more a complex human being."

He was paid $40,000 for his efforts, plus $150,000 for directing, and 10% of net profits.

Prior to going to Venice Peter had to go to New York to work with Olivier on his role switch in *Becket* and he took the opportunity to persuade Olivier to play Weir. He told the *Los Angeles Times*: "I felt that Larry was the perfect, and in many ways the only actor for the part . . . I had a copy of the book with me but he was working terribly hard, performing at night and rehearsing the King during the day. So it wasn't till after we opened *Becket* in Boston and Larry had received the glowing notices for his new performance that I suggested he read it.

"The suite we shared at the Ritz-Carlton was waist-deep in scripts which had already been sent to him. Larry protested that he really didn't have the time to read *Term of Trial* immediately. However, I persuaded him—wishfully thinking I might hear from him about it in a week or two."

Olivier accepted the part three days later. Peter then set his sights on earthy French actress Simone Signoret to play the schoolteacher's nagging wife, although she hadn't accepted any English-speaking roles since winning a Best Actress Oscar for *Room at the Top*. "She knew the picture was not a vehicle for her, but the role interested her and all she asked was that she have a reading with me to see if she felt she could play it," said Peter. "It's an unusual role in any respect, certainly an unusual one for Simone. After the reading we both knew she was exactly right."

It wasn't the first time Peter tried to hire the actress as Signoret revealed: "Glenville, whom I didn't know, came one day to ask me to do a film in Hollywood. . . . I explained politely even before I read the script, that he was wasting his time. I had no visa for America, I had never asked for one, and each time there had been a vague offer of my participating in an American production made in France, negotiations had rapidly broken off. . . . Peter Glenville replied, 'But McCarthy's dead!'

"Bill Goetz, his American producer, was in Paris and wanted to see me. So Mr. Goetz came. In the meantime, I had read the script. It was a comedy. I decided that I was neither young enough nor frivolous enough to play this archetypically French lady. I told them so. That's no snag, they said. They would change the character [to be] tailor made for me. . . .

"A few days later I received from Hollywood a long telegram of several pages. Bill Goetz explained to me that for reasons he couldn't explain, the dream he and Peter Glenville had had of seeing me in the film they were about to begin unfortunately had to be abandoned. . . . McCarthy was not dead, even if the citizens of his country thought they had buried him. . . . I was convinced that I would never see Bill Goetz or Peter Glenville again."

According to Signoret, Peter was irritated by her refusal but it did not put him off and he called the actress from the airport in Paris saying he wanted to meet her in the few hours he had while in transit from London to Los Angeles. Peter, thinking flattery might work, told Signoret that he had made the trip especially to ask her to be in his next film, which was to be English made with an English producer. Signoret agreed to see him saying: "Like a good director, he timed the scene carefully. He opened his suitcase and took out a book, covering the title with his hand for a second. He said, 'This is the book,' and put it down on the table."

It was '*Room at the Top*, by John Braine' and Peter was considering directing the film of the best-selling book. While any English actress would have jumped at the chance, Signoret was oblivious to its existence. Peter, undeterred, urged her to read it before leaving to catch his Los Angeles flight. "I didn't do *Room at the Top* with Peter Glenville directing, the film was directed by Jack Clayton. But it's impossible for me not to associate Peter with the watershed in my professional career this film proved to be," she recalled. He did Signoret a huge service by persuading her to do *Room at the Top* because she and her husband, actor Yves Montand, were political activists, and America's conservative establishment during the McCarthy era refused to give the couple entry visas. *Room at the Top* garnered Signoret international acclaim and a fistful of awards.

Peter then set about casting the role of the schoolgirl. He and Jimmy Woolf had seen a young actress fresh out of drama school performing at Worthing Repertory Company; it was the 18-year-old Sarah Miles. They contacted her agent and had her rush from a matinée performance at Worthing, only to arrive to discover there were two hundred other actresses in a queue, all of them blonde. When it came to her audition Peter told her to calm down and read some lines and Miles was one of a dozen hopefuls called back to read for a second time, this time opposite her idol, Olivier—she had kept a photo of the actor under her pillow for more than six years. Afterwards Peter asked her if she would die her hair blonde for the part: "I had died it brunette and was worried that [dying it once more would make it] fall out. Larry Olivier piped up that he would have cut off his right hand for the part, and then I burst into tears. Peter told me I could go. I replied, 'You can't let me go, it's not fair, it's a cliché wanting a blonde.' A tirade ensued and I had to be almost pushed out the door. Two weeks later my agent called and told me I had the part and could wear a wig." Peter said he believed she was "going to be an important actress."

The film quickly went into production to fit in with Olivier's busy schedule. The cast included Terence Stamp as one of Weir's nastier pupils, Mitchell—the 22-year-old actor had just finished making Sir Peter Ustinov's film adaptation of Herman Melville's *Billy Budd*, for which he won an Oscar nomination. Thora Hird played the schoolgirl's vindictive mother, and the supporting cast included Roland Culver, Frank Pettingell and Rosamund Greenwood.

Miles enjoyed her time on *Term of Trial*, and described Peter as "a good captain of a happy ship": "He was an absolute gentleman and good chap. I really respected and liked him. . . . He was a man of great manners and intelligence . . . and Larry had a lot of respect for him and that was very important. Peter was a man who was very generous of heart, something uncommon in this day and age." Peter's thoughtfulness and skill as a director were crucial when Miles doubted her performance during the filming of the trial scene: "It was the end of filming, the set was being dismantled and Larry was going home. I went back to my hotel and that night I realised I had done the scene wrong. I went to Larry and told him, who asked me, 'How should it be?' I showed him and he said, 'You're right, go to Peter and tell him you did it wrong.' I asked if he would back me up and he agreed to do so. I knocked on Peter's door and told him, 'I think I can do this a better way for your film.' He said, 'No.' I said, 'Please, and then performed the piece.' Peter agreed to let me redo the scene if Larry would stay on for free and they could keep up the set. What a great gift: he believed in me and his film."

The film's depiction of sex and violence among teenagers sailed close to what censors would accept at the time, but Peter remained adamant that its downbeat appearance was necessary, and was sufficiently concerned that he wrote to Warner Brothers in January to ensure that censors understood his position: "I want to make it clear that I am making what I sincerely consider to be a picture with a strong and impeccably moral point of view. In general the theme concerns a sensitive and intelligent man who is dedicated to teaching and to helping the young and who, because of his pacifist principles, finds himself teaching in a neighbourhood where the teenagers have succumbed to the influence of violence, cheap sexuality and an overall poverty of the spirit. He is also married to a woman with whom he is in love but who is herself, although attractive, an ordinary and rathercoarse and selfish woman who had hoped to better herself by the marriage and who now turns upon the hero the full measure of her discontent. . . .

"In order to properly illustrate this theme it is necessary to show the violence, vulgarity and sexuality of these people and their surroundings, not because as scriptwriter and director I have any preoccupation with these things (indeed they are always dismal), but in order to show the dilemma and the fight of a fine character at odds with his environment. Unless the cheapness and evil amongst which he finds himself are really strong and frightening, he will give the impression of being a goody-goody fool with no reason to suffer and the film will lose the possibility of making its impact and point, particularly from a moral point of view.

"I am convinced that unless we show clearly and forcefully what the hero is up against, he will not be a hero and if he is not and if the audience is not in a proper sense 'shocked' into identifying themselves with his point of view, the film runs the danger of losing any moral point whatsoever. On the other hand I think that the way it is being shot and acted will make it very clear that the cheapness, sexuality and violence (of which there is really very little) are unappetising, unattractive and give neither pleasure, satisfaction nor happiness to any of the participants. . . . The bitter irony of the ending is that the hero, who has a fine and sensitive nature, realises that his wife whom he loves is at heart a rather base and coarse person who does not appreciate either his moral standards or his ideals and in fact, although she is physically attracted to him, she rather dismisses him for being 'so bloody noble about everything.' In a moment of crisis when she threatens to leave him he makes one desperate compromise in pretending to her that she cannot be so sure of him or his behaviour and that he is capable of infidelity. Once the foolish woman suspects that she cannot be so sure of him and that he might be interested elsewhere, she becomes re-involved in the relationship but we know that this will be no solution. The man hates to tell the lie and the woman will later blame him for the very admission that he has made. The important point is that the audience should sympathise with the hero's point of view, and I am sure that as it is being played they will.

"However, I must repeat that if we tone down the ugliness

surrounding him there is a real danger that he will in fact appear to the audience to be what his wife accuses him of being, namely gutless, wet and over noble. If this should happen the whole point of view of the film becomes lopsided, the audience would then sympathise with the wife and the immoral implication that the Code officials wish to avoid in the ending would in fact be achieved."

Even with its great cast, the film failed to find favor when it premiered in London in August 1962 nor when it had its first showing in America early the following year. *The New York Times* said *Term of Trial* was "not an exciting picture" and *The New Yorker* went so far as to label it an "unnecessary" one.

The *Los Angeles Times* conceded that it was an absorbing film and Peter's "most incisively cinematic to date." However, reviewers did agree that Miles was a "discovery." They also agreed that Olivier's otherwise low-key performance was raised when he made his impassioned defence in the trial scene. Peter had decided to film it as one uninterrupted take and it certainly worked. In part the reviewers' difficulty with the film was accepting Olivier as a common man, verging on an underdog; the *Daily Express* complained: "[Olivier] can play a king—but he cannot play a mouse."

The film's grainy naturalism and Olivier's uncharacteristically subdued performance didn't deter awards judges. Olivier was nominated for a BAFTA as Best Actor and Miles won a BAFTA for Most Promising Newcomer to Leading Film Roles. Peter was nominated for a Golden Lion at the Venice Film Festival, and *Term of Trial* won the 1962 Grand Prix Award from the Office Catholique Internationale du Cinéma.

At the time of *Term of Trial*'s London premiere Peter and Bill were hard at work clearing two apartments on the principal floor of their Manhattan home, "the prize rooms of the building." They had done some renovations to the house, but having spent so time in Europe progress was slow. They considered selling it for an estimated $525,000. But their income from tenants was substantial $56,000 per annum, and their real desire was to make the two apartments into one and live there. They kept the house and began to formulate ideas with the help of a designer.

Peter was also back working on Broadway rehearsing *Tchin-Tchin*, adapted by Sidney Michaels from a French play by François Billetdoux. The show reunited Peter with Merrick, as producer, and Quinn and Leighton in the lead roles of Caesario Grimaldi and Pamela Pew-Pickett. Quinn played an Italian-American contractor and Leighton an uptight English woman married to a doctor. The pair arranges to meet at New York restaurant to discuss their respective spouses' affair and then find solace in each other when they make love in a tawdry hotel. Months later—and divorced—they meet again. Quinn's character is now a workaholic, and Leighton's an alcoholic. They decide to share their lives together in a sibling-like relationship as a way of avoiding their loneliness.

In his autobiography Quinn talked of how art partially reflected life as he managed to juggle three relationships while performing in *Tchin-Tchin*. He revealed how, in a desperate search for a place to conduct an affair with Leighton, they hired a limousine and turned their lovemaking into "a moveable feast": "We must have made a scandalous picture, me and my eager star, our asses pressed recklessly against the tinted windows as we toured New York City." At the time Quinn was married to the daughter of legendary film director Cecil B. DeMille, Canadian actress Katherine DeMille, and had a mistress, costume designer Iolanda Addolori, who was pregnant with their first child. Margaret Leighton was recently divorced from Laurence Harvey.

Some reviewers regarded the play as portraying two people who had lost their souls in alcohol, and others saw it as an allegory of Christian salvation. But its mix of intellectualism and gentle comedy managed to find an audience. After *Tchin-Tchin* opened at the Plymouth Theatre in October 1962 *Time* described it as "a Christian existential fable": "*Tchin-Tchin* is magical. It is also fragile, but it is saved from wispiness by Leighton and Quinn. . . . Director Peter Glenville propels the play toward its one compelling conclusion: that life is a fatal adventure." *Tchin-Tchin* was a success, although it courted controversy along the way. It played to packed house for the first six months of its seven-month run, and garnered Tony nominations for Best Play, Best Actress, Best Scenic Design and Best Direction.

During the run Quinn decided he had to end his affair with Leighton and made excuses to his wife saying he had to leave America to make a film in Rome, where he intended to join his mistress. When Quinn told Leighton of his departure, she decided to quit *Tchin-Tchin* and follow him to Europe. Merrick hired Jack Klugman and Arlene Francis to replace them. But the spell was broken and the play closed within a month. Quinn divorced DeMille and married Addolori.

Peter's take on Leighton's behavior was one of concern, and he wrote to his agent at the William Morris Agency: "Several reports have come back to me about Maggie [Leighton]'s health and state of mind. I felt very sad about her not appearing with the substitute when Tony Quinn left the play. Not of course on account of what it did to the production, but because of the shock and disappointment at hearing of behavior so unprofessional and uncharacteristic on the part on an actress usually known for her impeccable behaviour and general theatrical fortitude.

"I am also deeply fond of Maggie and can only imagine that she could conduct herself in this way if she were suffering under considerable strain and momentary loss of balance. I have been worried about her appearance for some time and I have heard it suggested that she may be using medicaments which are not good at all for her. Is it not possible that she should see a good doctor . . . who could take her in hand? I have a very strong hunch that somebody in a position to do so should persuade her to take a couple of weeks in a nice health clinic where she could eat and sleep properly. There is no doubt about the fact that everybody who has seen her agrees that she is not at all well and seems completely changed form what she was say a year ago. . . . I hate to think of Maggie going into a real decline. She has enough nervous wiry energy to keep going with her chin comparatively up when in fact she is in need of strong medical advice and attention."

Peter's next task was to step in as the director on a musical already up and running, *Tovarich*. It was based on a comedy by Jacques Deval and Robert E. Sherwood adapted from Duval's original French play that had been a hit on Broadway in 1936 and as a film in 1937. "Tovarich" means "comrade" in Russian and the story follows the fortunes of two Russian refugees, Tatiana and Mikail, who flee the Bolshevik Revolution. A duchess and a former general, they become a maid and a butler in Paris. The couple didn't escape their homeland empty-handed and have four million francs of the Tsar's money tucked away in a Swiss bank, which their former leader has entrusted them to keep safe. Headed by Soviet Commissar Gorotchenko, the Bolsheviks pursue the pair to France in an attempt to get hold of the loot.

Tovarich was choreographed by Peter's former colleague on *Take Me Along*, Herb Ross, and the libretto written by David Shaw. Music was by Lee Pockriss and lyrics by Anne Croswell. Pockriss had written the scores for several Broadway shows and films, as well as pop songs that included 1957's Grammy-nominated *Catch a Falling Star* and 1960's novelty hit, *Itsy Bitsy Teenie Weenie Yellow Polka Dot Bikini*. It was Vivien Leigh's debut as a singer and dancer but her erratic behavior meant that the production was fraught with difficulty.

After her divorce from Olivier, she found a new partner, actor Jack Merivale, but Leigh was in a fragile state of health; she had bipolar disorder and was prone to bouts of tuberculosis. Merivale was a stabilizing influence on the actress and she was persuaded to take on the role by the show's producer Abel

Farbman. Leigh was convinced that exploring a new medium would be exciting, but her nervousness about her role, the periods of separation from Merivale and her grief for her failed marriage to Olivier exacerbated her mood swings—and threatened the production.

Her co-star was French actor Jean-Pierre Aumont. Like Leigh the 50-year-old Aumont had never done a stage musical so unsurprisingly on the show's tryout tour in Philadelphia they found themselves floundering in an alien medium. Because of the singing and dancing scenes, timings change, tweaks are made and what arrives on Broadway may depart significantly from the tryout. During rehearsals Leigh and Aumont had sung and danced to a piano accompaniment. When they arrived in Philadelphia they performed with an orchestra for the first time. It was a nerve-wracking experience and Leigh started to hate the show and its director, Delbert Mann.

Despite the actors' qualms, critics were generous in their praise after the first night—thrilled by seeing the Oscar-winning star of *Gone with the Wind* and *A Streetcar Named Desire* dancing in a simple black dress and white organdie apron; they also felt it was dated. The worried Farbman dismissed Mann and hired Peter to try to sort out the problems. According to Aumont: "I knew Peter well. He had planned on producing *Un Beau Dimanche* (*A Beautiful Sunday*), a play of mine, in London. I was happy to work with him."

Peter was unquestionably a safe pair of hands and respected in the industry, but this production tested both his mettle and management skills. He immediately caused ructions by sacking two supporting actors as well as axing several numbers. Scenes were cut and lines changed—often to fit in with Leigh's caprice—as the show continued on tour to Boston, where it broke box-office records.

When the musical opened at Manhattan's Broadway Theatre in March 1963, critics praised the cast's comedy skills and Leigh's husky voice and sprightly dancing. The comedy's "visual splendors," the Motleys' "remarkable" quaint 1920s costumes and Peter's skill in bringing together his thirty-nine-strong cast were credited with creating "a sumptuous, amusing and tasteful show." The show ran until November and the writers won a Grammy nomination for Original Cast Album. Leigh won the 1963 Tony for Best Actress in a Musical.

All this was against a backdrop of backstage drama during the show's Broadway run. Leigh's moods constantly fluctuated and plans were made to close the show for a week in the autumn to allow her to recover from what was an exhausting role. As the production headed toward its proposed hiatus, disaster struck when Leigh broke down on stage. Aumont describes how prior to playing a matinée he found Leigh crying in her dressing room and listening to a tape of the theme tune to *Gone with the Wind*. Her performance in the first act was inconsistent and she sang too fast. In the following act the situation got worse according to Aumont: "The second act began without either of us speaking one word to the other. Then came the jealousy scene in which she was supposed to admit to having been raped by her jailer. At that moment, her old repulsion for these lines (that she'd expressed since the first rehearsals) rose up from the depths of her subconscious. She began to claw me, slap me in the face, and kick me in the balls. Since it was a quarrel scene I tried to make the audience believe that this boxing exhibition had been planned. . . .

"Unfortunately, Vivien [Leigh] stopped suddenly and, wrapping herself in total silence, looked at me, then through me at the entire world, with hatred. I began to improvise in an attempt to lead her back on the right track. . . . The explosive silence continued. . . . Then Vivien came to the edge of the stage. She looked out at the whole auditorium and spoke carefully enunciating each syllable: 'An actress has to think before answering,' and she walked off."

The curtain dropped, and two actors were then sent on to do a number they had performed already. Leigh made it back on stage for the closing waltz scene, although she refused to dance. When Aumont returned to his dressing room he found that his co-star had destroyed photographs of his wife and family, and that doctors were trying to sedate the actress with morphine. Leigh's understudy took over for the evening performance. Leigh fought to make her entrance and so was confined to her dressing room. The next day she was flown to London while under sedation and later underwent electric-shock therapy. When it was obvious Leigh would not be returning to *Tovarich*, Eva Gabor stepped in for the last three weeks of the run. Leigh died three years later from tuberculosis.

Peter had shown he was as much as a master on Broadway as in the West End, and that he was a steady hand when it came to managing the industry's top names—and their egos. Most people would have felt content. But Peter was always ambitious and must have been aware that a masterpiece in celluloid still eluded him. *Summer and Smoke* and *Term of Trial* had failed to establish his reputation as a top film director, and cinema was where he could create a work that would outlive him. Despite the plaudits his cast and crew achieved, he had yet to achieve the Holy Grail of movies for himself: an Oscar nomination. This must have been on his mind such was his desire for perfection and belief in his own talent.

10

A Canterbury Tale

1963-1964

After the drama of working with Vivien Leigh, Peter returned to familiar territory and a project that was arguably the pinnacle of his career. He had seen the cinematic potential of *Becket* long before he took it to Broadway and so Peter spent the summer of 1963 filming Anouilh's play. There is still debate as to whether it should be regarded as a good film or great film; a "club-footed drama" or worse. In any event Peter drew on the skills of friends and colleagues he had worked with for decades—bringing together a generation of actors on celluloid in itself was a major feat. Peter's persuasive skills reached new heights as he charmed, cajoled, wheedled and sweet-talked some of Britain's finest actors into working on the film and *Becket* would never have made it to the big screen without his doggedness and skill.

Casting Richard Burton and Peter O'Toole in *Becke*t was a stroke of genius. Their on-screen sparring as the cleric and the king is magnificent, their off-screen antics have made movie myth. But *Becket* is much more than just two actors playing at their peak. Its cast list reads like a "Who's Who" of British theater: John Gielgud as King Louis VII of France,

Donald Wolfit as the Bishop of London, Felix Aylmer as the Archbishop of Canterbury, Martita Hunt as Queen Matilda, Pamela Brown as Queen Eleanor and Frank Pettingell as the Bishop of York. In addition there are numerous lesser known, but nonetheless, fine actors. Two famous Italian actors, Paola Stoppi and Gino Cervi, played the men from the Vatican: Pope Alexander III and Cardinal Zambelli. Among the classical actors familiar to patrons of the Old Vic and Stratford Memorial Theatre were John Phillips as the Bishop of Winchester, Geoffrey Bayldon as Brother Philip, and Percy Herbert, Niall MacGinnis and Peter Jeffrey as King Henry II's barons. There were also some new faces, including O'Toole's wife Siân Phillips, as the ill-fated Gwendolen, and those yet to become big names—Victor Spinetti as the French Tailor and Edward Woodward as Clement.

Behind the scenes Peter put together a crew equal to the talents of his cast. Laurence Rosenthal wrote the score, Geoffrey Unsworth did the photography, Anne V. Coates the film editing, John Bryan the production design and Margaret Furse the costume design. Few could assemble such a cast and crew; movie history says this is because it was a Hal Wallis Production, and there is no denying Wallis played a major role in getting *Becket* on to the screen, but according to Rosenthal: "Peter Glenville triumphed over Hollywood. . . . *Becket* happened in spite of Hal Wallis, not because of him."

Before one camera turned Peter knew that working with Wallis could prove problematic. He wrote to his agent at William Morris in 1962: "There is . . . the question with a strong producer like Hal [Wallis] of what really eventuates when we get down to specifics about the whole film and what liberty he will permit me in the making of it."

Peter knew he would have to fight for recognition: "I notice that Hal makes a very special point of billing himself over the title in the same lettering and prominence as the stars . . . in *Summer and Smoke* he has billed me as director in rather smaller letters than Earl Holliman at the bottom of the advertisement and it is totally illegible because of the size of the letters." Peter found this "totally absurd." He didn't want the same treatment on *Becket* since he felt he had secured the film rights to the play and chased its stars: "In the case of *Becket* Hal Wallis has in fact bought the play on account of my production of it in New York where my contribution was billed above the title as 'Peter Glenville's production of –'. Naturally Hal will want this credit himself for the film but I suggest we should ask for 'Directed by Peter Glenville' directly under the title in, say, fifty per cent of the size of the title lettering."

His fears were not unfounded. Peter's contribution in bringing *Becket* to cinematic life has been overlooked; it tested his determination no end. He battled with Wallis to get what he wanted artistically and to see that Anouilh got the billing he was due. He fought over the Oscar-winning screenplay adaptation, doing a lot of work on it while getting no credit. All the while he managed to keep a sense of humor, particularly when Elizabeth Taylor arrived on set to be with her new lover, Richard Burton, and when the Welsh actor and O'Toole had a few too many drinks on a few too many occasions.

It is a film of sumptuous color, extravagant sets and opulent costumes; Gregorian chant and a rich score that add to its drama along with scenes of ecclesiastical sanctity that seem so plausible one can even smell a whiff of incense. It sparkles with wit, drama, passion and pain. O'Toole's manic beleaguered king jumps off the screen and Burton, known as hell raiser, makes a convincing saint, in a part that was one of the most challenging he ever played. The pair created a sense of bonhomie on screen that they shared off set.

The story of *Becket* began in February 1960 when Peter secured the go-ahead from Anouilh and translator Hill to make a pre-production film deal. For his services Peter asked for $200,000 plus 10% of grosses of the play in New York during winning weeks up to a limit of $450,000. He had the authority to seek a film-production deal by June 30, 1960. Hal Wallis' company bought the film rights, and Wallis produced *Becket* together with executive producer Joseph "Joe" H. Hazen.

Wallis had seen *Becket* on Broadway with Olivier and Quinn and was "completely enthralled" by it. He later said: "It struck me then that *Becket* would make a distinguished and exciting motion picture . . . [it] was that all too rare combination of dramatic ingredients: it had in it the elements of a big, spectacle picture and at the same time it was basically an intimate, literate, witty and adult drama. Against the sweep of medieval history, amidst the colour and pageantry, kings and palaces, courts, cathedrals and fields of battle, there was the underlying conflict of two friends who had turned against each other."

Wallis brought Peter onboard as director and asked him to adapt the existing script into a screenplay. They agreed that Peter would deliver a first draft screenplay by May 1, 1962, and that production would start in England about April 1, 1963. However, in August 1961 Hazen realized that the proposal would mean they would spend eight months unable to make commitments for studio space. They asked Peter for the screenplay by January 1, 1962, saying that if he couldn't do it, they were open to hiring a British screenwriter; they had nothing against Peter as the screenwriter, it was strictly a scheduling matter.

Peter suggested that he could find an English writer, mentioning dramatist Peter Shaffer to do the first draft instead of doing it himself—thereby using the period in which Peter would film *Term of Trial*. Peter wrote to Wallis while he was preparing to shoot *Term of Trial* in Ireland: "This would mean that by February we might have an interesting point of departure for the film, and I could then take on a script writing either alone or with the original writer and then use the time I was going to give you anyway before May to make the changes and rewrites that will undoubtedly be necessary." This would bring them nearer the goal of a "slightly earlier start date, namely around the New Year 1963." If Shaffer wasn't available, Peter suggested approaching John Mortimer.

In February 1962 Peter left Ireland to finish shooting *Term of Trial* in France. When March arrived, an anxious Wallis sent him a cable regarding the progress of the screenplay: "All plans for cast dependent on script and would appreciate your cabling advice how script progressing . . . when may I expect same or portion of it." Peter replied that he was finishing the last two days of on *Term of Trial* in Paris, and would then start scripting *Becket* to deliver in May. Wallis said there had been a misunderstanding and that he thought Peter would be writing the script during long evenings in Ireland when he had nothing to do. He wrote to Peter in March: "Frankly, I don't know how you can do a script between now and 1 May, but that is up to you."

Peter attempted to allay Wallis' fears by explaining that he had already done a large amount of preparatory work on *Becket*. He had amassed a large amount of historical material that, should they decide to deviate from Anouilh's interpretation of the saint's life, they could draw on, but he felt that the film should follow Anouilh's play for the first half of the story. He intended to depart from the play in the second half as he had "always felt that Becket's conversion to a religious way of life is sketched rather coldly in the play. The big prayer scene and another in which he confronts the bishops with his arguments for the independence of the Church are far too cerebral and intellectually sophisticated to hold on screen." He flagged up that his first draft of the script may not be completed until mid-May—he had to go to London to do ten days of dubbing on *Term of Trial*. He delivered the first draft on May 15. Wallis found it too verbose, so Peter set about changing it.

During this time Peter made his biggest mistake by failing to contact the Writers Guild of America to say he was writing the script; having done so much work on it he should have expected a credit. In fact he only began the process of attempting to get his credit in September 1963, by which time Edward Anhalt had also worked on the screenplay. Anhalt had worked for Wallis on the 1962 Elvis Presley vehicle *Girls! Girls! Girls!* and the 1965 Tony Curtis and Jerry Lewis comedy, *Boeing Boeing*, having previously won an Oscar for Elia Kazan's 1950 thriller *Panic in the Streets*. On September 9 a "notice of Tentative Writing Credits" was sent to the guild listing Anhalt, Anouilh, Peter and Wallis, in that order. But only "Screenplay by Edward Anhalt" and "Based on the Play by Jean Anouilh, as translated by Lucienne Hill and produced on the New York stage by David Merrick" were set to appear on screen. The producers gave the sole screen credit to Anhalt and left Peter to protest to the guild alone.

Wallis himself felt he had contributed sufficiently to the script to also ask for a co-credit, and based his decision to leave the accreditation as Anhalt's because he "wanted the movie to adhere as closely as possible to Hill's translation." Because Peter had worked on the translation when he staged *Becket*, he was less inclined to let the matter go.

Peter sent the guild a seven-page long assessment of the work he and Anhalt did on the script. He pointed out that he did the first draft with limited revisions by Wallis, and then Anhalt did a revised draft. Peter objected to many of the changes and "at meetings with Hal Wallis it was agreed that much of the original material should be restored and further revisions made." Wallis asked Anhalt to make the revisions, restoring much of the original script. Peter then went "to Hollywood in November and did his own revisions, and then in correspondence with Mr. Wallis continued to make further revisions and add material. [He] then returned to Hollywood for further meetings with Mr. Wallis and Mr. O'Toole, as a result of which additional material was incorporated into the script by [him. He] then went to England and in consultation with the producer did further work on the script, resulting in two more revised copies before the final shooting script. In the course of the film he also wrote additional material, including one completely new sequence, a copy of which is also enclosed."

On September 24, 1963, Peter wrote to the guild making his case for a screen credit on the film: "I had imagined that as I started work six months before the shooting of the film in a writing capacity that my rights in the matter would be those of any member of the Screen Writers Guild commencing exclusive work on the script. . . . I was responsible for the first draft treatment of the script, *Becket*, written between March 14 1962, and May 15 1962, which were sent to Mr. Hazen in Paris and a copy was sent to Mr. Wallis in Hollywood. Mr. Wallis then sent me some notes which required revisions on May 21 1962, which are enclosed, and I myself came to Hollywood from Europe and worked on these changes in July of 1962."

Peter said it had been agreed that a new writer would be brought in for additional dialogue and ideas: "I am afraid that I was not completely in agreement with his choice for this particular assignment. . . . Mr. Anhalt's revised script that it enclosed was given to me by Mr. Wallis at the end ofAugust when both Mr. Wallis and myself were in New York. I then sent him a letter on the 26 of August explaining that I could not go along with this new script . . . suggesting that I should retire from the production if he wished to proceed with the script as written. I then had a meeting with Mr. Wallis on the 28, and he admitted that he too was seriously disturbed by the Anhalt script as it stood and that before I made any final decision he would like me to give him my ideas for reconstruction and for restoring many of the values that had been lost from my original draft—most of which of course were the values that I felt necessary to retain from the original Anouilh play. I had several sessions with Mr. Wallis discussing this."

Peter received an amended script incorporating changes he requested and to which Wallis agreed. Peter still disagreed on a number of points, and went to Hollywood in November to revise the October script, which resulted in the script of December

5, 1962. On December 21, Peter returned to Hollywood again for a conference with Wallis and O'Toole. The actor made requests for scene changes, which were agreed. Peter returned to New York and incorporated the requested scenes and sent them to Wallis. Throughout the early part of the year Peter and Wallis corresponded, which resulted in a "fourth revised temporary yellow and a final shooting script." According to Peter, "I specifically claim ninety per cent of all the revisions made subsequent to Anhalt's revised script of 29 October."

The guild pooled together a team of arbitrators to decide on the issue and Peter sent in the two semi-final scripts and shooting script saying: "All revisions in these scripts were made by me." He included a detailed assessment of work done on script, saying: "I think it is an honest assessment of the work done by both parties." The guild found against Peter, and with a touch of irony awarded Anhalt the 1965 Writer Guild Award for Best Written Drama for *Becket*. History is written by the victors, and Peter was very definitely the loser. Whether he deserved a co-credit for the screenplay or not was judged by experts at the time. Nevertheless, Peter made a large contribution to the screenplay and it must have been bittersweet for him when Anhalt took home *Becket*'s one and only Oscar.

Peter also lost out when it came to the location shooting. If Wallis had been prepared to spend a little more money on location shoots *Becket* could have acquired an epic status. It could have avoided a theatrical look and feel that Peter was desperate to avoid, as he wrote to Wallis: "There are certain overall artistic production requirements that in my opinion as director are necessities to give the production reality and life so that it does not look like a theatrical pageant put on film. This in turn will involve questions of real and historic locations and varied exteriors and a proper measure of crowd scenes about which it is obviously very necessary for us to see eye to eye.

"I am sure you agree that we neither want a big spectacle of the *Spartacus* type nor on the other hand do we want a studio-made costume piece of the old MGM variety like *Diane de Poitiers*, *Desirée*, etc., which, however much they got by at the time would be considered very artificial and old-fashioned in terms of today's thinking."

Peter's vision for *Becket* was not to be. Nevertheless, he acknowledged that Wallis had been accommodating when it came to shooting the film outside of Hollywood: "Hal Wallis is a filmmaker firmly attached to the Hollywood scene, and ill at ease elsewhere. Even he did not ask me to do *Becket* there, although it was a studio picture with only ten days in exteriors. The film called for England and I could never have made the same film elsewhere."

The biggest challenge Peter and Wallis faced was who to cast as the King and Becket. Much has been made of Wallis' pursuit of O'Toole and Burton, and little of Peter's part in the process.

At that time O'Toole, known for his classical roles on stage in Britain, had just finished starring in *Lawrence of Arabia*. Casting began as early as October 1961 when Wallis was in London. Peter saw O'Toole as the natural choice for the King, while Wallis approached Albert Finney to play *Becket*. Peter pointed out that he doubted if Finney would be available as he was planning to do a year-long tour in repertory. Peter thought if they couldn't get exactly the right people, they could cast older actors, such as Olivier, of whose work they were very sure.

Peter met O'Toole at around the time he and Wallis discussed asking the actor to play the King. He hadn't realized that O'Toole already wanted to play what he saw as a great part with its "pithy" lines and Gallic edgy humor: "I happened to meet him for the first time at a dinner party in London. Before I had time to consider whether to broach the subject of the film, there and then, he turned the tables by telling me right away that he wanted to play Henry. Fixing me with a blazing blue eye, he said it was HIS part, so naturally and happily the part was his. As I watched him that evening, I was more than ever convinced that he was ideal for the role. O'Toole is a tall lanky Irishman, full of nervous energy. He is mischievous, sharp witted, uninhibited, extrovert and unquestionably as original. I discovered that he already knew all there was to know about the origins and background of the play and why and how it came to be written. Unknown to me (or to anyone else) he had flown to Paris and discussed the part with Anouilh. He had also flown to New York to see the theater production of *Becket* which I had directed. He is not a young man to leave a stone unturned."

In November Peter cabled Wallis from Ireland where he was filming saying he had met with O'Toole and the actor was willing to play the King in early 1963, after the Ontario Stratford Festival season: "*Becket* would be first film after *Lawrence* [*of Arabia*]. . . . Much hectic competition including from [Sam] Spiegel himself. . . . Writing fully meanwhile think important you authorise me encourage him regarding our intentions. . . . In view competition for services think you or Joe [Hazen] should fly over negotiate as he has personal manager not agent."

Days later Peter wrote to Wallis saying O'Toole "is willing to discuss here and now a commitment" to play the King: "Now I do not know whether the strong waves of excited opinion here have yet reached Hollywood about his performance as Lawrence. I can only say that everybody I have met connected with the picture . . . think that this film will make O'Toole a huge international star and of course the film is on a sufficiently large scale to justify worldwide exploitation and publicity that will help the actor's commercial value enormously."

Peter was aware of O'Toole's deal with film producer Spiegel to do three pictures over ten years but knew that O'Toole wanted to keep his hand in theater and was going to Stratford, Ontario next to play "exciting roles" including King Lear. But O'Toole wanted to do *Becket* near to January 1963, so he could do a film for Spiegel in the summer or autumn of that year. Peter told O'Toole that Wallis was unlikely to be able to give him a firm date as yet because *Becket* was a big film to prepare. Peter told Wallis that O'Toole "then persuaded me to go over and see his personal manager Mr. Jules Buck. At this meeting he was quite clear in his instructions to Buck that he would like to play in *Becket* and the discussion revolved around the question of how elastic the starting date would have to be from your point of view." Peter said that Wallis would be interested in principle but Peter couldn't commit then and there.

He told Wallis that if O'Toole took the part they needed an actor aged thirty to forty to play *Becket* with "considerable virility, strength and experience. Names that spring to my mind are Peter Finch and Richard Burton. I do not think we will get Finney as he seems completely tied up with his London Theatre Group and is, I understand, going to do a long worldwide tour after his next film which may take him well over a year.

"Of course there is still the question of Larry Harvey and I am aware of the advantages which your contract with him must suggest. However, most confidentially, Jimmy Woolf who, as you know, has Larry's very best interests at heart, is extremely sceptical about the wisdom of Larry playing opposite O'Toole in the part of the saint. . . . He feels that if a young actor of O'Toole's excitement played the King, it would then be very difficult for Larry to give a good performance in the more inward, determined mature role of *Becket*. He feels that Larry would be seen to great disadvantage and that a young man of O'Toole's talent and with all the histrionic colour that the part of the King provides, Larry would find it impossible not to compete in a way that would be bad both for the part and for him."

Peter closed his letter urging Wallis to act on the O'Toole matter "strongly and without delay." O'Toole's manager then said he was willing to fly to America to discuss the matter. In December Hazen cabled Peter in Ireland: "Buck cabled tersely quote 'Sorry your terms unacceptable' unquote. Please cable me whether you have spoken with O'Toole as I would like to discuss matter on the telephone with you before I have any further communication with Buck."

As Buck and Hazen hammered out the terms of the deal, Peter wrote to O'Toole in early January 1962. He said he was thrilled at the prospect of them doing *Becket* together and was "most earnestly hoping that nothing happens to obstruct the project." Negotiations continued over the next few months, and with it came pressure on Peter to write the screenplay.

Peter suggested starting shooting in May, and had another idea for who should play *Becket*: "I think [Maximilian Schell] would be most moving and sincere in the part which is very important, as in the first part Becket is rather elusive and supercilious and our belief in the strength of his final convictions in my opinion will determine the reaction to the whole film.

"Further, as Schell is rapidly rising to top stardom and even stands a chance with the Oscar [for *Judgment at Nuremberg*] I think we should put in our bid right away."

In May Peter wrote to Wallis after they had discussed the casting and outlined his wish list for *Becket*. Of several combinations his top one was O'Toole as the King and Burton or Finch as Becket. He dismissed the idea of Finney as the cleric thinking he would be better suited as the King: "Perhaps Finney could get away with robes and dignities of the Archbishop of Canterbury in spite of a slightly round baby face that suggests the middle twenties. However, it would be very difficult to imagine Finney giving lessons in grace, poise, table manners or sophisticated affairs to the King . . . what Finney would be doing with gold plate, velvet gloves, etc., I don't know.

"I think Burton would be splendid as Becket as he has great experience in playing classical parts and can suggest a stillness and intensity which is extremely convincing and moving in the right way. . . . Joe [Hazen] tells me that . . . the combination you would favour would be Burton as the King and Finney as Becket. My reaction is that they would make a splendid combination but that Finney should play the King and Burton should play Becket. Burton has considerably more authority and sophistication at his command than Finney and unquestionably looks a man around forty whereas Finney, juxtaposed to Burton, is bound to look definitely a younger and rougher type. This would be ideal in balance, age and style . . . the other way round . . . it would be obvious . . . that there was something wrong in presenting Finney as the older and more sophisticated figure tutoring Richard Burton about life and kingship."

Peter's discussion of Finney as the King was a practical one should they be unable to secure the Irishman's services. Peter urged Wallis and Hazen to stick with the "intolerably demanding" negotiations with his agent. He also revealed he had dismissed any idea of pursuing Guinness and Olivier, whom he considered too old and that he was afraid their emotional scenes could seem "unattractive."

In early June he wrote to Wallis from London saying he had had an evening with Oscar-winning production designer John Bryan, who was happy to say that in principle he was interested to forego his production plans for a period to work as art director on *Becket*. He sold Bryan to Wallis saying that he was without doubt "the finest and most experienced art director in England" and had experience as a film producer as well that would no doubt benefit the production: "While he would never wish to encroach upon your province as producer of the picture, his intimate knowledge of all the best key-men in England and their qualifications [his knowledge of unions, awareness of advance planning and costs would] be a very great insurance if he were in charge of arranging and designing the physical side of the production." Peter pointed out that hiring him would, however, be expensive, and that he wouldn't take less than the work he did as art director on *Lawrence of Arabia* but it would be worth paying the money.

Peter then prevaricated, saying he wanted O'Toole and Finney as the leads: "I hear . . . that Burton is unwilling to play the part of Becket for which, as you know, I think he is far more suitable, and that he is unwilling to play with O'Toole. For this I do not blame him as by all accounts the latter seems to make mincemeat of any other male actors around him. I do not think this would affect Finney—he has a talent of equal stature to O'Toole and knows it!

"Confidentially, I consider Burton a very secondary choice to these two and also I understand that his recent publicity has inflated his contractual demands enormously. I know the two other men are also very expensive but at least every time they have appeared so far they have completely hit the jackpot, whereas Burton has certainly had many, many chanced and whilst always being recognised as a fine and competent actor has always failed in the final analysis to really excite an audience."

By August Peter and Wallis had decided Burton was the right man for the role. But Peter became worried that his sacking the actor years before might make him averse to working with him. Peter wrote to Burton in Geneva in a somewhat disingenuous manner: "I was talking to Alan Lerner in New York the other day about the London production and subsequent filming of *Camelot* and he indicated to me that you were under the impression that I was less than enthusiastic about you in some indefinable way. Quite regardless of whether or not we do in fact get together on any project, I would like to clear up this point unequivocally.

"We certainly do not know each other very well personally so there could be no misunderstanding there. Professionally I can assure you I have been an open admirer of everything I have seen you do, so apart from a little contretemps a hundred years ago when we were both children over Terence Rattigan's play, I cannot imagine what could have given you the impression that I was less than enthusiastic about your work. Lord knows you made a magnificent job of Alexander when you played it—which still makes me think that you would not be ideal casting as his understanding pal! Anyway, maybe the boot's on the other foot and the reservations are really on your part, in which case there is nothing to be done!"

He said that Wallis would be flying to Geneva, and wanted to speak to the actor. Burton telegrammed back immediately:

"Would love to play Becket who plays king? . . . Love to see you and discuss Hal Wallis too. Hearken not to the scribe, sometimes one's funny stories are misinterpreted by Europe. . . . If all goes well shall have two hundred clauses absolutely forbidding you to fire me." Burton decided he could do a part carrying a crosier as much as part wearing a crown. He was also eager to perform opposite O'Toole.

Filmed in Technicolor and widescreen Panavision, shooting began in the summer of 1963 with a budget of approximately $3 million. *Becket* was one of the biggest film productions in Europe that year and filled most of Shepperton Studios. It was the first time Wallis had made a film outside Hollywood for eighteen years and only the second time he made a film in England. The set was enormous and Bryan's reconstruction of Canterbury Cathedral on Stage H, then the largest sound stage in Europe, was the largest interior set built in Europe. The cathedral took four months to build for ten days of shooting and just eight minutes of screen time. The original cathedral burnt down in 1174 and so five hundred drawings and blueprints were made to create its design. The crew also recreated the castles of Henry II, Louis VII's French court and the papal palace in Rome. Bryan admitted that Becket was the biggest job he had ever done, and it took a team of three hundred artists, draughtsmen and craftsmen to create the set. Bryan's work gained him an Oscar nomination for Best Art Direction-Set Decoration; he won a BAFTA for Best British Art Direction.

Margaret Furse's costumes on *Becket* changed in color according to the scene: earthy shades in the English scenes, pastels when the story moves to France and jewel-like hues for the ecclesiastical scenes. Her designs took great creative license to meet Peter's diktat that the film be "punctuated with bursts of spectacle" as 12th century fashions were coarse. So sumptuous were the costumes that Coco Chanel looked at them and said: "[These] could be one of mine." They won Furse her second Oscar nomination.

When it came to donning the costumes Burton and O'Toole's attitudes were quite opposite as Peter recalled: "By no means a natural extrovert, [Burton] has an innate shyness that sometimes makes him restless and unpredictable with strangers. This quality was evident in the many costume fittings that preceded the shooting of the film. Burton, though professional and cooperative, was ill at ease as he was being draped and adorned in the elaborate fineries necessary to the role of the Archbishop. He made no comment but it was clear that he found the process tedious and a little embarrassing. He desired only to get down to a discussion of the text. O'Toole, on the other hand, had a field day at the costumier's. He experimented with each garment in a hundred different ways, and was full of quips, cracks and suggestions. If the fitting was a lengthy one, he would divert himself (and us) by quickly converting the royal riches into a shape that made him look like a madcap comic—and a little patter and soft shoe shuffle would round off the divertissement."

Taylor and Burton were an item when the film was made, although Burton was yet to become Taylor's fifth husband and was still married to his first wife. According to Peter, Taylor was, "a constant visitor to the set" and he grew to like her. So frequent were her visits she had her own canvas-backed chair marked "Elizabeth Taylor." When she watched Burton and O'Toole rehearse the scene where they take shelter from a rainstorm in a peasant's hut and discover a young Saxon woman asleep on a pile of straw, Taylor had an idea. She spoke to Peter and when rehearsals resumed and Burton entered to see the young maiden in a blonde wig, he was startled to discover that Taylor had taken over the role.

The *Los Angeles Times* estimated that the prank cost $15,000 including studio time, the cost of lighting, film and cameras, and the actors' and crews' salaries. The newspaper didn't take into account what paying Taylor for two minutes acting a blonde may have cost. Prior to *Becket* she had filmed *Cleopatra*, the 1963 movie where she and Burton met. She was paid $1,000,000 to play Cleopatra, becoming the first female actress to earn that much for a film role.

Dealing with Taylor's visits on set at the height of her fame can't have been easy, but Phillips remembers that Peter "took it all in his stride, it was all in a day's work" managing everyone with "poise": "He directed anyone who was anyone—huge stars. He had very little ego, which is quite unusual for a top director. He knew how to let the author take first place, not the acting or the director. He didn't let things go off the rails but allowed the play to shine. Directors love to leave their mark; he never did that. He was skilful and knew when to be a show-off. When very famous people [became] insecure, he was diplomatic and was never phased. He knew when to move things along and make a joke, he never shouted or put his foot down."

Not that Peter was a pushover, and Phillips recalls that one day he lost his temper with Wallis: "We were stunned and amazed. [Hal Wallis] was interfering and Peter ordered him off set. . . . If you are a famous director and work a lot you've got to be like an army general and [be able] to throw people off set. He was incredibly organised and very efficient, [you could do] one take and it would be fine. He was very quick. . . . He came from the aristocracy of the showbiz world and had a gilded upbringing. . . . He understood show business . . . and knew everybody more than seems possible, but he did."

Peter's tact and humor served him well when the film unit moved on location to Northumberland and there were more high jinks. Burton and O'Toole had been friends for ten years, sharing a passion for rugby, songs and especially drinking. They would meet up in the mornings before going on set and do a crossword together. The first ten days they managed to stick to drinking tea but their resolve disappeared and they would have more than a few pints of beer on the way at a pub in the evening.

When they shot the beach scene their hangovers from the night before were evident, and they had trouble getting their horses to face in the right direction and the scene had to be reshot. Phillips remembered how everyone watched to see how Peter would react to his leading stars' misbehavior: "[The two] wild cards behaved like angels . . . as Peter laughed it off. [Afterwards] they behaved really well. I've worked with directors who [would have been] more difficult and nastier. Peter was unbelievably kind, reassuring and generous, and wonderful about making sure I felt comfortable when it came to my costume—I was very unconfident because I had just had a baby. He was articulate, witty, acerbic and looked much younger than he was—very good looking. He was funny, although he could be cutting, but he was very kind and made me laugh. . . . I admired his drive: from his earliest days he played at the top of the profession."

O'Toole enjoyed making *Becket*, especially after spending two years working on *Lawrence of Arabia*, drifting from country to country on location and on occasions enduring days in 103 Fahrenheit heat—being able to head home after a day working on set was a relief. Lawrence was difficult role, and one that saw him cast against type. According to O'Toole: "This is a part I could eat [and play as] a snarling butch geezer."

O'Toole described the cast of *Becket* as "a team of thoroughbreds," saying that he and Burton had to be on their "mettle" as they were conscious of being surrounded by actors whom they genuinely admired and respected. Ever since Burton had worked with Gielgud on *The Lady*'s *not for Burning*, he had looked on the senior actor as a mentor; meanwhile O'Toole was in awe of Wolfit, who had been a big influence on him.

O'Toole and Burton's mesmerizing performances and eloquent handling of the dialogue are much of what has made *Becket* enduringly popular. For his part Peter felt: "Their approach to the work was sophisticated, well informed and hard working. Each welcomed and admired the expertise of the other. . . . They were both fully versed in the entire text before the commencement of shooting. Small wonder, then, that directors prefer classically trained actors. Would there were more of them!"

With so many stars, coordinating their time was a feat in itself, and much of that was down to Peter's excellent organizational skills. O'Toole respected Peter as a man who had come from an acting family, been an actor himself and been in the "London theatre forever." It was that background and experience that enabled Peter to organize the shoot so that scenes were filmed in sequence, a method of working that O'Toole said made it so much easier for the actors when it came to performing. What makes Peter's skill even more extraordinary is that during the filming at Shepperton he left the studio to fly to Paris every evening, returning early the next morning. It was another of Peter's stratagems to avoid paying tax.

O'Toole and Burton warmed to acting "the disciplined old-fashioned way." They studied their lines at home, had a chat while putting on their makeup and then headed to the shoot. O'Toole said he and Burton choreographed their moves in rehearsals and Peter would say: "A bit louder, a bit softer, try this and off we'd go." Many of the scenes were filmed in one long shot and played as if a stage piece, although Peter was obviously on hand to edit. The shoot lasted twelve weeks; today it would likely take almost twice as long.

Anouilh was less happy about the experience. He liked the film when he saw it but was unhappy about his screen credit. Just when Peter's troubles over script attribution came to a close, the dramatist became outraged about his billing. On December 13, 1963, Anouilh's representative at international copyright agency, Dr. Jan Van Loewen Limited, wrote to Wallis and Hazen: "Apart from the fact that the card on which his [Anouilh's] named has been mentioned in very small print also bears the name of Miss Hill and the name of the adapter of the scenario, the difference in size between his name and that of the director and producers is such that it almost amounts to an insult."

The correspondent, Dr. Jan Van Loewen, said they would allow the translator, Hill, to appear on the credit "in very much smaller print in the left-hand corner." He demanded that "all copies of the film shall be changed accordingly before first showings." The same day Van Loewen sent a telegram to Peter saying: "[Anouilh] makes you the culprit as being finally responsible for the editing and says that unless he gets satisfaction on the point, it will seriously impair his relations with you.

"I am very sorry about all this and cannot understand why his name has not been mentioned on an individual card and, if nothing else, it seems to be a very short-sighted policy to snub an author of his standing in such a way. I trust you will see to it that things are put right without delay and certainly before the film opens."

Peter responded saying he wasn't consulted on the credits and would take up matter with Wallis. He immediately rang Wallis in Hollywood and Hazen in New York to urge them to do everything in their power "to satisfy so eminent an author as M. Anouilh and pointed out that any prominence they could give to his name would only reflect distinction on the film itself."

He wrote to Anouilh: "I am most upset that you should feel improperly treated in the credit cards of the film of *Becket*, and that you should hold me in any way responsible for it. The unfairness of this will be made clear to you by the enclosed correspondence between Dr. Van Loewen and myself. I can only add that I sincerely trust the producers are in a position to satisfy you in the matter and that incidentally you feel we have done some sort of justice to your magnificent play."

Van Loewen's accusations rankled Peter, and wrote to him: "I find it quite natural and excusable that M. Anouilh should be totally unacquainted with the current practice of Hollywood film making which might lead him to blame me for any inadequacies in the presentation of his name, but I really cannot understand that you yourself could write this letter, the wording of which presupposes an ignorance both of the producers' as opposed to the director's authority and responsibility in these matters, and indeed as I know find out, an apparent ignorance of the very contract you negotiated with the producers, which as far as I can now see has been most faithfully adhered to by them.

"I will deal with the two aspects of this matter separately, although it would seem to me that you must be fully aware of the facts that I am going to put before you, which is what makes your letter so mystifying.

"First of all, in the case of any film made by a Hollywood studio with an American producer, the director is entitled only to the first cut of the picture, and except in very rare cases which are specified in the contract, he has no control over the final editing. Furthermore, on the question of credits, the director is not even consulted nor does he know what they are until he sees the final answer print of the picture. The arrangement of the credit cards is exclusively the business of the producer, who has to satisfy the various clauses of each individual contract as well as the regulations set forth by the various unions involved—dramatists, directors, script writers, etc. I myself did not have the faintest knowledge of any of the contracts Mr. Wallis had negotiated with the persons concerned, nor did I even have any clause in my own contract calling for particular credit requirements myself. I must point out, however, that it is an inviolable rule agreed to by all parties concerned in union contracts that the name of the director automatically comes last on the list of credits. Apparently if this were not strictly adhered to the director's guild would immediately blackball any producer or production company who violated this rule. Needless to say, these union rules have nothing to do with me personally. Even when I telephoned Mr. Wallis and Mr. Hazen urging them to do everything in their power to satisfy M. Anouilh the premise of the conversation was that such credits were not affair of mine, and that in any case they could only act within the limits of such contracts as they had signed, the contents of which, of course, were unknown to me.

"The second aspect of the matter relates to the clauses concerning credits in the contract itself. I refer, of course, to the original contract for the sale of the film rights. I must reiterate that the handling of this contract had nothing to do with me and, until a few days ago, I was unaware of its contents. However, during my conversations with Mr. Hazan and with Mr. Wallis they pointed out to me as a matter of interest that the inclusion of Miss Lucienne Hill's name on the original author's credit card as well as the inclusion (both in much smaller print) of Mr. David Merrick's name as the original producer of the New York theater presentation, was made a condition of the sale of the rights. Furthermore, they pointed out that they were in principle extremely disinclined to accede to the inclusion of these two names as it is not normal practice to advertise the name of the translator of an original theater production or the name of the theater producer on the credits of a film which has been based on a play. They would have much preferred only to put M. Anouilh's name on the credit card, but were informed that the inclusion of the other two names was an absolute condition of the sale. Consequently I must say I cannot see it is their fault that these names are now included.

"I would certainly deeply regret, both personally and professionally, if my good relationship with M. Anouilh should in any way suffer on account of this matter. However, I must say that I feel it grossly unfair that I should be considered even remotely responsible for any aspect of it. If M. Anouilh should choose to hold me responsible for the invention of the atom bomb it would be equally regrettable from my point of view, and I would be equally unauthorised to do anything about it."

Van Loewen replied on January 14: "Permit me to avail myself of the prerogative of old friends: To call a spade a spade and to name things the right way, even if it hurts.

"Now then: I have received in the *Becket* affair a long letter from you and an equally long one from Messrs. Wallis-Hazen. The missiles coming from busy people in the U.S. are a sure sign that you all feel in the wrong, put up a lot of casuistry, but forget to do the only sensible thing, namely to placate Anouilh. You all mention things that can't be done—you do not say, what can be done. And as long as nothing comes forward from your side, the matter will rest, where it stands now, and you and the producers will have created an enemy whom they should not underrate. They also should not try to persuade two old hands, like Harold [Freeman] and myself, that we were negligent in contractual matters, but even had we been it would have only be [been] common sense on their part to be conciliatory over a—for them—small matter. Anouilh himself knows his *oignons* when it comes to motion pictures: he has written, produced and directed quite a number of them and he knows the rules and knows the practice.

"And the practice is that, notwithstanding all the union rules in the world, notwithstanding the humble picture you paint of a director of your eminence and notwithstanding the somewhat pig-headed *charme* of the producers, it would just need one word from the front-office to arrange matters in a way which would do justice to Anouilh and not offend anyone of the very talented gentlemen who are responsible for—as my spies tell me—a very remarkable picture.

"To sum up: If neither Messrs. Wallis-Hazen nor you will move in the matter, then my side will either have to mobilise the lawyers or, if we find that life is too short for that sort of thing, draw their own conclusions for the future. And the future, Peter, is a slippery affair, particularly in our profession and needs all the investment of good will of the past to give a reasonable dividend of security.

"Sorry to have to be so clear and outspoken, but time is short and I think these lines may prompt your side to some step in the right direction."

A few days later Peter had an emergency operation to remove his appendix. By January 22 he was fit enough to continue battling with Van Loewen—and in a remarkably dignified fashion: "Thank you for your letter. . . . I consider the tone of it to be most unfair and my first instinct was to be very angry about it, except that the interests of good sense and the truthful evaluations of a situation are never served by such emotions.

"It is ironic that I should be in any way blamed for M. Anouilh's credit, when I made my opinion so clear to the producers, namely that, irrespective of the contracts, they should do everything legally possible to feature M. Anouilh's name as importantly as is legally possible, not only to satisfy Anouilh's own feelings, but to confer added distinction to the film, since Anouilh's name is by far the most eminent of all the contributors. I made it clear that this was not merely to placate the author of the play, but that it would be in our own interests to insist on the prominence of so celebrated a dramatic writer.

"I must say, that their attitude seemed completely sympathetic and they assured me that they themselves in principle were against any diminution of M.Anouilh's name, but that they would have to look into the position of their contractual obligations which, of course, are not my concern and about which I have not been and never will be consulted.

"I could not have been more strong in my exhortation to them to do whatever could feasibly be done and any technical difficulties there are to the solving of this problem would seem to me to lie between you and the producers.

"If you do not believe me, my dear Jan, when I tell you that in America the director has no authority whatsoever in such matters as credits, publicity, advertising, etc. there is very little I can do to persuade you, but you could easily check this yourself.

"I had a long talk with Harold Freedman about it and he certainly understood my position. Since you must know what arrangements were originally entered into, would it not be best for you to make a specific suggestion to the producers? I am sure they would lend a sympathetic ear to any legally feasible suggestion you might make.

"As far as I am concerned, *Becket* will always be the literary creation of Anouilh and, any importance he may be given in the credit titles would only afford me pleasure.

"I can only say in conclusion if you and M. Anouilh are suspicious of my attitude you are not only doing me an injustice, but you could also be in error."

Van Loewen replied in a calmer tone: "Why . . . should not one be frank with one's friends? I would not be annoyed if you hit me hard if you thought I had slipped somewhere—as long as you didn't hit me below the belt.

"I do accept that you could not have been more instrumental in trying to reverse the awkward situation. However, the fact remains that Anouilh was and is dissatisfied with the way credit was given to him and while Wallis and Hazen can seek cover under the contractual terms, they are not willing to make a step in the right direction and there remains a feeling of displeasure as far as Anouilh is concerned. Needless to say, I have done everything to steer you clear of all this and in that respect our correspondence has been salutary. It is very strange that intelligent and experienced men like Wallis and Hazen, who will tell you over and over again that the script is the thing, behave rather short-sightedly when it comes to a minor matter like this one. I am quite sure they will regret their attitude one of these days."

The matter was resolved by early February, and Anouilh wrote to Peter thanking him for his efforts in attempting to solve the problem. Van Loewen, while excusing Peter, was disappointed with the outcome, replying: "Whatever you may say in excuse of Wallis and Hazen, they are not boiling over with courtesy. This goes so far that I have not even been invited to the trade showing of *Becket*, and this teaches one more lesson how to go with a fine tooth-comb through every film contract."

Anouilh's secondary billing did not go unnoticed by the press. When *The Times* reviewed the film it commented: "For though the name of the adaptor, Mr. Edward Anhalt, is featured at least twice as prominently as M. Anouilh's the adaptation stays in most respects remarkably close to the original." Working with Wallis was a battle and Anouilh became its casualty.

Another intimidated by Wallis was Rosenthal. Peter persuaded Wallis to hire the composer to write the film score. It was a risk because Rosenthal had never written a movie score of such epic proportions but Peter had complete faith in him. Rosenthal recalled that when Peter proposed him to Wallis the producer responded: "Who the hell is he? Never heard of him." Wallis wanted to use an A-list Hollywood composer, but Peter was equally adamant about employing Rosenthal. He was proved right; Rosenthal's score gained an Oscar nomination.

Rosenthal said: "They went into bat. Peter insisted and Wallis went away grumbling and muttering. I went to England to compose the score and I could feel Hal Wallis breathing down my neck and hoping I would fail so that he could say I was completely wrong for the job and he could then hire a top-flight composer. I had only done David Suskind's [1961 movie] *A Raisin in the Sun*—I wasn't a member of the Hollywood club and he was always huffing and puffing behind me. . . . Wallis would try to find out how the score was going, but he always got a good report.

"Then one morning at eight o'clock I got a phone call. 'Larry (Rosenthal).' It was Wallis, I was trembling and thought he was going to sack me. 'I heard some disturbing rumours.' He said he didn't want the film to end on a doleful and ironic note. He felt that the King had profited from Becket and was transformed and wanted the film to end in triumph. I thought, 'Does he understand the script?' I promised to keep his opinion in mind. I called Peter who told me, 'Don't worry, write the music and it will be right.'"

Rosenthal went away and mulled over Wallis' words. The producer had been in films a long time and Rosenthal took that on board: "I devised a way to satisfy his and my wishes, so that the film ends on a note of triumph but with tones of dissonance to add doubt," says Rosenthal, "When we recorded it with an orchestra, Hal Wallis walked in and I began sweating buckets that he would hate it and throw it out. The music was a pseudo-triumph with its doleful trombones. A smile spread across his face and he clapped me on the shoulder and said, 'You did it, my boy!' It was a relief. My final vindication came when he asked me to write the score on *Anne of the Thousand Days*."

Wallis continued to tinker when it came to the editing. Fresh from editing *Lawrence of Arabia* that won her an Oscar, Anne Coates said she was able to leave much of the film uncut because of the great team acting: "It was beautifully shot. . . . It seemed to work really well because [Peter] designed the shots. He never had people just standing about, they would always be people moving around each other. And he had a wonderful eye for colour; I remember the opening when [the King] goes up to the cathedral with his red cloak, it was just a stunning shot. . . . But [Peter] was given ten days . . . to do his director's cut—now they get ten weeks—and Hal Wallis took it over, and I thought, 'Oh, my God!' because the cut that Peter and I had got was pretty good, and Hal did practically nothing. I think he took out about three or four lines, tightened it up here and there. . . . I think that if Hal Wallis, who I did several films with and got on very well with, had spent just that little bit more money on *Becket* it would have become an epic. If he'd just put a little action into it and enlarged it a little bit it could have been a huge film. But as it was I think it was a beautiful film."

The film edited, a debate ensued about where it should premiere. Inevitably, Peter had strong views. In September 1963 he wrote to Hazen warning against opening *Becket* in London before New York. He felt there was a risk that the reaction of London critics, and their tastes, would seep over to America and cause problems: "The present critics, though generally very clever and sharp, are inclined to favour the more experimental type of picture and are inclined to be somewhat grudging about big productions presented in the classical manner such as *Becket*. [They are] more interested in the latest advances in film technique and contemporary subjects with a rather left-wing bias than in stellar acting or in the business of entertainment. They all have a slight suspicion of the theatre plays transferred to the screen and are also slightly prejudiced against the star system, believing that the truth of the camera eye can elicit more interesting and significant material from real life or specially selected unknown personalities than can be found in the more bravura technical techniques of stellar actors."

Peter felt that the British press might be less sympathetic towards *Becket*'s creative license and its liberties with historical fact; it might "serve as a platform for critics to show off their historical knowledge and to state their objections. . . . In America . . . I get the feeling that they are more interested in the overall entertainment gesture of a film, and oddly enough I think its religious and historical background will be more impressive to them and will be taken more seriously than in England where some of the critics have an undoubtedly left-wing and anti-religious bias. There is also no large Catholic influence in England."

Peter was also concerned how the press may react to his stars. Peter felt that Burton "at the moment is done rather less than justice by the English press on account of the overall publicity he has been receiving from the columnists." He was less concerned about O'Toole: "[He] has already been seen in England in many outstanding roles which show his power and versatility. He completely captured the national press when he played Shylock and his performance in *Becket* therefore would only be another magnificent portrayal in his gallery. On the other hand, in America they have only seen O'Toole playing Lawrence, and many people look on him as an attractive 'straight' personality actor. I think the real powers as an actor he shows as Henry will come over with a far greater impact to critics here than they would in England where his range his well known." Peter suggested the ideal solution would be to open the film simultaneously in New York and London.

Becket had its world premiere on March 11, 1964, at Broadway's now demolished Loew's State Theatre and it premiered in London at the Plaza Theatre near Piccadilly Circus on March 26. At the London premiere Peter became outraged. Wallis introduced an interval in the middle of the film. Peter's calm exterior fell away. The months of battling against Wallis had taken their toll. His struggle over the script attribution, his anger at being dragged into the debate regarding Anouilh's billing, and Wallis' general tinkering and overbearing attitude must have been exhausting for the director. Peter was happy with the film, but seeing it cut off in mid-flow so that the audience could buy popcorn was the last straw.

O'Toole was at the London premiere and saw the uncharacteristic display made by his "poor director" as Peter galloped across the cinema shouting: "You warthog!" Peter kicked Wallis out of the cinema and began to talk of lawyers. There was no lawsuit, but the fracas shows that even Peter's legendary cool had limits. It was an uncharacteristic outburst and is testament to how much making *Becket* had proved to be a trial. By the end of April Peter was hospitalized because of problems with his ulcer, once more stress affected his health.

Despite the tensions between Wallis and Peter, it didn't sour relations between them. In the spring of 1965 Hazen wrote to Peter saying that he and Wallis were keen for him to direct *Anne of the Thousand Days*. Peter's reply: "It is a story which has always fascinated me, as you know, and I think the script is extremely well done. However, my projects with MGM are making considerable progress, and as I am under a definite obligation to proceed with them, I am afraid it would be misleading for me to indicate an interest in directing your script."

Critical opinion was divided. *The New York Times*' Crowther had to admit it was a "magnificent picture." But *The Times* remained unconvinced: "[*Becket*] falls uncomfortably between two stools: too quiet and uneventful to be a spectacular, it is too large and cumbersome to be anything else."

However, *Becket* received twelve Oscar nominations, including that for Best Director. Peter lost out to George Cukor for *My Fair Lady*. That year two classic musicals swept the board: *My Fair Lady* won eight Oscars and *Mary Poppins* five. *Becket* only secured one—the ironic Oscar to Anhalt for Best Writing, Screenplay Based on Material from Another Medium. Never has a film been nominated for so many Oscars yet won so few. Only eleven films, among them *Gone with the Wind* and *Titanic*, have received more nominations.

There is no doubt *Becket* would never have happened without Wallis, and his contribution in raising finance and eye for what would be a commercial hit was extremely valuable. But the producer Peter jokingly referred to as "the old water buffalo" was eager to make an Oscar-winning hit. Despite his glorious reputation, Wallis hadn't won an Oscar nomination for Best Film since 1956 for *The Rose Tattoo*. He saw an excellent opportunity in *Becket* and its first-class company to achieve his dream. He often badgered Peter unnecessarily and was keen to assert his authority, which didn't make life easy for Peter. Wallis' own ambition lead him to tinker on occasion rather than trust. Whether that interference may have benefited the film is moot, perhaps he drove Peter to raising his game.

Peter's best chance as winning a coveted golden statue disappeared with *Becket*. He earned $200,000 ($1.5 million today) from the film, so the venture was hardly without financial reward, but money isn't everything. Three years later Wallis made *Barefoot in the Park*, followed by John Wayne's last great movie, *True Grit* and then *Rooster Cogburn* in 1975—John Wayne's penultimate film and Wallis' last-ever production.

11

The Revolutionary

1964-1967

The making of *Becket* encouraged Peter to seek greater autonomy and he started to explore the notion of producing films, although he told a reporter he had "no plans, I'm going through what you might call a pleasant little hovering period." In reality he was beginning to find it difficult to find projects that interested him; he was also struggling with changes in the industry. Peter believed in classical training for actors and was contemptuous of Method actors. He felt the commercial nature of Broadway theater allowed for little variety of parts, and when a young actor became successful in films they didn't dare go back to repertory for fear of losing their place on the ladder of film fame. Besides being frustrated he was bored.

After *Becke*t he returned to Broadway to direct a British actor he respected and admired in a play based on the life of Welsh poet Dylan Thomas. A sizeable production with twenty-two scenes and twenty-six characters, it called for creative lighting and a revolving stage. Written by *Tchin-Tchin* author Michaels, *Dylan* draws on accounts written by John Malcolm Brinnin and

Thomas' wife, Caitlin, about the poet's visit to America toward the end of his life. Peter said: "I find it excitingly written. I like the richness of the text and I like what appears to me to be its theatrical shape, fluidity and dynamics."

Dylan's melancholy account of the self-destructive last months of the poet's life spent in an alcoholic daze was far from commercial fare, needing a great actor in the lead to pull it off. Peter wheedled Alec Guinness in to taking on the difficult role; it would prove to be his greatest Broadway triumph. Initially Guinness wasn't convinced he was the man for the role—for a start he didn't like Thomas' poetry. To win him over Peter persuaded him to read Michaels' script. To cast the role of the poet's wife, Peter and the show's producers, George W. George and Frank Ganat, traveled to Canada's Stratford Festival to see Canadian actress Kate Reid; she readily agreed to the part.

The play had tryouts in New Haven and Toronto before opening at New York's Plymouth Theatre in January 1964. Days before the show hit Broadway Peter underwent an appendectomy in Toronto. Even without their director the cast rose to the occasion and the critics described Guinness' performance as "mesmerizing" and the *New York Herald Tribune* praised Peter for its "swiftness" and "visual gloss." The production, which ran on Broadway for nine months, gained three Tony nominations, including one for Reid, while Guinness won the Tony for Best Actor in a Play. Peter considered trying a film sale but decided that as a "serious straight play" it wouldn't do well in the contemporary market.

Two months after *Dylan* closed and *Becket* premiered Peter and Bill finally moved into East 68th Street and shipped over the contents of their house in Brompton Square. Their friend Tom Seligson said: "Bill handled all the practical details of their lives together: the upkeep of the building, which they owned and rented out. He also did the hiring and firing of the help." By this time they had a team of domestic staff, who cleaned, cooked, served at table and even a butler. Bill was a fair but strict landlord and boss, telling his staff they "must . . . keep the lower foyer in good condition and those louvers closed if they want people to think they are in Versailles as opposed to a film set with two Rin Tin Tins." The first people they hired were an Italian couple: "I have told them about the limitation of space at the moment and the confines of an American kitchen as opposed to the five-acre one they have [in Paris]. It doesn't seem to faze them and the woman . . . believes she can still manage her extraordinary French cuisine without huge marble slabs for rolling pastry and fish tables and pans, etc. . . . She also, between soufflés, does the laundry and irons the shirts beautifully which is a rarity . . . in New York. . . . My idea is that we use the 1A apartment for sleeping, bathroom, clothing, cupboard, etc, and Peter uses it during the day with his secretary for work."

Peter and Bill decorated their house exquisitely with art and antiques and they hosted numerous dinner parties for friends, among them the writers, Truman Capote, William F. Buckley, Jr., and Tennessee Williams, along with members of Manhattan's high society that included Drue Heinz, Brooke Astor and Kitty Carisle-Black. Peter loved socializing, and enjoying his home and his friends was becoming as important, and as interesting, as his work.

In his working life Peter then returned to familiar territory and made a film of *Hotel Paradiso*. Given the play's success on both sides of the Atlantic, a film adaptation was arguably the logical next step. Guinness reprised the role of Boniface and Byng that of Martin, and long-time collaborator Laurence Rosenthal wrote the score. The rest of the cast was equally impressive. Glamorous Italian actress Gina Lollobrigida played Marcelle, Robert Morley played Henri, British comedienne Peggy Mount the domineering Angélique and Akim Tamiroff the hotel owner Anniello. Among the younger faces in the cast were Derek Fowlds as Maxime and Leonard Rossiter as the Inspector, both of whom became much-loved stars of British comedy television.

The film marked Peter's last role as an actor when the role of the playwright Georges Feydeau was added in a new plot twist. Benedict and Marcelle are Feydeau's neighbors and the dramatist, who is suffering from writer's block, observes the action and transforms the characters' mishaps into a play. It was little more than a cameo role that Peter created after careful negotiations with Feydeau's estate. Peter also wrote the screenplay and co-produced the movie with Frenchman Pierre Jourdan.

Peter was prompted to become a producer because of his desire to do work he wanted, as he explained in a letter to Fred Kohlmar of 20th Century Fox rejecting an offer to direct a movie named *The Joyous Season.* "I started work on my own projects, through my company, because of a depression I had about the nature of the scripts I was being sent from outside sources. I found that, most of the time, I just did not like them and [in 1964 realized] that I would never settle down to do any of the projects that were being offered to me. Consequently, I started to work out my own little projects, knowing at least that the basic subject matter attracted me in the first place. This seems to be working very well but, of course, it does involve responsibilities which present difficulties when it comes to considering films outside the framework."

The lavish production of *Hotel Paradiso* was shot for MGM in France during the summer of 1965 in wide-screen sumptuous color. The cast and crew were mostly French and included Henri Decaë, who was one of the premiere cinematographers of the moment.

Although it is a film that is gorgeous to look at and is acted well, particularly by the rambunctious Mount as the domineering wife is a role she was made for, the film failed to live up to expectations on its American release in October 1966. Reviewers loved the acting but hated the movie, and Peter came in for a whipping. *Time* complained: "Putting the right people in the wrong beds is the principal preoccupation of French farce, but this sumptuous period piece gets rather confused about the sleeping arrangements: it's the moviegoer who does most of the yawning. . . . Glenville as Feydeau wears a wise, conspiratorial expression, presumably to suggest that middle-class morality can be terribly droll. But Glenville as Glenville hasn't the faintest idea of how to get the fun on film."

The New York Times was equally scornful: "As the man largely responsible for *Hotel Paradiso* . . . Peter Glenville . . . is split down the middle. He is so in love with beautiful objects that his camera can barely leave them alone—all of them in color: splendid gardens, weighty hangings, potted plants, ancient polished woods, pieces of sculpture, carpets both worn and new, a spacious landscape. Even the bath with its patterned blue marble and spouts that work like fountains has a museum-like finish that is a pleasure to the eye. . . . The trouble with this lavish care is that it conflicts with the idea of the film and its execution. . . . The result is that the picture is charming when it should be brisk, amiable when it should be ridiculous."

Only the cinematography seemed to meet with approval: "*Hotel Paradiso* is an eye opener only when photographer Henri Decaë has charge, for his views of Paris during *la belle époque* make decades melt away—particularly in a smoky, golden café scene reminiscent of [Toulouse] Lautrec, with portly naiads up to their chins in gym suits and a matronly stripper dismantling her corsetry on an overhead swing."

Peter was unfazed by the film's lack of commercial success, having planned it on a relatively minor budget of $1.75 million. Plans to distribute it in Britain were put on ice.

"I can only think that the circuits who show the films didn't like it," said Peter. "It wasn't a smash hit or anything in America, but it did quite well. I was disappointed originally but then other work came along, and I've almost forgotten all about it." It was a view confirmed by an MGM spokesperson: "We did have the idea that we'd premiere it in a plush West End theatre—it is after all a very artificial, stagey sort of farce—to get people in the right frame of mind, but so few theatres have projection equipment. It will be shown one day."

This was Peter's view in March 1971, fifteen years after his play was a hit on the London stage, and five years since the film was made. Time had helped to make the movie appear dated and out of touch. Guinness was still impeccable, although his age made him an unlikely suitor for a beauty as vibrant as Lollobrigida. *The Times* declared: "*Hotel Paradiso* is the latest addition to the ever-lengthening list of shelved and forgotten films now being dusted off and given an airing. . . . Though it does not really work, it has some quite funny moments, and it is, actually, a fair enough stab at a virtually impossible task: that of accommodating an entirely artificial farce to the naturalising medium of the cinema. . . . At least *Hotel Paradiso* keeps the pace up, and Alec Guinness' performance in particular often manages to strike the right note of mechanical-man stylisation. But alas! this is an area of film-making where there is no room to manoeuvre between triumph and disaster; and *Hotel Paradiso* is no triumph."

The Times described Peter's problem accurately as "virtually [an] impossible task": "The stage incarnations of the play were hailed for their brisk pace, and manifesting such a whirlwind frenzy to the screen doesn't work. The film is a visual joy with its opulent setting, but its realism causes a problem when viewing its flat characters." Rosenthal sums up the difficulties in the film: "Peter's error was in creating a sumptuous physical look that took away from the edge of the comedy. Its visual elegance was too rich and a miscalculation."

Moreover, times had changed. By 1971 the Beatles had been and gone, America was protesting against the Vietnam War, man had landed on the moon for the third time and the British public was more inclined to laugh at Monty Python than farce. A film spin-off from the TV sitcom, *On the Buses*, outgrossed James Bond's *Diamonds Are Forever*. The story of a bus driver and his troubles with female bus drivers proved that the cinema was no longer king; television now ruled. Between 1968 and 1980 more than thirty British films were adapted from successful TV shows. Peter's beautifully crafted film stood no chance.

A year before *Hotel Paradiso*'s American release Peter started work on another movie that would reunite him with old friends and colleagues. Greene, Burton, Taylor, Guinness, Gish, Decaë and Rosenthal all worked on a film that would take cast and crew to France and Africa. The film was *The Comedians*, an adaptation of a novel by Graham Greene. The $6 million movie proved to be something of a headache as Peter dealt with the demands of his star-studded cast and his desire to do justice to his friend's novel, it was a task made harder because Peter's Maximilian Productions company also produced the movie.

Greene always did have a nose for trouble. After he visited Mexico he wrote 1940's *The Power and the Glory*, after traveling to the Congo he penned 1948's *The Heart of the Matter*, and a trip to Cuba led to 1958's *Our Man in Havana*. *The Comedians* was written after he visited Haiti in the early sixties. Widely recognized as a Catholic novelist, Greene was very interested in international politics and the workings of espionage. *The Comedians* is commentary on life under the sinister rule of Haiti's leader François "Papa Doc" Duvalier, who, after becoming president in 1957, declared himself President for Life in 1964.

Duvalier ruled the Caribbean island until his death in 1971, aided by his private militia, the fearful Tonton Macoutes—Haitian slang for "bogey men." It is estimated that Duvalier was responsible for the deaths of 30,000 Haitians, sending thousands more into exile. The Tonton Macoutes were more powerful than the army and as the world became aware Duvalier's brutal regime, he and his country became increasingly isolated. By 1963 Duvalier, who declared himself a voodoo priest, had been excommunicated from the Catholic Church.

Greene visited Haiti twice before Duvalier took power; returning to the island in 1963 he was shocked by the cruelty and the demise of Port-au-Prince into a capital living under a curfew and surrounded by barricades. According to Greene: "I was haunted by Haiti for years after my last visit." *The Comedians* tells the story of an Englishman, Brown, who inherits a Port-au-Prince hotel.

As tourism plummets, Brown finds himself running a bankrupt business. Disillusioned with Haiti and life, the only reason the lapsed Catholic remains on the island is because of his love for a married woman, Martha Pineda, the wife of a Latin American ambassador. Martha refuses to leave her husband because she does not want to lose their son, Angelito.

Mr. and Mrs. Smith, two well-meaning American liberals, arrive at Brown's hotel and while their intentions are good, they are shocked as they witness the prevailing violence and injustice on the island. Another guest, Major H. O. Jones, a con man, is given to tall tales of his military experience in Burma in the Second World War; he's in Haiti to negotiate an arms deal. The main Haitian characters are Dr. Magiot, a former friend of Brown's mother, and opponent of the regime; Henri Philipot, a painter turned revolutionary; the pragmatic killer, Captain Concasseur; and the head of Haiti's public relations department, Petit Pierre.

All the film's characters are "comedians" of a sort—they all play a role of some kind. Pineda attempts to make out his marriage is still viable, the captain supposedly upholds the law, and Brown professes to prefer to stand on the sidelines and watch the brutality around him. Yet all of the characters are eventually drawn into the cycle of violence and forced to make choices. They are no longer able to fake.

The film had come about after MGM, acting on Greene's suggestion, sent Peter a synopsis of the film and a copy of the yet-to-be published novel in October 1965. Peter wrote back: "I enjoyed this book enormously and, if your colleagues were interested to buy the novel, I would certainly be interested to produce it. Of course, the book is a somewhat bitter pill to swallow but, on the other hand, it has such strong touches of compassion. . . . The strong action could, of course, make very exciting film material.

"It seems to me that its occasional criticism of the American policy of always supporting the Right, even to the point of condoning such a dictatorship as exists in Haiti, could very easily be left out of the film without damaging the story in any way. On the other hand, the implied criticism illustrated in the idealistic, vegetarian American who has his eyes finally opened during his stay on the island, is both amusing and inoffensive . . . I think that with really careful scripting, it could be moving, exciting, and exceedingly apposite both to today's political conditions and to modern filmmaking. Certainly, it is not sentimental, but what really good recent films are?"

The studio gave *The Comedians* the green light with Peter buying the film rights from Greene so he could both produce and direct it. Peter made it a condition that his friend adapt his story for the screen; he felt that no one else had Greene's knowledge of Haiti or was capable of the job. Greene was insistent that Peter visit Haiti before shooting began, but he needed to do this before the book was published and news of the film leaked out, as afterwards it would be too dangerous. In January 1966 Peter and *The Comedians*' art director François de Lamothe, who worked with Peter on *Hotel Paradiso*, set off for Haiti. The pair pretended to be researching a possible movie about the country's revolutionary hero turned unpopular monarch, King Henri Christophe I. They stayed in the Hotel Oloffson in Port-au-Prince, where Greene conceived his novel and upon which he based Brown's Hotel Trianon. They visited all the places in the novel, taking color photographs, "including the inside of the police headquarters where the photographs of the corpses of the rebel [Clement] Barbot and his aide, torn by gunfire, [we]re still pinned to the wall."

De Lamothe described Port-au-Prince as "a capital where the abandoned remnants of former wealth strangely contrast with the prevailing property; wonderful country-houses with carved-wood verandahs surrounded by gardens overgrown with a turmoil of vegetation. Large rectilinear avenues, dazzling with sun and colour, where a few old taxi-cabs wobble along; overpopulated slums, unfinished and aggressively modern constructions; sumptuous hotels and embassies—most of them empty—bumpy roads which dive into the night toward the voodoo rights . . . refugees. Everywhere appears the iron hand of Duvalier, president for life, and of his sinister militia: the glittering slogans day and night, the immaculate presidential palace with innumerable pillars and domes; the huge police buildings."

Peter later spoke of their cloak-and-dagger trip: "Two days after we arrived a PR man from the presidential palace dropped by the hotel. Fortunately, I had all the books with me to back me up. In fact, I'd really love to do a picture on Christophe. Soon we received an unofficial enquiry as to whether we would like to meet the president, who's very eager to have a picture made on Christophe. But I didn't want to. Quite honestly, he's no fool in his black-magicky way. I didn't want to be involved in a direct lie to him."

Peter and Lamothe planned to leave Haiti a day before *The Comedians* was to be published and were shocked when they arrived at the airport to see a military officer holding a copy of *The New York Times* open at the book-reviews section. A photograph of Greene and an article on *The Comedians* was clearly visible. Peter was, unsurprisingly, alarmed: "Naturally I had no way of knowing whether the movie had been mentioned or not and didn't dare show the least interest. Then there was a lot of Creole talk, then we heard over the loudspeakers that the flight had been delayed two hours.

"Then another man came up and handed the officer a six-page cable. At the end of every page he looked up at me. I tell you my heart was absolutely in [my] boots. 'You be here when I get back,' he said. It was two hours of absolute terror but he never got back."

In April 1966 Greene started adapting a screenplay from his novel and Peter joined him at his home in Cap Ferrat in France. It was no easy task—the first sixty-five pages of Greene's novel had to be condensed to just six minutes on screen. Greene told an interviewer: "I found working with Peter very exciting, especially the verbal sessions we'd have in the afternoons. He has enormous vitality. But the 'scientific' writing I found a bore, like the compressing of the opening chapter. That was terribly fatiguing work." The fatigue took its toll on Peter, as his ulcer problem flared up, and he was diagnosed with sub acute serum hepatitis, or hepatitis B.

Despite Peter's health issues they began searching for experts who could help to paint an authentic picture of life in Haiti: "Graham and I . . . gave a soirée for seventeen black Haitians—all most intelligent and interesting characters—who are going to help us with casting, research and voodoo experts, and I have several other contacts which will prove suitable for the rather enormous task of casting all the other coloured roles."

When Greene finished the screenplay a battle ensued. Peter knew that the affair conducted by Burton and Taylor's characters, and Brown and Jones' visit to a local brothel could cause problems with the censors. Draconian American censorship laws meant this fell under the terms of what was known as the "Production Code." Adultery and illicit sex, although recognized as sometimes necessary to the plot, could not be explicit or justified and were not supposed to be presented as an attractive option. Portrayals of miscegenation were forbidden and "excessive and lustful kissing" was to be avoided.

The Code fell by the wayside in 1968 because it became impossible to enforce it when studios began to release films without an approval certificate. Many of America's liberal movements that came to the fore during the sixties forced a reconsideration of how race, class, gender, violence, drugs and sexuality were depicted on screen. However, when Peter submitted *The Comedians* script for approval, the Code was still in force, albeit in its death throes.

Religion was equally problematic. In Greene's original script Brown says: "Suicide remains the courageous act." MGM was concerned and wrote to Peter in July 1966 to tell him that the censors' suggestion to cut the suicide dialogue "should be followed. It will be disliked intensely by Catholics and in this country the Catholic Film Office will almost surely request its elimination."

Peter replied in August: "In point of fact, this speech has been revised for other reasons but I would like to point out that the character making the speech is a lapsed Catholic and I cannot see any reason for a man characterised as such to speak orthodox Catholicism."

Peter agreed to revise a few lines deemed inappropriate and "recognise the need for restraint in the love sequences." Although he wrote to the censors saying: "Personally, I firmly believe that the effort to get around these technical schoolmasterish regulations has often influenced the less distinguished producers and directors to rely on horribly coy innuendos and *doubles entendres* which often result in something very near to adolescent smut. This accent on naughty but repressed 'sexiness' has been, I feel, the cause of much European criticism of the American attitude to emotional and sexual life as depicted in their films and has helped to create the legend that the Hollywood product is unadult."

But a potentially bizarre sticking point came over a line spoken by a young prostitute when she leaves the bordello where she works to chat with Brown, a former client. She tells the hotelier she made an excuse to leave saying she was going to the bathroom: "I told them I go *faire pipi*."

The studio wrote to Peter in September: "The Code people say that they personally still maintain the habit of urinating, but do not discuss it in polite society. While the habitués of a whorehouse may not be considered members of polite society, audiences are. They feel that we antagonise audiences needlessly with such a phrase, and in this connection it must be borne in mind that the U.S.A. still is a very puritanical nation." Peter was flabbergasted and wrote back: "Naturally, I am prepared to change this line as it is not important enough to justify making an issue of it. However, I am genuinely curious about the point of view of the Code people when they say that such things are not discussed in 'polite society.' I cannot help wondering what they mean by this very old-fashioned phrase which has not been used since [Anthony] Trollope or perhaps, at the latest, Sir Arthur Pinero.

"What is 'polite society'? They cannot mean by this a society of either aristocrats of eminent intellectuals since members of the upper classes are quite intolerant of false refinements and circumlocutions. Amongst the socially privileged, it is certainly considered extremely common to use words like 'toilet' and 'power room' instead of 'lavatory.' If, on the other hand, they are referring to every petty little housewife in the Baptist belt, the interesting question arises as to whether such rather limited outlooks have necessarily to be pandered to by the Code. I can imagine many people in the lower middle classes being extremely shocked by most of the great classics, from the Bible to Shakespeare to [Marcel] Proust. To people of limited education, a certain refinement in politeness is often a self-protective barrier against hearing any sort of truth.

"I would perfectly understand if you maintained that MGM, as a film company with films to sell, does not wish in any way to affront the conversational mores of any section of society. However, surely the Code people cannot think it part of their duty to protect the refined and often limited outlook of every moviegoers. The timidities and excessive refinement of some people are objectionable and childish to others. In any case, is the object of the Code to please everybody or to state what, in their opinion, is really objectionable for public performances? Surely salesmanship is one thing and public decency another.

"I would be most interested to hear what function the Code people are exercising, and on what principle, when they talk of things that are not mentioned in 'polite society.' I cannot see the relationship of politeness to censorship. Most serious works of art are impolite. Of course, very few films qualify as such but surely pleasing 'polite society' is a pretty nasty sort of limitation."

The censors gave up and wrote to Peter: "It is not a hanging matter . . . feel free to retain the line." It was like being back at the Oxford Union for Peter.

Preliminary casting began in April. Burton agreed to play the cynical hotelkeeper Brown and then Guinness accepted the role of the bogus Major. Burton was eager to work with Peter again and an admirer of Greene, as was Guinness, who had appeared in the 1959 film adaptation of *Our Man in Havana*; both actors also wanted to play opposite one another. Oscar-winning actor, playwright and director Peter Ustinov accepted the role of Ambassador Pineda, and silent-movie star Gish and comedian Paul Ford those of the do-gooding Smiths. Some of America's greatest contemporary black actors played the key Haitian characters. James Earl Jones took on the role of the fêted Magiot, Georg Stanford Brown the artist, Raymond St. Jacques the cool captain and Roscoe Lee Browne the public-relations man Petit Pierre. The problem was casting the minor role of the ambassador's German wife and Brown's mistress, Martha. MGM suggested Sophia Loren, but neither Peter nor Greene were enamored with the idea, and in July Peter wrote to the studio: "I don't think she is right, and neither does Graham Greene. We both feel she is too strong and volatile and clearly Italian. However, in the interest of box-office promotion I am willing to try to accommodate a major star even if it may give a somewhat theatrical and 'celluloid' look to the story."

Peter circumvented the dilemma by approaching Elizabeth Taylor, a star MGM would find hard to turn down. He went to Rome, where she and Burton were shooting Franco Zefferelli's

The Taming of the Shrew to secure their services in a somewhat unorthodox fashion. Peter had struck up a friendship with the couple since filming *Becket*, enough of one that he had accompanied Taylor to London premiere of *Cleopatra* three years earlier. By September 1966 the actress was on board and he wrote to her saying he was thrilled that "we will be working together for the first time." Peter famously persuaded Taylor to take a pay cut to earn $250,000 less than Burton's $750,000 ($5 million in today's money) fee plus percentages. Burton too had reduced his fee because he was by this time earning $1 million for a movie; Guinness received $250,000 ($1.7 million today).

Peter's version of events was that he approached the actress saying: "'Elizabeth, I'd love you to do it if you don't mind supporting your husband, for it's only a small role.' She said, 'There's nobody I'd rather support.'" Taylor had a different story. "I must have been out of my *tête* to take it. . . . It's the smallest part in the film. . . . Richard didn't want me to do it, but Peter Glenville conned me into it and got me at half pay. Do you know what he did? He said, 'You realise of course that Sophia Loren is dying to do it. You wouldn't want anyone else to do those kissing scenes with Richard.' Half pay . . . everyone's taking half pay."

Half pay or not, having Taylor on board threatened to incur extra costs. Insuring her was estimated to cost $187,000 and they would deduct the first $250,000 on any claim; Peter decided to take a risk and not insure the star. When it came to billing, Taylor was generous and suggested that all the other star cast members be billed first and she have "some kind of special billing which states 'and Elizabeth Taylor' or some special billing of such flavour." The studio had suggested that she only take second billing to her husband, which in itself would mean waiving its contract with the star that stated her name always appear first. Taylor then proposed that her name appear second, after her husband's. She asked that Guinness and Ustinov's names appear in the same print and with the same importance before the film title as herself and Burton. The names couldn't all fit on one line so Peter chose the order: Burton, Taylor, Guinness, Ustinov.

With the first draft script completed in May Peter rented a house in Paris, which served as the production center; he also started thinking about where to shoot it. Naturally shooting in Haiti was out of the question, in fact criticizing a dictatorship would be tricky to film in any "banana republic." He pondered a Lie political atlas to see the status of potential locations to see which party was dominant and why.

Peter and Lamothe started a globetrotting hunt for possible locations, beginning with Martinique and Guadeloupe. "These islands are delightful in themselves but their atmosphere suggests too strongly the fact that they remain dependencies of their mother country France. Their cultural links with Africa now seem remote. There are no African rites, no tribal dances and none of the mixture of uneasy sophistication and primitive force that we found in Haiti. Their mood is charmingly bourgeois and their towns are small and reminiscent of the comforts of a French provincial center transplanted to a tropical region. In spite of their occasional labor problems and a growing movement in favor of independent political status, they are quiet and pretty places—ideal holiday resorts for nice middle-class French citizens.

"We then flew to Bahia, the former capital of Brazil. The beauty and exoticism of this city was so compelling that it was tempting momentarily to forget the project in hand and to concentrate on the pure enjoyment of serious tourism. One of the disadvantages of 'scouting' locations for a film is that if you are at all curious by nature and if you enjoy sightseeing, it is frustrating to have to confine yourself to finding the bare requirements of a given film in a city of indigenous historical and artistic interest. The field of vision is necessarily narrowed. The eye has to be kept on the ball and the ball can only bounce so far. However, Bahia did have one advantage for the possible filming of *The Comedians*. The macumba rites are still celebrated and they are very near to the *vaudou* rites of Haiti. One of the major sequences in *The Comedians* is concerned with a *vaudou* ceremony. The scene dramatizes an invocation to Ogoun Ferraille, the God of War, by the *hougan* or priest. This would entail specific devotional chants and dances and the sacrifice of an animal to the god. The climax of the scene is reached when the spirit of the god enters the psyche of one of the celebrants and takes possession of his personality. The reason for this similarity of religious rites between Haiti and Brazil is that originally both countries were stocked with slaves from the same coastal area of Africa and specifically from Dahomey [now the Republic of Benin]. Although these slaves were induced to accept the Catholic religion in both Bahia and Haiti, they continued, more or less secretly, to practice their native rites and these in time developed into a strange mixture of Christian beliefs and ceremonies combined with the forms and observances of their ancient African heritage. Catholic saints, ancestral spirits and deified tribal heroes all became enshrined as patron guardian spirits in a complicated but nevertheless sincere and theocentric religious system.

"It was going to be important to film this *vaudou* ceremony with accuracy and with a proper respect for its dignity and sincerity, even if the form it would properly take might prove startling to Western audiences unacquainted with African religious customs. Professional actors or dancers would only be able to give a decorative or stylized version of what is in reality an ecstatic and transcendental religious experience. However, since Haiti itself was out of bounds, it would be difficult to find [100] French-speaking (and singing) practitioners of the *vaudou* cult. I had already made inquiries about the possible participation in this sequence of Haitian political refugees in New York and Paris. In nearly all cases they were afraid to appear in the film for fear of reprisals against their relatives still living in Haiti. Indeed, they claimed that if they were recognized in the film, stringent measures would be taken against any Haitian bearing the same name even if not related by blood.

"Meanwhile, we found that there were serious obstacles to the filming of this particular story in Bahia. The language of the people is Portuguese and only a small and privileged minority can speak French or English. Furthermore, the distance from our home base in Paris was too great. Telephonic communications with France were almost impossible and although air transport from Paris to Rio is frequent and direct, the customs procedure is apt to be lengthy and, in any case, Rio is several hundred miles from Bahia. The port (an important locale in the script) was too large to suggest Port-au-Prince and the city itself although magnificent was far too imposing for our purposes. After four days, we reluctantly gave up the idea of Bahia and returned to Paris."

In July MGM, worried about spiraling costs, suggested making the movie in Hollywood. Peter was adamant that it be shot in a sympathetic location and wrote to Ben Melniker at the studio.

"The question of doing the film in Hollywood seems to me to be pushing matters really too far in the wrong direction," wrote Peter. "You ask me to keep an open mind. Frankly my mind cannot possibly be open about a project on which I have been planning and working for the last four months. If my mind was still 'open,' it would be very damaging for the production in that I would obviously have no clear conception about how the film should be made."

Peter's letter continued: "There are many films that could be made in Hollywood. I myself would be quite happy occasionally to do one. However, more than any other film I have come across, *The Comedians* seems to need a location—and a genuine negro French Caribbean one at that. I have worked in Hollywood and I once had to find there an exterior locale situated on a road suggesting the South of France. The search was exhaustive and the result unsatisfactory. There is nothing less American than the atmosphere of a French colonial island now entirely run by coloured people . . . believe me, if we ever attempted to build in America the streets and the buildings and the market square, ports, slums, etc., needed for this film, the costs would be phenomenal and the results ersatz."

As he so often did Peter got his way and in October he flew to the former French colony of Dahomey; he knew immediately that his problems were solved: "Within a few hours of our arrival there, we knew that this would be the location for the exterior shooting of the film. Many of the elements were already there. A small port and jetty, recently superseded, would be at our disposition and the grand esplanade with its extravagant government buildings, the colourful poorer sections, the vegetation, the French-speaking natives, the smart modern villas and embassies were all suitable to our purpose and needed very little reconstruction or alteration. . . . There were good construction firms with available personnel, although it would of course be necessary to bring over our head construction men and some scenic painters from France. Local wood for building was abundant and although reasonably priced was of superb quality mahogany (at first, it seemed almost shocking to use such wood for so transitory a purpose as set construction). Excellent hotel accommodation for the entire unit was available. Air-conditioning was also provided—an important factor for when actors and crew have been working all day in 100 degrees in the shade, the relief of a cool bedroom to sleep in is a major consideration. Telephonic communication with France was quick and reliable and direct flights to and from Paris were scheduled twice a week. Furthermore, the old fetishist religions were still practiced in much the same way as the *vaudou* rites in Haiti. Ogoun Ferraille is still invoked and animals are still killed as sacrificial offerings. It was obvious that with a Haitian assistant and a Haitian *hougan* to conduct the ceremony, the variations that had been introduced in the Haitian branch of the cult could be incorporated without much difficulty.

"Our production manager then joined us to discuss the various contracts and permits necessary to our purposes. In Dahomey, authority is benign but centralised. Labour for building, for transport and for crowd work was not only available but extremely willing. Dahomey is not a rich country and the employment we were to provide for quite a number of the inhabitants in its principle city would be a real boon. . . .

"One final location problem remained to be solved. Three weeks of intensive work would be necessary in and around the décor on the Trianon Hotel which, in the story, is owned and managed by the principal character. This gothic hotel, its grounds, its swimming pool, its porch, its bar, staircase and offices would all have to be constructed. Many of the sequences set in this décor would have to be filmed at night (since much of the action takes place in the black-out), and long important dialogue scenes were involved. This would be the most ambitious single décor of the film and even the facilities of Dahomey were not going to be equal to such a construction which really required the servicing of an adjacent studio to make the operation feasible. Furthermore, foreign location shooting with a large cast and crew is extremely costly and the rhythm of work is apt to be slow. The hotel sequences at night would require a much greater quantity of special lighting equipment than would be necessary for the daylight sequences in other décors. All lighting equipment would in any case have to be shipped from France. On the other hand, the Paris studios do not have 'lots,' i.e. nearby terrain in open air on which the sets can be built while the shooting is still being serviced by the studio facilities. Some London studios have such terrain but there the weather is far from dependable and the wind and the rain can be a serious obstacle to the progress of exterior shooting. Accordingly, we decided to shoot all the other exteriors in Cotonou, the interiors in a Paris studio and then complete the shooting of the hotel sequences at the Victorine Studios in Nice, in the South of France."

Dahomey's largest city, the sleepy port of Cotonou, was to substitute for Port-au-Prince. The French-speaking nation of two million people was ideal because it is the ancestral home of many Haitians and of Haitian voodoo. Both races are descendants of the Yoruba and Hausa tribes, and the Haitians can trace their ancestors back to people transported to the island as slaves centuries earlier. The decision sparked a protest from the Haitian ambassador in Benin, Jean Cordin, and he was recalled to Haiti when the film unit started to arrive in December.

Locations were one thing but housing such a famous cast for a six-week shoot was quite another task. Fortunately Benin's President, Christophe Soglo, came to the rescue. About a mile out of Cotonou was a cluster of government villas in a white-washed walled compound, surrounded by scrub and pineapple groves that faced a palm-fringed sandy beach. Normally used by distinguished official visitors Soglo put them at Peter's disposal for $1,000 a month each (around $7,000 in today's money). Peter immediately slated one for Burton and Taylor, took one for himself and Bill, and used another as a production office. The remaining two were used by actors with star billing such as Gish and Guinness, as well as Greene, when they arrived on set.

Peter was very grateful: "[Soglo] offered the palace cars for our future transport needs and his palace projection room for our rushes. He would arrange for the customs procedure to be speedy and cooperative. . . . Tourism is not yet highly developed in the country and the president welcomed the extra business that would result form the presence of the stars. He gave the project invaluable cooperation."

The arrival of more than 100 cast and crew and ten tons of equipment in the tiny nation was a huge event. Cotonou's hotels became so full that some of the crew slept in a monastery. President Soglo did everything possible to help, even keeping oil tankers waiting off shore so that the small harbor was clear for filming the dockside scenes. He also permitted them to deck the town with a sign saying "Welcome to Haiti" and billboards praising Duvalier. It was a wise move—the shoot poured $500,000 into the economy of a country whose national budget was $10 million. Nor did all the money disappear into government coffers—the hundreds of locals hired as extras, including the city's beggars and cripples, earned $4 a day—great money by Dahomey standards. The extras even had their own fans, as relatives came to watch them on set.

Shooting was scheduled to start January 9, 1967, to coincide with a chartered cargo boat used in the opening scenes in Cotonou's port. Burton and Taylor agreed to arrive two days earlier, but getting them there was no easy task. The couple were extremely rich, owning houses in Mexico and Switzerland, and were ostentatious in their spending: Taylor's dresses, furs and jewelry, the couple's jet and yacht, and charity donations and benefits were all over the newspapers. They travelled with a large entourage costing $2,450 per week ($18,000 in today's money); each had their own make-up man and dresser, Taylor her own hairdresser and they shared a press secretary. Peter warned the couple it would take a few days to get used to the high temperatures; arriving on January 7 to start shooting four days later was ideal. He told them their "little villas" were comfortable and air conditioned, but that Taylor would have to bring silk or linen sheets if cotton ones weren't good enough for her.

Dahomey's poverty and the possibility of falling ill—travelers were advised to have inoculations against yellow fever—didn't seem to register with the Burtons, and Peter had to advise them against bringing their pets: "Much as I love the idea of seeing the dogs around, I must tell you that I have been advised that the climate here is not at all good for high pedigree dogs, particularly young ones, and the officials take a very serious view of any dog that gets very sick and could be suspected of catching rabies. . . . I have seen some dogs around but none of them were high-strung pedigree dogs—just large mongrels sitting in the shade."

The Burtons, nevertheless, arrived with two Pekingese dogs, one brown, and one white. The stars were given a huge welcome—even a somnolent little town in West Africa was star struck by the luster of showbiz's pre-eminent glamorous husband and wife. The president lent them his air-conditioned Mercedes when they arrived at Lagos airport in neighboring Nigeria and allowed them to keep it throughout the duration of their stay. Naturally there was a reception at the presidential palace. According to Peter, "all the black gentlemen whirled around the floor with Elizabeth [Taylor] apparently to their mutual satisfaction. . . . Like something from one of Ronald Firbank's novels." The palace was hardly luxurious by Western—and Burton—standards, with washing clearly visible on the clothesline when the couple visited. But the couple were charmed by the stocky, bow-legged Soglo in his ill-made clothes, as the *Los Angeles Times* reported: "Burton is convinced that Soglo's wit and salaciousness must derive from a few drops of Welsh blood and says Miss Taylor 'is absolutely in love with him.'"

When shooting began reporters poured into Cotonou. *Time* described it as "further out than the location of any movie since Nanook of the North . . . [it] is a jerry-built outcropping of grandiose, half-filled government buildings and a splendid four-lane boulevard that runs straight and proud to the weeds and sand at the city's edge." It was an era when the press were fascinated by the Burtons' every move, and to find them in such an out-of-the-way place made for a great stories: "When not on camera call, Burton spent amiable hours in the bar of the Hôtel de la Plage, talking of baseball and Vietnam, reminiscing about Dylan Thomas and Wales, and doing his famous imitation of himself imitating Winston Churchill. . . . Elizabeth sat conjugally by his side, interrupting every hour or so to ask: 'Don't you think it's time we went home, Richard?' 'Yes,' replied the bilingual Burton. 'When I've finished my drink. *Garçon! Donnez-moi une autre bouteille de* rotgut, *s'il vous plaît.*'"

Newspapers described every detail of life in their "holiday village," mostly concentrating on what Taylor was wearing, her husband was drinking, and what together they were eating. As the violet-eyed Taylor sipped Jack Daniels and soda dressed in a "low-cut white linen dress" and the greying Burton drank a vodka tonic, a still youthful-looking Peter would knock back a whisky. The Burtons' assistant, Gaston Sanz, would lay out the hors d'oeuvres on a dining-room table and dispense Champagne that had been shipped in from France. Taylor planned what they would eat—anything from chicken to shrimp or steak-and-kidney pie with cabbage and mashed potatoes.

In truth the press could find little else to say. Cotonou was a small town of mud-walled houses with tin roofs and oil-lit dirt-track streets. It had a few coffee shops, two hotels, two cinemas, one dance hall and an ice cream parlor. Other than occasional invites to the palace and parties at various consuls, the stars entertained themselves by a mix of eating, boozing and banter. With a man as vocal and opinionated as Burton that wasn't hard as conversations veered from politics to religion, usually taking in his favorite topics of Wales and Welshness somewhere en route. The marital bickering took up newspaper column inches as they argued about mundane topics like her driving and more volatile ones such as whether they should adopt one of the local children.

The bored, heavy drinking Burton would often head out to one of the local hotels for a snifter, leaving his wife to ring around the city's few watering holes late at night to persuade him to head home.

According to writer Melvyn Bragg, when the couple left they missed the comparative privacy of life in a backwater. Burton wrote in his diary that he and his wife retained "a certain nostalgia for Dahomey. The house, the lizards, the palm trees, the unit intrigues, the arrogance of the American negroes with the West Africans, the dangerous fascinating sea only a couple of sand trumps away from the house, the mad Palace, the

President and his dowdy provincial wife. The Palace receptions and the fetes."

The high point away from the filming for Burton and Taylor was when Marlon Brando arrived on set to give the actress a New York Film Critics Circle Award for her performance in *Who's Afraid of Virginia Woolf?* Brando had been her co-star in 1967's *Reflections in a Golden Eye*—a film Peter was originally slated to direct. The Burtons had asked Brando to pick up the award, after which he decided to fly to Africa to deliver it personally; the stars played charades all evening. Peter had written to the Burtons before shooting began: "I hope all goes well with *Reflections* [*in a Golden Eye*] and that Elizabeth is squeezing a couple of laughs out of all that Method [acting]. I want a full description when you arrive of the scene when Elizabeth, quite unclothed, threatens to thrash a by no means emaciated looking Marlon. Something tells me there must have be a giggle or two somewhere along the line there." He no doubt got his description, and from both parties involved.

It wasn't all fun and games. There was talk that Duvalier had sent a voodoo priest to disrupt the film. More seriously, there were rumors that two of Haiti's Tonton Macoutes were in Benin to assassinate Peter, Burton, Taylor, Guinness and the film's technical adviser, who was described as "a young political exile whose back bears the scars of Tonton Macoutes' lashes." Greene's reaction in a letter to Peter was typically mischievous: "I read in the papers about the threats to the Burtons and I hope you won't be having any trouble. Of course if there is a real menace I would like to be there!"

No assassinations took place, but the hot humid weather, mosquito bites and shark-infested seas took their toll. Such was the sweltering heat that shooting began at sunrise and sometimes continued through the night. The cast and crew became dehydrated, suffering from headaches and breathlessness, and some were flown home. Things were exacerbated by the fact that sometimes scenes had to be shot many times; the well-behaved locals, among them babies and children, were unaccustomed to performing. One day Burton took the temperature under the lights in the afternoon, it was 138 Fahrenheit, causing him to joke that if it was any higher the cast could fry eggs on their heads, although he said he had worked in worse places: "the Sahara Desert . . . South Wales."

The unit was most concerned about the 73-year-old Gish. Frail in appearance, on the day where she had to shoot the scene when she is pushed to the ground by Duvalier's henchmen, an anxious and gentlemanly Burton suggested they halt the shooting because the temperatures were more than 130 Fahrenheit. Gish refused to give up insisting they carry on filming until sundown. Peter praised the star as an "old trouper" as she managed to join him for dinner later that evening.

More tragically, a member of the film unit drowned on the first day. Peter and Bill also had a narrow escape when they went swimming on the beach near the compound as Guinness recounts in his autobiography. On a rare day off from shooting the couple headed to the beach. They had been warned that the sea had a dangerous undertow and they should not stray out of their depth. Guinness looked on at his friends waving to him while he read a book sitting on a sand dune. He soon realized that their waves were cries for help. A fierce wind had picked up and the tide was carrying them out to sea. Guinness attempted to go in and pull them back to shore, but Peter told him to get help, least he too be dragged under. No help was available as Guinness looked on and prayed. Suddenly, a wave miraculously appeared and brought Peter to shore, seconds later another plopped Bill on to the sand. That evening, when Peter and Bill had recovered, the trio went to the local Catholic church to offer up prayers.

Bizarrely, Peter was repeating history. In 1912 his parents had nearly drowned at St. Margaret's Bay in Dover, Kent when were cut off by the tide. They tried to swim around a rock and back to shore, but neither were strong swimmers and they found themselves stranded. Their cries for help were eventually heard by passers-by and coastguards came to their rescue.

On set, life was less dramatic and generally good-humored. Peter's policy of employing people he had worked with before meant he picked many of the crew personally, even down to the grip men. Peter's quiet cool and friendliness helped as many flagged under the scorching sun.

As make-up man Ron Berkley said: "Working with him makes a big difference. There's hardly a guy on this set he doesn't know by his first name." Chief soundman Cyril Swern concurred: "He's not one of those shouters. Some directors you want to kick in the teeth."

Not that it meant Peter was a pushover. If anything he was incredibly efficient, and Burton joked that the cast and crew called their director "That's-Perfect-Let's-Just-Do-One-More." Peter finished *The Comedians* three weeks ahead of schedule after eighteen weeks of shooting in Cotonou, Paris and Nice and brought it in almost $117,000 under budget.

Ustinov summed up the experience in a letter to Peter in December: "Thank you, my task in your film was really made terribly easy by the presence of the Burtons and of Alec [Guinness]—to say nothing of your infrequent but telling *sotto voces.* It is very rare that one is able to work in an atmosphere of practically wordless intelligence, where every tiny indication is understood without fuss, and, as a consequence, one begins to rely on . . . oneself. That is a colossal privilege—the instinctive comprehension worthy of a sporting team—and that is flattery, Peter, since it is the antithesis of the Strassbergian Flatulence (this sounds like a heresy put forward at the Diet of Worms).

"I am glad [to tell] you how much I enjoyed working in your film, and how satisfied I was artistically that you find a niche for me among such august yet accessible creatures as Elizabeth [Taylor], Richard [Burton] and Alec—to whom, my love and my respect."

After leaving Dahomey in February the cast were reunited in Paris for about a month of shooting interiors at Franstudio in St. Maurice. They were allotted apartments and continued to mix with the local worthies, in this case Peter's friends the Duke and Duchess of Windsor. Bragg reveals that Burton wrote in his diary that the royal outcasts went back to the Burtons' apartment at the Plaza and Burton and the duke sang the Welsh national anthem. When Peter's troupe arrived at the French capital the paparazzi followed in the hope of tracking down the Burtons. They did—catching them late at night drinking in bars—and took joy in reporting on their woozy debates.

The Burtons' contract stated that they would be released in order to fly to London at the end of February for the Royal Command Performance of *The Taming of the Shrew*. For Burton it was something of a reunion as he invited 150 friends and relatives from the Welsh valleys, paying for them to stay in the Dorchester Hotel and party the night away. But the biggest news was that the couple had both been nominated for Oscars for *Who's Afraid of Virginia Woolf?* Yet despite pleading, Taylor refused to take time off from filming *The Comedians* to accept her award in April.

Jack Warner, the head of Warner Brothers, cabled Peter in Nice imploring him to persuade her to go. He didn't beg him to ask Burton, so it was obvious she would be a winner and Burton a loser. "Dear Peter, Sent the following cable to Elizabeth quote Dear Elizabeth distressed is a mild expression if you not here for Academy as agreed by you personally and publicised by all media you just cannot do this. You must be here otherwise your image in eyes of motion picture industry and particularly all members of Academy will be damaged. Have not informed anyone you not coming as you must come. Any schedule ever made can always be changed for a few days. I implore you not to burn all bridges you have built. Sincerely Jack Warner unquote I implore you personally Peter to aid Academy membership board governors and entire industry at this critical time I know you can shoot around her as originally planned particularly when we had her assurance she would attend awards please phone me or cable immediately Miss Taylor will leave in time to be here for Academy Monday evening. Kindest personal regards Jack Warner." Peter sent a cable back immediately saying: "The decision for Elizabeth not to come for the awards is a personal matter in which regretfully I have no power to interfere."

Taylor won her second Oscar for Best Actress, and actress Anne Bancroft accepted it on her behalf. Perhaps she chose to stay with her husband as a show of loyalty knowing he wouldn't win an award, or maybe she just was too in love to leave him.

The cast and crew had moved on to Nice for seven weeks—the hills of the Côte d'Azur matched those in Haiti and Greene lived nearby. Peter hired some villas, which were a cut above those they used in Africa. The Burtons' La Fiorentina had extensive gardens, tennis courts, croquet lawns, staff and a huge swimming pool, which they rented for six weeks for $10,000 ($70,000 today). Peter rented a smaller house within walking distance. The cast hung out with more of Peter's royal friends, Rainier III, Prince of Monaco and his wife, former actress Grace Kelly.

Laurence Rosenthal joined them: "Peter was a very practical man and knew how to turn every situation to his advantage. He rented a beautiful villa on the French Riviera near Antibes for him and Bill, and an even more magnificent one for Richard Burton and Elizabeth Taylor. I arrived to do work on post-production in Studios La Victorine in Nice and he found me a villa at St. Paul de Vince next door to Marc Chagall with a piano and a swimming pool—he knew how to live it up! I loved doing that score with Haitian drums and voodoo rhythms. Graham Greene lived in Antibes so he would often drive over to see Peter socially—they were both semi-lapsed Catholics and I heard endless long conversations and theological discussions."

But Peter's friendship and respect for Greene caused the first and only problem in his relationship with Rosenthal. Greene felt *The Comedians* should have a hard and gritty atmosphere reflecting life in a police state. Rosenthal knew this, and had no intention of composing music that would soften the movie. But when it came to writing the music to accompany the ill-fated, illicit romance of Brown and Martha, Rosenthal wrote a sad, melancholy waltz to echo the feeling of a romance without resolution. Peter became nervous when he heard what he felt was romantic music and said to Rosenthal he was missing the point. Rosenthal replied: "Can't you hear the dismal hopelessness and bleakness?"

He couldn't. Rosenthal went away to rethink. The next day was the last day of recording and he had seventy musicians lined up. He was pressed for time. The composer got up at six o'clock the morning of the recording to rewrite the piece and then headed to the studio for a nine o'clock start. The orchestra played a waltz but used the dialogue as the melody. Rosenthal played it to Peter who thought it was perfect and that his fears were allayed. Rosenthal finished the post-production in Paris and the recording in London: "Drifting from capital to capital was Peter's style."

When the film premiered late October 1967 at New York's Coronet Theatre, Rosenthal went along to the gala evening with the Burtons and a host of stars. Afterwards they went to a party at The Rainbow Room on the 65th floor of 30 Rockefeller Plaza—the epitome of Manhattan sophistication. "It was a great evening," said Rosenthal, "but when I'd watched the film I'd heard the music dialed in and out all the way through the film. I thought, 'What's he done? He's butchered the score!'

"In terror Peter had redubbed the entire film because of his fear of Greene. He'd done it in a very crude manner. I thought, 'Why didn't he call me back and not do this in an amateurish way? He's usually so impeccable.' I went to see Beatrice Straight at her apartment, sputtering to her that I needed a drink. She suggested I return to The Rainbow Room and find Peter and make a rapprochement. It was a gamble, but I went back. Peter came over and sat on my table. My anger had subsided but I told him I was hurt that he'd done something so crude. I was very nervous.

"He asked for my pardon and said he hoped it wouldn't injure our artistic partnership. That was the only time it was, and it was only for a moment."

Earlier, when Peter had shown the movie to MGM the studio bosses they were enthusiastic. He wrote to Burton at his home in Gstaad, Switzerland in April: "Well, we had the big slam-bang showing for MGM and for the sales people yesterday of *The Comedians*. The reaction was enthusiastic enough to make one highly nervous. In their opinion, you had already gained an Oscar and they are even now counting the money at the box office.

"Heaven knows they may be wrong but I mean it quite seriously when I say that your performance is one of the finest not only that you have given but that I have ever seen on the screen. I am embarrassed at writing eulogistically and the Lord knows you are quite successful enough to do without praise. However, I feel impelled to say that every time I watch your performance in *The Comedians* I am astonished by the truth of its detail and by the persuasiveness of the undercurrent of emotion. Very little credit for this is due to me as you are not an actor who needs detailed direction. I think by this time it would be difficult for a director to get a really bad performance out of you. I can only hope that I was of some help in the original scripting and in the editing and camera work which frame your performance.

"The MGM people were very enthusiastic also about Elizabeth and found her completely persuasive and moving as the Ambassador's wife."

Reviewers liked Burton but felt the movie was too long.

"Running two hours and forty minutes, *The Comedians* has everything but economy, and director Peter Glenville has tarried with a story that might have been twice as good at half the length. . . .

"Ironically, the film's most stirring moments are not its overheated love scenes but the brief encounters between Burton and Guinness. In one, Guinness, a short day's journey from death, recounts his wasted life of lies in a graveyard retreat. Priest-like, Burton answers the tortured confession with a symbolic absolution. At such moments of transcendent drama—and there are enough to make it worthwhile—*The Comedians* is easily forgiven its other sins," said *Time*.

The New York Times registered the film's sense of unease: "By far the most agitating aspect of the film Peter Glenville has made from Graham Greene's novel, *The Comedians*, is the sinister image it presents of a rigid reign of terror in a Caribbean country under a black dictatorship. . . . Never mind that the country represented in this amazingly forthright film is specifically present-day Haiti under Papa Doc Duvalier—or it could just as well be [Fidel] Castro's Cuba or Hitler's Germany. . . . This sudden and vivid implication of pertinent menace in this straight American film . . . is the most forceful thing about it. . . .

"But what is arresting and disturbing is the atmosphere. . . . Mr. Glenville has crowded his picture with a vivid and convincing *mise-en-scène* of a hot country boiling with anger and frustration under an unseen dictator (he is glimpsed just once from the side) and with characters and cultural indications that reek of menace and mystery. . . . Mr. Glenville made a lot of his picture in Dahomey, West Africa, so that he has a true look of a tropical country and its swarms of natives up there in the colour on the Panavision screen. It is a picture to make us apprehensive. Haiti suddenly seems a bit too close."

The film was cut heavily for second-run theaters. The cuts seemed to lessen rather than enhance its appeal and when it opened in Britain in January 1968 *The Times* damned Greene's stereotypical characters and the film's lack of style, declaring it a "very glum trudge": "M. Decaë's photography is muddy and unappealing, Miss Taylor's 'German' accent (French, surely, if anything) comes and goes from scene to scene, and Mr. Glenville's attempts to galvanise the picture into occasional life with short-cuts from sequence to sequence are wrecked by his fatal habit of signalling each supposed shock at least ten seconds early."

The film's ironic title didn't help it at the box office and it did moderately well taking $5,200,000 in America; by way of comparison the 10th highest grossing movie of the year, *A Lion in Winter*, took $10 million. However, this was the first Burton-Taylor collaboration to have lost money at the box office. Gish was nominated for a Golden Globe as Best Supporting Actress and there were a couple of other low-key awards. Its mix of a doomed romance portrayed by two superstars and political commentary meant it fell between two stools. *The Comedians* was perhaps too gruesome for some and insufficiently punchy for others.

Critics in the 21st century may be less harsh and see that the film is far from boring, as some at the time felt. The film's subject matter still resonates given tin-pot regimes still rule parts of the globe and it had a stellar cast to match the subject matter. *The Comedians* creates a feeling of disquieting menace. It is unapologetic in its portrayal of the prevarications of the white man and the last-ditch heroics of a handful of them. If anything it seems remarkably prescient and less a depiction of stereotypes than a rather depressing accurate generalization.

Whatever the critics felt *The Comedians* highlighted Haiti's problems as Duvalier's reaction reveals. Peter sent a cable about it to Greene in November: "The following official protest has been sent to Washington by the United States Haitian Ambassador and we are being asked by the press to issue a reply to it stop I think it would be a good publicity for the film and also for the Haitian opposition if you would cable us your own answer to this protest stop If you telephone Bill Edwards at Metro Goldwyn Mayer in Paris . . . he will cable me direct stop Here is quote.

"The embassy of Haiti strong[ly] protests against Metro Goldwyn Mayer the film *The Comedians* which constitutes an inflammatory . . . [against] Haiti and has been publicly released to mislead American people stop . . . [It is] not less than a character assassination of an entire nation stop From first to last the film presents an utterly distorted picture of Haiti its people and its government stop Filmed in Dahomey *The Comedians* shows Haiti with a wrecked fort dirty customs shabby taxis dilapidated hotels and houses broken up streets . . . a nation [of] voodoo worshippers and killers . . . This is not only a character assassination . . . is a characterised indirect aggression against a government representative of the masses stop It is also an economic assault and a propaganda aimed at disgusting and scaring the American tourist at the beginning of the season stop Haiti is one of the most beautiful peaceful and safe countries in the Caribbean stop End of quote."

Greene cabled his reply to MGM and Peter: "Suggest following: The ruler of Haiti responsible for the murder and exile of thousands of his countrymen is really protesting against his own image in the looking glass stop Like the ugly queen in Snow White he will have to destroy all the mirrors stop But perhaps someone with a sense of humour drafted the official protest with its reference to 'One of the most peaceful and safe countries in the Caribbean' from which even his own family has fled stop I would like to challenge Duvalier to take a fortnight's holiday in the outside world away from the security of his Tontons."

MGM President, Robert H. O'Brien told the press that *The Comedians* was based on Greene's "extensive experiences in Haiti"—much of the story draws on real events and people—"The situation dramatised in both the novel and the film can be supported by numerous news accounts which have appeared in respected publications during the last few years." Duvalier himself criticised Greene calling him "a liar, a cretin, a stool-pigeon . . . unbalanced, sadistic, perverted . . . a perfect ignoramus . . . lying to his heart's content . . . the shame of proud and noble England . . . a spy . . . a drug addict . . . a torturer."

Although the film raised awareness of Haiti's problems, it failed to raise any more than a ripple in political circles. Haiti was a bulwark against Communism for America and Duvalier remained in power until his death, only to be succeeded by his son Jean-Claude "Baby Doc" Duvalier. Haiti continued as a police state until 1986 when Baby Doc was ousted. What is significant is that a film about Third World politics and life under an existing harsh regime was made at all. A tale of how American and British tourists get caught up in political unrest in Haiti was unusual fare. As Peter said just prior to *The Comedians*' release: "Ours is the only movie ever made that overtly attacks another existing regime in a time of peace."

Greene's intention in adapting his novel into a movie was to widen its political impact: "Back in 1935 if someone had done a film on German concentration camps, I suppose no one would have believed it. . . . If anything the real Haiti is blacker than I have portrayed it. . . . The execution scene—which all the children were made to watch on Papa Doc's orders—actually happened. Papa Doc even had the execution filmed and he made every theatre in Haiti show it for two weeks running. I saw it myself."

Peter's involvement in Haiti's political affairs went far deeper than simply making a controversial movie. He contacted Father Jean Baptiste Georges, a former priest who was once Education Minister under Duvalier, for advice on how to stage the voodoo ceremony and help find someone to coach actors in a Haitian accent; Georges was living in exile in America.

On August 26, 1966, Peter wrote to Georges in New York in a letter headed "STRICTLY CONFIDENTIAL": "I was glad to be able to speak to you last. . . . I sincerely hope that I shall be in a position to help you. I think that [my lawyer] Aaron [Frosch] may feel that there are certain dangers to me *vis-à-vis* official US circles. As you know, I am not an American citizen and only come to work in America on a temporary permit. I am hoping therefore that Mr. Frosch can regulate these matters so that he will allow me to proceed.

"About your Haitian friend who is willing to have some chats and go through the text with one or two of the actors I have in mind, I think the best plan would be for you to give me his name and either address or telephone number and I will then tell the actors to get in touch with him directly. . . .

"I had several conversations with Graham Greene about you and the project. He had heard of you often in Santo Domingo and he said that should the project come about, he would very much like to accompany you, naturally without mentioning a word to anyone. Subsequently, he could give the matter world coverage and in the most favourable light possible on account of the eminence of his name, his many connections and his intense sympathy with your aims. I understand that this may not be possible but, in any case, you can rely upon his total discretion at all times.

"I am looking forward to seeing you when I am next in New York. Let us hope that, by that time, considerable progress will have been made.

"Please say a prayer for me from time to time.

". . . P.S. On account of mentioning Mr. Greene, I think it would be better if you destroyed this letter."

"The project" that Peter alluded to was not the film, but plans to overthrow Duvalier.

Georges and Peter corresponded throughout 1966, and Georges recommended fellow Haitians Albert Chassagne as the voice coach and René Lilavois to aid with the voodoo ceremony. In December Peter told the cast not to use Chassagne because he had had "far too broad an accent" and wanted to charge an "exorbitant" fee of $15 per hour for a six-hour course. On September 27 drafts from Peter's account at the Bank of Bermuda "in full compensation for services rendered in connection with casting and technical advice relating to *The Comedians*" were sent to Georges: $10,000 for Georges, $5,000 for Lilavois and $5,000 for Chassagne. So Chassagne had supposedly already been paid. The amounts themselves are also high, in comparison the actor who played Petit Pierre, Browne, was paid $500 a day for a minimum of ten days, plus $30 a day expenses.

Georges' cryptic reply to Peter was: "I, the undersigned certify that the sum of twenty thousand dollars ($20,000) received from Mr. Peter Glenville on this day 27 September 1966, as well as an equal sum of $20,000 to be paid later, will be used exclusively for the liberation of Haiti." Today that would equate to around £150,000.

American Customs officials foiled an attempted invasion of Haiti, on November 29, 1966, by a group of Haitian and Cuban exiles along with some Americans. *The New York Times* reported that CBS reporters, in the hope of getting a scoop, had monitored the attempt for months. Georges was the leader of the Haitians and was to replace Duvalier if the invasion worked, Rolando Masferrer headed the Cubans; Masferrer had been in charge of a special police unit under former Cuba's President Fulgencio Batista. The group intended to topple Duvalier and to use Haiti as a base to wage a war against President Fidel Castro on nearby Cuba. The leaders moved between New York and Miami, while the weapons were smuggled from one place to another. They recruited 300 men, acquired hundreds of weapons—including bomber aircraft—and spent some $250,000 (somewhere around $1.8 million today).

As the day of the invasion drew nearer, Georges hid out in various "safe" houses and motels in Miami. Other TV stations got wind of the plan and while ABC interviewed Masferrer an NBC crew was sent to Port-au-Prince. But America did not sanction armed expeditions from its shores, and officials said: "Those men are not even going to get their feet wet." CBS didn't get to film an invasion and customs officials warned the would-be rebels off their expedition. On December 14, Peter wrote to his agent at William Morris, Charles Baker, to discuss casting and mentioned the recall of the Haitian ambassador from Dahomey: "I suppose you read in the papers about the so very sad development of my enterprise with Father Georges and his merry men. Perhaps something will still come of it but the signs are not good so far."

Georges did not give up easily. On January 3, 1967, he was taken into custody in Key West with 24 other revolutionaries who were bound for Haiti. Another fifty-one Haitian and Cuban exiles were jailed in Miami, while more than 200 managed to escape an American Coast Guard's raid on the small island of Cocoa Plum in the Florida Keys. According to *The Washington Post*, "A company commander who escaped, Anton Constanzo, detailed the invasion plans, which were compact but ambitious. He said twenty exiles had already been sneaked into Haiti and were set to attack and capture a small airport at Cape Haitien, a port on the remote north coast what is a favorite target of numerous plotters against dictator François Duvalier.

"A miniature air force of five planes was to use the field for staging runs at the garrison next to the presidential palace at Port-au-Prince. Then, as rebels rallied and confusion spread in the tiny Haitian army, a seaborne commando band of [100] men or more was to go ashore at Port-au-Prince and oust Duvalier. . . . But customs agents, who had staked out the island hideaway for days, stopped the Haitian adventure before it got started. When the commandos were spotted loading a 55-foot shrimp boat last night, agents decided to strike. . . . They surrounded a large two-story concrete blockhouse, and exiles came tumbling out.

"The agents explained that everybody was under arrest. After mutterings and shouts in Spanish and French, the commandos lined up in a military formation and began marching toward U.S. Highway 1. They said they were going to march to Miami to protest their arrest. Outnumbered custom agents called for help. Twenty sheriff's deputies roared in. but the men did not stop marching until cruisers blocked the road.

"Inside the house, agents found an arsenal. Masferrer said it included 100 M-1 rifles, fifty carbines, ten automatic rifles, fifteen .30-caliber machine guns, ten .50-caliber machine guns, six 60-millimeter mortars, three 81-mm mortars and fifty Belgian rifles."

The son of pantomime performers, Jesuit-educated, Oxford University student, actor turned director and producer, and a very charming English gentleman proved at heart he was a revolutionary. Much to Peter's disappointment, the revolution never happened. But the lack of plaudits for *Hotel Paradiso* and *The Comedians* after the Oscar nominated glory of *Becket* was a much greater blow. Peter's career was on the wane. For Peter a life spent on location, far from the opulence of his New York home while dealing with actors' egos, and producing films meant he had more responsibility and more to worry about. It was all beginning to appear to be more effort than it was worth.

12

No 'Out Cry'

1967-1973

As the 1960s drew to a close Peter's life away from the stage and screen was changing. It part it was a change brought about by shifting styles, fresh faces and new ideas in the theater and in film. His attempts at bringing projects to the screen had failed; he worked on a screen adaptation of a Proust novel and *The Tower of Babel*, a film set in the Middle East—neither came to fruition. Neither was his collateral what it had been, despite the fact that he could still command the opportunity to work with some of the very best writers and actors. Whereas many people have to work to live, Peter had lived to work; yet he had so many interests away from the theater. But it was still work and in order to pursue the other areas of life that were important to Peter he was contemplating retirement. Peter's character meant that whatever he threw himself into became all-consuming; for him "retirement" was what other people might well call work.

The lease on his house on Brompton Square had also expired and he wasn't given the opportunity to renew it. Although Peter had sublet the house in order to establish his non-resident tax status, he still used it on occasional visits and was sad to lose the home he had lived in, on and off, for over twenty years. It was the last place in England that he could call home. From then on whenever he visited London he stayed in rented properties on short lets or in hotels.

Once *The Comedians* was done Peter returned to the theater to direct Albee's *Everything in the Garden* on Broadway; it had a strange genesis. Albee, the leading American playwright had adapted a play written by Giles Cooper, an Irishman known for his scriptwriting work for the BBC. Cooper met a tragic end in December 1966, when, aged just forty-eight, he fell from a train and was killed. Albee dedicated his adaptation of *Everything in the Garden* to his memory. An absurdist comedy, it tells the story of a middle-class couple who make money from the wife's extra-curricular activity as a prostitute.

The Pulitzer Prize–winning Albee transposed Cooper's tale of keeping up with the Joneses to American suburbia. The result is a long way from Albee's 1962 masterpiece *Who's Afraid of Virginia Woolf?* Although it still explores themes that satirize the "American Dream" and life behind the picket fences of the middle-class. The production reunited Peter with actresses Barbara Bel Geddes and Beatrice Straight, who he had worked with on *Silent Night, Lonely Night* and *The Innocents* respectively. Bel Geddes played the lead role of the wife and part-time hooker, Jenny, and Barry Nelson her husband, Richard; they were frequent collaborators having played opposite each other in popular Broadway plays including 1961's *Mary, Mary*. Casting them in *Everything in the Garden* was Albee's call, as he wanted to recall the feel of these light-hearted comedies, and thereby sharpen the barbs of his hard-hitting black comedy. Straight played Mrs. Toothe, the Madame who runs the bordello that pays for the suburban inhabitants' lawn mowers and cocktail parties.

Rehearsals began in late October 1967 at the dramatist's Manhattan townhouse on West 10th Street. When the eleven cast members assembled for their first reading Peter informed them of some "tiny nipettes" he and Albee had made to the script, and "chortled" as Bel Geddes and Nelson read their lines. Rehearsals then shifted to the Plymouth Theatre (now The Gerald Schoenfeld Theatre) as they prepared for the opening night a month later.

As the previews got underway Peter wrote to his friend Gore Vidal: "The comedic side certainly goes well, but I have no means yet to know what the audience reaction is to the blacker side of the play, which takes over in the third act. It is certainly an interesting evening with good performances, but it is anybody's guess what the critical reaction will be to it. I imagine theatre people will find it pretty fascinating."

Peter was right; Albee's play met a mixed reception from reviewers. They found its condemnation of materialism and cynical view of a smug, but hypocritical, America uncomfortable to watch. *Time* saluted it as "Albee's most satisfying dramatic effort since Virginia Woolf" and the *New York Post* declared it as the best American play of the season. *The Times* said: "Peter Glenville's direction intensifies Mr. Albee's sombre approach and permits that expert light comedian Barry Nelson to give an unaccustomed display of overpowering grief. Barbara Bel Geddes does less well as the wife, remaining resolutely but inexplicably dowdy throughout her rise to sudden wealth." *The New York Times* was less convinced, questioning Albee's purpose: "Wrong as the play is in its moment-by-moment and then in its final effect, we listen to every word that is spoken, commanded by the author's deliberateness, alarmed by its self-destructive drift. Mr. Albee's capacities are not in question. His pointlessly convoluted, stylistically perverse use of them is."

Comparisons were drawn between Albee's adaptation and Cooper's original, to Albee's detriment, with critics preferring Cooper's subtlety. In the end the production was a modest success and ran until February 1968.

Peter then moved on to take over as the director of *Dear World*. It proved to be a disaster. The musical which was based on Giraudoux's 1943 comedy *La Folle de Chaillot* (*The Madwoman of Chaillot*) tells the story of an eccentric Parisian Countess, who tackles a group of oil speculators set to ruin the city shortly after the Second World War. The play was transformed into a musical by Jerome Lawrence, the composer-lyricist of the massive 1960s Broadway hits, *Hello, Dolly!* and *Mame* along with librettists Robert E. Lee and Jerry Herman, who were also behind *Mame*. The $720,000 production got off to a troubled start well before Peter's involvement—its original director Lucia Victor resigned after two-and-a half weeks of rehearsals citing artistic differences with its authors and star, Angela Lansbury. By the time of Peter's arrival in late October what had started out as a chamber musical had evolved into an overblown Pandora's box with a huge cast performing numerous ballet and dance sequences. When the critics panned *Dear World* at its Boston opening on November 11 Peter resigned and the creative team immediately set about rewriting the entire show.

The musical, which was planned to open in late December, was all set to become the most expensive flop in Broadway history. It eventually opened on Broadway in February 1969 receiving a chilly response from the critics. It was only Lansbury's Tony Award-winning performance that saved the day, allowing it to run for 132 performances.

Peter had little time to reflect on either his performance as director, or the production, as his father suffered a stroke. Shaun passed away in his sleep at his home in London on December 28 at the age of eighty-four. Peter was in England when his father died and was able to help Dorothy organize the funeral. A service was held at St. James' church in Spanish Place in Marylebone and Peter read from the Bible to a large gathering of mourners, many from the theater world. Afterward Shaun's body was cremated and buried at Kensal Green Cemetery in North London. A graveyard favored by Victorians, the cemetery is where Anthony Trollope and Harold Pinter are buried, and it was immortalized by Catholic writer G.K Chesterton in a poem he wrote: "For there is good news yet to hear and fine things to be seen; Before we go to Paradise by way of Kensal Green." Peter and other family members held a wake at Dorothy's home.

Taking time to mourn Shaun, Peter only directed only one production in 1969. It was Osborne's play *A Patriot for Me*, set during the last years of the Austro-Hungarian Empire. Although regarded as one of Osborne's lesser works when first performed in London in 1965 it still managed to cause a huge outcry. The tale of *fin de siècle* homosexuality was refused a license by the Lord Chamberlain's Office so it was shown at a private members' club at the Royal Court Theatre; the drama is regarded as instrumental in the demise of Britain's outdated institution for censorship. It is based on the true story of Lieutenant Alfred Redl, a soldier from humble beginnings, who rises through the ranks to become deputy chief of the army's espionage service. Simultaneously he becomes aware of his own homosexuality, and as he explores his sexuality he lays himself open to blackmail by the Russians. Once exposed as a traitor, he shoots himself.

Peter finally got to work with Austrian actor and Oscar winner Maximillan Schell, whom he had considered casting in *Becket*. Schell played the tormented Redl, Dennis King the aging homosexual Baron von Epp, and Salome Jens the Russian spy, Countess Sophia Delyanoff. Rehearsals began in September and the production opened in October at the Imperial Theatre.

Critics pronounced *A Patriot for Me* pointless. They disliked Osborne's trawl into history, asserting that the dramatist's best works came about when he stuck to the present. They had little praise for the cast and *Time* bemoaned: "Dennis King plays the role in tiara and gown, and flutters an imperious fan with the regal disdain of a queen of players. At no other point does the play rise to this level of theatricality. Salome Jens adorns the evening physically as a Russian Mata Hari, but she delivers her lines like a fishwife. As for Maximilian Schell, he is frostily remote. Director Peter Glenville doubtless tried to coax some emotion out of Schell, but he might as well have pleaded with a two-by-four." The *Los Angeles Times* was even more vehement in its putdown saying Osborne's work was "a dreary, static play in which resemblances to anything living is coincidental." Once again Schell's performance was pronounced "wooden," and Peter was deemed inept: "Peter Glenville . . . has made a good stab but we find that he's aimed his sabre at a dummy, a punching bag, kapok-filled, and unworthy of anyone's concern."

Rosenthal, however, contradicts the reviewers' assessment of the "fascinating play" he was able to "drench with music." He composed 45 minutes of music for the dance scenes—a mêlée of waltzes, gavottes and minuets. He said Peter was thrilled and that Schell gave a magnificent performance. However well Crowley's play may have done off-Broadway, *A Patriot for Me* was shown on Broadway, and its subject matter didn't have commercial appeal. "In 1969 homosexuality was a touchy subject in New York or anywhere," said Rosenthal. "People were uncomfortable despite the fact that the production dealt with it tastefully and decorously. The play wasn't a smash hit but it should have been a brilliant production. I met Peter at a party afterwards, he told me was, 'tired of beating his head against a stone wall' and wanted to enjoy the rest of his life." It was the last time Peter and Rosenthal worked together in the theater.

The production wasn't a complete wash out, and King's performance as the aging Baron won him a Tony nomination for best featured actor in a play. Nor did Freddy Wittop's extravagant costumes go unnoticed, gaining him a Tony nomination and winning him a Drama Desk Award for outstanding costume design.

There was also a young man among the cast for whom the play made a huge difference. For the 23-year-old, future Oscar-winning actor Tommy Lee Jones, *A Patriot for Me* was his Broadway debut, and moreover won him a coveted actors' union card. The Texan-born Jones moved to New York after graduating from Harvard to try his luck at acting. To get a job he needed to be a member of the Actors' Equity Association, to become a member of the union he needed a job. Jones recalled how he circumvented the Catch-22 situation: "If you didn't have a union card, you insinuated that you did by suddenly frantically searching for your wallet and then saying you'd left it at home."

Jones went to an open-call audition for *A Patriot for Me* and by the combination of his subterfuge and nascent talent won a part—actually, three parts. The play demanded a huge cast, and Jones was one of those given a chorus contract, which meant he played three roles: a Private, a Boy and an Orthodox Priest. But he only had one line. Jones was ebullient: "I was very happy, it was the beginning of my professional working life."

The young actor found Peter "just fine" as a director, although he had little interaction with him until he thought about leaving. When the play arrived on Broadway after a short provincial tour, Jones was offered another, and bigger, role off-Broadway. "I thought I'd got a better part, so I could just move along," said Jones, "I asked to speak to Peter, and I remember sitting at the back of the theatre and telling him this. He was very amused and patient with my naivety. He said to me, 'You've made a commitment and if you know what's good for you, you'll stay.' I did, and it worked out for me because when it closed I went from this play to the next. Peter was generous, kind and understanding to me even though I had been a bit stupid." He did not have to wait long as it ran for forty-nine performances.

Peter returned to England to direct his first West End play for fourteen years, Rattigan's *A Bequest to the Nation*. It wasn't just a homecoming for Peter; it was a return to the fold for its author. Peter and Rattigan stayed in touch even when they weren't collaborating, and the writer valued Peter's opinion sufficiently that he sent him scripts to read. The 1960s had been a tough decade for Rattigan as kitchen-sink realism took hold his plays fell out of fashion with the backlash against him being churlish as well as verging on cruel. He had also suffered personal problems that stalled his output: he was diagnosed with leukemia in 1962; the original diagnosis was found to be incorrect it was a virus. Rattigan fell ill again in 1968 and alienated by England, and its culture, tired of poor notices, he moved to Bermuda to live in semi-retirement writing lucrative screenplays and plays for television.

There had not been a new Rattigan play since *Man and Boy*. Yet Rattigan was convinced that the cultural *volte-face* was a fad: "I've seen other fashions come and go. The wheel will eventually come around full circle. And we'll have actors wearing clothes again and a curtain that opens and closes. When the maid answers the telephone, everyone will be terribly moved because it will look new." Rattigan's optimism was rewarded. *A Bequest to the Nation* awakened a fresh interest in his work, and it prompted a successful revival of *The Winslow Boy* only six weeks after its opening.

A Bequest to the Nation is based on the dramatist's 1966 TV play, *Nelson—A Portrait in Miniature*. The proceeds went to Prince Philip's Duke of Edinburgh's Award scheme and the Cutty Sark Society; it had been Prince Philip who had encouraged Rattigan to write the play. The author said he had always thought of the British naval hero, Vice-Admiral Viscount Horatio Nelson, as "a dull fellow" to which the Prince retorted: "Well, if you write about him, you might make him interesting."

The play recounts the story of the last three months of Nelson's life, and his death at the Battle of Trafalgar in 1805. Its title refers to a document written by Nelson on the eve of the confrontation in which he bequeaths his mistress Lady Emma Hamilton and their daughter Horatia to king and country: "that they will give her an ample pension to maintain her rank in life."

Although the nation remembered Nelson's relatives generously, it ignored his request regarding his paramour. Hamilton died in Calais from dysentery, nine years after her lover, in straitened circumstances.

Peter began rehearsals in August with a cast headed by Zoe Caldwell as Hamilton, Ian Holm as Nelson, Leueen MacGrath as his forgiving wife Lady Frances Nelson and Michael Aldridge as the Scottish nobleman Lord Gilbert Minto, readying for a first night at the Theatre Royal Haymarket in September. Binkie Beaumont staged *A Bequest to the Nation* together with Caldwell's husband, Robert Whitehead and with a strong gallery of players and Rattigan's name on the bill—"a class of professional writer that has vanished"—the play drew massive press attention, with reporters lining up for interviews. Rattigan was forthright with his views. "The play is about Nelson at the age of forty-seven, but he's not a burnt-out case. He has this wild infatuation for the plump lady and doesn't mind about the scandal he is causing. . . . The English theatre is settling down now. Just after John Osborne one was written off before one came in as an old traditionalist. But now, I think, people are getting some perspective. There is room for all kinds of theatre." He was correct, as the *Daily Mail* revealed: "Who would have predicted that in 1970, the year of *Oh! Calcutta!*, the West End would be dominated by Coward, Priestley, Rattigan and [Robert] Bolt? Ibsen, Shaw, Chekov, even Maugham and Boucicault, have provided some of the biggest successes."

The redheaded Australian Zoe Caldwell had played at Stratford and London's Royal Court before trying her luck in America, where she won acclaim on Broadway as the Scottish teacher in *The Pride of Miss Jean Brodie*. After a ten-year absence Caldwell returned to Britain together with two Tony Awards to play the blowsy Hamilton—Peter and Rattigan had waited two years for her to be available at the same time as Holm. Caldwell had recently given birth, and they were keen for her to maintain her curvaceous appearance, saying: "That's marvelous, keep it, keep it." The actress gained a stone to play Hamilton at ten stones seven pounds, eating potatoes, bread and Yorkshire puddings to maintain her weight. Caldwell played Hamilton as a bawdy, foul-mouthed trollop and stole the show. Rattigan's Hamilton had lost her ravishing beauty, she was a woman dissipated by drink and gluttony and given to sexual innuendo and raucousness that would "cause Aunt Edna to raise an eyebrow" with lines like: "I don't give a fart." Rattigan was uninterested in shocking theatergoers, telling *The Scotsman* that by then Aunt Edna would wear "blue jeans and go to the Royal Court."

Ian Holm was another Tony Award winner, and at thirty-eight years old was yet another Shakespearian actor from Stratford and the Royal Shakespeare Company whom the newspapers touted as Olivier's successor. He won good notices as Nelson but in his autobiography he revealed that he didn't enjoy the experience: "I couldn't help feeling that I was participating in a relic, that the play was somehow out of its time and the goodish notices were inspired by nostalgic generosity as much as anything else. It wasn't a bad piece of work and it wasn't a bad production, but a story set almost two hundred years ago was hardly at the cutting edge. Rattigan was a refugee from a time when writers were forced to hide their ideas behind a story audiences would accept, and increasingly I felt awkward in the role. It did pay well . . . but somehow it wasn't the meaningful soul-saving work for which I had been searching."

The production was the stage debut of former wrestler and schoolteacher Brian Glover as Nelson's staunch Flag Captain, Thomas Hardy. A colleague at Glover's school, Barry Hines, wrote *A Kestrel for a Knave* that was made into the 1968 Ken Loach movie, *Kes*. The director approached Glover to play the bullying games master and his performance was regarded a success. Glover returned to teaching, but when Beaumont saw the film he thought he would be ideal in the role of Hardy and made him an offer. "I wanted a stalwart, heart-of-oak man for Hardy," said Peter. "Because film acting is easier for beginners, I put him through a testing stage audition. But he did it extremely well."

Peter brought designer Oliver Smith over from America to do the sets. After Messel had moved on to a career in architecture and interior design, Smith had become one Peter's favorite designers. Smith was then fifty years old with white hair in a crew cut and a tall, lanky frame. Trained as an architect during the Great Depression, the lack of new buildings forced him towards a career in the theater. Smith, the designer behind the 1961 Broadway hit *West Side Story* and films including 1955's *Guys and Dolls*, was widely respected. His designs for Hamilton's bedroom and Nelson's Surrey home at Merton Place were described as "a joy to behold."

When *A Bequest to the Nation* premiered in the West End Dorothy was there along with a host of Nelson's relatives and a fair smattering of the great and the wealthy. It won warm reviews. "A play of weight, entertainment and shapeliness which earns full honours by the ingredients of a fascinating human situation and by the cunning of its preparation. Mr. Rattigan has produced a genuine theatrical shock without looking as though he was trying to in the least," said the *Daily Mail*. The *Financial Times* gushed: "In Mr. Rattigan's hands this is tremendous theatre. . . . This is a splendid romantic composition, the work of a master of entertainment." As did *The Stage*: "Rattigan, like Shaw, achieves a triumph of showing genius in flower."

Not that *A Bequest to the Nation* had an entirely easy ride from reviewers.

Some, like Holm, found the play old fashioned, while others thought Peter's direction "staid"—and by contemporary standards they were. Rattigan's most successful plays were written when he had to grapple with the censors and was forced to subterfuge as his biographers Darlow and Hodson pointed out: "Rattigan made his art depend on the oblique, the implicit, the struggle of frightened, damaged people to find self-expression and fulfilment in a society whose strict moral codes inhibited them. Once the moral codes had been relaxed in the theatre, Rattigan was not only out of fashion, he was stranded. . . . The result was that when he tried to confront sex in his writing, however frankly and sincerely, in the permissive atmosphere of, he seemed evasive, insincere the post-Osborne theatre and sometimes actually embarrassing."

But others liked the play. *The Observer*, called Rattigan "the playwright we lost to permissiveness": "Against the gains our new theatrical freedoms have brought us should be set one major loss: Terence Rattigan." *The Illustrated London News* said the production "remains under Peter Glenville's direction a strong and pleasantly debatable theatrical experience in the old style of portrait play, with less cardboard then one might have feared." *The Daily Telegraph* was full of admiration: "Glenville has directed . . . his fine company with a discretion and imagination too long missing from the London theatre. . . . [He and Rattigan] are senior craftsmen, and their names guarantee an evening with a certain quality of pleasure."

In March 1971 Peter began working on a new film, *Man of La Mancha*. Based on the Broadway musical of the same name, it is an adaptation of Miguel de Cervantes' 17th-century novel, *Don Quixote*. It tells the story of the eccentric Spanish knight, Don Quixote de la Mancha, as a play within a play performed by Cervantes and his fellow prisoners as he awaits trial before the Spanish Inquisition. The original 1965 play ran for 2,328 performances and won five Tony Awards. The musical's book was written by Dale Wasserman, the lyrics by Joe Darion and the music by Mitch Leigh. Wasserman, Leigh and the director of the stage production, Albert Marre, were hired to make the movie, while the Broadway stars, Richard Kiley and Joan Diener were screen tested in anticipation of the two actors repeating their stage roles. Following a dispute with United Artists Marre was fired, and Wasserman, Leigh, Kiley and Diener left the project.

Peter was brought in on the understanding that Wasserman's script was dropped, and a version written by John Hopkins was used. Hopkins, a British writer known for his work on the popular TV drama series *Z Cars*, was no stranger to writing for the big screen having received a co-screenwriter credit for the 1965 James Bond film *Thunderball* as well as writing the screenplay for 1969's *The Virgin Soldiers*. When United Artists' Charles Adams Baker read Hopkins' script in May he wrote to Peter: "I am as pleased with his work as I was critical of the original script which I found false and common in the extreme."

The film was to be shot in Italy and so Peter and Bill rented an apartment in Rome to begin the hunt for locations and a cast. O'Toole agreed to play the lead role of Don Quixote/Cervantes/Alonso Quijana and Sophia Loren that of Aldonza/Dulcinea. Peter wasn't looking for singing actors because, apart from the two principals, each character only had one song: "and so I am concentrating on acting performances with dubbed singing, since the script is very much an actor's vehicle rather than a musical in the ordinary sense of the word."

Peter was keen to hire James Coco, with whom he had worked on in *Hotel Paradiso* to play Don Quixote's sidekick, Sancho Panza and Cervantes' Manservant. Coco cabled Peter in June saying: "I was born to play Sancho." Peter also hired John Castle as the Duke/Dr. Sanson Carrasco and Ian Richardson as the Padre. Peter brought Rosenthal onboard too. Although Leigh was off the project and in dispute with United Artists, he had powers of approval regarding the music. He wasn't keen on Rosenthal but Peter fought to hire his composer of choice almost from the moment he took over as director.

He wrote to his agent Paul Rosen explaining his choice of Rosenthal: "Apart from being a brilliant classical composer (he got an Oscar nomination for his work . . . in *Becket*), [he] would make my schedule here much easier since I am so used to working with him. . . . In view of the fact that the new script will have scenes with quite different moods and more subtle implications, I urgently need a musician who, while using the melodic themes of the original compositions—as is required by contract—can translate them into the new action and implications required by the Hopkins script. It is a great bore and I am nervous about the timing of the orchestral arrangements and songs which will have to be pre-recorded prior to shooting, which gives us very little time."

By the beginning of July Leigh agreed to Rosenthal prompting Peter to write to Paul Rosen: "Frankly, I think he [Leigh] should be extremely happy that a musician of Rosenthal's calibre is interested to do so much legwork on a project, especially in view of the contract which ties down the musician so very tightly to the themes as already written by Leigh. I certainly think the film calls for more than a musical comedy orchestrator and I know of very few talented composer orchestrator conductors who would be willing to spend a year on a project which gives them no opportunity for original composition." Rosenthal went on to gain an Oscar nomination for Original Song Score and Adaptation for his work on *Man of La Mancha*.

Another difficulty for Peter was his billing—always a touchy subject with directors and producers. When he agreed to do the film he negotiated a contract as director and replaced Alberto Grimaldi as producer. The studio wrote to Peter saying: "It was agreed by United Artists that they would use their best efforts to style the film somewhat along the lines of 'Peter Glenville's production of' or 'Peter Glenville's film of' with, of course, separate producer and director billing." Peter was unhappy about their vagueness and wrote to Rosen: "What is the inference [in] United Artists' 'best efforts' cannot arrange for 'Peter Glenville production of'? As things are working out in practice, I could not possibly, with any degree of sense or logic, agree to anyone else being given production credit, since in fact nobody else is producing in any accepted sense of the word."

United Artists wanted to leave Grimaldi with the role of Italian producer but Peter disagreed: "Personally I get along very well with Grimaldi whom I find to be a most pleasant person and, I would think, extremely honest and well-meaning. However, he is not in any sense an active administrator or producer, but is a promotional and legal figure who has had considerable success in setting up and financing some Italian westerns which did extremely well.

"The main problem with his office is that for all positive and executive decisions and actions he has to rely entirely on his staff. It was apparent that he had a preference for rather minor employees who, albeit probably very efficient, were too much in the nature of dependents without the necessary strength of authority to help organise a big American musical."

Peter was worried about practicalities. Grimaldi relied on a production manager who only spoke Italian who would be unable to communicate with Peter's English-speaking technicians. Peter wanted the contract amended so that his own production credit would appear on the film everywhere bar Italy. At the end of June he wrote to United Artists again: "You have always been a little vague about the exact credit situation in regard to this film and if you remember, I wrote to you before about the need for extremely strong specifics on this point, not only in regard to the title itself but also with regard to size and style of type and position on the bills. If these things are not worked out well in advance, they can poison the entire period of post-production and first exposure of the film for the people concerned."

Peter wanted a guarantee that the film credit would say "Produced and directed by Peter Glenville" and that the billing should not be equal in size or type by that of Grimaldi. Correspondence was batted back and forth and in July the studio agreed that Peter would receive "a presentation credit above the title in substantially the form of 'A Peter Greenville Film'" throughout the world and "Produced and directed by

Peter Glenville" below the title throughout the world "ex Italy," where it would be "Directed by Peter Glenville." After five months of work Peter was relieved that United Artists "are now ready to discuss the detailed terms of my contract."

In reality the terms of Peter's billing was potentially irrelevant as he outlined to Rosen in July: "We have prepared an Italian and post-production budget, leaving certain of the above-the-line items out, which totals four million seven [dollars], excluding the two-hundred-and-fifty-thousand [dollars] spent by Grimaldi, Leigh and Marre on tests and various expenses, none of which constitutes realisable items in the actual production. In other words: total loss."

Peter had taken over a production that had already blown a significant amount of money: "[the] test costs were . . . ridiculously high. . . . I don't honestly think that any effort was ever made to reduce whatever requests were made for payment." One way he thought of cutting costs was to ask the British and American crew to fly tourist class to the shoot, and, by way of a first, to do so himself to set an example.

He was aghast at the deal Grimaldi had negotiated with costume designer [Luciano] Damiani telling his agent: "I have now read it and find that it is extravagant and untenable to the point of absurdity. It guarantees him high payment and living expenses until the end of shooting, with no possibility of a cut off or termination of services." Because of five months of postponements of original filming dates he pointed out that this "will make his total payments about three times that of any star designer in America; that is to say, impermissibly high."

Peter had come to the realization that he had inherited a poisoned chalice: "From a practical and producing point of view, I would never again wish to be associated with a film in which the organising and producing elements had already been set up in so unprofessional and risky a manner." In early August matters got worse when United Artists wanted to use a meld of the original and latest script. Peter wrote to Rosen: "I am sure you will understand that a very serious situation might arise if on Sunday it turns out that [U.A.] really wishes us to return half way to the Wasserman script, which as you know I twice declined when the film was originally proposed to me. I think any attempt to combine Hopkins and Wasserman would have an even worse result as the two writing styles are so different. This would be getting the worst of all possible worlds."

By August 12 it was all over. United Artists thought the budget was too high and Peter was off the project: "United Artists have decided to do a much smaller production and asked me to go back to the original theatre version which . . . I turned down when they first mentioned the project to me. There is no doubt that Hopkins' version would require a higher budget, but personally I am too out of sympathy with the Broadway-Wasserman version to agree to direct it."

As Peter wrote to Rosen, "I suspect that the *volte-face* about the Hopkins script is largely based on the question of the budget . . . that they wanted to spend less money and do a smaller production. . . . However this is now a thing of the past. I just think it is regrettable that if the budget for the new script is the basic problem, as I am inclined now to think it is, it would have been more sensible for them to have asked us to adjust it to a given figure, which I have never shown any disinclination to do—unless of course they really love the Wasserman version, in which case the whole situation was indeed impossible. However, it seems outrageous to me that they should have had such a change of front after six months, when I had already made my position perfectly clear about that script when they first proposed the film to me. Moreover, both John [Hopkins] and I have had letters indicating no only their acceptance of the Hopkins' version but also their enthusiasm for it. Indeed it was an enthusiasm which did not even provide for any minor criticisms along the way."

Arthur Hiller was brought in as director and Saul Chaplin as associate producer. Hiller had been nominated for a Best

Director Oscar for 1970's *Love Story*. Chaplin was a composer who moved into producing and was behind 1965's *The Sound of Music*. Those that Peter left behind were nervous. Rosenthal said that when Peter walked off that he, Coco, Loren, O'Toole, Castle and Richardson were "dismayed"—Peter as "the captain of the ship" was why they were there. Rosenthal said he agreed to work on a film where he couldn't write the score because, "I wanted to work with Peter again and spend a year in Rome. We had a wonderful cast and I got to work with Peter O'Toole and Sophia Loren."

He said Hiller was an unexpected choice as replacement and the director admitted to his cast he wasn't really used to musicals or costume dramas; he also knew nothing about Don Quixote or Cervantes. Rosenthal revealed: "We wondered what we'd got into as what we had got us to do the film was the director. Peter had known a lot about Cervantes. Things went from bad to worse, it wasn't much fun. [U.A.] then started to worry that Arthur Hiller was inexperienced so they sent in Saul Chaplin, and we were even more miserable."

Chaplin's experience on *Man of La Mancha* was an unhappy one. He wasn't pleased that non-singing actors had been hired, although quite why, as the hit musical *My Fair Lady* had had Sir Rex Harrison and Audrey Hepburn in the lead role; O'Toole had also played the lead in the musical *Goodbye, Mr. Chips* three years earlier. When the film came out in 1972, reactions were mixed. But along with Coco and Rosenthal, O'Toole's efforts were recognized; his performance earned him a Golden Globe nomination for Best Motion Picture Actor in a Musical/Comedy and he won the National Board of Review Award for Best Actor, while Coco won a Golden Globe Award for Best Supporting Actor.

After Peter's Roman holiday it was back to the theater and a chance to work with a playwright he respected. He was to direct Tennessee Williams' play *Out Cry*, a revised version of the playwright's *The Two-Character Play* produced in 1967.

Williams' work tells of the relationship of a brother and sister, Felice and Clare, who are locked in a "State Theatre of a state unknown." Believing they have been deserted by their manager and fellow actors and that an audience is arriving they decide to perform the one two-character play they know. The dramatist had worked on his play on and off for a decade and it is a surreal piece focusing on the state of mind of its two performers.

Williams admitted it was a reflection on his own relationship with his sister Rose and a period when he undergone an emotional crisis. In 1963 Williams lost his long-time companion Frank Merlo, who died of cancer, after which his work took on an experimental nature and became more akin to that of Sartre and Becket in its abstraction. The man who had been on the front cover of *Time* in March 1962 and described as the "world's greatest living playwright" had become less popular with the critics. They found his later plays baffling and longed for the lyricism of his previous realistic work. His 1969 play *In the Bar of a Tokyo Hotel* fell foul of reviewers and Time-Life Corporation placed a full-page ad in a June edition of *The New York Times*; beneath a head shot of Williams were the words "Played Out?" printed in large type. In September the burnt-out writer spent two months on a detoxification program, intended to free him from a prolonged dependency on alcohol, amphetamines and barbiturates.

By the time Peter directed *Out Cry*, few directors and producers were keen to work with the playwright. *Out Cry* portrays his alcoholism and self-doubts about his role as an artist in society. But his attempt to tackle his personal demons did not always make for easy viewing. It is a sign of both Peter and David Merrick's loyalty that they even agreed to take on what most people considered a doomed production. In fact, Merrick had wanted to put on Williams' new play *Red Devil Battery Sign*, but the writer had insisted that, in order to obtain the rights, Merrick would have to mount a production of *Out Cry* first. Merrick did so, but put no real commercial wind behind its sails, so his loyalty may have been tinged with altruism. The play was staged by the John F. Kennedy Center for the Performing Arts and Merrick's Arts Foundation, which he founded to stage plays he didn't think would be commercially successful but deserved a chance.

Peter had become a friend of the playwright, who frequently dined at Peter and Bill's Manhattan home. Williams was one of many respected writers with whom Peter was friendly. He knew Rattigan and Wilson from Oxford and became close to Greene through work. Peter always had a fascination with writers and loved the company of Vidal, Capote and Norman Mailer. He loved reading, and such was Peter's passion that he told Vidal when renting his apartment in Rome that he always traveled "with an absurd number of books (three trunks full)": "Usually when one rents a place there is a dreadful dearth of good books, which is most depressing. Anyway we obviously share some mutual interests—all the Byzantine stuff, [Marcel] Proust . . . [Benjamin] Disraeli, the buried city, the Middle Ages, the Dark Ages and heaps of others, so I have just left mine in trunks."

He even once wrote to a friend: "I think if it were not quite the active busybody I am, I would really have enjoyed studying and, even possibly, writing history more than anything else. Indeed, one of my problems is that instead of reading the sort of books that could provide me with interesting new projects for films in the commercial market, I get buried in historical works which, to me, have more interest than any thriller or romantic mishmash."

Peter's fascination with writers was no doubt based on the intellectual banter and stimulation they provided. Yet his practice of tinkering with the text of plays perhaps reveals his own desire to write. He may have professed wanting to be an academic, it seems more plausible that he was a frustrated writer.

His friendship with Williams was par for the course, but Peter actively courted the writer according to Williams' biographer, Dotson Rader, who was a friend of both Peter and the playwright. Peter was keen to work with the best people, and although Williams' career was by then in free fall, Peter still rated him.

Casting *Out Cry* was simpler than most plays as it requires just two performers. English actor Michael York played Felice in what was his Broadway debut and Canadian actress Cara Duff-MacCormick his sister. Both were rising talents with York having joined Olivier's new National Theatre Company in 1965 and a year later made his film debut in Zefferelli's *The Taming of the Shrew*. Duff-MacCormick had been nominated for a Tony for her performance in Michael Weller's 1972 play *Moonchildren*. Williams had approached York to take on the role when they met at the Venice Film Festival, Peter hired Duff-MacCormick after being convinced by her instinctive interpretation at her reading.

York first met Peter when they started rehearsing *Out Cry* in December 1972 at Peter's home: "Peter was always elegantly attired and perfectly groomed—qualities you don't immediately associate with theatre folk. He wore cardigans—like Henry Higgins—and Cara and I were in many ways his relatively inexperienced Eliza Doolittles that he molded into shape. His beautiful apartment reflected this good taste. This was a world away from the cold, inhospitable theatre where Tennessee had set his drama.

"Peter may have looked like an aesthete but his direction was entirely down-to-earth, practical. (Although his choice of [Olivier] Messiaen [theme] music [for *Out Cry*] suggests an ethereal side to his imagination—and wide cultural grounding.) He also had a pervasive sense of humour that relaxed any potential tension and made the work enjoyable. . . . Working with him was a genuine pleasure. . . . Also, with such a small cast our work was concentrated, direct and personal. . . . He was always polite—but at times he could be very firm and direct—which, of course was immensely helpful."

The 31-year-old York was impressed with Peter and admired the way he had conducted his career: "[It was] a relief to have a director with a clear idea and understanding, also a great pleasure to work with someone so profoundly civilised, had a way with words and had profound experience. We were both born in England, both educated at Oxford and both worked in film, but I was establishing a reputation and he had extraordinary reputation. He was doing things I wanted to do, which was not to be pigeonholed as either movie or television or stage actors . . . and I suspect Peter [benefited] by moving from one to another as they feed into each other."

With characteristic meticulousness, Peter prepared a sheaf of notes after a first reading of the play. His initial response was that *Out Cry* was a poetic allegory and "a study of fear developing into panic": "Many artists, especially in their middle years, have been impelled to devote at least one work to the remembrance of a crisis of the spirit—a dark night of the soul, of a moment in time when the landscape of their lives seemed barren and threatening. In literature they have sometimes described their fears during this period of crisis: fear of neglect, of being misunderstood, of being considered abnormal, freakish, which in a magnificent way, the more talented artists often are. Some have feared the exposure of their work to an alien public and so have retreated into a total solitude and into a world of hallucination. Some have become mad and some have killed themselves. For almost all cases there has been the fear of lunacy and of death. This period of spiritual panic has often been endured even by the most urbane and sophisticated writers. (Two recent examples come to mind: [F.] Scott Fitzgerald's *Crack Up* and Evelyn Waugh's *The Ordeal of Mr. Pinfold.*) *Out Cry* seems to me to be a disturbing personal description of this inner crisis of the artist—a *cri de coeur* in a moment of despair. . . .

"As I read the scenes describing the fears of brother and sister of moving out of the house, or even of picking up the telephone, or again the scenes in which as actors they realise that the theatre has neither windows nor doors and is instead a dark prison in which they may be fated endlessly to play out the drama of their early lives, I was reminded of the black period of [Francisco] Goya's paintings. His huge complacent vultures and his cannibal dog bats flitted across my mind; his murky old women sitting at night on the dead branches of ugly trees. The play seems too, to belong to the world of the graceful nightmares of [Henry] Fuseli, and to the last terror filled landscapes of [Vincent] van Gogh. For me, scene after scene, evoked the mood of Van Gogh's vines and cornfields that stretch out towards you and shriek their panic—that terror of lunacy which was a very real threat to both the painter and the dramatists."

Williams, more than most playwrights, was known for rewriting his plays while on tour, as he freely admitted. York found this stimulating yet respected the way Peter dealt with the continual changes—sometimes scribbled on napkins—and how he managed to freeze the process in preparation for its first night on Broadway: "I was enormously impressed with Peter's cutting a firm path through the spatial inexactitudes of Williams' poetic writing—and dealing with the constant rewriting (which for me was one of the most exciting parts of the enterprise). Peter was always in control and yet dealt with Williams with his usual courtesy and deference. A wonderful director to have! Someone to trust—and believe me I've suffered under the opposite kind of director."

The actor kept a diary during rehearsals and when the production went on its Broadway tour. Williams arrived to be with the troupe in New York on December 24 and joined in on rehearsals at the Longacre Theatre west of Broadway four days later. Peter warned his players not to let their "performances reflect subconsciously the presence of the author." On January 5, 1973, they gave their first run through of the play to Mielziner and the designer tried out "on the back wall of the theatre, of the beautiful projections he [had] designed. Images melt into images." Williams supplied some textural emendations.

Two weeks later the play had its world premiere in New Haven. Reviewers were encouraging but found *Out Cry* "too opaque and obscure." Williams set off to do more rewrites. Three days later they headed to Philadelphia. When the play opened there critics were still bemused, and Williams decided to postpone a trip to London to "devote more time to the play." He rewrote the ending while Peter made cuts to lines that seemed to antagonise the audience. By the end of January cuts were made to the "abstruse" opening dialogue. They were insufficient and the scene went through several versions before Williams arrived at a satisfactory rewrite "just before the opening night in New York."

York and Duff-MacCormick acted with their new lines ready for a move to the Eisenhower Theatre in Washington, D.C., where the play opened on February 5. They decided "to wait up for the reviews, alleviating anxiety and a monstrous thirst with champagne." *Out Cry* had a positive reception and Williams was deeply moved: "He interpret[ed] it as an authorisation to continue writing for the theatre."

The box office started to be busy and the production averaged $45,000 a week. Three days later Williams suggested introducing a third character before heading off home to Key West. On February 10 they rehearsed a new ending for the first act. Three days later Peter felt that part of the new rewrite was wrong, on February 23, with the opening speech smoothed out, Peter said the play had to be frozen.

When *Out Cry* opened on Broadway in March reviewers found it as intangible as Williams' other recent plays. *Time*'s somber review was headed "The Crack-Up": "The appearance of *Out Cry* is immensely saddening. Here, the man who suffers and the mind which creates are no more separate than a drunk and his crying jag. In the plays that earned Williams his reputation as America's finest dramatist, he showed that he could impose the order of art on his darkling terrors and forge passion and compassion out of pain. *Out Cry* is devoid of those gifts. . . . Most of [it] is rendered in maundering monologues and non-sequiturish asides. A Williams groping for words, parched for images, fumbling in dramatic craft—all this seems incredible, but alas, it is true."

The New York Times reviewer was more hopeful: "Undoubtedly *Out Cry* is a very brave and very difficult play. It is not ordinary Broadway fare, and seen in the context of Broadway show business its situation and its poetry, its demands on ears and mind, may seem to many merely pretentious. Yet this is an adventure into drama at which many, perhaps the majority, will scoff at, but some will find stimulating. Minorities, needless to say, are not always wrong.

"Peter Glenville's mostly humourless staging struck me as only acceptable, although the two performances were, admittedly, remarkable."

Out Cry closed after ten days.

York said of the play's reception: "The reviews were indeed mixed. I think many reviewers had written Williams off and were upset that he refused to lie down and play dead. But we had enough positive reaction—from audiences and critics alike—to justify the enterprise. Peter himself later said he felt the production would have fared better off-Broadway and described *Out Cry* as . . . a *cri de coeur* from a highly talented and special man. But it's not tragedy because it's not universal enough. It's too subjective, too concerned with his own hang-ups and complexes. It's poetic drama of a high order, but it falls short of tragedy because it's so personal."

Williams' reaction was to blame everyone, and Peter in particular: "I had a number of references to sunflowers in the script; they had these huge projections of sunflowers on the back wall. They weren't necessary, unfortunately. I don't blame it on the gentleman who designed the set, because he was encouraged in this. Everything had to be literally shown. If they were in prison, there had to bars, or trapped figures projected in huge size on the cyclorama of the set. It was put together by Mr. Peter Glenville the director. He arbitrarily took out whatever he thought what he wanted from all the versions. I had practically nothing to do with it. For instance, Genevieve Bujold came down from Canada twice to read the part for the girl. I was not permitted to hear her. She would have been perfect opposite Michael York."

Of the reworking of the play on an ongoing basis while touring he complained: "He did consult me to some extent about it. But I was so overawed by the prospect of having a Broadway production for this little play that I just let him go ahead. Things only got a bit uptight when we were on the road. I felt that I was not being allowed to cut and revise as I should. The time seemed wasted."

The play caused a rift between Peter and Williams from which they never really recovered. *Out Cry* was a highly personal work for Williams so his judgment was a particularly emotional one. Peter had tinkered with the script, often making sheaves of notes that Williams ignored. But the playwright seemed unable to desist from revising his play, and the stress of the process and its poor reception left both of them unhappy. *Out Cry*'s failure was too tough to take, following as it did on the heals of *A Patriot for Me*, *Dear World* and the massive disappointment of *Man of La Mancha*. Whereas *Out Cry* was meant to be a come back for both Peter and Tennessee Williams it was a disappointment for both men. When Williams blamed Peter for casting the female role without his input he may have been right, but it's just as likely that the play was wrong. Peter Glenville had had enough. He decided to retire. He was fifty-nine years old.

Peter had loved everything about the theater but he was falling out of love with what he felt the theater had become. He was used to working at the top level with prominent directors, actors and playwrights. Not everything he had done had found favor with critics and audiences, but he was well respected by his peers, those he worked with and the critics. It was not a case of quitting while he was ahead, nor was he quitting because he had in any way failed. For Peter life held other challenges and it was time to move on.

13

Forgetting Those Things Which Lie Behind

1973-1996

When Peter retired in 1973 he had, just like his Stonyhurst motto, done as much as he could. The changes that had come about in the entertainment industry in 1968 on both sides of the Atlantic had more than likely played a part in his decision. In Britain theatrical censorship ended, and London's theater land celebrated with the opening of *Hair*, the hippy musical known for its irreverence, nudity and four-letter words. London's West End had changed and in America the Production Code was dismantled, and films started to become more violent and sexually explicit. In the year that Peter retired from directing his close friends and collaborators Noël Coward and Beaumont passed away. It really was the end of an era.

Broadway had also gone through some significant changes. The year Peter directed *Out Cry*, it was one of only nine new shows; in the 1970s dozens of old Broadway theaters would be demolished, and many that were left fell into disrepair. By the middle of the decade the fabled street of dreams had lost much of its glitz; Times Square and 42nd Street became a downbeat area populated by seedy bars, strip clubs and sex shops. Merrick produced less shows, choosing instead to head to Hollywood to produce *The Great Gatsby*. The theatrical impresarios were becoming dinosaurs as investors began to hold greater sway. The public's taste had changed and the kind of star-vehicle, extravagant, often highbrow, plays and films that Peter wanted to direct were falling out of fashion.

According to family and friends Peter's decision to retire was an easy one. He had done everything he wanted to do professionally, his passion and his drive had placed him at the top table he had worked with film and theater's greatest writers, actors, directors, composers, designers and costume makers. He was used to success and the respect it garnered; to continue courting mediocrity was impossible to contemplate. Nor did he have to work; he had invested his money wisely. Peter was sixty years old and had worked in the theater and films for forty years. Peter was smart enough to realize that the industry was moving in another direction, a direction he did not want to take himself.

Society columnist Aileen Mehle got to know Peter through mutual friends at parties and dinners, soon after he finished making *The Comedians*. She loved the house on East 68th Street, and when one of its apartments, The Grande Ballroom, became free in the early 1970s she moved there. She remembered when Peter retired: "He told me, 'No more of this, this is it. I don't want to do this any more. . . . I love it but I've done it so long and I'm finished.'" Mehle said that Peter's agent at William Morris attempted to dissuade him, and even begged Mehle to try and persuade Peter to continue directing, all to no avail: "At the end he was still in demand but he didn't want to be in demand. When he'd made up his mind nothing was going to bring him back."

Peter was tempted out of retirement in March 1977 when he signed a contract with an Irish production company, Surprise Productions, to direction an adaptation of Joyce Cary's 1941 novel *Herself Surprised*. His contract reveals that Bill would have acted as assistant director, and Peter had agreed to direct on the understanding he approved the screenplay and Burton starred in the movie. Peter never directed the movie although the project lingered on for some years. In 1982 *People* reported that Burton and Taylor were going to star in the film, by which time the director was slated as Ronald Neame. In 1977 Burton's by then ailing career had a boost when he starred in *Equus*, which won him a Best Actor Oscar nomination the following year. The actor then made *The Medusa Touch* and *The Wild Geese*. Whether Burton's other commitments meant *Herself Surprised* was put on hold, Peter lost interest, or Peter simply didn't like the screenplay is unknown. So despite what he told Mehle, Peter's signing of a contract shows that he would still prepared to work if the right project and cast came along.

He did make a rare appearance on TV in 1982. His friend William F. Buckley Jr., interviewed him to discuss the screening of Granada Television's 1981 TV series *Brideshead Revisited* in America on PBS. Based on Waugh's 1944 novel of the same name the series tell a story of student life at Oxford University between the two world wars, male love and its characters' Catholic faith. Peter was the perfect choice as a commentator. The producer of *Brideshead Revisited* was Charles Sturridge, a former pupil at Stonyhurst, and it is very redolent of Peter's old school. Waugh was a frequent visitor to Stonyhurst in the late 1920s and early 1930s when he went to see a friend from his Oxford days, Christopher Hollis—the history teacher "who changed [Peter's] life." Waugh was influenced by Hollis' spirituality, and after Waugh became a Catholic in 1930 the first person he went to see was Hollis. Stonyhurst is one of the locations at which Waugh wrote 1932's *Black Mischief*.

Apart from this brief TV appearance, Peter's life in entertainment was over and his social and home life became the focus of his considerable energy. Peter and Bill's Manhattan home was the epitome of elegant grandeur. They had called upon the services of an old friend, the designer Geoffrey Bennison, to decorate it. Bennison helped them furnish Brompton Square, but his work on East 68th Street reached fresh heights. Peter's friend, the biographer John Richardson, revealed how Peter got to know Bennison during the Second World War: "Geoffrey and I had been students at London's Slade School of Art where Geoffrey was by far and away the most gifted pupil. [He was] a demon draughtsman and budding theatrical designer who had benefited from studying under Vladimir Polunin, the great scene painter who had taught Picasso much of what he knew about stagecraft and executed his hugely influential design for Diaghilev's Ballet Ruses. Geoffrey was looking forward to becoming a set designer but he got tuberculosis and was packed off to a sanatorium in Cornwall. On a trip to London in about 1946 he met Peter and Bill, who were fascinated by Geoffrey's innate flair for theatre design . . . and they were very concerned by Geoffrey's deteriorating health. 'You're only hope is to go to Davos,' Peter said."

Peter was appalled at the situation, and regardless of Bennison's reservations, he arranged for him to have a cure at the world-famous Wald sanatorium in Davos in the Swiss Alps where Thomas Mann wrote *The Magic Mountain*. The cure took seven years and Bennison nearly died but, thanks to Peter's kind intervention, he was eventually able to return to London. Peter continued to be a valuable help by introducing Bennison to people in the theater world because he wanted to be a set designer. But Peter then told Bennison he was wasting his time as set designer, suggesting he become an interior designer, and he started out by sourcing furniture for Peter's home at Brompton Square. By the time Bill acquired East 68th Street, Bennison had become an antiques dealer and interior designer with several shops, and was known for his eccentric take on classical style and his eye for luxurious fabrics. He said that he felt that Peter had saved him from certain death and agreed to decorate the *piano nobile* free of charge, and scoured antique markets and auction houses for furniture and upholstery. Although the house had once belonged to Standard Oil heiress Millicent Rogers, who was famed for her panache and elegance, its rooms needed rethinking and furbishing.

Peter wrote an article about Bennison for *World of Interiors* in 1985, describing him as: "Funny and endearing, eccentric and affectionately bossy, he had the infallible colour sense of the fine painter he would certainly have become if tuberculosis . . . had not cut short that promising career. But he had no self-pity because of his ordeal, and his view of the world remained keenly satirical. A Yorkshireman with a firm sense of reality, he was sophisticated, sensual, and at times sentimental. Although not interested in any form of intellectualism, he was extraordinarily bright."

The result of Bennison's two-year-long endeavor was an apartment in the grand style. The living room, hall and study were filled with tapestries, Turkish carpets, oil paintings, marble and bronze busts, gilt mirrors, 18th-century furniture and chandeliers. The drawing room was reminiscent of the Versailles Hall of Mirrors with mirrors set in *boiserie* to reflect one another, and the library contained a portrait of Fernando II of Medici, a coffee table of petrified wood, a 17th-century brass Dutch chandelier and Regency sofas. Peter and Bill had separate bedrooms, and Peter's contained a Chippendale four-poster bed that once belonged to 18th-century actor, director and playwright David Garrick. The Louis XVI *boiserie* in the dining room was lit by candlelight from an 18th-century carved wood-and-crystal chandelier and 18th-century *torchers* topped with French Empire candelabras carved to resemble Egyptian figures, at its center was an octagonal marble table. A friend of Peter's, novelist Fernanda Eberstadt, described the apartment:

"[It] looked as if an English duke had gone mad on a Grand Tour of Asia Minor, and plundered a few Medici palaces on his way home. Much bronze, silk, and marbled magnificence, not much daylight." Bennison's work on the house served him well. His reputation soared and he went on to decorate the homes of wealthy clients including Isabel Goldsmith and the Rothschilds.

Peter threw dinner parties when everything was done with great style and panache. The silver cutlery from Asprey's that included prawn forks and grape scissors, Waterford cut glass, 19th-century gold-edged Limoges dinner service, silver goblets and candlesticks were laid, and flowers adorned the room. Peter had lists of grand, smart and beautiful guests, who would prove to be genial company and provide for some lively intellectual banter. Peter was the perfect host and entertained his guests with stories—he was a superb raconteur and mimic. Janet Ward said: "He'd sit and tell you stories and you'd be mesmerised. He spoke such beautiful English and never took on a twang of an Americanism. He had a way of phrasing [such] that he could tell a story and pause at the right part. It was wonderful."

He was embraced by New York society: no gossip column or social event was complete without him and he attended concerts, shows, parties and benefits. His guests found as much entertainment in his home as they would have had at an evening at the theater, and they were attracted by his mischievous humor, love of gossip, youthful zest for life, engaging manner, sharp intellect, generosity and kindness. Mehle said: "He knew everyone and he was a friend to everyone; he was very much in demand. He had such a marvellous personality: wit, charm, intelligence and then of course he looked rather like a matinée idol. . . . He was a fine-looking man with great features and he had that British look . . . he was very distinguished looking."

Spending time with Peter was never dull and his guests would provide provocative debate, ranging as they did from priests to the publisher of *The Washington Post*, Katharine Graham. As much as Peter liked to mix things up a little, the one thing he did insist on was that his guests have good manners, Peter didn't like swearing, inappropriate sexual conversations or drunken behavior, and was insistent that his guests behave with a sense of decorum in his home.

Photographer and psychotherapist Frederick Eberstadt, and his wife, novelist Isabel Eberstadt, got to know Peter at this time, and said that even when Peter didn't like someone he managed to make it amusing: "He had a very pleasant way of putting people down. He was always polite but when he would discuss certain people he didn't have a high opinion of it was always entertaining. He had an unfailing eye for the details of people's behaviour which gave you an insight, into what at least he thought, was interesting and sometimes unfortunate about them."

One of Peter's friends, writer and biographer, Dotson Rader, said: "I felt Peter led a remarkably unexamined life, he had great reluctance to make any judgment on himself by himself you'd never hear Peter say, 'I was such a fool then' or 'I made such a mistake' . . . he never expressed regret. He never made any moral judgment on his life or what he was doing with his life. He could be very critical of people he knew, and severely critical of people he didn't know, but he was never critical of himself at all. I used to wonder why he was so resistant to self examination. . . . [But] he loved gossip. . . . I always thought that was a writerly quality, all the writers [I've known] have all had something in common in their interest in the intimacies of other people's lives—a kind of novelistic gift, that deep interest in other people's lives—which he had. In a sense that is a writer's gift not a theatrical gift . . . he had no narcissism. . . . He was very courtly, had a great insistence on correct manners, and was a very kind man when you were around him. He had no vanity about his money, he had never boasted about being rich, he never boasted who he knew, he was modest about all that [but] it was very difficult to get him to talk about his own life."

Peter and Bill were avid film and theatergoers but Peter's retirement saw him distance himself from the world of theater and film, professing a sense of "fashionable ennui." He shunned the jet-set lifestyle he had previously lived, where he flew on a private plane to a ball in Venice given by Italian nobility and partied with film stars. He became less interested in the world of show business. He maintained contact with old friends like Angus Wilson, and such was his concern for Wilson that when the writer was placed in a nursing home in 1991, suffering from dementia, Peter offered Wilson's partner, Bernard Treneman, money towards his care.

He also kept in close touch with Alec Guinness and his wife, Merula. When the couple visited New York in 1975 Peter held a dinner party at East 68th Street in their honor. The line up was typical and reveals the social circle Peter moved in. Mehle listed the guests as herself; "man of property" Bill; wealthy socialites Brooke Astor and Drue Heinz; record tycoon Ahmet Ertegun and his wife Mica; William F. Buckley Jr.'s son, Christopher; film director Franco Rosellini; and Ilaria Rattazzi, daughter of future Italian politician Susanna "Suni" Agnelli, and granddaughter of Fiat founder, Giovanni Agnelli. Mehle reported on the gathering: "After dinner, Dolly, Mr. Glenville's adorable tame robin, was let out of her cage to fly around the room and make friends with everybody. She landed on Merula's head, dunked herself in a bowl of ice on the bar, broke a crystal goblet—and well, you can see what a darling bird she is."

Peter's friends came from Manhattan's establishment: the city's socialites, writers, and political movers and shakers. Although he was a staunch Republican his interest in politics saw him move in both conservative and liberal political circles. He became friends with former American Secretary of State Henry Kissinger and his second wife, Nancy. Peter met the couple before they were married at a formal dinner given by a Republican senator, which brought

Kissinger together with the head of the Chinese delegation to America. Peter recalled his "enjoyment was marred" when a pudding was served, and its bubbling red hot sauce spilt was spilt over Peter's upper torso: "A charming lady on my right, whose name was Nancy, helped me to remove my coat, my waistcoat, my tie . . . my very braces. Her humour, her candour and liveliness managed completely to overcome my shame, my pain, and a very pungent odour of somewhat overripe raspberries. I realised at once that I was sitting next to an enormously likeable young lady of great personal style." The lady was Kissinger's future wife, Nancy Maginnes. Peter traveled with the couple to Spain in 1982 to watch the soccer World Cup, and five years later accompanied them on a trip to Nepal and China. His friendship with the couple no doubt laid the ground to an invite from President Gerald Ford to an evening at the White House in 1975.

He was also friendly with writer and conservative icon William F. Buckley, Jr., and his wife Patricia Taylor Buckley, one of New York's most popular socialites. Politics wasn't the only thing Peter had in common with the couple; they were both staunch Catholics. Peter often spent weekends and Thanksgivings on the couple's yacht, and got to know their son Christopher well. Christopher went on to become a satirist and author.

After Peter's death, Christopher gave a speech at a memorial service in his honor: "[Peter] was a fixture in my life for over a quarter of a century. I first experienced him at the home of my parents . . . who loved Peter very dearly. . . . I was nineteen when we met, and was immediately smitten with him. The handsome face, the elegant air, astounding erudition, the pearly conversation, the larky twinkling of his eyes, the upturned badger's eyebrows, his extraordinary gentleness and patient attentiveness to one so young and unknowing—all this drew me to this exotic, *mechant* autocrat of my parents' dinner table.

"In time he became my friend too, and I was very proud of that. Imagine: Peter Glenville, who had directed *Becket*, who knew—my Lord, who didn't he know? Alec Guinness, Graham Greene, Evelyn Waugh, Kim Philby, Guy Burgess, John Gielgud, Samuel Beckett, [Jean] Cocteau, Mick Jagger. . . . Anecdotes dropped from him like flawless, juicy peaches from an abundant bough: the time Ken[neth] Tynan knocked frantically on the door of his London [home], stark naked, in extremis, and on the run from an enraged wife who had discovered him in the act of—well, not a suitable story for [a church]. . . .

"One time I brought home a college English paper [on *Hamlet*] that I was quite proud of, that had gotten an enthusiastic A from my professor, a rather distinguished Yale [University] critic. I showed it to Peter, imaging with a sophomore's cockiness that I would be providing him with fresh insight into the tortured Dane's psyche. Twenty-five years later I can only cringe to think of this pathetic lump of coal that I was presenting with such sureness to the Lord High Chancellor of Newcastle, he who had made his first success playing Hamlet. Peter read my onion-skin exegesis, pursed his lips in that portentous pout of his. One eyebrow majestically arched. 'Well,' he said, 'It's very interesting, of course, but I'm not *entirely* sure we can say with anything resembling certainty that Hamlet's struggling to repress his *feminine* side.'

"In later years, as we grew closer, he dropped the Socratic mode and would challenge my intellectual gambits with a more direct, 'I don't believe it for a second!' His intelligence, as fine as any I have ever known, was uncompromising, illuminating. He was the most literate man I knew. Listening to him speak, made me think of what André Gide once said of an evening spent in the company of Oscar Wilde: '*Il rayonnait*. [He shines.]' For twenty-five years he was my Oxford don."

Peter's paternal relationship with Christopher Buckley was one of many that he had with a younger generation. Peter never had children and he enjoyed the company of some of his friends' offspring. Among those was Fernanda Eberstadt, daughter of Frederick and Isabel. She said of her friendship: "I first met Peter at the now defunct restaurant Mortimer's in New York in 1979. I was eighteen years old, an over-sophisticated Manhattanite heading off for my first year as an Oxford undergraduate, and somebody was giving me a going-away party. Peter later told me, 'When I first met you, I didn't care for you a bit. You were wearing a little black velvet pill-box hat with a black veil, and I thought you were a pert little thing far too pleased with yourself and conscious of the impression you made on others.' That was typical Peter—brutally frank, sharp eye for detail.

"Our next meeting, also at a dinner-party at Mortimer's, was almost ten years later. I was about to go to Sicily, which was a place he knew well and loved, and we talked about Byzantine mosaics and the Rococo sculptor [Giacomo] Serpotta, and by dessert, we were friends. Between the first meeting and the second, I had also been on a trip through the former Soviet Union that had turned me into a rabid anti-Communist, and that was an additional bond between us—two Reaganites in a largely Democratic world.

"Our friendship was a source of passionate delight to both of us. A cousin of mine [visited] Peter and Bill, and came back much amused because Peter had told her that if it weren't for the age difference between us (forty-seven years!), he and I would have been made for each other. She found the idea that age was the only obstacle pretty comic. I found him both physically very beautiful—the rich colours of his rosy cheeks and black hair and dark-blue eyes, the proud chin and craggy nose—and morally uplifting. I could think of him if I felt downhearted, and immediately be cheered. He was a rock. Sweetness, vigour, fierce intelligence. You would want him at your side in battle, or in a shipwreck. And he made me laugh more than anyone I knew—he did love fun! I sometimes wondered whether his willpower might not have been a bit bulldozer-like when he was younger. It was obvious from his stories that he had had a painful damaging childhood, and yet he had emerged from his early unhappiness not just successful but a whole, happy man, loving, fearless, sunny natured, who was immensely generous to his friends without being overly desirous to please.

"Of course he had an acid tongue and a devastating wit, but he was never petty. He was full of contradictions—being a gay theatre director who was also a devout Catholic and a conservative Republican—and although the political and religious faiths were genuine, I also think he enjoyed provoking his more liberal-minded friends. . . . I imagine Catholicism was a lone source of moral stability and intellectual rigor to him, growing up with a capricious manipulative pantomime-star mother, and perhaps his politics provided the same kind of antidote."

Another of Peter's young friends, and one whose politics were more liberal minded, was Rader: "Peter really liked knowing what was going on in the world. What was fun about being with him is that he was open to anyone, at least once. People fascinated him, and the less like him they were and the farther outside his social world, the better he liked it. . . .

"Politically, he was on the Right. That said he enjoyed being with people on the Left. He loved debate, and he was good at it. I once took him to a Communist Party rally for Angela Davis. He ate it up."

Rader said Peter was fascinated by what was going on in left-wing circles and enjoyed being taken to places that he wouldn't normally visit: radical meetings, anti-war rallies and venues such as Max's Kansas City—the nightclub on 213 Park Avenue South was a hangout for musicians, poets, writers, artists and politicians in the 1960s and 1970s, frequented by Andy Warhol, Lou Reed and Iggy Pop. Rader said Peter may have arrived dressed as if he was going to "La Cirque for dinner" but was curious to know what people outside of his customary circle were thinking: "He was terribly proper and yet I could get him to places where he really didn't belong . . . but he tried to belong. . . . Peter would have a ball and an hour later I'd find him sitting on a sofa holding court. Because what people responded to in Peter was his intense interest in other people and when you are young and you meet someone like Peter even if you don't know who he is you can tell by his accent and manners he just bled class. To have a man of such apparent distinction pay you such regard, and listen, and ask you questions about your life and what you were interested in whether it was stopping the [Vietnam] war or underground movies was immensely flattering . . . I always loved that about Peter. . . . He was open to experience."

Rader introduced Peter to a friend of his, producer Tom Seligson, in 1973. They met at a benefit concert for an anti-war group held at the Cathedral of Saint John the Divine. Seligson remembered: "He wasn't there because of politics, but because of the participants; Tennessee Williams was speaking and Norman Mailer put on a play. Peter stood out because of the dashing figure he cut in an elegant black sport coat that looked like a smoking jacket. He was always the most elegant person in the room, no matter where. He wore cologne that was distinctive, masculine, but not clawing. We became friendly, and started a special relationship that went on until he died, although in his later years, when he spent most of his time in Mexico I saw him much less frequently. It was paternal in nature. He was very interested in my work as a writer. His support didn't involve any artistic judgment, but about the practicalities of the work. I remember him saying, 'You're going to make a lot of money as a writer,' which, of course, was great to hear. Also, Dotson [Rader] and I had written a play, which Peter read and was enthusiastic about. He was surprised when it failed to be picked up."

Seligson said that he and Peter chatted about anything from politics to the death penalty and Peter "held court even when there was an audience of one": "We got together every couple of weeks. I would come to his home for tea, or to have a drink.

His house was the most elegant and lavishly furnished home I think I'd ever seen. . . . I remember thinking that each piece was probably more than I was making in a year. It wasn't the kind of place you visited in blue jeans and a sweatshirt and I would always dress for the occasion. Tea with Peter was always a special event. In addition to the tea, we'd have a sweet of some kind, a pastry or plate of cookies. And certainly not store bought, they were from some high-end bakery in the neighbourhood. The cookies would be brought in by the Spanish housekeeper, or by Bill Smith, who would then join us. [It] was always an intellectually vigorous event.

"Peter's great gift was conversation. He had an extraordinary interest in ideas, political or philosophical ideas, and he loved discussing them, analysing their implications. I couldn't call what we did a debate, but a rigorous exchange about ideas. I remember always feeling pushed to explain what I thought. As if often the case when in such circumstances, you actually learn what you believe in the process of discussion. I would always leave my time with Peter feeling mentally exhilarated. I also would be invited to dinner, which was always an elegant event. He had a very small dining room, the table sat no more than six, and so you were very close to the other guests, which made the dinner especially intimate."

Being friends with couples was an important part of Peter's life, too. He was friends with husbands and wives, and Mehle said: "He was wonderful with women. He gave them little presents, and [Peter and Bill] were wonderfully polite and complimentary, [noticing] your hair, your makeup, your jewellery." His favorite female friends were Astor, Mehle, Agnelli, Nancy Kissinger, Patricia Buckley and Rosamond Bernier Russell.

Peter definitely loved female company, and had women friends. But he also made the ideal male companion, and throughout his life he made a habit of adopting *la bella figura* by accompanying women to functions.

Seligson said: "Peter was an elegant escort, he loved the parties, and he was no sexual threat to the husbands. I always felt sorry for Bill Smith, who was left home when Peter went out with these ladies. I think none of his lady friends wanted to admit that Peter was gay, and the presence of Bill would make that difficult to deny. There were times when the two of them were at the same event. And Aileen [Mehle] when writing about the event, would refer to Peter as the 'well-known director', and Bill as a 'man of property.'"

Peter's retirement wasn't just confined to Manhattan. He wanted to buy a second home somewhere warm, safe and quiet. Once he retired he started to consider where to live. He thought of Paraguay and Cartagena in Colombia but decided they were too far away for friends to visit. He'd been to Oaxaca in Mexico in 1971 and wrote to a friend: "[It has] a most extraordinary climate, hot in the day with clear bright dry sun and marvellously cool in the evenings. . . . Some day I must have a house in that country."

Mexico fitted his criteria and he bought a house in San Miguel de Allende, a picturesque town 140 miles north of Mexico City in the hills of Guanajuato. San Miguel de Allende became popular with American tourists after the war because of its beautiful colonial architecture and thermal springs. By the time Peter bought a house there in 1978 the town was home to a small but lively expatriate community of Americans, Canadians and Europeans comprised primarily of retirees. Peter enjoyed the sun, reading and getting to know Mexico and new people. Among them were writers Anita Anton von Bleyleben and her husband Karl, who lived nearby: "Peter reconstructed the existing house . . . with very good taste including a little pond with a duck. He bought an adjoining lot which provided space for the long stretched pool and guest house which was built around an enormous tree trunk. . . . At night the luxuriant garden was illuminated in such a way [that] only someone from the theatre could do it."

Situated on an acre of land, five minutes' walk from the center of town, the house Peter bought was ten years old but seemed older because it of its Spanish Colonial style. Peter and Bill set about transforming the house into an elegant home that featured in lifestyle magazines including *House & Garden* and *Elle Décor*. The main house has three bedrooms, a kitchen, library and dining room. It has a view across a shaded terrace and 70-foot-long pool surrounded by Italian Cypress trees with fountains inspired by the Alhambra in Granada, Spain. In the distance lies the town, plains and mountains. The lush garden contains a cabana and a two-story guesthouse with a large living room, kitchenette and winding staircase leading to a circular bedroom with a domed ceiling.

Peter and Bill worked on the house without the aid of a designer; Peter concentrated on improving the house and Bill on the garden. Peter furnished his home in a traditional European style, but that wasn't easy to do. The Mexican government forbad imports of furniture unless the importer was a permanent resident. One of the reasons Peter wanted a second home was to make sure he was out of America often enough to maintain his non-resident tax status, and he didn't want to then have to become a resident somewhere else.

He had a flair for learning languages, speaking fluent French and passable Italian, so he set about learning Spanish, eventually good enough to speak it colloquially. He approached local artisans to make imitations of French and English eighteenth-century furniture to his own specifications. He also visited the local potteries to make tiles for the swimming pool, a crusader's tent ceiling in one of the bedrooms, and plates to adorn the walls instead of paintings. He employed local metalworkers to make Gothic garden furniture and Art Nouveau style lamp stands, and masons at the nearby quarries to make stone obelisks and fluted columns. The result was a stylish but eclectic home that Peter devoted as much attention to creating as a film set.

The guesthouse came about when he decided to landscape the garden in 1981. John Richardson came up with the idea of a "folly"—a domed temple with arcaded wings surrounded by stone steps. Russell admitted his idea was "grandiose" but an idea was sown. Peter hired Boston architect Donald Jasinski, who was used to working on curved architecture and earth-sheltered dwellings to come up with a plan. He rejected Richardson's ideas as unsuitable for the site and designed a rotunda guesthouse that took eighteen months to complete. Jasinski said: "That started what became a friendship. . . . Peter was an extremely engaging person and we almost had a father-and-son relationship; he was very caring and lots of fun. . . . He was a big man. He liked to do things in a big way and present himself in a big way—in a very careful artistic way. His level of artistry in presenting himself was very high. He was an actor—it was a natural thing, you didn't feel it was acting—it was a great presence to witness when you were with him but he was kind on top of that, a rare personality."

The guest house was an important feature because Peter entertained as frequently in San Miguel de Allende as he did in Manhattan, and distinguished guests including jewelry designer Kenneth Jay Lane, Laurence and Mary Rockefeller, and novelist Edna O'Brien, flew in from all over the world. What made Peter unusual was that he had Mexican friends too, drawn from Mexico's intelligentsia, many of whom lived and worked in Mexico City, but had country houses in San Miguel de Allende.

Art lecturer and editor, Rosomond Bernier Russell, and her husband, art critic and author John, met Peter when they went to San Miguel de Allende on holiday. Peter invited them for lunch, and they quickly became friends. The Russells warmed to Peter's lack of pretension and "exquisite politeness": "He was immensely charismatic because not only was he extremely good looking, he had great effortless charm. . . . He was the kind of person with whom you felt immediately at ease, there was absolutely no side, no feeling of him being a celebrity. . . .

His relationship with Bill was very touching: Peter was the glamorous one, the handsome one, but there was such a real bond between those two in the nicest way. . . . Peter was there—the king—and Bill accompanied him, and it seemed totally cloudless. I never heard any kind of irritation. There was never any sense of competition. It always seemed totally harmonious with each one in his role."

The lunch and dinner parties in Mexico were made possible with the aid of their staff, primarily their major domo a former boxing champion Carmello Luno, and his wife, Tomasina. Peter sent Carmello on *cordon bleu* cookery course so that he could prepare the kind of exquisite meals Peter wanted served to his guests. Carmello's culinary skills became so good that Peter flew the Mexican couple back and forth between San Miguel de Allende and Manhattan. Fernanda Eberstadt said: "Peter and Bill adored [them], and were intimately absorbed by their goings-on, happinesses, concerns. It was clearly an old-fashioned paternal relationship, but [Peter's] devotion to them, and theirs to him, was very real. After Peter died, Carmello ran Bill's life and practical affairs for him." When Peter passed away he bequeathed the couple a sizeable bequest of money as well as the house directly across the street from his own.

As the years passed, Peter's happy retirement was inevitably punctured by the loss of friends and family: Mielziner died in 1976, Rattigan in 1977, Messel in 1978, Burton in 1984, Boland in 1988, Olivier in 1989, and both Wilson and Greene in 1991.

His two biggest losses came when Bill's mother, Lucy, and his own mother passed away. Lucy died in 1978. Peter had had a warm relationship with her for more than thirty years, so much so that he wrote a eulogy to her that was read out at her funeral service. Peter described her as "a gentle and feminine lady of the old days and ways, when women gave their interests, their energies, their lives, to their husbands, to their families, and even to their friends. . . . She was instinctively, and without effort or calculation, a Christian lady, a fond and perfect wife and parent, and a beloved friend to many."

Peter appears to have looked upon Bill's mother as the perfect mother figure. She was obviously very different from Dorothy, who made Peter dance with her when he was a young man, and then once she'd propelled him close to whichever man she was interested in, she would shriek out to him: "Keep your paws off me, you wicked boy!" Coping with his mother's attention-seeking ego must have been difficult, as Bill once wrote to Peter: "She is always a star and a very remarkable woman." Peter's habit of telling affectionate stories about her behavior, albeit with some asperity, may have been his way of laughing that off. According to Holly Book, her grandmother Lucy was "one of the most amazing women I have ever known—and a 'lady' in every sense of the word, dignified, noble, kind, incredibly sweet and enormously generous. I now understand how wonderful she would have been to Peter, no question and very motherly indeed." This was of course something that Peter had lacked in his own mother.

But there is no doubt at all that Dorothy adored him and was proud of her son's achievements. She was careful with her money, too, and in 1954 had organized her own significant finances so that Peter would benefit, and the pair held a joint American bank account. When he was a young director it was her generosity that gave Peter the financial security to do the projects of his choosing.

In old age she lived alone with her housekeeper at her flat at 85 Berkeley Court in London's Baker Street before she grew too frail to be at home and Peter's cousin John helped find a nursing home for her. Peter visited his mother every day when he went to London. Dorothy died in her sleep of pneumonia on March 30, 1987, aged ninety-seven. Peter was holidaying in the Florida Keys when she died and he rushed to London to help organize the funeral.

As for Shaun, the service was held at St. James' church in Marylebone and Peter chose the hymns and read from the Bible. Family members attended a wake at the house of Peter's friend Marguerite Lipman. Dorothy was buried beside Shaun at Kensal Green Cemetery.

After she died *The Stage* wrote: "She kept up a loyal network of friendships, and . . . would send out 400 Christmas cards, writing them in bed with a large box of chocolates for refreshment. . . . Her recipe for keeping young could well be followed by thousands: 'Stay interested in today's less gracious world.'" She was an old trouper to the end—in keeping with her wishes, Dorothy was buried in her make up, and Peter thought she looked "lovely."

Peter did not live to such an old age. He died on June 3, 1996, aged 82. Friends and family say that it was clear that his health was failing in the last few years of his life. He complained of "a mystery pain" and was diagnosed with diverticulitis. He preferred to stay in Mexico, which he loved, rather than get first-rate medical care in New York. When he attended a family wedding that year in February, he looked frail and was unable to go out to dinner.

He died in his sleep of a heart attack at his Manhattan home. Fernanda Eberstadt said: "I don't think he was a bit scared of dying. I don't think he was scared of anything." Bill found Peter and was distraught. He was never the same again and found it hard to recover from his grief.

A funeral service was held at the Roman Catholic Church of Saint Vincent Ferrer on New York's Upper East Side and Peter was laid to rest north of Manhattan at the Gate of Heaven Cemetery in Hawthorne, Westchester County, on June 7. His remains lie in a white stone mausoleum. The words "Glenville Smith" are carved above its small gated entrance. Inside the mausoleum carved on marble are the words to Peter's favorite prayer, written by Cardinal John Henry Newman:

May he support us all the day long,
till the shades lengthen and the evening comes,
and the busy world is hushed
and the fever of life is over and our work is done.
Then in his mercy may he give us a safe lodging
and a holy rest and peace at the last.

Peter had been a member of Newman Society when he was at Oxford, and the society chose its name in tribute to the priest, who had done so much to advance the cause of Catholicism in Oxford, both as an Anglican attempting to recover Anglicanism's Catholic roots, and later as a Catholic convert. Peter never forgot what he owed to Stonyhurst and Oxford. Throughout his life he made monthly contributions to the old school that had been like a family home to him, and to the OUDS that gave him his theatrical training.

A Requiem Mass was held in London at Brompton Oratory on June 26. At Peter's old church his friend from Stonyhurst, the Jesuit priest Philip Caraman officiated. Family and friends attended it, but as Guinness wrote in *My Name Escapes Me: The Diary of a Retiring Actor* when he was helping arrange the mass: "The trouble is that there can be only a handful of his English friends still alive." Guinness was devastated at the loss of his close friend of more than fifty years and wrote the day after Peter's death: "My mind remains numbly blank. And my heart, too, curiously enough. Sorrow will come for sure, in its own time and, I am sure, dozens of happy or absurdly funny memories; but for the moment all is grey, in spite of brilliant sunshine."

Bill died on October 3, 2001. He took to sleeping in Peter's bed when he became ill, and died there. He was buried in the same mausoleum as Peter. Bill never recovered from losing Peter. Mehle explained: "He could not possibly be comforted."

She described Peter and Bill as: "The nicest people, more than nice: they were sophisticated and worldly, they were divine. . . . They were opposite in many ways but Bill had been with Peter so long that in many ways they were alike. However, Peter was the star. Peter was a star and the star of that couple. Not that Bill was pushed in the background, he never was. Peter never belittled him ever in any and there was nothing to belittle. Bill was very intelligent and very much knew what was going on. He was very sweet and darling and did a lot of things for Peter. . . . He did all the ordering, the shopping, that sort of thing, but he was always treated as the equal that he was in every way, and I think he helped Peter a lot in his career."

Fernanda Eberstadt said of their relationship: "Peter was a very dominating character. Bill was definitely the long-suffering wife in this fifty-year-long marriage, and was not allowed much attention. I remember Bill trying and trying and trying to interject his own impressions mid-stream into a story Peter was telling, 'Now Peter, it wasn't like that, it was —' 'Peter, it wasn't —' 'Peter, she didn't say—' 'Peter—' and at last subsiding with a ruefully resigned, 'He never listens—not to a word I say—not to a single word!'"

Easy going, funny, intelligent and gentle in nature, Bill was the more humble and quieter of the two men, and he allowed Peter to shine with a sense of affection. This was an asset and made for a stable and balanced relationship. It made Bill easier to be with than Peter too, whose snobbery could be off-putting on occasion. Seligson pointed out: "I liked Bill enormously. He was very down to earth, and actually easier to talk to than Peter. There wasn't this sense of debate, and he loved to gossip. He was also more practical than Peter."

Peter was aware of Bill's many good qualities, and his selflessness. He was devoted to Bill, sending him cards: "Dearest B, as usual you have made it all possible!—And think of all the fun ahead! Love P." After thirty years together he wrote a note to him to accompany a gift: "For a wonderful creature who has made three decades of life possible, happy and exciting. Love P." After Peter died, Bill came out from his shell and began telling the same stories Peter had told for so many years—without interruption. Their good friends remained friendly and supportive of Bill, but without Peter around parts of Manhattan society no longer bothered with Bill. One friend commented that Bill was "running a museum but no one came to see the exhibit" because Peter was not there. Nevertheless Bill remained at East 68th Street and there was always a sense of Peter in the house.

Peter and Bill appeared to have a relationship akin to a monogamous marriage, and friends and family have said they never appeared camp nor made any open displays of affection. Their relationship was founded on mutual respect, need, friendship and love.

Frederick Eberstadt observed: "They were a very connubial couple. But Peter was very much against [what he regarded as] 'gay' behaviour. He was as strict as a bishop of Boston—things had to be done in a correct way and he was strong on manners." Peter grew up at a time when homosexuality was illegal, and even when he was older, gay men were often still referred to as "fairies" or "queens." He was traditional in his outlook and chose to keep his own life private.

When Bill died his will stated that a foundation be set up in Peter's name. Their fabulous home on East 68th Street was sold and after various generous bequests to family and friends were fulfilled, The Peter Glenville Foundation was established to fund artistic endeavors that will help aspiring actors and directors deliver inspiring projects that honor Peter's legacy. The foundation had a naming opportunity for the prestigious Professional Children's School, the Peter Glenville Theatre, to honor Peter; it's just a few blocks from East 68th Street, on 132 West 60th Street. It was officially opened in March 2005 by Holly Book, Bill Smith's niece, and the Foundation's Director along with Peter and Bill's close friend, John

Richardson. The theater is part of New York's Professional Children's School and is used by its students for theatrical, dance and musical performances.

Two ardent theatergoers, Jane Harris Hall and Jean Greer Robinson, founded the school in 1914. The women had learned that the city's child actors were missing out on an education because local schools couldn't accommodate their schedule and set up the school to fill the gap. It enrolled more than 100 students within its first year and among the school's former alumni are Elliot Gould, Scarlett Johansson and Uma Thurman. Peter directed at least two of the school's students, Isobel Elsom in his Broadway production of *The Innocents* and Rita Moreno in the film *Summer and Smoke*.

How Peter reconciled his Catholicism with his sexuality is unknown. Richardson suggested it was via the practice of confession. Peter told Radar he was celibate. Revealingly, there was a handwritten note pinned up in East 68th Street when Peter lived there: "I count not myself to have apprehended, but this one thing I do, forgetting those things which are behind, and making forth with these things which are before . . ." Whether Bill or Peter wrote it is unknown. The words are taken from the Bible, and come from *Philippians*, chapter 3, verses 13 to 14. They were written by Saint Paul when he was in prison, as he acknowledged his past mistakes, drew upon God's mercy, and then focused on becoming more like Christ. The apostle concentrates on the concept that salvation cannot be achieved by merit or good works, stressing the notion that it is a free gift: a matter of God's grace. It was clearly a precept that guided both Bill and Peter throughout their lives, a life together that was very private, yet they shared their good fortune and their hospitality with many. For Peter believed he always believed his faith would help him to do what was right, and to keep trying to do that when he failed. He trusted God to judge him.

Peter's apparent lack of angst fits with a man of contradiction, who mixed in political circles, held conservative beliefs but spent half of his life avoiding paying taxes. Peter became the man he most wanted to be—an English upper-class gentleman, one that courted intellectual circles and the very best that life had to offer. On the one hand it gave him a sense of validation, while also distancing himself from what was not the happiest of childhoods. Peter had talent and ambition, and most importantly the drive to succeed. Peter also enjoyed the trappings off his success, a success that could more readily enjoyed in America. In London, Peter's background was known, in America, with his partner of 50 years, he was able to be the man he had become without ever being reminded of where he had come from.

He was more successful as a theater director than as a film director. George Cukor once said that Peter's problem was that he thought too much. His sense that theater and film were art rather than business meant he obsessed about making things perfect, and his tinkering doesn't always seem to have enhanced the final product. His choice of theater and film work was eclectic, and his financial independence meant that he could make that choice. Peter's meticulousness is perhaps what made him fall short of being a great director rather than the good one that he was; a director whom actors could trust to help them bring home a coveted award. He had flashes of brilliance and because most of those were in the theater rather than on celluloid he has been forgotten, a lost British treasure. Maybe he did not quit while he was ahead, but he was still among the frontrunners. But above all else Peter Glenville was an intelligent man, he chose what work he wanted to do and how he wanted to live. He was old fashioned and when his ways went out of fashion he simply withdrew into a world of his own creation. He wanted to be happy in life more than anything else and ultimately placed that above ambition or any desire for kudos. He did what he wanted to do, and only what he wanted to do.

Appendix

Peter Glenville's career as an actor and director on stage and on screen.

Play Opens February 9, 1933. *Edward II* by Christopher Marlowe for the OUDS at the University of Oxford, Oxford. PG plays Edward II.

Play Opens c. February 16, 1933. *King John* by William Shakespeare for the OUDS at the New Theatre, Oxford. PG plays Cardinal Pandulph.

Play Opens June 15, 1933. *A Midsummer Night's Dream* by William Shakespeare for the OUDS at South Park, Headington Hill, Oxford. PG plays Puck.

Radio Play September 11 and 12, 1933. *The Fantastic Battle* by Leslie Baily based on the story by C.R. Burns for the BBC. PG plays an unknown role.

Play November 17, 1933. *The Masterpiece* by Paul Dehn for the OUDS at the University of Oxford, Oxford. PG directs.

Play Opens November 23, 1933. *Rope* by Patrick Hamilton for the St. John's Mummers at the University of Oxford, Oxford. PG directs.

Play December 1933. *King Richard II* by William Shakespeare for the Oxford University Stonyhurst Dramatic Society at Stonyhurst College, Lancashire. PG directs and plays King Richard II.

Play Opens February 20, 1934 *Doctor Faustus* by Christopher Marlowe for the OUDS at Oxford Town Hall, Oxford. PG plays Mephistopheles.

Play Opens March 7, 1934. *Pass the Salt* by Peter Glenville for the OUDS at the University of Oxford, Oxford. PG writes, directs and plays The Husband and Doctor Faustus.

Radio Play April 13, 1934. *Doctor Faustus* by Christopher Marlowe for the OUDS and the BBC. PG plays Mephistopheles.

Play Opens June 13, 1934. *Richard III* by William Shakespeare for the OUDS at Oxford University, Oxford. PG plays Richard III.

Play Opens June 26, 1934. *Richard III* by William Shakespeare for the OUDS at the Regent's Park Open Air Theatre, London. PG plays Richard III.

Plays September, October and Christmas season 1934. For the Manchester Repertory Company, Manchester. *The Swan* by Ference Molnár; PG plays Dr. Agi. *On the Spot* by Edgar Wallace; PG plays Tony Pirelli. *The Maitlands* by Ronald Mackenzie; PG plays Jack Maitland. *Candida* by George Bernard Shaw; PG plays Eugene Marchbanks. *To What Red Hell* by Percy Robinson; PG plays Jim Nolan.

Play Opens February 19, 1935. *Hamlet* by William Shakespeare for the OUDS at the New Oxford Theatre, Oxford. PG plays Hamlet.

Play May 1935. *Rossetti* by R.L. Megroz and Herbert de Hamel for the People's National Theatre at the Arts Theatre Club, Great Newport Street, London. PG plays Dante Gabriel Rossetti.

Play Opens June 18, 1935. *Twelfth Night* by William Shakespeare at the Regent's Park Open Air Theatre, London. PG plays Orsino, Duke of Illyria.

Play Opens August 12, 1935. *Man and Superman* by George Bernard Shaw for the Macdona Players at the Cambridge Theatre, Earlham Street, London. PG plays Octavius Robinson.

Play Opens October 21, 1935. *The Hangman* by Pär Lagerkvist at the Duke of York's Theatre, St. Martin's Lane, London. PG plays Bödeln.

Play Opens November 14, 1935. *Theatre Royal* by George S. Kaugman and Edna Ferber at the Oxford Playhouse, Oxford. PG plays Anthony Cavendish.

Plays November 1 to December 6, 1935. For the Swansea Repertory Company at the Fforestfach Cross Theatre (later Fforestfach Welfare Hall), Swansea, Glamorgan. *The Late Christopher Bean* by Sidney Howard. *The Shining Hour* by Keith Winter. *Payment Deferred* an adaptation by Gilbert Miller of the novel by C.S. Forester. *They Knew What They Wanted* by Sidney Howard. *Private Lives* by Noël Coward. PG plays unknown roles.

Plays April 13 to September 26, 1936. Shakespeare Festival for the New Shakespeare Company at The Memorial Theatre (now Royal Shakespeare Theatre), Stratford-upon-Avon, Warwickshire. *The Taming of the Shrew* by William Shakespeare; PG plays Petruchio. *Julius Caesar* by William Shakespeare; PG plays Marcus Antonius. *Romeo and Juliet* by William Shakespeare; PG plays Romeo. *Twelfth Night* by William Shakespeare; PG plays Feste. *King Lear* by William Shakespeare; PG plays Edgar. *Much Ado About Nothing* by William Shakespeare; PG plays Claudio. *Troilus and Cressida* by William Shakespeare; PG plays Hector.

Plays May 3 to August 1937. For Margate Repertory at the Theatre Royal, Margate, Kent. *Tonight at 8.30* by Noël Coward; PG plays unknown role. *The Dominant Sex* by Michael Egan; PG plays unknown role. *Someone at the Door* by Dorothy and Campbell Christie; PG plays unknown role. *Heroes Don't Care* by Margot Neville; PG plays unknown role. *Anthony and Anna* by St. John G. Ervine; PG plays unknown role. *Romeo and Juliet* by William Shakespeare; PG plays unknown role. *Call it a Day* by Dodie Smith; PG plays unknown role. *On the Spot* by Edgar Wallace; PG plays tony Pirelli. *White Cargo* by Leon Gordon; PG plays Harry Witzel. *Still Life* by Noël Coward; PG plays Alec Harvey. *Anna Christie* by Eugene O'Neill; PG plays Mat Burke.

Plays September 6, 1937 to December 1937. For John Baxter-Somerville's Repertory Players at the Springfield Theatre, St. Helier, Jersey. *The Amazing Dr. Clitterhouse* by Barré Lyndon; PG plays Dr. Clitterhouse. *Busman's Honeymoon* by Dorothy L. Sayers and M. St. Clare Byrne; PG plays Lord Peter Wimsey.

Plays March 28 to July 1938. For the Q Theatre Company at the Q Theatre, Kew, Surrey. *Beyond the Horizon* by Eugene O'Neill; PG plays Robert Mayo. *Blind Corners* by Mary Frances Flack; PG plays unknown role. *The Green Holly* by Edward Percy and Reginald Denham; PG plays unknown role. *Diversion* by John van Druten; PG plays Wyn Hayward.

Radio Play November 14, 1938. *Hassan* by James Elroy Flecker for the BBC. PG plays unknown role.

Play Opens February 19, 1939. *The Courageous Sex* by Mary D. Sheridan at the Globe Theatre (now Gielgud Theatre), Shaftesbury Avenue, London. PG plays Martin Diggle.

Play Opens March 19, 1939. *To Be Or Not To Be* by Eleanor Kalkowska at the Phoenix Theatre, Charing Cross Road, London. PG plays Raymond Lefort.

Play Opens March 28, 1939. *The Taming of the Shrew* by William Shakespeare for the Old Vic Company, Old Vic Theatre, The Cut, Waterloo Road, London. PG plays Lucentio.

Play April 24, 1939. *Othello* by Shakespeare for the Old Vic Company, for Shakespeare's Birthday Festival, Old Vic Theatre, The Cut, Waterloo Road, London. PG plays an unknown role in the "Handkerchief" scene.

Play Opens January 8, 1940. *Behind the Schemes!* By George H. Grimaldi at the Shaftesbury Theatre, Shaftesbury Avenue, London. PG plays Tony Howard.

Film Released January 27, 1940. *His Brother's Keeper* from Warner Brothers-First National Productions. PG plays Hicky Cornell.

Play Opens January 30, 1940. *Down Our Street* by Ernest George for the People's National Theatre at the Tavistock Little Theatre, Tavistock Place, Russell Square, London. PG plays Charlie Stubbs.

Film Released March 9, 1940. *Return to Yesterday* from Ealing Studios. PG plays an undetermined role.

Play April 22, 1940. Shakespeare's Birthday Festival for the Old Vic Company, Old Vic Theatre, The Cut, Waterloo Road, London. PG performs an unknown role.

Play Opens July 22, 1940. *Murder in Mayfair* by Ivor Novello for the Q Theatre Company, Kew, Surrey. PG plays Bill Sherry.

Play Opens September 5, 1940. *The Infernal Machine* by Jean Cocteau at the Arts Theatre Club, Great Newport Street, London. PG plays Oedipus.

Play Opens October 3, 1940. *All's Well That Ends Well* by William Shakespeare at the Vaudeville Theatre, the Strand, London. PG plays Bertram.

Film Released October 19, 1940. *Two for Danger* from Warner Brothers-First National Productions. PG plays a Young Latin.

Play Opens October 23, 1940. *Henry IV Part One* by William Shakespeare at the Vaudeville Theatre, The Strand, London. PG plays Prince Hall.

Play Opens June 4, 1941. *The Light of Heart* by Emlyn Williams at the Globe Theatre (now Gielgud Theatre), Shaftesbury Avenue, London. PG plays Robert.

Play January 18, 1942. *The Merchant of Venice* by William Shakespeare for a Green Room Benevolent Fund and Green Room Rags Society fundraiser at The Palladium, Argyll Street, London. PG plays an unknown role in a scene from the play.

Play Takes over role March 28, 1942. *The Doctor's Dilemma* by George Bernard Shaw at the Theatre Royal, Haymarket, London. PG plays Louis Dubedat.

Film Released August 24, 1942. *Uncensored* from Gainsborough Pictures. PG plays Charles Neele.

Film Released April 10, 1944. *Heaven Is Round the Corner* from British National Films. PG plays Donald McKay.

Play Opens August 16, 1944. *John Gabriel Borkman* by Henrick Ibsen for the Old Vic Company at the Liverpool Playhouse, Williamson Square, Liverpool, Lancashire. PG directs.

Play Opens September 6, 1944. *Lisa* an adaptation by Peter Glenville of *A House of Gentlefolk* by Ivan Turgenev for the Old Vic Company at the Liverpool Playhouse, Williamson Square, Liverpool, Lancashire. PG adapts and directs.

Play Opens October 18, 1944. *Point Valaine* by Noël Coward for the Old Vic Company at the Liverpool Playhouse, Williamson Square, Liverpool, Lancashire. PG directs.

Play Opens November 22, 1944. *Uneasy Laughter* an adaptation by Judith Guthrie of *He Who Gets Slapped* by Leonid Andreyev for the Old Vic Company at the Liverpool Playhouse, Williamson Square, Liverpool, Lancashire. PG plays Funny the Clown.

Film Released c. December 18, 1944. *Madonna of the Seven Moons* from Gainsborough Pictures. PG plays Sandro Barucci.

Play Opens December 20, 1944. *The School for Scandal* by Richard Brinsley Sheridan for the Old Vic Company at the Liverpool Playhouse, Williamson Square, Liverpool, Lancashire. PG directs.

Play Opens January 31, 1945. *Anna Christie* by Eugene O'Neill for the Old Vic Company at the Liverpool Playhouse, Williamson Square, Liverpool, Lancashire. PG directs.

Play Opens February 28, 1945. *Hamlet* by William Shakespeare for the Old Vic Company at the Liverpool Playhouse, Williamson Square, Liverpool, Lancashire. PG plays Hamlet.

Play Opens April 16, 1945. *The Alchemist* by Ben Jonson for the Old Vic Company at the Liverpool Playhouse, Williamson Square, Liverpool, Lancashire. PG plays Face.

Play Opens May 9, 1945. *His Excellency the Governor* by Robert Marshall for the Old Vic Company at the Liverpool Playhouse, Williamson Square, Liverpool, Lancashire. PG directs.

Play September 1945 to April 1946. *Duet for Two Hands* by Mary Hayley Bell at the Lyric Theatre, Shaftesbury Avenue, London. PG plays Stephen Cass.

Play Opens February 14, 1946. *The Time of Your Life* by William Saroyan at the Lyric Theatre, King's Street, London. PG directs.

Play Opens October 16, 1946. *The Assassin* by Peter Yates at the Lyric Theatre, King's Street, Hammersmith, London. PG plays John Wilkes Booth.

Play Opens September 3, 1947. *Point Valaine* by Noël Coward at the Embassy Theatre, High Holborn, London. PG directs.

Play Opens March 30, 1948. *Major Barbara* by George Bernard Shaw at the Arts Theatre, Great Newport Street, London. PG directs.

Film Released April 28, 1948. *Good-Time Girl* from Gainsborough Pictures. PG plays Jimmy Rosso.

Play Opens June 3, 1948. *The Gioconda Smile* by Aldous Huxley at the New Theatre (now Noël Coward Theatre), St. Martin's Lane, London. PG directs.

Play Opens June 16, 1948. *Crime Passionel* by Jean-Paul Sartre, adapted by Kitty Black, at the Lyric Theatre, King's Street, Hammersmith, London; transfers to the Garrick Theatre, Charing Cross Road, London on August 4. PG directs.

Play Opens September 8, 1948. *Playbill* (comprising *Harlequinade* and *The Browning Version*) by Terence Rattigan at the Phoenix Theatre, Charing Cross Road, London. PG directs.

Play Opens November 24, 1948. *The Return of the Prodigal* by St. John Hankin at the Globe Theatre (now Gielgud Theatre), Shaftesbury Avenue, London. PG directs.

Play Opens March 17, 1949. *Adventure Story* by Terence Rattigan at the St. James' Theatre (now demolished), King Street, London. PG directs.

Play Opens April 28, 1949. *The Power of Darkness* an adaptation by Peter Glenville of Leo Tolstoy's play at the Lyric Theatre, Shaftesbury Avenue, London. PG adapts and directs.

Play Opens October 12, 1949. *Playbill* (comprising *Harlequinade* and *The Browning Version*) by Terence Rattigan at the Coronet Theatre (now Eugene O'Neill Theatre), 230 West 49th Street, New York. PG directs.

Play Opens February 1, 1950. *The Innocents* an adaptation by William Archibald of *The Turn of the Screw* by Henry James at the

Playhouse Theatre (now demolished), 137 West 48th Street, New York. PG directs.

Play Opens October 24, 1950. *The Curious Savage* by John Patrick at the Martin Beck Theatre (now the Al Hirschfeld Theatre), 302 West 45th Street, New York. PG directs.

Play Opens March 10, 1951. *Romeo and Juliet* by William Shakespeare at the Broadhurst Theatre, 235 West 44th Street, New York. PG directs.

Play Opens November 22, 1951. *Summer and Smoke* by Tennessee Williams at the Lyric Theatre, Hammersmith, London; transfers to the Duchess Theatre, Catherine Street, London on January 23, 1952. PG directs.

Play Opens April 23, 1952. *Under the Sycamore Tree* by Sam Spewack at the Aldwych Theatre, Aldwych, London. PG directs.

Play Opens July 3, 1952. *The Innocents* an adaptation by William Archibald of *The Turn of the Screw* by Henry James at Her Majesty's Theatre, Haymarket, London. PG directs.

Play Opens October 10, 1952. *Letter from Paris* an adaptation by Dodie Smith of *The Reverberator* by Henry James at the Aldwych Theatre, London. PG directs.

Play Opens April 16, 1953. *The Living Room* by Graham Greene at Wyndham's Theatre, Charing Cross Road, London. PG produces and directs.

Play Opens April 14, 1954. *The Prisoner* by Bridget Boland at the Globe Theatre (now Gielgud Theatre), Shaftesbury Avenue, London. PG produces and directs.

Play Opens September 22, 1954. *Separate Tables* (comprising *Table by the Window* and *Table Number Seven*) by Terence Rattigan at the St. James' Theatre, King Street, Piccadilly, London. PG directs.

Play Opens October 4, 1955. *Island of Goats* an adaptation by Henry Reed of *Delitto all'isola delle capre* by Ugo Betti at the Fulton Theatre (now demolished), 210 West 46th Street, New York. PG produces and directs.

Film Released December 11, 1955. *The Prisoner* from London Independent Producers Limited, B&D Film Corporation and Columbia Pictures Corporation. PG directs.

Play Opens May 2, 1956. *Hotel Paradiso* an adaptation by Peter Glenville of *L'Hôtel du libre échange* by Georges Feydeau and Maurice Desvallierès at the Winter Garden Theatre (now New London Theatre), Drury Lane, London. PG adapts, produces and directs.

Play Opens October 25, 1956. *Separate Tables* (comprising *Table by the Window* and *Table Number Seven*) by Terence Rattigan at the Music Box Theatre, 239 West 45th Street, New York. PG directs.

Play Opens April 11, 1957. *Hotel Paradiso* an adaptation by Peter Glenville of *L'Hôtel du libre échange* by Georges Feydeau and Maurice Desvallierès at Henry Miller's Theatre (now the Stephen Sondheim Theatre), 124 West 43rd Street, New York. PG adapts, produces and directs.

Film Released August 26, 1958. *Me and the Colonel* from William Goetz Productions and Columbia Pictures. PG directs and plays British Submarine Commander.

Play Opens January 27, 1959. *Rashomon* an adaptation by Mike and Fay Kanin from stories by Ryunosuke Akutagawa at the Music Box Theatre, 239 West 45th Street, New York. PG produces and directs.

Musical Opens October 22, 1959. *Take Me Along* music and lyrics by Bob Merrill, book by Joseph Stein and Robert Russell and based on Eugene O'Neill's play *Ah, Wilderness!* at the Shubert Theatre, 225 West 44th Street, New York. PG directs.

Play Opens December 3, 1959. *Silent Night, Lonely Night* by Robert Anderson at the Morosco Theatre (now demolished) on 217 West 45th Street, New York. PG directs.

Play Opens October 5, 1960. *Becket* adapted by Lucienne Hill from *Becket ou l'honneur de Dieu* by Jean Anouilh at the St. James Theatre, 246 West 44th Street, New York; transfers to the Royale Theatre (now Bernard B. Jacobs Theatre), 242 West 45th Street, New York on December 19, 1960. PG directs.

Play Opens May 8, 1961. *Becket* adapted by Lucienne Hill from *Becket ou l'honneur de Dieu* by Jean Anouilh at the Hudson Theatre (now a conference centre), 141 West 44th Street, New York. PG directs.

Play Opens November 16, 1961. *Summer and Smoke* from Hal Wallis Productions and Paramount Pictures. PG directs.

Film Released August 16, 1962. *Term of Trial* from Romulus Films and Warner Brothers Pictures. PG adapts and directs.

Play Opens October 25, 1962. *Tchin-Tchin* adapted by Sidney Michaels from the play by François Billetdoux at the Plymouth Theatre (now Gerald Schoenfeld Theatre), 236 West 45th Street, New York; transfers to the Ethel Barrymore Theatre, 243 West 47th Street, New York on February 11, 1963. PG directs.

Musical Opens March 18, 1963. *Tovarich* music by Lee Pockriss, lyrics by Anne Crosswell based on the play by Jacques Deval and Robert E. Sherwood at the Broadway Theatre, 1681 Broadway, New York; transfers to Majestic Theatre, 247 West 44th Street, New York on June 10, 1963 and the Winter Garden Theatre, 1634 Broadway on October 7, 1963. PG directs.

Play Opens January 18, 1964. *Dylan* by Sidney Michaels at the Plymouth Theatre (now Gerald Schoenfeld Theatre), 236 West 45th Street, New York. PG directs.

Film Released March 11, 1964. *Becket* from Hal Wallis and Paramount Pictures. PG directs.

Film Released October 14, 1966. *Hotel Paradiso* from MGM. PG adapts, produces, directs and plays Georges Feydeau.

Film Released October 31, 1967. *The Comedians* from Maximilian Productions, MGM and Trianon Films. PG directs and produces.

Play Opens November 29, 1967. *Everything in the Garden* by Edward Albee based on the play by Giles Cooper at the Plymouth Theatre (now Gerald Schoenfeld Theatre), 236 West 45th Street, New York. PG directs.

Play Opens October 6, 1969. *A Patriot for Me* by John Osborne at the Imperial Theatre, 249 West 45th Street, New York. PG directs.

Play Opens 23 September 1970. *A Bequest to the Nation* by Terence Rattigan at the Theatre Royal, Haymarket, London. PG directs.

Play Opens March 1, 1973. *Out Cry* by Tennessee Williams at the Lyceum Theatre, 149 West 45th Street, New York. PG directs.

Bibliography

Lillian Gish: Her Legend, Her Life, by Charles Affron, University of California Press, 2001
Ego 2, by James Agate, Victor Gollancz, 1936
Ego 5, by James Agate, George G. Harrap, 1946
Ego 8, by James Agate, George G. Harrap, 1942
Sun and Shadow, by Jean-Pierre Aumont, W.W. Norton, 1977
Flora: An Appreciation of the Life and Work of Dame Flora Robson, by Kenneth Barrow, Heinemann, 1981
On Q: Jack and Beatie de Leon and the Q Theatre, by Kenneth Barrow, The De Leon Memorial Fund in association with Heritage Publications and Hounslow Leisure Services, 1992
The Royal Shakespeare Company: A History of Ten Decades, by Sally Beauman, Oxford University Press, 1982
State of the Nation: British Theatre since 1945, by Michael Billington, Faber & Faber, 2007
Upper Circle: A Theatrical Chronicle, by Kitty Black, Methuen, 1984
Limelight and After: The Education of an Actress, by Claire Bloom, Weidenfeld & Nicolson, 1982
Notebooks, Tennessee Williams, edited by Margaret Bradham Thornton, Yale University Press, 2006
Laurence Olivier, by Melvyn Bragg, Hutchinson, 1984
Rich: The Life of Richard Burton, by Melvyn Bragg, Coronet Books, 1989
Great Acting, edited by Hal Burton, British Broadcasting Corporation, 1967
Growing Opinions: A Symposium of British Youth Outlook, edited by Alan Campbell Johnson, Methuen and Company, 1934
OUDS: A Centenary History of the Oxford University Dramatic Society 1885-1985, by Humphrey Carpenter, Oxford University Press, 1985
The Folies Bergère, by Charles Castle, Methuen, 1982
Oliver Messel: A biography, by Charles Castle, Thames & Hudson, 1986
Lord Snowdon, by Helen Cathcart, W.H. Allen, 1968
Idols of the 'Halls', by H. Chance Newton, E.P. Publishing, 1975
The Golden Age of Movie Musicals and Me, by Saul Chaplin, University of Oklahoma Press, 1994
The Park: The Story of the Regent's Park Open Air Theatre, by David Conville, Oberon Books, 2007
Gainsborough Pictures: Rethinking British Cinema, edited by Pam Cook, Cassell, 1997
Present Indicative, by Noël Coward, William Heinemann, 1937
The Coming of Godot: A Short History of a Masterpiece, by Jonathan Croall, Oberon Books, 2005
The Letters of Noël Coward, edited by Barry Day, Methuen Drama, 2007
Terence Rattigan, by Michael Darlow and Gillian Hodson, Quartet Books, 1979
The Selected Letters of Tennessee Williams Vol. II 1945-1957, by Albert J. Devlin, Tennessee Williams, and Nancy Marie Patterson Tischler, New Directions Publishing, 2004

Conversations with Tennessee Williams, edited by Albert J. Devlin, University Press of Mississippi, 1986
Hal Wallis: Producer to the Stars, by Bernard F. Dick, University Press of Kentucky, 2004
Conversations with Graham Greene, edited by Henry J. Donaghy, University Press of Mississippi, 1992
Angus Wilson: A Biography, by Margaret Drabble, Minerva, 1996
The Finest Years: British Cinema of the 1940s, by Charles Drazin, Andre Deutsch, 1998
Those Dancing Years: An Autobiography, by Mary Ellis, John Murray, 1982
Missing Believed Lost: The Great British Film Search, edited by Allen Eyles and David Meeker, BFI Publishing, 1992
"Oh, Yes it is!" A History of Pantomime, by Gerald Frow, British Broadcasting Corporation, 1985
The Movies, Mr. Griffith, and Me, by Lillian Gish with Ann Pinchot, W.H. Allen, 1969
Nobody's Fool: The Lives of Danny Kaye, by Martin Gottfried, Simon & Schuster, 1994
Olivier, edited by Logan Gourlay, Weidenfeld & Nicolson, 1973
Sparks Fly Upward, by Stewart Granger, Granada, 1981
Landmarks of World Literature: Samuel Beckett, Waiting for Godot, by Lawrence Graver, Cambridge University Press, 1989
Fragments of an Autobiography, by Graham Greene, Penguin Books, 1981
Blessings in Disguise, by Alec Guinness, Book Club Associates, 1985
My Name Escapes Me: The Diary of a Retiring Actor, by Alec Guinness, Hamish Hamilton, 1996
A Positively Final Appearance: A Journal 1996-98, by Alec Guinness, Hamish Hamilton, 1999
A Life in the Theatre, by Tyrone Guthrie, Hamish Hamilton, 1960
To Fall Like Lucifer, by Ian Harvey, Sidgwick & Jackson, 1971
Sir Donald Wolfit, C.B.E.: his life and work in the unfashionable theatre, by Ronald Harwood, Secker & Warburg, 1971
Anything for a Quiet Life, by Jack Hawkins, Elm Tree Books, 1973
Mielziner: Master of Modern Stage Design, by Mary C. Henderson, Backstage Books, 2001
The First Three Years of the War: A Day-by-day Record, by Harold Hobson, Hutchinson, 1942
Verdict at Midnight: Sixty Years of Drama Criticism, by Harold Hobson, Longmans, Green and Company, 1952
Indirect Journey, by Harold Hobson, Weidenfeld & Nicolson, 1978
The Oxford Union, by Christopher Hollis, Evans Brothers, 1965
Acting My Life: The Autobiography, by Ian Holm with Steven Jacobi, Corgi Books, 2006
The Thirties, by Ian Jenkins, Heinemann, 1976
David Merrick: The Abominable Showman, by Howard Kissel, Applause, 1993
Years of Upheaval, by Henry Kissinger, Phoenix Press, 2000
The Prince: The Public and Private Life of Laurence Harvey, by Des Hickey and Gus Smith, Leslie Frewin, 1975
Music Hall, by Roy Hudd, Eyre Methuen, 1976

Roy Hudd's Book of Music-Hall, Variety and Showbiz Anecdotes, by Roy Hudd, Robson Books, 1993
Binkie Beaumont: Eminence Grise of the West End Theatre, 1933-73, by Richard Huggett, Hodder & Stoughton, 1989
Samuel Beckett's Waiting for Godot, by William Hutchings, Praeger, 2005
Rod Steiger, by Tom Hutchinson, Gollancz, 1998
The Stratford Festival: A History of the Shakespeare Memorial Theatre, by T.C. Kemp and J.C. Trewin, Cornish Brothers, 1953